A proper dyaloge betwene a Gentillman and an Husbandman

A proper dyaloge betwene a Gentillman and an Husbandman

Edited by Douglas H. Parker

UNIVERSITY OF TORONTO PRESS

Toronto Buffalo London

© University of Toronto Press Incorporated 1996
Toronto Buffalo London
Printed in Canada

ISBN 0-8020-0735-X

Printed on acid-free paper

Canadian Cataloguing in Publication Data

Main entry under title:

A proper dyaloge betwene a gentillman and an
husbandman

Includes bibliographical references and index.
ISBN 0-8020-0735-X

1. Reformation – Early works to 1800.
I. Parker, Douglas H. (Douglas Harold), 1942–   .

BR304.P76 1996   270.6   C95-932003-2

University of Toronto Press acknowledges the
financial assistance to its publishing program of the
Canada Council and the Ontario Arts Council.

For my father Harold Parker
and my two sisters
Beverley Simpson and Margaret Daly

Contents

Acknowledgments ix

Introduction 1

Contents and Structure 3
Authorship 22
Sources and Analogues 51
The Tradition of Complaint:
  Sampler of Texts 67
The Tradition of Complaint:
  Themes in *A proper dyaloge* 80
Interrelation of Editions 102
Bibliographical Descriptions 105
Notes 108

**A proper dyaloge betwene a Gentillman
and an Husbandman** 123

Commentary 174
Glossary 241
Emendations 251
Variants 254
Appendix A 258
Appendix B 262
Bibliography 269
Index 281

Acknowledgments

I am indebted to the generosity of the librarians of the following institutions: British Library, London; Bodleian Library, Oxford; Huntington Library, San Marino, California. I am especially grateful to the staff of the libraries at University of Ottawa; Carleton University, Ottawa; St Paul's University, Ottawa; Laurentian University, Sudbury. I owe special thanks to Dr Michael Welsh, Department of Classical Studies, Carleton University for the English translations of Latin passages in the Commentary, to Dr Paul Colilli, Dean of Humanities, Laurentian University for technical support, to Dr Paul Cappon, Vice-President, Laurentian University for financial assistance, to Ms Suzanne Rancourt, University of Toronto Press for her remarkable efficiency, competence, and good humour, and to Ms Judy Williams for her careful editorial work.

As always, my final debt is to my wife, Hilary, and my two sons, Geoffrey and Jonathan.

Introduction

Contents and Structure

A proper dyaloge betwene a Gentillman and an Husbandman is in some ways a puzzling and anomalous text. Its actual title has been the source of some confusion both in its day and our own. It was published twice in a short period of time, the second version appearing in 1530 only months after the publication of the first, which appeared probably in late 1529. Although both versions were published by Hans Luft of Antwerp (ie Johannes Hoochstraten), neither appeared with any indication of author or authors, and the first version gave no indication of publisher.[1] And finally, it is a hybrid text, made up in its first version of an original dialogue and a borrowed Lollard tract of the late fourteenth century attacking clerical possessions, and in its final version of a dialogue plus the Lollard tract just mentioned *and* a second prose piece written probably in the early fifteenth century and arguing for the Bible in the vernacular. It is this latter version which serves as the basis for this critical edition.

The work opens with a 684-line original composition made up of some preliminary material followed by a lengthy dialogue between a gentleman and a husbandman or farmer. The preliminary material begins with a rime-royal acrostic (minus the letters 'x' and 'z') of twenty-one lines followed by ten more rime-royal stanzas. This gives way to a thirteen-rime-royal stanza monologue spoken by the gentleman, after which the husbandman enters and the dialogue proper begins and continues for 491 lines.

The acrostic, entitled 'An A.B.C. to the spiritualte,' a title which was often used in the sixteenth century to describe the work as a whole (see Authors), is addressed to the entire church hierarchy – 'Bothe preste / pope / bisshoppe and Cardinall' (8) – and warns it to mend its way or risk 'a fall' (10). In the first stanza of the acrostic the hierarchy is accused generally of 'mischefe' (11), a charge that is more precisely defined in stanza 2, where the tract states that the clergy has held Christendom in 'bondage / of mennes tradiciones' (15) and deprived 'Kynges and Emperoures' (16) of 'their chefe possessiones' (17). The accusation is developed at great length in the dialogue itself, and especially in the first Lollard tract, which attacks clerical possessions and calls for disendowment. The third stanza of the acrostic moves from kings and emperors to the 'Poore people' (21) whom the clergy are accused of oppressing in order to satisfy the lust of their 'godde / the belly' (24). The exact nature of the oppression against the poor is not mentioned but becomes clear once the husbandman enters the dialogue and speaks on behalf of his socioeconomic group. At this point one sees that it is clerical possession of temporal goods, especially land and land claims, that is the source of the complaint against the clergy. Finally, the acrostic ends where it began with a warning to the clergy that 'god will be revenged at the last' (27).

The ten-stanza rime-royal segment which follows opens and closes with stanzas addressed to the 'Christen reder' (28 and 91). These opening and closing stanzas exhort the reader not to judge the tract hastily or rashly when it exposes the clergy's malevolence, or to assume that the accusations brought against the clergy are the product of perversity on the part of the accusers. The stanzas between the opening and closing ones imply that the majority of Christians have been hoodwinked by the clergy's appearances of holiness. The refrain at the end of each stanza, which focuses on demonstrating the clergy's hypocrisy, sums up the tract's sense of its own mission: it will expose the hypocritical jugglers (55), the modern-day magicians Iannes and Iambres (50), the descendants of the Pharisees (57), the usurpers of God's power (79), for what they truly are. In this ten-stanza attack on clerics, the tract brings no specific charges against them, as it did in the acrostic where clerical possessions were attacked. Here the emphasis is on showing the general hypocrisy, in preparation for a more specific exposé of individual manifestations and examples of this hypocrisy.

Although we are told after this ten-stanza segment that 'Here foloweth the Dialoge' (99), the dialogue, in fact, begins as a twelve-rime-royal-stanza monologue spoken by the 'Gentillman' (101). In this monologue the gentleman 'With soroufull harte' (102) explains the reasons for his present miserable condition. In the first stanza he makes clear that he has lost his 'enheritaunce and patrimony' (106) and in subsequent stanzas clarifies how this came about. Speaking on his own behalf, but representing as well, one feels, the majority of his social group, he states how at an earlier and better time his worthy ancestors, secure in their own wealth, provided for their own welfare and advancement, and, as a result, were able to assist those with fewer means. The fact that the gentleman sums up this happy state of affairs in only four lines (109–12) and then devotes the rest of his lengthy monologue to the universally unhappy consequences of paying too much attention to the hypocritical clergy suggests that the good old days were brief indeed and that the present intolerable situation has been going on for some time. Social harmony, peace, and prosperity amongst members of the commonwealth started to disintegrate once this gentleman's ancestors – indeed all gentlemen's ancestors – began to be seduced by the clerics who promised spiritual assistance and rewards to those who turned over their properties to them. Hoodwinked into believing the wily and vain arguments of priests and other members of the spiritual estate (138), these ancestors gave them their lands, goods, and possessions (144–5), thereby disinheriting 'their right successyon' (147). The result in the here and now is that gentlemen are no longer affluent and, consequently, are unable to help themselves or the poor. Indeed their indigence forces them 'to theft or mourder' (153) in order to survive, with the result that the fabric of society is torn asunder. Families suffer enormously, and clerics, now living 'in welthe aboundantly' (167) because of the indecent swapping of temporal possessions for fraudulent spiritual promises, are deaf to the pleas of those who seek their material assistance, a situation which stands in stark contrast to the happier days when land was held by the laity. Now everyone is poor except the clergy. As the gentleman puts it in his final summary stanza: 'They haue richesse / and we calamyte I Their honour encreaced / oures must dekaye' (190–1).

As was the case with the ten stanzas preceding the gentleman's monologue, these stanzas conclude with a refrain which repeatedly reminds the reader that the true culprit in the seemingly hopeless impoverishment of society that the gentleman outlines is the Catholic church's doctrine of purgatory. The clergy has seduced society and won temporal possessions from it by promising to pray for the souls of those who give their lands and goods to the church. This obscene bartering of temporal goods for spiritual ones repels the gentleman, who has lost out because of the gullibility of his ancestors. For its part, the church, through the papacy, claims the authority to bind and loose sinners, to keep them in purgatory or to release them from it. Although priests and prelates take upon themselves the authority of the apostles, and often preach about Christ's own poverty (172–4), their words are clearly at odds with their actions: society suffers from the 'ambicious tyranny' (182) created by their fraudulent power to bind and loose souls.

The husbandman, who has been waiting in the wings as it were, and overheard at least part of the gentleman's complaint, now enters to bring the dialogue to a true beginning. The shift in stanzaic and rhyme pattern also signals a new development as the tract abandons the rime-royal form for a relentless six-line pattern rhyming *a a b c c b*. Logically perhaps, this bringing together of a farmer and a gentleman to discuss a matter of pressing mutual concern might strain credibility. However, within the philosophical framework of this particular tract, the yoking is altogether appropriate, since the work is demonstrating that the entire socio-economic hierarchy has been adversely affected by the clergy's greed, as the gentleman intimates in his earlier monologue. Whatever differences exist between them – and in the normal course of events there would be many – the gentleman and husbandman are surely joined by a common complaint: both have lost their respective stations, positions, and relative economic security as a result of the appropriation of 'lordships' by the clergy.[2]

In order to give the dialogue some sense of immediacy and drama and to carry it beyond the level of prosaic mutual complaint, the author(s) allow the two characters to engage in what might be called a dramatic agon. The husbandman, while sympathizing with the gentleman's 'sorowe' (195) and claiming to understand its cause, namely 'the oppression intollerable / Of thes monstres so vncharitable / Whom men call the spiritualte' (197–9), argues that he and 'husbandmen euery where' (203) are in far worse shape than the gentleman and his ilk. This 'challenge' allows the gentleman to reiterate and expand on the reasons for his poverty. The reiteration, in turn, permits the reader to learn more about the pernicious practices of the clergy, which, according to the gentleman, is intent on taking over the land of the entire country. The husbandman responds to the gentleman's statement that the clergy is gradually absorbing into its kingdom 'baronries and erldomes / With esquyres landes and knightes fees' (217–18) by arguing that these possessions were freely given to clerics by the gentleman's ancestors, a claim which gives the gentleman the opportunity to question the word 'Freely' (224). The gentleman responds that his ancestors were 'constreyned' (225) into giving up their temporal possessions by a deceitful and fraudulent clergy who variously frightened and charmed them into acquiescence with the doctrine of purgatory. The husbandman then comments on the false nature of prayer as practised by the clerics and states that such prayer 'is not worthe a rotten aye' (255). The gentleman, showing more wisdom than his ancestors, closes this initial section of the dialogue by pointing out that purgatory does not exist, despite the clergy's attempts to render it frighteningly real. The husbandman, who has earlier demonstrated a wry sense of humour by stating that the clergy has already prayed so long that it has 'brought the lande to beggery' (247–8), now states that he hopes the prayers of the clergy will soon cease. If they continue, the country will be 'worsse than nought' (266).

The husbandman changes the direction of the dialogue to show how he and his colleagues have suffered. Harking back, as the gentleman did earlier, to a time when 'temporall gouernoures' (271) knew no 'spirituall iurisdiccion' (272), he conjures up an image of social harmony and economic prosperity throughout the kingdom in order to contrast it with the present state of affairs which began as soon as the clergy 'Gatt to theym worldly dominacion' (290). Since clerics began taking over property, rents on land have been raised beyond what any husbandman can afford, and priests' wages, the costs of repairing altars and churches, and the like, have impoverished farmers to the point where they are 'fayne to dryncke whygge and whaye' (307). Additionally, the clergy, by combining many small farms into single large ones, makes such properties rentable only to gentlemen who can afford the high tariffs. The result is the decay of households, villages, and towns, since farmers can no longer work the land in order to maintain themselves, their families and communities. The gentleman responds to the criticism of himself and his colleagues implied in the husbandman's claim that only gentleman can now afford rents on enlarged farms by pointing out that the gentlemanly class has been 'so beggeryd' (351) through the loss of its inheritance and patrimony that it is 'compelled / With fearmes soche shyft to make' (352–3). The essence of the argument is that the greedy clergy turns fellow citizens against each other as gentlemen take over land formerly rented to farmers, and farmers, in turn, are reduced in status to beggars.

Momentarily at least, in this occasionally wayward tract, the argument moves away from economic considerations to a general indictment of the life and practices of clerics. The husbandman, who has spent his life working with his hands, states that the clergy refuses to work on behalf of the prince or the commonwealth (364), using its spiritual calling and duties as an excuse. The gentleman, not fearful of redundancy, points out that clerical prayers have made the world worse rather than better and argues that the spiritual order should engage in 'labour bodely' (391). This discussion leads to a consideration of the clergy's legitimate predecessors, the apostles, who were 'gostely' (395) like the clerics, but who, unlike them, did not display pomp or greed. The husbandman makes clear that one of the main reasons the scriptures are not allowed in English is to keep hidden the differences between the humble lives of Christ and the apostles and the lives of clergy of his own day. This first mention of a vernacular Bible is important, since it helps justify the addition of the second prose tract on the history of the vernacular Bible to the second edition of *A proper dyaloge*. In what follows the gentleman states that clerics are either spiritual or worldly depending on which characteristic suits their immediate purpose: they justify their refusal to work and their reluctance to defend their prince on grounds that they are spiritual; on the other hand, they see nothing wrong with acting the part of the most worldly of landowners and landlords.

After this summary of clerical shortcomings, the husbandman suggests that he and the gentleman make their way to London to present their complaints before parliament. The gentleman, however, is not optimistic about the outcome of such a decision in light of what happened to the petition of the 'poore beggers / For thir pituous supplicacyon' (486–7). The allusion here is to Simon Fish's *A Supplicacyon for the Beggers* published early in 1529. With this reference to Fish's vitriolic little satire, *A proper dyaloge* introduces for the first time and in rapid succession a series of contemporary or near-contemporary events, all of which dramatize the malevolence and strength of the traditional church in its struggles to maintain its perceived superiority over man and state. The husbandman has just referred to the Reformation Parliament which opened in London in 1529; then follows a reference to Fish's tract and Thomas More's prolix response to it, *The supplycacyon of soulys* published in 1529, in which More defends purgatory against Fish's attacks. A few lines later the gentleman mentions the unjust treatment of 'kynge Ihon' (531) at the hands of the clergy, and the ill-fated 1414 rebellion and deaths of the Lollard Sir John Oldcastle (538–42), and Humphrey, duke of Gloucester (544). Beginning at line 575, the gentleman alludes to Cuthbert

Tunstal's burning of Tyndale's New Testament in 1526 and later to the persecution of the Lollards during Henry V's reign.

As quickly as they began, the historical allusions, introduced by husbandman and gentleman to justify their accusations against the clergy, are abandoned, and this lengthy segment of the dialogue closes with a comment designed to prepare the reader for the first Lollard prose tract on the evils of clerical possessions. In response to the husbandman's question whether the clerics deny God's word as found in the scriptures, the gentleman states that although they don't deny it, they interpret it in a sense 'clene contrary' (628) to the one intended. In addition, in order to trick the simple Christian, they assert 'the popes auctorite' (629) and warn others 'To beware of thes heretikes Lutheranes. / Whom they saye is a secte newe fangled' (646–7) and who they claim are the ones who began to express concern over legitimate clerical possessions. This last statement provokes the husbandman to argue that concern about clerical possessions has a legitimate history and is not simply something dreamt up by the new Lutheran sect resident in England. And to justify his claim he alludes to a book 'aboue an hundred yere olde' (661) that makes the same accusations against the church. That it is the humble farmer rather than the gentleman who should know about and have a copy of this book will come as no surprise to those who are aware of the strong appeal Lollardy had for common folk.[3] In any case the husbandman needs little encouragement from the gentleman to read the work. With this reading the second major section of *A proper dyaloge* begins.

The 'olde treatyse made aboute the tyme of kinge Rycharde the seconde' (685–7) is the first major Lollard borrowing in *A proper dyaloge*, although various echoes of Lollard 'doctrine' have already been heard in the exchanges between the two speakers. Its intent is to demonstrate that the claims made against the clergy by both gentleman and husbandman in the dialogue itself are not novel or newfangled, but rather form part of a long tradition stretching back into Lollard times. In fact, the borrowing of this tract by the probable Lutheran authors demonstrates the continuity between Lollard and Lutheran thinking at least on the matter of clerical worldliness and temporal possessions held by clerics. The tract is published in its entirety in Matthew's edition of *The English Works of Wyclif*. Matthew states that 'No external evidence authorizes us to attribute' it to Wycliffe (359), although if it is by him it would probably date from between 1365 and 1375, since it has more similarities to his works of this period than to his later ones (359). In *A proper dyaloge* it is stated by the husbandman that it was written 'aboute the tyme of kinge Rycharde the seconde,' whose dates were 1377–99. Putting these two pieces of evidence (or speculation) together, one might conclude that it was composed in the later 1370s or early 1380s.

The tract itself is a shamelessly repetitive document which uses a common rhetorical device of the time, namely the piling up of documented evidence in the form of scriptural citations and contemporary records, to prove that the clergy has no right to the temporal possessions it has gained over the years. The crux of the argument, anticipated in the conversation between the gentleman and husbandman, is that the clergy cannot assert its spiritual authority at the same time as it demonstrates an all-too-eager involvement in worldly matters, especially as these pertain to the accumulation of property and land. Numerous examples from the gospels plus St Bernard's words to Pope Eugenius in his tract *De consideratione* prove that 'lordships' are not appropriate to the priestly role (698–732). Clerics respond to this charge by countering with two arguments: first they claim that they do not hold lands as private domains but rather in common, and secondly they argue that they were given these properties 'by tytle of perpetuall allmes' (746), that is by generous benefactors for life, the very situation the gentleman complained about when he spoke of his gulled ancestors' having given away his inheritance and patrimony. The Lollard author responds to the first claim by calling on scripture: rather than believing what the clergy says about the difference between holding land in private and in common, pay attention to the clergy's actions, which are clear for all to see. Despite their words, clerics treat their property and those who question their right to it in the same way as do 'the secular lordshyppe' (761). Therefore by their works – rather than by their words – you shall know them. As for the clerics' second claim that they receive their lands by virtue of perpetual alms, the author cites Robert Grosseteste (a regular source for Lollard writers and polemicists) and scripture to prove that alms are only legitimate when they are given to those in need by those who can well afford to give them. And since the clergy is not in need, because God provides for all states, secular and religious alike – consider the lilies of the field – and since many benefactors impoverish themselves and their descendants in the false belief that they are building up spiritual capital by giving away their possessions, these perpetual alms are not true alms and therefore cannot be construed as free, legitimate, and lawful gifts from secular benefactors (733–962).

Indeed the effects of these generous if foolhardy donations of property to the clergy are the impoverishment of families, towns, and, finally, the commonwealth itself – consequences which both the husbandman and gentleman expressed in their earlier dialogue.

After this prolix statement of the thesis and detailed response to objections complete with chapter and verse documentation, the author draws the inevitable conclusion. In order to obey God's word, which was supported by the prudent and judicious advice of experts in such matters, and avoid the dire social and economic consequences of clerical possessions, the clergy should be disendowed: 'it may be vnderstonde of this processe / that withdrawyng of this lordshippes from the clergy and restoringe againe of them to the states that god hathe assigned them to / shuld not be called robbery of holy chirche as oure clerkes saye / but rather rightwise restitucion of good wrongfully and theefly withold' (915–20). It is, therefore, the responsibility of the laity who have unwisely donated lands to the clergy to break their oaths in order to put an end to this heresy and simony 'the which oure clerkes call perpetuall allmes' (933). Furthermore, since God was responsible for entailing land to secular lordships, these latter have no right to violate that entailment by giving such lands and possessions to the priestly order. For their part, clerics should realize that just as they and not the secular order are entitled to tithes by virtue of God's entailment of tithes to priests in the old law, so the secular arm of the commonweal is the only state entitled to temporal possessions (971ff). In addition, tithes are abundant and therefore sufficient to maintain the clergy. As a result, there is no justification for clergy 'to amorteyse secular lordshippes' (1026). As well as receiving tithes, clerics have a number of other perquisites 'whiche smacke of symonye and extorcion' (1031–2), such as first fruits, fees for 'prouynge of testamentes' (1033), and the like.

Following this exhaustive examination of the reasons why clerics should not hold secular lordships, the treatise pauses for breath for the space of fourteen lines so that the husbandman can tell the gentleman (and the reader) that there is indeed legitimate precedent for his own views on the evils of the clergy holding temporal possessions. The husbandman also introduces the next part of the tract devoted to showing how the clergy has no right to hold secular office, a position at least as old as Marsilius of Padua's *Defensor Pacis* (see Sources). These two segments of the tract, the first holding forth on the inappropriateness of the clergy possessing lordships which properly belong to the laity, and the second speaking out against the clergy holding secular office, effectively disenfranchise the clergy from involvement in the secular life of the commonwealth and marginalize it to the point where its 'power' resides only within the spiritual realm. It is an ironic reversal of the church's own attempts throughout these years to disempower heretics by extirpating them from the commonwealth and by undermining their pernicious doctrines.

The shorter and less repetitive second part of this Lollard tract is printed in Matthew as an appendix to the first part and is addressed to secular lords who appoint clerics to high office within the government. The author cites St Cyprian, St Gregory, a pope, and, of course, scripture to demonstrate that members of the clerical estate have no right serving in government. Their true, if unexciting, tasks are defined as 'contemplacion / studye / prayer and preachinge of goddes worde and ministrynge to poore folke' (1096–7). Although this tract was written well before Henry VIII's reign, one can understand how the author(s) of *A proper dyaloge* would see the appropriateness of this admonition for Henry himself, many of whose high-flying ministers – including the amazing lord chancellor, Cardinal Thomas Wolsey – were also members of the clerical order.

To this point in the tract at least, both husbandman and gentleman, as well as the author of the Lollard addition, make clear that the clergy has capitalized on opportunities and done well for itself largely because it has been assisted by a compliant lay element within society: not only have gentlemen lost their livelihood and enriched the spiritual estate through their thoughtless donations of land to it, but also kings and princes themselves have handed clerics more secular authority than they are entitled to by appointing them to positions of power. There is no doubt that *A proper dyaloge* is a tract designed to expose various manifestations of clerical abuse, but, as important, it is also a wake-up call to the laity – kings, gentlemen, and farmers alike – to pay attention to what it is giving away.

The dialogue begins again immediately following the conclusion of the second part of the first Lollard tract. The gentleman and husbandman express pleasure at the thesis of the Lollard text and once more emphasize its vintage so as to reiterate the claim that their own complaints against clerical possessions have a legitimate historical pedigree.

Historical allusions comprise the next part of the dialogue in order to show clerical atrocities over the centuries and to demonstrate once more that these present complaints have a genuine, if regrettable, history. The husbandman begins by giving a revisionist and skewed view of church abuse during the reign of Henry v (1164ff), when Lollards were slain at the instigation of the clerics and the king hoodwinked by clerics' malicious subtleties, as was the case in earlier reigns, particularly King John's. The gentleman credits King John with trying to disendow the clergy and suffering death as a result (1220ff). The burning of the New Testament (the context here suggests the so-called Wycliffe Bible) was carried out not because of errors therein, as the clergy claimed, but rather because the clerics were afraid that the truth would emerge if the Bible were allowed in the vernacular, a comment we shall hear again in the introduction to the second prose tract. The husbandman states that the church burns more than books and chronicles, as the number of Christians burnt in his own day attests.

As this part of the dialogue closes, the gentleman promises that he will say more about the clergy's behaviour 'another tyme at leyser' (1285), and the husbandman bids him adieu and hopes that 'the trouth [will be] knowen openly' (1291), the very intent of this tract itself. What follows these farewells is the second prose addition on the vernacular Bible entitled 'A compendious olde treatyse / shewynge / howe that we ought to haue the scripture in Englysshe' (1292).

Unlike that part of the dialogue which immediately precedes the beginning of the first Lollard addition on clerical possessions, there is no smooth lead-in to the second tract, although occasional references throughout the entire dialogue to the English New Testament and attempts made to suppress it make the transition less abrupt here than it might otherwise be. The fact that there is no prelude in the dialogue to this second tract indicates that probably the tract was added as an afterthought, after it appeared as a separate publication in its own right early in 1530 (STC 3021; see Authors). Despite its status as an afterthought, it is a crucial addition to this text and must have been seen as such in its own day, since it appeared as part of the second edition of A proper dyaloge only some months after the appearance of the first edition published without it. Probably it would have been regarded as an important text, since it provides, after its fashion, some historical justification for the existence of an English Bible and serves as a vindication of the Tyndale New Testament, which appeared as a complete text in 1526 but was subsequently and summarily condemned and burned under orders from Cuthbert Tunstal. As was the case with the first Lollard addition to A proper dyaloge, this second prose text also links past religious protest with contemporary Protestant criticisms in the face of government and church opposition.

'A compendious olde treatyse' begins with two rime-royal stanzas, a prose apology entitled 'Vnto the Reader,' and a concluding rime-royal stanza, none of which is part of the original tract written by either Purvey or Ullerston, depending on the source one consults (see Authors). The treatise speaks in its own person in the rime-royal stanzas apologizing for its 'barbarous wede' (1297) and lack of 'gaye eloquency' (1298), yet, at the same time, claiming that it tells the truth about the arrogant and wealthy clerics who refuse to allow 'goddes worde in their natyfe langage' (1303). The prose tract 'Vnto the Reader' mentions Tyndale's translation of the New Testament and points out that the present tract 'wrytten aboute the yere of oure lorde a thousande foure hundryd' (1321–2) demonstrates that clerics, from earliest times, were reluctant to have any vernacular translations of scripture made available 'to the laye people' (1323–4). The conclusion that the writer of the apology draws in showing the relevance of this tract for his own time is that now, as in times past, those who objected to a vernacular scripture did so because they feared that such a text would expose 'the inward malyce' (1319) of the clerics. The final rime-royal stanza sums up what has gone before and claims that it is the 'frowarde presumpcion' (1340) of the clergy which stands in the way of a vernacular scripture.

The tract begins with the author excoriating present-day clerics for burning God's word and comparing such activities to those of 'king Antioche' (1347), who also 'brent the bokes of gods lawe' (1348). This opening, the product of a contemporary hand and not the work of the original author, whoever he might have been (see Authors), leads into the tract proper where this original author, in true medieval rhetorical fashion, calls upon renowned authorities such as Boethius, Seneca, and Al-Ghazali to demonstrate that people from an earlier age were encouraged to learn the path of virtue. If such 'hethen philosophers' insist that people profit from 'naturall science' (1374–5), it is all the more important that Christians 'profyt in science of vertues' (1376), which is best found in the Bible. Then follows an extensive list of biblical allusions to demonstrate that God gave his laws to his people in their own tongues. The conclusion based upon analogy seems compelling: 'And of this it is notabyll sithen the laye people in the olde lawe had their lawe in ther mother tounge / that the lay englishe people in the newe lawe haue it as all other nacions haue /

syns Christ bought vs as he did other and hath geuen to vs the same grace as to other' (1410–15).

The rest of the tract, and the longest part by far, expands on the thesis stated above with references to the Bible and contemporary documentation as support: St Peter showed greater tolerance and magnanimity by baptizing heathen men than do present-day clerics, who are less trusting of the laity (1416ff). Both St Paul and Nicholas of Lyra recognized the importance of speaking in a language that people can understand (1422–31). The seventy famous doctors translated the Bible 'out of Ebrue into Greke' (1431), and Spaniards, Germans, Italians, and the French have had vernacular Bibles for many years (1433–4). 'Iames Merland' (1435–6) is cited as an example of someone who translated the Bible, and was persecuted for it by the church and later vindicated. An anecdote in Bede's *Ecclesiastical History* shows that there is a Christian precedent for translating biblical narratives into English (1440ff), and worthies such as Robert Grosseteste, Thomas Aquinas, William Thorisby, Richard de Rolle, and King Alfred himself all demonstrate, state, or imply that a vernacular scripture is legitimate (1460–1500).

Near-contemporary incidents within the political sphere are called upon to support the thesis for a vernacular scripture. John of Lancaster's stalwart defence of an English Bible during Richard II's reign is referred to, and even the arch-conservative Archbishop Thomas Arundel, instigator of the 1408 Oxford Constitutions prohibiting an English Bible, is shown to have defended the gospels in English on one occasion at least, although he later withdrew his support and suffered a horrible death as a consequence (1513–27). Naturally, as one might expect, there is a good deal of revisionist history in this tract in order for the author to convincingly convey what in today's critical terms might be called his ideology. I have tried to record many of these tendentious claims in the Commentary.

Since, at this point, much of the tract as printed in *A proper dyaloge* deviates from the original version, the issue of editor-/authorship of this 'revised' prose tract is crucial (see Authors). New material and a new more aggressive tone mark the transition from one author to another. References to the Roman church as Antichrist increase, as do attacks against bishops who deceive their princes into believing that a vernacular scripture is both spiritually and politically threatening. These defensive conservatives mount a counter-attack by burning both books and so-called heretics (1569ff).

Finally, the tract reverts to calling upon further precedents for a vernacular Bible. We learn that the four evangelists wrote their gospels 'in diuerse langages' (1596), and the chronicle *Polychronicon* (ie, 'in cronicis Cistercien,' 1627) is invoked to demonstrate Origen's, Theodosion's, Aquila's, and Symmachus's part in biblical translation (1619–26). References to St Jerome's Old Testament prologues draw the work to a close, and the author of the revision concludes by hoping that 'all christen men and women / praye that the worde of god maye be vnbounde / and deliuered from the power of Antichrist / and renne amonge his people' (1675–8). This version of the tract ends more naturally than the original English translation printed in Deanesly and Bühler (see Authors), which bumps and jerks to an abrupt stop, leaving the reader wondering what might be missing. The editor of the revised version has a better and more felicitous sense of an ending.

Despite the fact that less than one half of *A proper dyaloge* is in actual dialogue form, thereby making the title something of a misnomer if it was meant to apply to the entire tract, a few words need to be said about this particular literary genre. The origins of the form are traced by Atkins in the introduction to his edition of *The Owl and the Nightingale* (early thirteenth century), which, he claims, is the earliest example of the debate form in England. Atkins states that the debate or dialogue originated in the Latin tradition with the pastoral eclogues of Theocritus and Virgil; its prominence during the Carolingian era is attested to by Alcuin's Latin debate *Conflictus veris et hiemis* and Sedulius Scotus's *De rosae liliique certamine* (*The Owl and the Nightingale* xlvii). The popularity of the form during the medieval period can be attributed to Abelard and his *Sic et Non* method of pursuing, without necessarily resolving, conflicting ideas (xlviii). Its ready application to theological discussion is evident in Peter Lombard's *Sentences* and Thomas Aquinas's *Summa Theologiae*, and its suitability to legal debate in Gratian's *Decretum aut Concordia discordantum canonum* (xlix). Atkins concludes that 'the debate in the 12th and early 13th centuries became everywhere a favourite literary device' (xlix). *The Owl and the Nightingale* itself, a dialogue of some 1795 lines, pits the representative of the serious life, the Owl, against the Nightingale, the upholder of the joyous life. As for its tone, Eric Stanley states that 'there is an element of direct and honest obscenity, not of sniggering obscenity, half-concealing, half-revealing; but of vulgarity there is not a trace. The tone is light, but much of the matter is serious' (*The Owl and the Nightingale* ed

Stanley 22). The restrained nature of the combatants' disagreement stands in marked contrast to later manifestations of the form, especially in its anti-genre manifestations (see below).

Charles Herford's old but still valuable study examines dialogue's history and importance in the sixteenth century and refers to it as 'among the classics of modern pamphleteering' (21). Arguing that the sixteenth-century dialogue combines 'literary distinction and popular persuasiveness' (21), he also claims that the German dialogue in particular shows a judicious blend of 'literary culture with moral and religious fervour' (21). It would, of course, be overstating the case to argue that *A proper dyaloge* shows significant literary distinction; but there can be no doubt about its moral and religious fervour or its desire to persuade and appeal to a popular audience at a particular moment in history and within the context of a particular culture.[4] Its stridently anti-papal stance, its tendentious distortions of history, and its exchange of 'enlightened' opinion between two speakers whose views on the contemporary church coincide – despite the large social divide between them – demonstrate its adherence to the terms of Herford's definition.

Herford claims that the dialogue form, popular during the Middle Ages despite its limited range as a 'simple debate between two opponents' (22) often reflecting the common medieval method of debate known as scholastic disputation, was 'released' from its strictures principally by Erasmus and Ulrich von Hutten. Their contributions to the form were to make the dialogue travel along more informal lines rather than follow the 'pedantic symmetry' (25) of the medieval debate. Indeed one recent critic argues that 'the concreteness of Renaissance dialogue appears as a deliberate riposte to the abstraction of medieval debate' (Chuilleanáin 388).[5] According to Herford, Erasmus and Hutten were also responsible for replacing personified abstractions or types with 'real figures drawn not seldom with the pencil of Holbein, and of every grade of society' (25), and introducing a degree of 'refined satire' and 'the scathing and implacable laughter of Aristophanes and Lucian' (25) in place of the 'heavy bludgeon' (25) of the medieval practitioners of the form.

Even though their contributions to the form were significant, Hutten and Erasmus's satiric methods differed in what one might call 'touch.' If Erasmus attacked deviations from what he defined as common sense by exposing 'types' who strayed beyond the Erasmian norm, Hutten's method was to attack individuals directly with a no-holds-barred approach. Herford claims that Hutten 'founded the literature of personal invective in which the Reformation was so profuse and at times so great' (26).[6] My own view is that both Hutten and Erasmus, rather than their medieval or classical predecessors or Hutten alone, must be seen as the tonic inspiration for works such as Jerome Barlowe and William Roye's scurrilous attack on Cardinal Wolsey, *Rede Me and Be Nott Wrothe* (1528), a work, I argue later, written by the authors of *A proper dyaloge* and very much in evidence in the latter. Despite its indebtedness to *Rede Me*'s verse form, diction, and imagery, *A proper dyaloge* is more restrained in tone and less satiric, and its attacks less particularized and pointed, as it prefers to attack institutions rather than individuals.

Although Hutten's dialogues began in 1517 with the *Phalarismus* and ended only four years later with the *Bulla*, the *Monitor*, and the *Praedones*, Herford claims that his example gave rise to an enormous number of German dialogues extending from 1521 to 1526 and beyond. One group was characterized by its debate set within the context of a strong 'imaginative background,' another by its range of characters, and a third by its 'dramatic action' (27–31).

Herford argues that the dialogue in England did not have the same degree of popularity as it did in Germany.[7] Although he states that the form was 'scattered through the literature of the [sixteenth] century' (31), it seems clear that at certain times it was more popular than at others. For example, a cluster of dialogues concerned with issues dear to the hearts of the reformers made dialogue's presence felt in the late 1520s through to the early 1530s. Certainly one of the first and one of the most popular, if not the most important, is *Rede Me and Be Nott Wrothe*. Like *A proper dyaloge* and unlike many of its medieval predecessors, *Rede Me* does not pit ideological opponents against each other in debate. Rather both speakers, Watkyn and Ieffraye, represent reformist views and fulminate against the abuses that they see within the church. Occasionally, as a formal bow in the direction of controversy, one accuses the other of exaggeration or overstatement, or plays the role of the disingenuous naïf, but both speakers are committed to radical reform, and satirize an enemy which is never allowed to defend itself within the poem. Essentially the same dynamic obtains in *A proper dyaloge*. The gentleman and husbandman both rail against clerical possessions and the reluctance of the church to allow a vernacular Bible. Sporadic disagreements arise between them not because of conflicting ideologies – both are clearly committed to reformist positions – but rather because the husbandman occasionally accuses the gentleman of making the husbandman's state worse than it might otherwise be. If the essence of dialogue is the exchange of varying and contrasting points of view, even if one of these viewpoints is made to appear ridiculous so as to provoke the reader's scorn, then these two works do not qualify as true dialogues. Both voices in each poem represent the same ideological stance and chime together; the works are dialogues only in so far as two speakers exchange comments.

Roger Deakins, the author of a more recent study than Herford's, has refined the category of dialogue, dividing it into two types, genre and anti-genre. Genre dialogue, defined and explained in Carlo Sigonio's *De Dialogo* (1561), is a serious form devoid of satire, wit, cheap humour, *ad hominen* attack, and jokes; it is characterized by decorum and good taste and has a clear structure made up of two parts, a 'vestibule' and a 'contention' (Deakins 11–12). Deakins claims that of approximately 230 Tudor dialogues extant, only five conform to this type, two of the most famous being Thomas More's *Utopia* and Thomas Starkey's *Dialogue between Pole and Lupset* (16). Both *Rede Me and Be Nott Wrothe* and *A proper dyaloge* clearly stand outside of this convention and conform to the anti-genre type, the immediate inspiration for which is, according to Deakins, Erasmus's *Colloquies*.[8] Lacking the decorum, good taste, and emotional restraint of the genre dialogue, the anti-genre dialogue is satiric, addresses questions of particular immediacy, and is prone to hyperbole and stylistic inconsistency. Although Deakins argues that the anti-genre dialogue flourished between the 'Great Divorce and the middle years of Elizabeth's reign' (22), and although both *Rede Me* and *A proper dyaloge* antedate this period and do not subscribe to all of the form's characteristics, it seems clear that they were precursors of it and, in their own idiosyncratic way, helped set the stage for its full-blown development in later dialogues.[9]

One of the most important dialogues of the period is *The Plowman's Tale* (see below, 'The Tradition of Complaint: A Sampler of Texts'). Probably written for the most part at the beginning of the fifteenth century by a strong Lollard sympathizer, it was printed for the first time in English by Thomas Godfray around 1536, probably for the purposes of advancing the Henrician reform agenda (Wawn 'Chaucer'). Falsely associated with Chaucer's name for a canonical stamp of approval, the tale is a dialogue between two birds, a Pelican and a Griffon, the former holding Lollard views, the latter the views of the Catholic church. The dialogue clearly fits into Deakins's anti-genre type: it is a violent attack against essentially all aspects of the

Catholic church. Summing up its targets, Wawn calls it 'anti-papal, anti-curial, anti-monastic, anti-mendicant, anti-clerical and pro-royalist in sympathy' ('Chaucer' 177). More than three-quarters of the poem is a monologue uttered by the loquacious Pelican, who has much to say against the church. The Griffon, initially playing the part of straight man, asks leading questions which the Pelican responds to at great length. Only near the end of the poem does any dialogue as such enter this 1380-line poem. The Griffon weakly rebuts the Pelican's attacks on the church and insists that he recant; when the Pelican refuses the Griffon enlists the support of his feathered friends, who are summarily routed by the Pelican's ally, the Phoenix.

Unlike *A proper dyaloge* and *Rede Me and Be Nott Wrothe*, both of whose two speakers support radical reform within the church, thereby nullifying the possibility of true debate, *The Plowman's Tale* does have two speakers representing different sides of an issue. However, the Lollard sympathies of the author stack the cards against the Griffon by effectively rendering him mute until near the end of the poem. As a result, the tale gives only the illusion of dialogue; it is, in fact, a propagandistic monologue. To borrow Victoria Kahn's terms, the goal in this dialogue, like *Rede Me* and *A proper dyaloge*, is not 'to educate the reader's prudential judgment or practical reason' (ix) by arguing 'in utramque partem or on both sides of a question' (ix). Rather, the goal is to persuade through rhetorical bludgeoning, exaggeration, and undermining the opposition by giving it no – or very little – chance of responding.

Another dialogue of the mid-1520s used to advance reformist views is William Roye's *A Brefe Dialoge bitwene a Christen Father and his stobborne Sonne* 1527 (STC 24223.3), called by the editors of *The Complete Works of St. Thomas More* 'the first attempt at systematic exposition of reformed doctrine in the vernacular' (8 iii 1172) and 'the first Protestant theological tract in English' (11 xxviii). Its importance is also attested to by Hume, who refers to it as only the third printed work of an English Protestant, coming after Tyndale's translation of the New Testament and his Epistle to the Romans ('William Roye's *Brefe Dialoge*' 307). Based upon a work by the German reformer Wolfgang Capito, as Hume has convincingly demonstrated (308), Roye's English version, like its original, uses the Creed and the Lord's Prayer as points of departure for the justification of Protestant theology and for attacks on the church.

For the purposes of this discussion on dialogue, what is important is the dramatic alteration Roye makes to the role of the two speakers in the tract. In the Capito original, the father poses questions and the son supplies the answers. Roye, however, reverses the roles, making the father the respondent to the questioning son. Hume argues that the change in roles 'gave the work an unexpected flavour in the context of the normal anticlerical tradition; and it reflected appropriately the situation in England, where the regular Protestant catechising of children was hardly a possibility, while the close questioning of a believing adult was a more probable formula' (310). Although Herford finds this assignment of roles unusual, since, he argues 'the genius of the Protestant dialogue tended to put the defence of the new teaching into the mouth of the younger, or the poorer man, while the elder, or the more powerful, or the superior in social ranks defended tradition' (44), Roye's alteration of speaking roles fits nicely into Deakins's categorization of speaker functions in Tudor prose dialogues where the son plays the part of the pupil and the father the teaching master.

Authorship

It should come as no surprise to anyone aware of Henry VIII's doctrinal conservatism throughout the majority of his reign (see, for example, the early chapters in Dickens) that both editions of *A proper dyaloge* were printed without any indication of author. On the basis of what we know about its reception, it seems clear that it was generally regarded as a subversive and dangerous document worthy of suppression. Foxe cites 'A Proclamation for the resisting and with-standing of most damnable Heresies' (IV 676) issued by Henry VIII in 1530 and mentions a number of books 'restrained and forbidden,' among which are '*A Disputation between the Father and the Son*,' a work of William Roye published in 1526–7 in Strassburg by Johann Schott (Clebsch 232–5; Rupp 53–4; Hume, 'English Protestant Books Printed Abroad' 1069; STC 24223.3); '*the burying of the Mass*,' published in 1528 in Strassburg by Schott and also known as *Rede Me and Be Nott Wrothe* (STC 21427; *Rede Me and Be Nott Wrothe* ed Parker); a number of William Tyndale's works; and, significantly, this work, *A proper dyaloge*, entitled 'A.B.C. against the Clergy' and so named, it would appear, for the rime-royal three-stanza poem on its title page.[10] Foxe again mentions the work or part of it in a section of *Acts and Monuments* entitled 'Prophecies and Proverbs of the Church of Rome' (IV 259) and reprints the three-stanza poem, entitling it 'The A,B,C, against the pride of the Clergy.' He wrongly attributes it to William Thorpe, which leads Arber to conclude erroneously that '*The A.B.C. to the spiritualte* must be distinguished from *The A.B.C agenste the Clergye* prohibited at Paul's Cross on Advent Sunday, 3d Dec. 1531' (Arber 128). In fact, the two works are the same. The three-stanza poem quoted by Foxe is identical to the poem entitled 'An A.B.C. to the spiritualte' published as a three-stanza acrostic in the printed text.

The work is mentioned again by Foxe in connection with a list of 'Persons Abjured in the Diocese of London.' One 'John Mel, of Boxted, A.D. 1532' is cited 'For having read the New Testament in English, the Psalter in English, and the book called "ABC"' (v 38). We hear of it again, with yet another twist to its title, in Richard Bayfield's answer to the heresy charges brought against him in 1531.[11] In a response to a question about which heretical books he might have read, Bayfield 'confessed that he had read "The Obedience of a Christian Man" and the "Sum of Scripture" among company, and also, "The Dialogue betwixt the Ploughman and the Gentleman," among company, as he thought ...' (IV 683). And finally, in a list of books prohibited in 1542, drawn from Bishop Bonner's Register, we once again see the book entitled 'The ABC agaynst the Clergy' (Foxe v appendix x). It would be difficult, perhaps impossible, to determine which of the two versions of A proper dyaloge published by 1530 these citations refer to, just as it is impossible to know to what extent the second edition, complete with the additional tract on the value of a vernacular Bible, superseded the first. Probably both versions of the work were condemned as one, since both contained what would have been seen as stridently heretical material, the first focusing on clerical greed as manifested in land grabs, and the second adding to the first its own claims for the translation of the Bible into the vernacular.

Much like Rede Me and Be Nott Wrothe, which was also called The Burying of the Mass, this tract seems to have had some difficulty over the years establishing a firm identity based upon a fixed title.[12] And occasionally, the criticism of our own day has added to the confusion. Commenting on books smuggled into England from abroad during the 1520s, the editor of volume 9 of The Complete Works of St. Thomas More lists the following titles, which he attributes to Jerome Barlowe: a 'Proper Dialogue between a Gentleman and a Husbandman and the ABC to the Spirituality in two editions' (xxix). Not only does this statement falsely lead one to conclude that the one work with two titles is two entirely different works, but it also suggests that the latter of these 'two' was issued in two editions and that the former was not.[13] Clebsch also manages to confuse matters. At one point he refers to 'A proper dyaloge betwene a Gentillman and a husbandman' as a work attributed to Roye or Barlowe (236–8); but a few pages later, in discussing the battle against Protestant books waged by the church, he refers quite specifically to Roye's Dialogue of the Gentleman and Ploughman (265) without stating that the two works are the same and without apparently seeing that he had earlier referred to the tract, under one of its other names, as being by either Roye or Barlowe.

As was evident in the first part of this introduction on the contents and structure of this tract, I plan to call this text *A proper dyaloge betwene a Gentillman and an Husbandman* – regularly shortened to *A proper dyaloge* – since the ABC titles found in contemporary records – 'ABC against the Clergy' or 'A.B.C. to the spirtualte' or 'ABC of the Prelacy' or simply 'ABC' – refer, in fact, to only the three-stanza poem at the beginning of the work in the printed text, and since the other contemporary title, *Dialogue of the Gentleman and the Ploughman*, has no textual justification at all.[14] Although the title *A proper dyaloge* does not capture the essence of the entire tract, since in its final version the work is an amalgam of three separate documents and not simply a dialogue, it does, nevertheless, better serve our purposes than any of the ABC titles because it both contains the latter and also appears in large black-letter type on the title page of both printed editions. On the other hand, one can understand why the work was often referred to in its own day by the various ABC designations since to refer to it as *A proper dyaloge* might have been to confuse it with two other dialogues published within the same general time period, *Rede Me and Be Nott Wrothe* and *A Brefe Dialoge bitwene a Christen Father and his stobborne Sonne*.

As mentioned earlier, neither edition of *A proper dyaloge* gives any indication of author or authors, although the complete second edition has the colophon 'Emprented at Marborow in the lande of Hessen / by me Hans Luft / in the yere of oure lorde. M.CCCCC. and .XXX' and was probably based on the earlier edition also printed by Luft (Johannes Hoochstraten), an Antwerp printer who may have published as many as eleven English Protestant books between 1528 and 1530 (Hume 'English Protestant Books Printed Abroad' 1071–8). In the brief, non-textual, introductory material to the Bodleian copy of the first edition (STC 1462.3), the work is initially attributed to William Barlow, bishop of St Asaph and of Chichester, although only a few lines later it is tentatively attributed to 'W. Roy,' that is, William Roye, one of the probable authors of *Rede Me and Be Nott Wrothe* and of *A Brefe Dialoge bitwene a Christen Father and his stobborne Sonne*. Somewhat surprisingly, the revised STC lists *A proper dyaloge* under William Barlow's name too, although it adds William Roye's name as a possible author in its notes to this edition, and further adds Jerome Barlowe's name as possible collaborator in the 'Addenda and Corrigenda' to volume 1 (613). The attribution of the first edition of *A proper dyaloge* to William Barlow can be dismissed, since it is based on the probably mistaken theory that this Bishop William Barlow, rather than Jerome Barlowe and William Roye, was the author of *Rede Me and Be Nott Wrothe*, a theory once proposed by Koszul (25–34) and the editors of the *Dictionary of National Biography*, but subsequently disproved by Rupp (67–73), whose views are upheld by Hume (*English Protestant Exiles* 79–80) and McLean (173–85).[15] The degree of present-day confusion surrounding the authorship of this tract is evident not only in the fact that the revised STC covers all of the bases by listing it under William Barlow's name and then adding Roye and then Jerome Barlowe to the list of possible authors, but also in conflicting commentary in the Yale edition of *The Complete Works of St. Thomas More*: three volumes make contradictory comments on Gordon Rupp's statement about the confusion over William Barlow and Jerome Barlowe. In volume 6, for instance, the editors state correctly that 'Rupp concludes, tentatively, that [Jerome Barlowe] was not that William Barlow who later became Bishop of St Asaph's and St David' (6 II 683). Comments in volume 7 are in accord with this claim (275). However, in volume 8 the editors, obviously misreading Rupp, state that 'William Barlowe [sic] is not to be identified with the Franciscan Jerome Barlowe, friend of Roye and collaborator with him on the *Burial of the Mass* [ie, *Rede Me and Be Nott Wrothe*]. Rupp's suggestion that the two are the same man has been effectively refuted by Anthea Hume ...' (8 III 1249). Those who attribute *A proper dyaloge* to William Barlow the bishop are no doubt confounding him with Jerome Barlowe, but probably also sense similarities between *A proper dyaloge* and *Rede Me* – a work which, we have seen, was also at one time attributed to William Barlow. They are right to sense a relationship between these two works – though, since no comparative study exists, it is doubtful that they have been able to read them carefully – but their attribution of authorship is incorrect, since in my view, *A proper dyaloge* was written or (perhaps better) written and edited by one or both of the actual authors of *Rede Me and Be Nott Wrothe*, namely Jerome Barlowe and William Roye.[16]

Even though we cannot be entirely certain what part Barlowe and Roye may have played in the production of the popular *Rede Me and Be Nott Wrothe* – indeed some critics maintain that Roye had the idea and that Barlowe was responsible for the execution, whereas others claim that Roye had no part at all in the authorship – it is my view that both men to some degree were involved in it and that *Rede Me* was, finally, a work of joint authorship. Even the scholarly *Complete Works of St. Thomas More* seems baffled by the problem of authorial attribution to the point where the editors, ignoring More himself, who attributes the work to both Barlowe and Roye in *The supplycacyon of soulys* (7 161 STC 18092), contradict themselves: in three instances the work is definitely attributed to Jerome Barlowe (6 II 683; 8 II 1070; 9 xxvi), but in four others it is seen as the work of Barlowe *and* Roye (8 III 1160, 1249, 1466, 1632). It is also my view that the two men were involved in the composition of the two editions of *A proper dyaloge*, although the exact degree of involvement is impossible to determine. Certainly Barlowe's participation is definite and without question: in his recanting letter to Henry VIII in 1533, he confesses to having 'made certayne bookes, and suffred theym to be emprynted,' naming 'the Treatyse of the Buryall of the Masse' (*Rede me*), and 'Dyaloge betwene the gentyllman and Husbandman,' this latter doubtless being *A proper dyaloge* (quoted in Clebsch 236). Clebsch mentions that Rupp attributes *Rede Me* and *A proper dyaloge* to Barlowe alone, but he himself seems less certain (and, as we have seen above, contradicts himself) and adds that Rupp 'exhibited a marked animus against Roy' (236). Hume feels that *A proper dyaloge* is Barlowe's work, although she is less assertive than Rupp ('English Protestant Books Printed Abroad' 1076) and Aston, muddying the already murky water, adds that the *dyaloge* 'was by Jerome Barlow working for William Roye' (*Lollards and Reformers* 233).[17] In light of these conflicting opinions, Clebsch is doubtless correct when he states that 'The association of Roy and Barlowe seems impervious to all attempts at disentanglement' (237). The perceptive reader has perhaps noticed that critics seem unable to agree even on the spelling of the two putative authors' family names: some leave both without a terminal 'e'; others give both the final 'e'; while some reserve it for one (but not necessarily the same one) and not the other.

Near the conclusion of the prefatory letter to *Rede Me and Be Nott Wrothe*, the correspondent, writing from the continent to his colleague in England, assures him 'that the fyre which Christ cam to kyndle on erth, cannott butt burne' (147–8). However, in order to ensure that this fire will not go out, he encourages his friend to send him other tracts which he refers to as 'smale stickes [that] come vnto youre hondes, which ye shall iudge apte vnto the augmentacion of this fyre ... yf in englonde they maye not be publisshed ...' (150–3).

The correspondent wants these 'smale stickes' so that he might arrange for their publication on the more reformist continent and have them smuggled into England for the greater edification of the population. It is altogether possible that Barlowe and Roye in 1528, the date when *Rede Me and Be Nott Wrothe* was published, were preparing their readers for the appearance of yet another 'stick': *A proper dyaloge*, published on the continent only about one year after the appearance of their comments in the prefatory letter to *Rede Me*. Rupp speaks briefly but knowledgeably about the traffic in contraband books travelling from the continent into England or within England itself through the agency of the Christian Brethren or the Brethren of Christ – one of whose members, Richard Bayfield, was mentioned earlier (More 8, 3, 1385). This group worked to ensure the dissemination of the tracts of the 'known men' or Lollards. Rupp adds that 'It is significant that when William Roye, as Tyndale said, "gat him new friends", he was engaged with Jerome Barlow in an enterprise which included the reissue of two fragments of Lollard tracts from the preceding century' (9). Although Rupp does not mention the titles of the two fragments and later denies Roye any part in the writing of *A proper dyaloge*, which, he claims, is Barlowe's work and 'much inferior' to *Rede Me* (59), it is possible that the 'two fragments of Lollard tracts' Rupp has in mind are the two prose pieces that end up forming central components of *A proper dyaloge*.

There are some striking similarities between portions of *A proper dyaloge* and *Rede Me and Be Nott Wrothe* which suggest either that the authors of both works are the same, or that someone very familiar with the latter work used it to write the dialogue section of the former. In general terms, both works open with three rime-royal stanzas directed against offending clergy. *Rede Me*'s attack against Cardinal Wolsey, the main target of the work, is made through an exegesis of the cardinal's escutcheon, appropriately modified to emphasize Wolsey's cruelty. *A proper dyaloge*'s is a direct attack against the church hierarchy in general. On *Rede Me*'s title page the authors claim that 'With confusion thou [Wolsey] shalt have a fall' (6), and in the first stanza of *A proper dyaloge*'s three-stanza attack, the authors predict that the clergy 'Daungerously [be] lyke to haue a fall' (10). Authors of both works must have known that their predictions were, in fact, rather timid prognostications. Wolsey's fall occurred in 1529 and was imminent in 1528 when *Rede Me* appeared, and by 1529–30, the dates of the appearance of both editions of *A proper dyaloge*, the clergy was fighting a rearguard action against a plethora of reformist writings.

Following the brief prefatory letter and the thirteen-rime-royal-stanza-dialogue between 'Author' and 'Treatous' in *Rede Me*, in which the treatise complains that it will not be believed when it brings its various charges against the traditional church, is another rime-royal segment in which a priest laments the death of the mass because of the consequent loss of privileges traditionally associated with it. The corresponding sections in *A proper dyaloge* are found immediately after the three-stanza acrostic directed against the clergy (6–27). In the first ten-rime-royal-stanza segment, the authors direct the 'Christen reder' (28) not to judge hastily or rashly what they say or dismiss it as untrue. In the last stanza in this section (91–7), they reiterate their concern that they will be misunderstood when they bring charges against the clergy, and once again exhort the reader to have 'pacience' (92). This segment is not unlike that part of *Rede Me* where the treatise fears being misunderstood and, consequently, written off by readers for the apparently preposterous claims it makes against the clergy. The parallel is further strengthened when both works bring each of the stanzas in this section to a conclusion with a refrain.

Rede Me's rime-royal lamentation finds a parallel in *A proper dyaloge*'s rime-royal stanzas of complaint put into the mouth of the Gentleman, one of the two principals in the dialogue. Although the priest's lament in *Rede Me* is meant to be ironic – we are to rejoice at the losses he incurs because of the death of the mass – and the gentleman's is meant to be seen as legitimate, both sections in both works lament major losses resulting in a substantial reduction in the standard of living of both complainants. And again, the parallel between the two works is strengthened in this section because, as earlier, each stanza concludes with a refrain.

It would be stacking the cards in favour of my argument – namely, that the authors of *Rede Me* were also responsible for *A proper dyaloge* – to list thematic parallels between the two works, since most of the reformist literature of the period focuses on a limited number of themes which are repeated time and again in all of these proto-Protestant, pro-Lutheran, Lollard-inspired texts. More convincing, in my view, are the shared verse forms and linguistic echoes which carry the common themes in each text. The authors of *A proper dyaloge* show themselves to be as adept at doggerel as those of *Rede Me*. Once the preliminary material in both works is over and the dialogue itself begins, rime royal in both works gives way to a new verse form that is used to convey the conversation and the point of view of each of their two speakers. Both *Rede Me* and *A proper dyaloge* work in

six-line units rhyming *a a b c c b*. The pattern is so strictly adhered
to that even when units are divided between the two speakers in each
work, the rhyme scheme is never violated.

Linguistic parallels are evident too. In the opening three-stanza
segment of *A proper dyaloge*, we hear the authors complain about
the clergy 'Sekynge the lust / of [their] godde / the belly' (24), a
phrase reminiscent of *Rede Me*'s similar attack on clerical greed,
expressed in the phrase 'their god which is their belly' (3665). In
a section of *A proper dyaloge* where the husbandman is expressing how the clergy forces men of his occupation into poverty, he
states: 'We tourmoyle oure selfes nyght and daye / And are
fayne to dryncke whygge and whaye / For to maynteyne the
clargyes facciones' (306-8). In *Rede Me*, Ieffraye, one of the
speakers, complains in a similar vein about the harm the clergy
does to farmers: 'Pover cilly shepperdes they gett, / Whome into
their fearmes they sett, / Lyvynge on mylke, whyg, and whey'
(2812-14). Focusing once more on how the clergy deprives the
farmer of what is rightfully his, the husbandman complains
(326-33):

> But nowe their ambicious suttlete
> Makyth one fearme of two or thre
>   Ye some tyme they bringe .vi. to one.
> Which to gentillmen they let in farmage
> Or elles to ryche marchauntes for avauntage
>   To the vndoynge of husbandemen echone.
> Wherby the comones sufferinge damage
> The hole lande is brought in to rerage

And in *Rede Me* Ieffraye states (2789-93):

> A newe waye they do invent,
>   Lettynge a dosen farmes vnder one.
> Which one or two ryche francklynges,
> Occupyinge a dosen mens lyvynges,
>   Take all in their owne hondes a lone.

And a few lines later we read (2863-5):

> And even as they do by farmage,
> Brynge the londe into a rearage,
> Contempnynge the state temporall.

Even though common themes are off-limits for the purposes of this comparison for reasons given above, the articulation of these themes through similar examples in both works is striking and worthy of note. Both works, for example, mention that the clergy refuses to come to the support of its king or prince in times of need, citing spiritual duties as an excuse (*Rede Me* 2488–93; *A proper dyaloge* 363–6); both criticize the fact that clerics refuse to perform manual labour (*Rede Me* 1621–35; *A proper dyaloge* 391ff); both refer to Cuthbert Tunstal's burning of Tyndale's New Testament in 1526 (*Rede Me* 702–20; *A proper dyaloge* 575–7); and both stress throughout the economic hardship under which the country labours as a result of the selfish actions of all levels of the spiritual hierarchy. Both works as well tinker or play with historical events in order to depict the traditional church in the worst light possible. In doing this they subscribe to what Aston calls the 'Tudor propensity to make history a moral hunting ground' (*Lollards and Reformers* 222).[18]

Finally, the relationship between the speakers in both dialogues is not dissimilar. In both, speakers take turns disabusing their interlocutors of misguided opinions or informing them of facts of which they seem to be ignorant. Such devices move the dialogue along and sustain the sense of dramatic action. In *Rede Me and Be Nott Wrothe*, for example, Ieffraye and Watkyn, the tracts' two major characters, each possess areas of knowledge unknown to the other. Watkyn's expertise is in religious events that have occurred on the continent; Ieffraye's on the state of England under an oppressive, traditional, and corrupt church. In *A proper dyaloge* both the gentleman and husbandman know what effects the traditional church and clerical greed, as manifested principally in land take-overs, have had on their lives, and the gentleman seeks to justify his class's apparent hard-heartedness towards husbandmen in general by pointing out that gentlemen have been forced to behave as they do because of the clergy. The husbandman, for his part, sees his state as worse than the gentleman's and the dialogue proceeds as each makes clear his plight to the other. The fact that two extremes of the social hierarchy share a common plight shows that Barlowe and Roye, here and in *Rede Me*, are convinced that the pernicious practices of the clergy run the entire social gamut and affect deleteriously all its members spiritually, economically, and socially.

Naturally, as one might expect, there are major differences between the two tracts. Most significantly, I think, *Rede Me and Be Nott Wrothe* is, in the strict sense of the term, a more heretical tract than *A proper dyaloge*. It does not shrink from attacking church doctrine: it excoriates not only the clergy, but also the mass, auricular confession, the veneration of saints, pilgrimages, and the doctrine of purgatory, to name a few. On the other hand, *A proper dyaloge*, in its dialogue sections at least, is eager to emphasize the economic hardship brought on by the greed of the clergy as it obtains, one way or another, an increasing number of 'lordships' and temporal possessions which belong properly in the hands of the secular order. Such church doctrine as, for instance, that of purgatory comes under fire only in so far as it contributes to the proliferation of this abuse. To this extent at least, *A proper dyaloge* is a far more focused text than *Rede Me*, but for this very reason, perhaps, a far less interesting one. *Rede Me* gives a broader, if distorted, picture of pressing reformist concerns.

This analysis of similarities between the dialogue section of *A proper dyaloge* and *Rede Me and Be Nott Wrothe*, an extended dialogue of some 3500 lines, makes it clear that the two works were the brain-children of the same authors, Jerome Barlowe and William Roye, although the extent to which each contributed to either text is still unclear and probably unsolvable. My hunch is that the authors, keen on disseminating pro-Lutheran-Lollard tracts, worked quickly to ensure that such works reached the general public with dispatch. Exiled on the relatively safe continent (although both Tyndale and Roye would die as Protestant martyrs there in the 1530s), they would have been aware of the growing importance of Protestant literature in England and the church's struggle to suppress it. By 1526 Tyndale's New Testament had been published and quickly suppressed and burnt, and by the time *A proper dyaloge* appeared, Tyndale's influential *Parable of the Wicked Mammon* and *Obedience of a Christian Man* had also been published. By this time as well, Roye had written his *Brefe Dialoge bitwene a Christen Father and his stobborne Sonne*, to say nothing of *Rede Me and Be Nott Wrothe*, the work for which both he and Barlowe are best remembered. But perhaps what served as their strongest motivation for issuing the hybrid *A proper dyaloge* was the appearance of Simon Fish's notorious but influential pamphlet *A Supplicacyon for the Beggers* (STC 10883; More 7), printed by Johannes Grapheus in Antwerp in early 1529 (Hume 'English Protestant Books Printed Abroad' 1071–2). The importance and popularity of this work were out of all proportion to its size. Fish's scurrilous attack on clerical possessions and greed and the sacrosanct doctrine of purgatory provoked Thomas More's prolix response, *The supplycacyon of soulys*, in 1529. *A proper dyaloge*, which, in my view, relies on Fish's tract as a partial source and puts Fish's complaints against the church in dialogue form, was probably quickly put together late in 1529 by Barlowe and Roye to capitalize on the popularity of Fish's *Supplicacyon* and to give its complaints, through the inclusion of a vintage Lollard document which expresses many of the same concerns, a legitimate historical pedigree (see Sources). Doubtless, the authors would not have been shy to borrow from Fish, but also from their own earlier work, *Rede Me and Be Nott Wrothe*, to get their reformist opinions into the public domain as quickly as possible.

Although it is my contention that Jerome Barlowe and William Roye were the authors of the dialogue sections of *A proper dyaloge*, they were not, clearly, responsible for the two prose additions, except in an editorial capacity. At this stage in our knowledge of Wycliffite or Lollard writings we cannot say who wrote the first Lollard tract on clerical possessions that appears in *A proper dyaloge*. As mentioned above, the entire text of this work, copied from the Lambeth manuscript, is printed in Matthew's edition of Wycliffe's writings under the title 'The Clergy May Not Hold Property' (359–404), although Matthew is by no means certain that the work is from Wycliffe's pen. In his introduction to it in *A proper dyaloge*, the husbandman claims that he has only 'a remenant From the begynnynge of the .vi. chapter' (672–3), and that 'halfe the boke we want' (ie, lack) (671). In fact, if Matthew's chapter divisions are correct, the husbandman actually begins his reading from the text at a point not quite half-way through the seventh chapter; in addition, about half of the first sentence in our text, up to the mention of the names 'Seynt Huge and seynt Swithune' (690–1), is not in the original and therefore must be by Barlowe and Roye. This half-sentence is designed to serve as a smooth entry into the Lollard text itself. Finally, although the husbandman claims to have only part of the text, the entire tract, that is, that section which appears in *A proper dyaloge* and the first six chapters, is printed in Matthew.[19]

About the occasion for the writing of this text one can only speculate. Matthew claims that if the work is by Wycliffe (and it seems to be a big 'if'), it was probably written between 1365 and 1375. *A proper dyaloge* states that this 'olde treatyse [was] made aboute the tyme of kinge Rycharde the seconde' (685–7). Richard reigned from 1377 to 1399. If the work were written early in Richard's reign, and if one does not hold too rigidly to Matthew's terminal date, one might guess, given the subject matter of the tract, that it was written in perhaps late 1381 or early 1382 as a document supporting one of the major concerns in the 1381 Peasants' Revolt. Aston, among others, tells us that 'the question of temporalities [had] a prominent place in the rebels' demands' (*Lollards* 10).

As mentioned above, the second edition of *A proper dyaloge*, published by Hans Luft in 1530, is the only text that contains both prose additions, the one concerned with clerical possessions, which also appears in the first edition of *A proper dyaloge*, and the other dealing with the history of the Bible in the vernacular, which does not appear in the first edition. This second addition, published in our text under the title 'A compendious olde treatyse / shewynge / howe that we ought to haue the scripture in Englysshe' (1292–5), is, in my view, based on the same text published separately and under the same title in 1530 by Hans Luft (*STC* 3021). The title reads: 'A compendious olde treatyse / shewynge / howe that we ought to haue the scripture in Englysshe' (A1r), and the colophon states: 'Emprented at Marlborow in the lande of Hessen / be my [sic] Hans Luft / in the yere of owre lorde M.CCCCC.and.XXX.' (A8v).

This text, without authorial attribution, is, in turn, based on the original work which Margaret Deanesly claims was written by John Purvey, a significant Lollard scholar before his recantation, in a Latin version entitled *De Versione Bibliorum* and later translated by him into English (Deanesly 437–45). Deanesly, who reprints the original English translation, further claims that *De Versione Bibliorum* was 'founded on the debate on biblical translations between the Lollard, Peter Payne, and the Dominican, Thomas Palmer, at Oxford, 1403–05' (437). The original English text of 'A compendious olde treatyse' was also edited and published by Curt F. Bühler in *Medium Aevum* in 1938, although Bühler, wisely perhaps, does not speculate on the tract's author and does not mention either Purvey or *De Versione Bibliorum* (167–83). More recently, Anne Hudson ('The Debate on Bible Translation, Oxford 1401') has argued that the Latin text was not by John Purvey but rather by one Richard Ullerston and that the title that Deanesly gives it, *De Versione Bibliorum*, has no manuscript justification. Unlike Deanesly, she also claims that the original English text is very different from the Latin original: it is very much longer, better organized, and far more detailed. And finally, rejecting Deanesly's intimation that the original English version might be by Purvey himself, she claims that, because it is 'a typical Lollard pro-

duction,' (14) it is 'useless to speculate about its authorship' (15).[20]
Margaret Aston does nothing to convince us that she is clear on the
issue of authorship: at one point in her book she refers to a section in
the original English version of this tract and calls it 'Richard Ullerston's early fifteenth-century defence of Bible translation' (209), but
later she refers to it as 'John Purvey's defence of the translation of the
Bible' (Aston *Lollards* 221). And Anthea Hume, citing Deanesly,
states without qualification that 'The treatise was the work of John
Purvey' ('English Protestant Books Printed Abroad' 1077).[21]

The sixteenth-century English version of Deanesly/Bühler, published separately in 1530 and then again as part of *A proper dyaloge*
in the same year, is quite a different document from the original
English version edited by Deanesly and Buhler. What I hope to show
as I try to determine authorship/editorship of the sixteenth-century
edition of this tract is that the version of 'A compendious olde treatyse' published as part of *A proper dyaloge* in 1530 actually followed
the publication of the separate English edition published in 1530 simply because the editor of at least part of the latter was probably William Tyndale. It is my view that the authors and/or printer of the first
edition of *A proper dyaloge* published in late 1529 or early 1530 acted
quickly, because of Tyndale's popularity, to add Tyndale's edition of
the Deanesly/Bühler translation to the edition of *A proper dyaloge*
published in 1530, thereby enlarging it and making it reflect more of
the pressing reformist issues of the time, one of which was the
importance of a vernacular Bible.

John Foxe thought 'A compendious olde treatyse' important
enough to reprint it in his *Acts and Monuments* (IV 671–6). In his
brief preface to the tract, he speaks as if he is actually reprinting the
original Deanesly/Bühler version of the text. With a view to supporting his position that the bishops under Henry VIII were responsible
for preventing the Bible from appearing in the vernacular, he states:
'Against the proceedings of these bishops, in forbidding the Scripture
in English, instead of an answer to the same, I have thought meet to
adjoin a certain old treatise, found in a certain ancient English book;
which, as it may well serve for a confutation of the bishops' doings in
this behalf, so have I thought not to defraud the reader of the profit
thereof' (671). In fact, a study of Foxe's text shows that the version he
prints is based not on Deanesly/Bühler but rather on one or both of
the sixteenth-century editions published in 1530.

Deanesly, who bases her text of Deanesly/Bühler on the Trinity
College, Cambridge manuscript, which, she claims, has the 'com-

plete tract' (437), argues that Foxe's version 'was not founded on the complete Ms., but on his own transcript of the [incomplete] Worc[ester] Ms. ... and the early printed editions founded on the Worc. Ms., which included those of Hans Luft' (437). She continues, 'Foxe copied the first paragraph from Hans Luft's ed., then inserted two from his own transcript, then followed the printed ed. substantially to the end, but without acquainting the reader that the printed ed. contained about half as much again of new matter as the Worc. Ms.' (437–8). Although I have not examined the incomplete Worcester manuscript version of Deanesly/Bühler, or any of the other manuscripts which Deanesly claims are copied from Worcester, I can say with some degree of certainty, based upon my study of Foxe's text and the two 1530 editions of 'A compendious olde treatyse,' that the Worcester manuscript probably plays very little, if any, part in Foxe's version. Deanesly's statement that 'Foxe copied the first paragraph from Hans Luft's ed., then inserted two from his own transcript' of the Worcester manuscript does not stand up to scrutiny. By stating this Deanesly is suggesting that there are some significant differences between the two inserted paragraphs supposedly from Worcester and the rest of the Foxe version taken principally from the 1530 editions. I have collated the Foxe text with both 1530 printed texts and conclude that the *entire* Foxe text is essentially identical with the two 1530 editions. Even in Foxe's second paragraph, which Deanesly claims he transcribed from his copy of the Worcester manuscript, an error in both 1530 printed texts – the repetition of the phrase 'a cleane myrror new pullished' (1366–7) – is included in Foxe. And in the next paragraph, which Deanesly also claims Foxe transcribed from his transcript of Worcester, Foxe includes two references, found in the 1530 editions, to the term 'mother tonge' (1378, 1381) which are not in Deanesly/Bühler, or presumably in Worcester either. If they were, Deanesly would not be able to distinguish the 1530 texts from the Worcester transcript, which she implies she can do by pointing out (erroneously) that Foxe used Worcester for his second and third paragraphs and the 1530 versions for the rest. Consequently, I am unable to detect two paragraphs near the beginning of Foxe or anywhere else in his text which deviate from the 1530 editions enough to suggest that another source, ie, the Worcester manuscript, was used along with the 1530 editions to construct Foxe's text. Using this evidence, one might even conclude that Foxe worked only with the two 1530 texts – or perhaps only one of them – and didn't have to hand a manuscript version at all.[22] It is, therefore, possible that Deanesly may have been taken in by Foxe's statement that the text he reprints was 'found in a certain ancient English book' (671) and simply assumed that he was working, in part at least, from a printed version of a manuscript. For his source on the work's antiquity, Foxe need only have turned to the information which precedes the tract in the printed versions where it is called 'A compendious olde treatyse' (1292–3), where it refers to itself as 'olde' and 'clothed in barbarous wede' (1297), and where it is dated from 'the yere of our lorde a thousande foure hundryd' (1321–2). Despite its vintage, and whatever alterations may have been made to Deanesly/Bühler to make it reflect its new sixteenth-century context, the 1530 editions of 'A compendious olde treatyse' were seen in their own day as the legitimate text, with little regard paid to the work's original shape, orientation, or *raison d'être*. Despite what Foxe might have said about the work's antiquity, his interest was in using the text for his own immediate purposes, and for him the sixteenth-century editions probably suited those purposes better than the original English version. Naturally, of course, he was keen to show that his complaint about bishops had a legitimate ancestry, but beyond that the original text probably held little interest for him.

A comparison of the two 1530 Luft editions with Deanesly/Bühler shows significant additions and major differences over and above the minor differences which exist between the 1530 texts themselves. Not content to simply reproduce the Deanesly/Bühler version, the author/editor of 1530 adds new material, particularly in the latter half of the work, liberally sprinkles the entire text with marginal glosses, excises some of Deanesly/Bühler's text, moves other bits of it around to suit his purposes, and includes a preface at the beginning of the tract. Aston dates the Deanesly/Bühler text at about 1400 (*Lollards and Reformers* 221), Deanesly between 1403 and 1405 (437). Although Arber in his nineteenth-century reprint of the entire 1530 *A proper dyaloge* seems to acknowledge the presence of a sixteenth-century editor for 'A compendious olde treatyse' – he speculates on which reformer might have produced *A proper dyaloge*, and states, referring to 'A compendious olde treatyse,' 'The Protestant setting supplied by the Englishman at Marburg consists of *all* the verse, "Unto the reader" ... and nearly all the side notes' (127–8) – nevertheless, he also sounds as if he has not seen Deanesly/Bühler but only the 1530 edition. In that part of the text where Bishop Richard Fleming is mentioned (1522–3), Arber states in a note that 'Bp Fleming's death seems the latest personal allusion in the text. It is alluded to in so distant a manner as to afford a presumption that the treatise was not written for a number of years later' (178). Here Arber speaks as if the Fleming reference appears in Deanesly/Bühler, and based on this he dates the work 'as clearly not much earlier than 1450, A.D.' (128), since Fleming died in 1431.[23] But careful study of Deanesly/Bühler shows that the Fleming reference does not appear in it, and, therefore, is probably the addition of a later hand, possibly the author/editor of the 1530 Luft texts.[24] Furthermore, Arber never comments on the additions to and deletions from Deanesly/Bühler, a fact which also indicates that he may not have seen any copies of it.

The question now arises who this sixteenth-century author/editor might have been. Deanesly seems quite comfortable with the name William Tyndale. In the introduction to her reprint of Deanesly/Bühler she states: 'The editor of Hans Luft's 1530 ed. was probably Tindale [sic], who published the work as part of his controversy with sir Thomas More' (438). She supports her position by pointing out that in 1528 More had published his *A Dialogue Concerning Heresies*, directed in large measure against both Tyndale and vernacular Bibles, and that between 1530 and 1534 Tyndale was busy working on his English version of the Pentateuch (eventually published by Luft) and, as a result, did not answer More's *Dialogue* until 1531 (see *Answer to Sir Thomas More's Dialogue* 1–215). Deanesly seems to imply that 'A compendious olde treatyse' served as Tyndale's stopgap response to More's *Dialogue* until he was free to respond more fully in an altogether original tract. To demonstrate Tyndale's editorial talents and his interest in Lollard tracts, she cites *Acts and Monuments* (III 249), where Foxe claims that Tyndale edited William Thorpe's *Defence* against Thomas Arundel, a figure who also gets mentioned in 'A compendious olde treatyse' in a not altogether flattering way (1513–27). Foxe, summing up Tyndale's contribution to Thorpe's *Defence* – also published by Hans Luft after Tyndale's work on it – states: 'the said Master Tindal (albeit he did somewhat alter and amend the English therof, and frame it after our manner), yet not fully in all words but that something doth remain, savouring of the old speech of that time.' Deanesly concludes that 'In the case of the *Compendious Treatise*, however, Tindale added very long passages' (438).

Although, for reasons I shall state below, I am inclined to agree with Deanesly's conclusion about the identity of the author/editor, I am not altogether certain that her slight external evidence based on Tyndale's involvement in Thorpe's *Defence* justifies her conclusion, nor am I sure that Tyndale's is the only hand involved in reworking

Deanesly/Buhler. Indeed, based on my study of this tract within the context of *A proper dyaloge* in particular and earlier Reformation literature in general, I am prepared at least to consider that 'A compendious olde treatyse,' as it appears in its sixteenth-century manifestations, might be the work of at least a couple of people with Tyndale playing the major, but not the only, part. In my view the side-notes, the apologia entitled 'Vnto the Reader,' and some of the additions, deletions, and rearrangements of parts of Deanesly/Bühler are possibly Tyndale's responsibility. But I am not certain that the three-stanza poem – which is not part of Deanesly/Bühler – entitled 'The excusacyon of the treatyse' is from Tyndale's pen, simply because Tyndale, as far as we know, never wrote a line of poetry – even doggerel – in his life. If he did, he never published it. Furthermore, two of the three rime-royal stanzas are similar in form and have linguistic and verbal echoes with *Rede Me and Be Nott Wrothe* by Barlowe and Roye, the authors, I argued earlier, of the dialogue section of *A proper dyaloge*.

Throughout its preliminary sections, *Rede Me and Be Nott Wrothe* makes a point of stressing that it tells the truth despite the seemingly outrageous claims it makes against the church. Indeed the second line of its title – 'For I saye no thynge but trothe' (2) – introduces what becomes a leitmotif in the work. In the third line of the first stanza of 'The excusacyon,' 'A compendious olde treatyse,' somewhat preposterously speaking in its own 'person' (a device no more realistically used in *Rede Me*), insists that 'I tell the truth' (1299). This appeal to be believed strikes one as bizarre in a tract which brings so much historical material to the service of its own argument. The appeal to the reader is appropriate in *Rede Me*, given some of the emotionally charged and outrageous statements made therein, but it seems unnecessary in a work which is more controlled and more self-consciously aware of a historical tradition – even a distorted one – to which it can allude to defend its measured statements. The trope, then, seems unnecessary for 'A compendious olde treatyse,' a curious add-on perhaps unthinkingly borrowed from a popular contemporary document close at hand.

Additionally, one finds common sentiments against the clergy in both *Rede Me* and the opening poem of 'A compendious olde treatyse,' sentiments which seem appropriate to the former, given its strident tone, but inappropriate to the latter. In the first stanza of 'The excusacyon,' the clergy is characterized in general as having a 'frowarde / furious frenesy' (1300), words which suggest irrational,

erratic, and frightening madness and are not in accord with the tone
of the prose tract which follows. In early lines of *Rede Me* the church
hierarchy is described variously as 'ravenynge wolves' (82) and 'ves-
sels of wrath' (117). It is composed of individuals who 'crye and roare'
(82), who can scarcely contain 'their outragious furoure' (74), and
who condemn with 'furious sentence' (14). Once again, the tone of a
work like *Rede Me*, as reflected in its diction, to say nothing of the
rime-royal stanzas themselves, seems to be borrowed by 'A compendious olde treatyse' for reasons best known to the person or persons
responsible for these pilfered additions. Perhaps someone felt that if
the work began with a poem reminiscent of *Rede Me and Be Nott
Wrothe*, it too would attain the same degree of attention as Barlowe
and Roye's popular satire.

Finally, the expression 'goddes worde' in the final line of stanza 1
(1303) echoes the same expression repeated seven times in a refrain
near the end of *Rede Me* (3370ff), and the first two metonymic lines
of stanza 2 – 'Enemyes I shall haue / many a shoren crowne With
forked cappes and gaye croosys of golde' (1304–5) – can clearly be
heard in *Rede Me*'s lines 'Com hither monkes: with brode shaven
crounes' (134) and 'A due forked mitres and crosses of golde' (164).
These two stanzas, with their similarities to *Rede Me*, and the third,
which follows the brief section 'Vnto the Reader,' were clearly put
together by someone other than Tyndale, whose affection for Roye
and *Rede Me* was not strong,[25] and whose temperament and talents
did not run to poetry. Indeed, Tyndale may have simply handed over
his portion of the tract to Luft, thinking it complete, and it may have
been the enterprising Luft himself, and not Barlowe and/or Roye per-
sonally, who saw to the poetic additions in order to make the work
appear, on the surface at least, more like something readers would
have already known or, at least, known about.

The prefatory statement 'Vnto the Reader' (1311) and some of the
editorial work in the treatise itself could be Tyndale's. The opening
Pauline sentence of the prefatory statement – 'Grace and peace: not
that the worlde geuyth / but from god the father and oure sauioure
Iesu Christ with increace of the holy spryt be with the and all that
thurste the truthe. Amen' (1312–14) – is not unlike salutations found
in other works we know to be by Tyndale. For example, in his 'Preface' to the *Parable of the Wicked Mammon* he states, 'Grace and
peace, with all manner spiritual feeling and living, worthy of the
kindness of Christ, be with the reader, and with all that thirst the
will of God. Amen' (*Doctrinal Treatises* 37). Again in his 'Preface' to

his *Answer to Sir Thomas More's Dialogue*, he greets the reader as follows: 'The grace of our Lord, the light of his Spirit to see and to judge, true repentance towards God's law, a fast faith in the merciful promises that are in our Saviour Christ, fervent love toward thy neighbour after the ensample of Christ and his saints, be with thee, O reader, and with all that love the truth, and long for the redemption of God's elect. Amen' (5). And finally in the 'Preface' to *The Parable of the Wicked Mammon* he states: 'Grace and peace, with all manner spiritual feeling and living, worthy of the kindness of Christ, be with the reader, and with all that thirst the will of God. Amen' (*Doctrinal Treatises* 37).

The preface expresses the views of a man whose life-work was the translation of the Bible into English and whose lifetime struggle was against a church which consistently and systematically tried to frustrate his goal. That Tyndale should have been keen to edit a tract which established a legitimate pedigree for his own biblical translation and commentary and which proved that the church consistently stood in the way of all such translations is not surprising, given his views on the importance of his own task for all reformed English Christians. Throughout the preface we hear echoes of a complaint that is everywhere evident in Tyndale's various writings; that complaint – that the traditional church finds Tyndale's biblical translation corrupt because his English Bible would act to expose the rottenness and hypocrisy within it – is the major Tyndalian attack upon Catholicism and the papacy and the goal of all his writing, polemical and non-polemical alike.

Although the argument is apparent throughout his work, it is nowhere more eloquently expressed or more closely aligned with the sentiments expressed in this preface than it is in his *Preface to the Five Books of Moses* (*Doctrinal Treatises* 392–3), a work, interestingly, published in 1530, the same year as 'A compendious olde treatyse.' Here is the author in the introduction to 'A compendious olde treatyse:'

Consyderynge the malyciousnes of our prelatz and theyr adherentes whiche so furiously barke ageynst the worde of God / and specially the new testament translatyd and set forthe by Master William Tyndale / which they falsely pretende to be sore corrupte. That ye may knowe that yt is only the inward malyce whiche they haue euer had ageynst the worde of God. I haue here put in prynte a tretyse wrytten aboute the yere of oure

lorde a thousande foure hundryd. By which thou shalte playnly
perceyue / that they wolde yet neuer from the begynnynge
admytte any translacion to the laye people / so that it is not the
corrupte translacion that they withstonde. For yf that were true
the ydle bellyes wolde haue had leyser Inough to put forth a
nother well translated. ... Thus mayst thou se that bycause their
workes are nought and not bycause yt is euill translatyd / they
so furiously resyste the worde of god whiche is the trew lyght.
(1315–32).

And here is Tyndale in his *Preface to the Five Books of Moses*:

When I had translated the New Testament, I added an epistle
unto the latter end, in which I desired them that were learned to
amend if ought were found amiss. But our malicious and wily
hypocrites, which are so stubborn and hard-hearted in their
wicked abominations, that it is not possible for them to amend
any thing at all ... say, some of them,that it is impossible to
translate the scripture into English; some, that it is not lawful
for the lay-people to have it in their mother-tongue; some, that
it would make them all heretics; as it would, no doubt, from
many things which they of long time have falsely taught; and
that is the whole cause wherefore they forbid it, though they
other cloaks pretend. ...

And as for my translation, in which they affirm unto the lay-
people (as I have heard say) to be I wot not how many thousand
heresies, so that it cannot be mended or correct; they have yet
taken so great pain to examine it, and to compare it unto that
they would fain have it, and to their own imaginations and juggling terms, and to have somewhat to rail at, and under that
cloak to blaspheme the truth; that they might with as little
labour ... have translated the most part of the bible. For they
which in times past were wont to look on no more scripture
than they found in their Duns, or such like devilish doctrine,
have yet now so narrowly looked on my translation, that there
is not so much as one *i* therein, if it lack a tittle over his head,
but they have noted it, and number it unto the ignorant people
for an heresy. Finally, in this they be all agreed, to drive you
from the knowledge of the scripture, and that ye shall not have
the text thereof in the mother-tongue, and to keep the world
still in darkness, to the intent they might sit in the consciences

of the people, through vain superstition and false doctrine, to satisfy their filthy lusts, their proud ambition, and unsatiable covetousness, and to exalt their own honour above king and emperor, yea, and above God himself.

There are clues within the text of 'A compendious olde treatyse' itself which point to Tyndale as its editor. The first are the side-notes, and three of them in particular. Even a cursory look at Tyndale's writings shows that he seemed almost constitutionally incapable of not inserting side-notes and marginal glosses throughout his texts. He obviously regarded them as essential and handy summaries, directives, and pointers to his readers; in his prefatory letter 'unto the reader' in the 1534 edition of the *New Testament*, he refers to them as devices which 'set light in the margin' (*Tyndale's New Testament* ed Daniell 3).

As far as I can judge from Deanesly/Bühler, there are no side-notes in the text which shape the reader's response to the material, or try to convey a point a view, although there are indications within the text itself (rather than in the margins) as to the source of certain biblical references or citations. In Tyndale's text these latter are sometimes found in the tract, as in the original, and sometimes in the margins when Deanesly/Buhler has left some biblical sources unidentified. However, of the twenty-one side-notes in the sixteenth-century edition, only four are directives to a biblical source. The majority of the rest are less objective and meant to shape the reader's attitude towards the material in the text itself. At least three of these are significant, since they help to prove Tyndale's involvement with the tract. The first appears with reference to lines 1370–2 and states 'Reade robyn hode / saye our masters.' At this point in the tract Deanesly/Bühler is talking about Bede's comments on the importance of children learning virtue. Bede mentions the value of Seneca as attested to by Boethius in *de disciplia scolarium*. Nowhere in this section of the tract, or anywhere else for that matter, is Robin Hood mentioned; therefore the reference to him in the side-note seems gratuitous, even puzzling. However, an examination of some of Tyndale's other writings shows that Robin Hood is a particular favourite of his, and that he often makes reference to this figure from popular lore to point to the frivolity and deceit of Roman Catholicism, or to the way in which the church encourages reading of tales of romance at the expense of more efficacious reading of the scripture, or to the church's refusal to interpret scripture in the appropriate fashion.[26] In

The Parable of the Wicked Mammon, for example, Tyndale states: 'He that hath not the Spirit hath no feeling ... neither abhorreth the pleasures of sin, neither hath any more certainty of the promises of God, than I have of a tale of Robin Hood' (*Doctrinal Treatises* 80). In *Obedience of a Christian Man* he states 'that this threatening and forbidding the lay people to read the scripture is not for the love of your souls ... is evident, and clearer than the sun; inasmuch as they permit and suffer you to read Robin Hood, and Bevis of Hampton, Hercules, Hector and Troilus, with a thousand histories and fables of love and wantonness, and of ribaldry, as filthy as heart can think, to corrupt the minds of youth withal, clean contrary to the doctrine of Christ and his apostles' (*Doctrinal Treatises* 161). In the same work he states: 'yea, verily, Aristotle and Plato, and even very Robin Hood, is to be believed in such a point, that so greatly maintaineth our holy father's authority, and all his disguisings' (220). And again: 'if I could not prove with an open text that which the allegory doth express, then were the allegory a thing to be jested at, and of no greater value than a tale of Robin Hood' (306). And finally: '"Gird on thee the sword of the Spirit, which is God's word, and take to thee the shield of faith:" which is, not to believe a tale of Robin Hood, or Gesta Romanorum, or of the Chronicles, but to believe God's word that lasteth ever' (328). In *The Prologue to the Book of Genesis*, Robin Hood makes another appearance: 'And when some, which seem to themselves great clerks, say, "They wot not what more profit is in many gests of the scripture, if they be read without an allegory, than in a tale of Robin Hood:" say thou, "That they were written for our consolation and comfort"' (*Doctrinal Treatises* 400). In a marginal gloss to Deuteronomy, Tyndale alludes to present-day prelates who encourage the laity to 'Talk of Robin Hood' (*Tyndale's Old Testament* 273). And finally, in the *Prologue to the Book of Jonas* he states: 'And the lives, stories, and gests of men, which are contained in the Bible, they read as things no more pertaining unto them than a tale of Robin Hood, and as things they wot whereto they serve, save to feign false descant and juggling allegories, to stablish their kingdom withal' (*Tyndale's Old Testament* 450).

These numerous references to Robin Hood demonstrate that Tyndale enjoyed using the figure to expose the church in various ways. And here, in this side-note reference in 'A compendious olde treatyse,' he once again employs Robin Hood to call down scorn upon the church, whose scholars (ie, 'masters') encourage one kind of reading at the expense of another. The reference is, of course, gratuitous, since the relation to material within the text is tangential at best. But the reference loses its puzzling quality when seen in the context of Tyndale's other writings.[27]

The second side-note worthy of consideration for the light it sheds on the identity of the editor occurs about three-quarters of the way through the tract (1576–7) in one of the sections that does not appear in Deanesly/Bühler. At this stage the author has just shown how, by not allowing the scriptures to be read in English, the clergy is responsible for creating heretics by forcing those interested in Bible study to do it secretly and risk error because of their isolation. The tract concludes that the clergy is responsible for turning God's law as found in the Bible into a source of damnation for those who study it privately and err as a result. Here the marginal note reads 'Is not this turninge the rotys of the tres vpward.' This use of an inverted tree is an attempt on the author's part to show the unnatural consequences of the clergy's ban on an open, accessible, and vernacular Bible. It is an image I have found nowhere else in the literature of the period before Tyndale's *Obedience of a Christian Man*, where it occurs twice, each time in the text as well as in the margin.[28] Additionally, one reference to the inverted tree in *Obedience* is used in connection with the interpretation of scripture, the identical situation to the one in 'A compendious olde treatyse.' In the first instance, Tyndale is concerned with the church's insistence that we believe the scholarly interpreters of scripture before scripture itself, a situation which he regards as unnatural. He states, 'If I must first believe the doctor, then is the doctor first true, and the truth of the scripture dependeth of his truth; and so the truth of God springeth of the truth of man. Thus antichrist turneth the roots of the trees upward' (*Doctrinal Treatises* 154). The marginal note next to this comment reads, 'Antichrist turneth the roots of the tree upward.'

The second use of this image occurs in connection with the vexed and complex relationship between faith and good works, a major point of contention between the reformers and the traditional church. Tyndale states, 'Our good deeds do but testify only that we are justified and beloved. For except we were beloved, and had God's Spirit, we could neither do, nor yet consent unto any good deed. Antichrist turneth the roots of the trees upward. He maketh the goodness of God the branches, and our goodness the roots. We must be first good, after antichrist's doctrine, and move God, and compel him to be good again for our goodness's sake: so must God's goodness spring out of our goodness. Nay, verily; God's goodness is the root of all goodness; and our goodness, if we have any, springeth out of his good-ness' (295–6). And once more the marginal gloss reiterates the graphic image by stating, 'Antichrist turneth the roots of the trees upward.'

One final side-note in the text of 'A compendious olde treatyse' supports my view that Tyndale was the probable editor of portions of this tract. Early in the text Deanesly/Bühler cites Nicholas of Lyra, almost in passing, immediately after two references to Corinthians, to prove that people can only truly assimilate information when they are addressed in a language they understand. The Lyra quotation is as follows: 'Yf the people vnderstonde the prayer of the priest it shall the better be ledde vnto god / and the more deuoutly answere Amen' (1425–7). Tyndale jumps on this reference to Lyra with the following marginal gloss: 'Here youre owne master Lire yf ye wil not here Paul.' This rather aggressive injunction is obviously directed at the tradi-tional church and those who subscribe to it. By phrasing the side-note in this fashion, Tyndale immediately distances himself from Lyra and suggests that the 'master' is one of the clergy's own, a view not suggested in the innocuous textual reference to him. An exami-nation of Tyndale's two references to Lyra in his other works shows why he responds in this way. In the *Obedience of a Christian Man* he lumps Lyra together with other medieval scholastic philosophers and theologians who, in his view, cloud rather than clarify the truth of God's word. He states, 'Moreover, seeing that one of you ever prea-cheth contrary to another; and when two of you meet, the one dis-puteth and brawleth with the other, as it were two scolds; and forasmuch as one holdeth this doctor, and another that; one fol-loweth Duns, another St Thomas, another Bonaventure, Alexander de Hales, Rayomond, Lyre ... and such like out of number; so that if thou hadst but of every author one book, thou couldst not pile them up in any warehouse in London, and every author is one contrary unto another. ... Whereby shall I try and judge them? Verily by God's word, which only is true. But how shall I that do, when thou wilt not let me see scripture?' (149–53). His second reference to Nicholas of Lyra, if somewhat more humorous, is no more complimentary; it occurs in his *Answer to Sir Thomas More's Dialogue*: 'And when More, to utter his darkness and blind ignorance saith, that "they which were overwhelmed with Noe's flood had a good faith," and bringeth for him Nicolas de Lyra; I answer that Nicolas de Lyra *delirat*' (133–4).[29]

According to Deanesly, Lyra's work was attractive to 'the first generation of scholarly Lollards' who 'appealed to [him] freely to justify their disregard for the secondary interpretations of the text'; she adds that 'Purvey translated and incorporated large portions of Lyra's prologue into his own work' (166). In his uncomplimentary marginal gloss, Tyndale's association of Lyra with the other 'masters' he despised so vigorously is an ironic distortion of Deanesly/Bühler's apparent regard for him. But Tyndale's negative view of Lyra here is altogether consistent with his other references to him in the two works just cited. Since Tyndale seems to despise Lyra, it is interesting to speculate on why he did not simply excise the reference to him in the text. The answer, I think, is that he was too tempted by the opportunity to attack his opponents in the gloss by suggesting, first of all, that they disregard Paul's epistles, and secondly, that even one of their own benighted allies was, on this occasion at least, bright enough to recognize what they themselves refuse to understand: people can only appreciate what is being said to them when they understand the language in which it is being said. In a backhanded way, therefore, Nicholas of Lyra, whom Tyndale clearly dislikes, come to his aid to attack those whom he dislikes even more.

Further pieces of evidence to show that Tyndale may have edited parts of 'A compendious olde treatyse' come from the body of the text itself. The first thing that the decisions taken by the sixteenth-century editor of this work lead us to say is that he is not someone who simply tinkers with or makes minor adjustments to Deanesly/Bühler. There is tinkering to be sure: a careful comparison of Deanesly/Bühler with the sixteenth-century version shows that the editor moves around some of the original's passages to suit his own purposes. But changes do not stop there; in fact, well over half of the tract is made up of material which does not appear in Deanesly/Bühler and, therefore, might represent additions made by the sixteenth-century editor. The majority of these changes show that the editor is very concerned with strengthening the original's already strong argument for a vernacular Bible, and, more important perhaps, demonstrating how the church has stood in the way of vernacular scriptures over the centuries. And who more than Tyndale, the translator of the Bible *par excellence*, and recently under heavy verbal fire from Thomas More, would have had a greater stake in disseminating this information to the public?

A study of some of the additions shows that a large number focus on proving the importance of a vernacular Bible and exemplifying the malevolence of those who work against this goal. This latter point is especially important because in these additions one feels a greater sense of animosity towards the enemy, indeed a greater sense of enemy presence, than at any point in Deanesly/Bühler. The additions are more emotionally charged than the Deanesly/Bühler text. For instance, only once in Deanesly/Bühler is the word 'antichrist' used to refer to the papacy or the spiritual hierarchy. In the additions, however, it appears ten times, and although Tyndale did not coin the expression as it applies to the church or have a monopoly on its use, he may have appropriated it here for his own purposes, as he did in his other writings.

The additions also focus largely on the traditional church's actions to suppress a vernacular Bible. Within five lines of the opening, the editor attacks 'Antichrist the kinge off clergy' (1349) for the burning of the New Testament – undoubtedly an allusion to the fate of Tyndale's own translation, consigned to the flames under order of Cuthbert Tunstal, bishop of London, in 1526. This first additional passage also closes with a reference to scriptural burning. The editor states that 'now oure bisshopes dampne and bren goddes lawe / for bycause it is drawen into our mother tounge' (1357–8). In another long insertion he excoriates 'oure bisshops' because 'they brenne gods worde' (1530–1). In the same passage he attacks the church for burning those who seek to have God's law in English (1539). On 1560ff he speaks out against those who burn English books but adds that they cannot burn them as fast as others can be produced; and on 1580ff he mentions the work of those who labour to produce books and those who labour to burn them.

The editor's focus on the importance of a vernacular Bible in this tract is also evident in his repetition of the phrase 'mother tongue.' In Tyndale's writings centring on his own work of biblical translation the phrase appears often. In the 'Preface' to *Obedience of a Christian Man* it appears ten times; in the *Preface to the Five Books of Moses*, three times; and in *A Pathway into the Holy Scripture*, once. In Deanesly/Bühler it appears twice, and the English editor, naturally, keeps it. But in the additions, he uses the phrase eight times, and on three other occasions he adds it to sections of Deanesly/Bühler that he reproduces in his own version, once interrupting a biblical citation to slip it in (1381). The implication seems clear: either Tyndale or someone very familiar with his work had a hand in this version.

The editor of 'A compendious olde treatyse,' is content to use Deanesly/Bühler's English translations of biblical citations in those sections of the text where he merely copies the original English translation. By the time the translator of Deanesly/Bühler (whoever he was) began working on his text, he probably would have had two versions of the so-called Wycliffe Bible to draw on if he so desired (John Wycliffe: *The Holy Bible, Containing The Old and New Testaments* ed Forshall and Madden). After examining scriptural citations in Deanesly/Bühler and comparing them with both versions of the Wycliffe Bible, I have concluded that the latter played very little part in Deanesly/Bühler. What is significant, however, is that Tyndale, my candidate as editor of some portion of this version, allowed Deanesly/Bühler's version to stand for the most part, even when he had his own work to draw on. A brief sampler of Deanesly/Bühler's renderings, the Wycliffe versions, and the Tyndale renderings (where applicable) follows.

At line 1368, Deanesly/Buhler's version of Wisdom 1:4 is 'Wisdome shall not enter into a wicked soule.' This version is not close to Wycliffe: 'For in to an euell willi soule shal not gon in wisdam' ('For whi wisdom schal not entre in to an yuel willid soule' Forshall and Madden III 86). In 'A compendious olde treatyse' (1397–8), Numbers 11:29 reads as follows: 'And Moses sayde / what enviest thou for me? Who shall let that all the people prophesye / yf god gyue them his spirite?' The Wycliffe versions are somewhat contorted, at least to modern ears: 'And he, What, he seith enuyest thou for me? who gyueth that the puple prophecie, and God gyue to hem his spiryt?' ('And he seide, What hast thou enuye for me? who gyueth that al the puple profesie, and that God gyue his spirit to hem?' I 398). The Tyndale version (not used in 'A compendious olde treatyse') is a model of clarity by comparison: 'And Moses sayed vnto him: enuyest thou for my sake? wolde God that all the Lordes people coude prophecye, and that the Lorde wolde put his spirite apon them' (*William Tyndale's Five Books of Moses Called the Pentateuch* 438). In 1418–19 one reads the following citation from Acts 11:17: 'Yf god haue gevyn the same grace to them that he hath to vs / who am I that may forbyd god?' The Wycliffe Bible also uses the important word 'grace' in both versions: 'Therfore if God gaf to hem the same grace, as and to vs ... who was I, that mygte forbede the Lord' ('Therfore if God gaf to hem the same grace, as to vs ... who was Y, that mygte forbeede the Lord' IV 541). Tyndale, the possible editor, suppresses his own preference for the word 'gift' in place of 'grace' in order to follow Deanesly/ Bühler. His own version reads: 'Forasmuch then as God gave them like gifts, as he did unto us ... what was I that should have withstood God' (*Tyndale's New Testament* ed Daniell 181). In almost all other

instances where the editor copies Deanesly/Bühler, he also sub-
scribes to its biblical translations.

Naturally, my case that Tyndale was the sixteenth-century editor
of the Deanesly/Bühler text would be considerably strengthened if I
could show that the biblical citations within the textual additions
were identical to those in Tyndale's edition of the New Testament.
Unfortunately, this cannot be done, since the editor appears to translate New Testament citations in the text directly from the Latin, and
in two instances quotes the Latin, or part of it, after his rendering
(1497–8; 1665–7). Even so, one can see Tyndalian turns of phrase in
these biblical quotations which might suggest that Tyndale tinkered
with the English in some of them. The citation from Luke 9 which
reads in the text as 'saynct Ihon euangelist said vnto Christ / lorde
we shall forbid one that casteth out spirites in thy name / which
foloweth not vs. And Christ said do not forbid for who so is not
against vs is with vs' (1399–1402) appears in the 1534 New Testament as 'And John answered and said: Master we saw one casting out
devils in thy name, and we forbade him, because he foloweth not
with us. And Jesus said unto him: forbid ye him not. For he that is
not against us, is with us' (*Tyndale's New Testament* ed Daniell 107)
(1526 has 'For he that is nott agaynst you, is with you' (*William Tyndale's Five Books of Moses* ed Mombert 438).[30] Again, Acts 2 is rendered as follows in 'A compendious olde treatyse': 'That god nowe in
the laste dayes shall shede out his spirite vpon euery flesch. For god
sayeth your sonnes and doughters shuld prophesy / and your yong
men shall se visyons' (1405–8). In the 1534 New Testament this is
rendered: 'It shall be in the last days saith God: of my spirit I will
pour out upon all flesh. And your sons and daughters shall prophesy,
and your young men shall see visions' (Daniell 166). And in a textual
addition to Deanesly/Bühler, 1 John 2 is rendered: 'they haue gonn
owt of vs but they were not of vs' (1559–60). In Tyndale 1534 we read,
'They went out from us but they were not of us' (Daniell 339).

Given the tone, certain distinctive Tyndalian marginal glosses, an
inordinate focus on the importance of a vernacular Bible evident in
the repetition of certain themes and even words and phrases, and linguistic parallels between biblical quotations here and in Tyndale's
New Testament, it seems probable that the sixteenth-century editor
of this short tract was William Tyndale himself.[31] Tyndale would
have found some comfort in discovering in this work another voice,
albeit one not as loud or persistent as his, or altogether in harmony
with him, that recognized the importance of the Bible in the vernacu-

lar and was able to show a legitimate pedigree for its translations over the centuries leading up to the production of his own monumental work and the various strong reactions to it.[32]

It now remains to firm up briefly my earlier speculations on the order of publication of these various tracts. On the strength of my claim that 'A compendious olde treatyse,' issued as a separate text in 1530, was in part a modified Tyndalian version of Deanesly/Bühler, I conclude that *A proper dyaloge* without the 'compendious olde treatyse' addition was published by Luft in either late 1529 or early 1530,[33] and that *after* printing the Tyndale edition of Deanesly/Bühler in 1530, Luft quickly printed another edition of *A proper dyaloge* in the same year with the Tyndale text appended to it. My reasons for establishing this order are as follows: obviously anything from Tyndale's pen – even something not openly acknowledged – would attract widespread interest amongst Protestant polemicists, given Tyndale's stature at this time. By 1530 he had produced a number of influential works, including *The Parable of the Wicked Mammon* and *Obedience of a Christian Man*, to say nothing of his 1526 edition of the New Testament. Secondly, since in its original version *A proper dyaloge* was already a medley or hybrid text made up of a dialogue and a prose tract from a Lollard source, there would be no reason not to add another tract; and thirdly, since *A proper dyaloge* in its earliest version mentions both the reluctance of the church to allow the Bible in the vernacular and its perverse readings of scripture to suit its own ends, the Tyndale text would be a perfect graft onto material already thematically prepared to receive it.

Sources and Analogues

Rede Me and Be Nott Wrothe

I have already shown how *A proper dyaloge* is indebted to *Rede Me and Be Nott Wrothe* in certain formal ways: how it borrows its literary type, the dialogue; how it uses a similar rime-royal pattern which shifts to a pattern of tightly rhyming doggerel once the dialogue proper begins; how it, like *Rede Me*, makes use of refrains and a lamentation; how it sets up an interesting dramatic tension between the characters as *Rede Me* does; and how it goes as far as to borrow certain key words and phrases from the earlier work. The technique of borrowing devices from themselves would not have seemed unusual to the authors' contemporaries, since plagiarism as we know it did not exist at this time, nor would recycling one's own material have been seen as anything but good sense, especially if that material struck a sensitive chord and proved popular.[34]

It should, therefore, come as no surprise to discover that *Rede Me and Be Nott Wrothe*, a source of borrowings of a structural and formal nature for *A proper dyaloge*, also served as a potentially rich repository of reformist concepts that Barlowe and Roye could use to help construct their new work designed to attack certain aspects of the traditional church that *Rede Me* had also felt compelled to expose.

However, before thematic connections between the two works are made, a proviso on indebtedness and borrowing during this period should be stated. In general terms, since the English reformers of the 1520s and 1530s were interested in a rather small range of religious issues directed against the traditional church, it is all too easy to fall prey to the *post hoc ergo propter hoc* fallacy and see areas of direct indebtedness based on chronology, when, in fact none might actually exist. Rather than borrowing from his predecessor(s), an author might simply share an identical position, hold the same attitude, attack the same abuse.[35] During the period under discussion here, roughly the years between 1527 and 1530, a number of English reformist works, critical of the religious establishment and published on the continent, appeared on the scene. There were, of course, the block-busters: Tyndale's *The Parable of the Wicked Mammon* and *Obedience of a Christian Man*, published in 1527 and 1528 respectively (Tyndale *Doctrinal Treatises*); but there were also many other influential and thematically related tracts: Roye's *A Brefe Dialoge bitwene a Christen Father and his stobborne Sonne* (1527), *Rede Me and Be Nott Wrothe* (1528), Frith's *The Revelation of Antichrist* (1529), Roye's *An exhortation to the diligent studye of scripture* (1529), Simon Fish's *A Supplicacyon for the Beggers* (1529), and, of course, two editions of *A proper dyaloge*, and 'A compendious olde treatyse' (Hume 'English Protestant Books Printed Abroad'). Theoretically at least, one could find God's plenty of 'sources' for subsequent works by simply focusing on Tyndale's two works mentioned above, to say nothing of the source-hunting one could do by working through Tyndale's writings themselves to find the number of times he serves as his own source, since he was not reluctant to repeat himself.

A second element of the proviso applies specifically to *Rede Me and Be Nott Wrothe*. Since it is both structurally and from the point of view of content a somewhat chaotic work that touches on an enormous number of perceived abuses in the church – the mass, auricular confession, purgatory, the papacy, monks, friars, pilgrimages, the veneration of saints, Thomas Wolsey himself – it is, or can be perceived as being, a 'barber's chair to fit all buttocks,' that is, a source – to some extent – for whatever reformist tract might follow it. With this in mind, one can, nevertheless, see that *Rede Me* does provide concepts – however undeveloped, inchoate, or truncated – which *A proper dyaloge* could have grasped and developed.

Like many other English reformist works of the period, *Rede Me and Be Nott Wrothe* became the object of official government proscription and banning, which Clebsch summarizes under the title 'The Battle against Books' (258–70). For some reason it missed being included in Archbishop Warham's extended list of heretical books circulated probably sometime in 1529, although Roye's 'A dialogue betwixt the father and the son,' as it was called, did make the list. *Rede Me* was also omitted from the list issued by Henry's ecclesiastical commission in May 1530, made up of William Warham, Thomas More, Cuthbert Tunstal, and Stephen Gardiner and 'four Cambridge liberals' (263). However, it was included in the 1530–1 list of proscribed books under the title 'The burying of the mass,' and in two of the three subsequent lists, one issued in 1531 by Stokesley and another undated list, it also makes an appearance.

A proper dyaloge's critical focus is essentially on three elements: in the first edition the main concern is on the economic abuses against society brought about by a greedy and acquisitive clergy keen on obtaining land that rightly belongs to the laity; this element in the dialogue is given added strength and historical validity through the inclusion of the first Lollard tract. Closely tied to the notion of landgrabbing is the tract's attack on the doctrine of purgatory, which is seen as the lever used by the clergy to pry land from the intimidated and frightened laity. The final element on which the tract focuses is the importance of a vernacular scripture, alluded to from time to time in the dialogue itself, but given its greatest development in the prose tract added to the second edition.

In the first part of the dialogue in *Rede Me and Be Nott Wrothe*, the impoverishment of the laity is not attributed to the impropriation of secular lands and farms squeezed from the gullible solely through the use of the doctrine of purgatory but rather to the Roman Catholic mass. The mass proves to be the major source of clerical wealth because of the fraudulent powers the clergy associate with it, including remission of temporal punishment due to sin and the consequent reduction of time one might have to spend in purgatory in the afterlife. However, even within the first part of the dialogue where discussions of the mass predominate, *Rede Me*, because of its shotgun approach to a wide variety of topics, turns its attention, however fleetingly, to other abuses committed by 'religious folke' (1307), by which the speaker means 'possessioners' or monks rather than friars or 'seculer prestes' (1287). At one point Ieffraye explains to Watkyn how 'religious folke' make do. His comments are reminiscent of those made in *A proper dyaloge* when the gentleman complains about clerical takeover of his land and the loss of his patrimony. Early in the tract the gentleman complains against the clerics: 'My enheritaunce and patrimony. Agaynst right / from me they kepe awaye' (106–7). Later (144–50) he complains about his ancestors:

> Their chefe lordshippes and londes principall
> With commodytes of their possessyon

> Vnto the clergye they gaue forthe with all
> Dysheretinge their right successyon.
> Which to receiue without excepcion
> The couetous clergy made no denay
> Sayenge that they wold for their soules praye.

And when the husbandman enters, the gentleman reiterates the point (213–18) so that the reader cannot possibly miss the nature and source of the problem:

> They haue oure aunceters lyuelood and rentes
> Their principall fearmes and teneamentes
> With temporall fredomes and libertees.
> They haue gotten vnto their kingdomes
> Many noble baronries and erldomes
>   With esquyres landes and knightes fees.

The husbandman responds that he and his ilk are impoverished too and claims that the gentleman's ancestors have lost all by bartering lands for spiritual promises and prayers for their souls.

These notions are identical to Ieffraye's in *Rede Me* (1307–15):

> As for religious folke to be brefe,
> In all Englonde they have the chefe,
>   And most plesaunt commoditees.
> The goodly soyles, the goodly londes,
> Wrongfully they holde in their hondes,
>   Endued with many knyghtes fees.
> By coloure of their faulce prayres,
> Defrauded are the ryght heyres,
>   From their true inheritaunce.

and they re-echo in his song to Watkyn near the end of part one (1530–1; 1537–8):

> The ryches and gooddes of the common weall,
> Hath sett theym in their honoure full hye.
> ...
> The laboure of the povre people they devower
> And of nobles they waste the patrimony.

Additionally, near the conclusion of the song one can hear a comment about purgatory which is reminiscent of *A proper dyaloge*'s view on this church abuse (1593–6; 1600–1):

> Christes fredom they have brought in bondage
> Of hevenly rightes makynge marchandyse
> In gostly workes they covett avauntage,
> To fede their insaciate covetyse.
> ...
> Of hell and heven they make chevesance
> Faynynge as they lyst a purgatory.

Naturally, someone involved in the production of Tyndale's New Testament – to whatever extent – would not pass up an opportunity to comment on its destruction at the hands of the church. Barlowe and Roye's lengthy comment on this action in *Rede Me* – 'they sett hym a fyre, Openly in London cite' (711ff) – is repeated in *A proper dyaloge* (572–7):

> ... they haue commaunded straytely
> That none vnder great payne be so hardye
>   To haue in englishe the testament.
> Which as thou knowest at London
> The bisshop makinge ther a sermon
>   With shamefull blasphemy was brent.

In part two of *Rede Me and Be Nott Wrothe* the authors, through their speakers, turn away from Wolsey and the mass, for a while at least, to pay greater attention to the insatiable greed of the clergy as manifested not only in the behaviour of the friars but, more importantly for our purposes, in the successful take-over of lands and farms by avaricious possessioners. As a result, this part of the work is more in tune with the economic orientation of the dialogue section of *A proper dyaloge*. In describing the craftiness of the monks, who took advantage of the laity before the arrival on the scene of the friars, Barlowe and Roye concentrate on their theft of temporal possessions, an indictment we heard earlier in part one of *Rede Me* and one that permeates the dialogue sections of *A proper dyaloge*, although in this latter work the clergy in general, rather than just monks, is under attack. Notice how in the following quotation Ieffraye, the expert on affairs in England, focuses on the loss of patrimony consequent upon the take-over of property by the clergy, an idée fixe for the gentleman in *A proper dyaloge*. Ieffraye states (1897–1905):

> By their coloured devocion,
> To the people they gave a mocion,
>   Their favoure craftly purchasynge.
> And so by their contrivynge cast,
> They gott clene a waye at the last,
>   Their chefe possessions temporally.
> Wherby laye people opressed sore,
> Scant coulde they geve eny more,
> Concernynge londes and patrimony.

One hears of the clergy's greed and wealth and the notion of patrimony again later in the work (2516–23):

> They have in maner the ryches,
> Of every londe and nacion.
> Namly in Englonde region,
> They excede in possession
>   And lordly dominacion.
> The blacke order hath more alone,
> Then all the nobles every chone
>   As touchynge their patrimony.

And finally, both *Rede Me* (2789ff) and *A proper dyaloge* (320ff) complain about the way in which individual farms taken over by the clergy are combined into single large ones so that only the rich can afford to rent them. The terms in which this complaint is uttered in both works are so close that I used them as an example earlier to help demonstrate that the authors of the one work also wrote the other.

To further vilify clerics, *Rede Me* complains that members of the priestly order do nothing to contribute to the welfare of the commonwealth and when called upon to do so use their spiritual calling as an excuse for inactivity (2488–93):

> Wher as the religious sectes,
> Vnto no lawes are subiectes,
>   Obeyinge nether god nor kynge.
> Yf the kynge will their service vse,

> Forthwith they laye for an excuse,
>   That they must do goddes busines.

A similar sentiment is expressed in *A proper dyaloge* (449–54):

> But is the realme in any necessyte
> Where as they shuld condescend of duete
>   To stande by their prince with soccour.
> Than to be of the world they denye
> Sayenge that their helpe is spiritually
>   From the worlde makinge a separacion.

The fact that clerics refuse to participate in the world when their own skin might be at risk, and behave in such a way as to suggest that they are being untrue to their spiritual calling, indicate that they are neither part of this world nor a part of the legitimate spiritual realm. Both works express this notion in similar ways. In *Rede Me* (2902–4) Ieffraye says that

> They are nether gostly ner worldly,
> Rather divlysshe then godly
>   With out eny goode properte.

In *A proper dyaloge* the husbandman, referring to clerics, asks the gentleman, 'Are they worldly or gostely to saye the trothe?' And the gentleman replies: 'So god helpe me I trowe none of bothe / As it apperyth by their fasshion' (439–42).

In both works the speakers complain about the exalted position of the spiritual orders within the political sphere by referring to their presence in parliament. Here is *Rede Me* (2536–8):

> Divers of theym have the degre,
> Of worthy Erles in dignite,
>   And are lordes of the parlement.

And here *A proper dyaloge* (519–21):

> Thou knowest that in the parlament
> The chefe of the clergye are resident
>   In a maruelous great multitude.

With a view to indicating that the present state of affairs has not always obtained, both speakers in each work hark back to a happier time when clerics did not have the possessions they now hold and, as a result, the laity were happier, more prosperous, and better able to be charitable to those in need. Watkyn and Ieffraye put it as follows (2776–81):

> Wat. I have hearde saye of myne elders,
> That in Englonde many fermers,
> Kept gaye housholdes in tymes passed.
> Ief. Ye that they did with liberalite,
> Sheawynge to povre people charite,
> But nowe all together is dasshed.

In *A proper dyaloge* the gentleman reminisces on essentially the same subject (109–13):

> Myne aunceteres of worthy progeny
> With rentes and lyuelood largely endued
> Mayntayned their estates honorably
> Aydynge the poore / indigence to exclude.
> Tyll at the last / the clergy to them sued.

And later in the tract the husbandman expresses the same sentiments from his own point of view (270–2; 282–7):

> Fyrst whan englonde was in his floures
> Ordred by the temporall gouernoures
> Knowenge no spirituall iurisdiccion.
> ...
> We husband men lyke wise prosperously
> Occupyenge the feates of husbandry
> Hyerd fearmes of pryce competent.
> Wherby oure lyuinge honestly we wanne
> And had ynough to paye every manne
> Helpinge other that were indigent.

And finally, each work gives the same explanation for why the church objects to having a vernacular Bible: if the people could understand the word of God in their own language they would immediately perceive how the clergy violates God's law through its pernicious actions. *Rede Me* states (3164–71):

> Ief.   They despyse Christ oure saveoure,
>   Labourynge his worde to exclude.
> Wat. Canst thou prove this in dede?
> Ief.   Whosoever will the gospell rede,
>   To prove it shall nede no testes.
>
> Wat. Peraventure they wolde have it hid,
>   Wherfore to rede it they forbid
>   Lest men shulde knowe their wickednes.

And in *A proper dyaloge* the husbandman states (409–16):

> In fayth syr I coniecture some what
> And I suppose I do not moche erre.
> Might men the scripture in Englishe rede
> We secular people should than se in dede
> What Christ and the apostles lyves were.
> Which I dout nothinge are contrarye
> Vnto the lyuynge of oure clargye
>   Geuyn to pompous ydlenes euery where.

A Supplicacyon for the Beggers

About two-thirds of the way through the dialogue portion of *A proper dyaloge*, the gentleman and husbandman, after expressing their concerns about clerical impropriations and the profound effects such actions have had on them and on the country as a whole, consider the possibility of taking their complaints to London, where, they have learned, a new session of parliament (the so-called Reformation Parliament whose first session convened in November 1529) is being held. When the gentleman asks the husbandman what purpose this might serve, the husbandman responds that they would be able 'to declare' before parliament 'The constraynte of oure myserye ... Vnder a meke forme of lamentacion' (482–3). The gentleman's less than enthusiastic response to this proposal is interesting from a number of points of view, not least because it alludes to two contemporary documents, one of which serves as a possible source for *A proper dyaloge* (485–93):

So shuld we be sure of soche answeres
As were made vnto the poore beggers
For thir pituous supplicacyon.
Against whom the clergyes resons nought worthe
The soules of purgatory they brought forthe
　The beggers complaynte to discomfyte.
Wherfore against oure peticion I the tell
They wold bringe out all the deuells in hell
　For to do vs some shamefull despyte.

The gentleman's reference to the 'pituous supplicacyon' of 'the poore beggers' is an allusion to Simon Fish's *A Supplicacyon for the Beggers* (*STC* 10883), a vitriolic attack on all forms of clerical power and the doctrine of purgatory, probably published by Johannes Grapheus of Antwerp in early 1529 (More 7 409; Hume 'English Protestant Books Printed Abroad' 1071-2).[36] Fish's slim work, referred to in its own day as a *libretto* (More 7 lxviii), created an enormous and instant stir amongst church traditionalists, as witnessed by Thomas More's quick response, ten times the length of Fish's tract, entitled *The supplycacyon of soulys*, published probably in September or October of 1529, only months after the appearance of Fish's work (More 7 lxv–lxvi).[37]

The gentleman's reference to the church's response to Fish's tract requires clarification. The line 'Against whom the clergyes resons nought worthe' (488) is misleading, since the response to Fish was not the clergy's, but Thomas More's and his alone. The use of the plural 'clergyes resons' may refer simply to More's function as spokesman *on behalf of* the church: in March 1528 he received a commission from Bishops Tunstal and Stokesley to act as official reader of Protestant tracts so as 'to meet the danger by quickly putting forth sound books in the vernacular on the catholic side' (cited in Clebsch 286). More, then, became church spokesman and polemicist against heretical books and to this extent at least his written responses to such works represented the church's official position.[38]

The further reference in the gentleman's response to the clergy bringing forth 'the soules of purgatory' 'to discomfyte' 'The beggers complaynte' (489–90) alludes to More's technique in his response to Fish. More 'devotes the entire second half of his treatise to a defense of [the doctrine of purgatory], and further emphasizes the point by presenting his pleas and arguments through the assembled voices of the souls now suffering in the fire of purgatory' (More 7 lxviii).

As a biased reformist tract, strongly supporting the Protestant cause, *A proper dyaloge* presents a skewed portrait of the polemical war between Fish and More, clearly stating that Fish was the victor and that More's tract relied solely on the voices of purgatory to score his very weak points. The husbandman poses the following question (495–7):

> And was ther none other waye at all
> But the soules of purgatory to call
> In ayde and assistence of the clergye?

And the gentleman responds (499–504):

> It was the suerest waye by seynt Ihone
> For had they to playne scripture gone
>   I wousse they hadde be taken tardye.
> The beggers complaynte was so grounded
> That the clargye hadde be confounded
>   Had they not to purgatory hasted.

In fact, careful study, especially of the second part of More's *Supply-cacyon*, shows that he does rely heavily on scriptural citations and allusions to defend the doctrine of purgatory, and that Barlowe and Roye here are probably simply repeating Fish's view uttered in *A Supplicacyon* that 'there is not one word spoken of hit in al holy scripture' (419, 17–18) to justify their claim that More could not defend his position on purgatory with scripture's aid. To argue that More does not make use of scripture in his response to Fish when it is clear that he does and when anyone who wanted to certify the claim could do so by examining his work, written only four years prior to the publication of *A proper dyaloge*, is a stunning example of how the authors of this work attempt to manipulate even so recent a part of the historical record to generate their propaganda. Naturally, to admit that More did use the Bible in his response to Fish on the question of purgatory would require the authors of *A proper dyaloge* to go deeper into this matter than they want to or have time for. Additionally, it would undercut their ubiquitous ideological position that the traditional church shuns the Bible in order to hide the truth from those it wishes to keep in a state of blissful ignorance.[39]

An allusion to a work within another one does not mean, of course, that the work alluded to was an actual source, but in the case of

Fish's *Supplicacyon* there is sufficient internal textual evidence to conclude that Barlowe and Roye knew the work well. Indeed, one might even make a case to demonstrate that Fish's tract shows some indebtedness to Barlowe and Roye's earlier work, *Rede Me and Be Nott Wrothe*, especially in its withering depiction of friars, although as Knowles has made clear, the various orders of friars came under attack from several sources – some of them from within the church itself – almost from the moment of their inception (*Religious Orders* 2 90ff).

At first glance it might appear that there are few similarities or areas of indebtedness between the two works: large parts of *A proper dyaloge* are written in poetry; *A Supplicacyon* is a relatively short document in prose. Despite the obvious artificiality of its form, *A proper dyaloge* goes some distance to convey its legitimacy and versimilitude; it is, in essence, a conversation between two aggrieved members of society who have little in common except their economic plight and their criticisms of a corrupt clergy with too much secular power and land. Fish's *Supplicacyon* is a masterpiece of rhetorical artifice which moves beyond a dramatic portrayal of Roman Catholicism's gross enormities to the borders of melodrama. Its rhetorical devices strive with each other for supremacy: its sentences are lengthy, even breathless; its plethora of rhetorical questions and balanced repetitions impressive; and its language of attack extreme, intemperate, and unrelenting. Its verve and energetic diction convey a sense of urgency to the message that Fish wants the king to receive, but at the same time, its careful rhetorical contrivances – its artifice if you will – work to deconstruct its powerful sense of immediacy and national crisis. Compared to it, *A proper dyaloge* is a measured and temperate document, despite the involvement of the personae in the issues they present. Fish is his tract's narrator; the gentleman and husbandman are both narrators and victims of the stories they tell. From the point of view of energy, Fish's work is closer in spirit to *Rede Me and Be Nott Wrothe*, a frequently intemperate and angry work to which Fish may have been indebted, if not for content at least for tone.

Qualifications apart, there is much in *A Supplicacyon* that could find its way into *A proper dyaloge*. The human targets of attack in both works are members of the clerical hierarchy, and the major area of concern is the unseemly involvement of the church in the economic and political life of the country. In the opening few lines of *A proper dyaloge*, the speaker warns 'preste / pope / bisshoppe and Cardinall' (8), later collectively referred to as 'wolffes' (350), that they are likely to have a fall. Early in *A Supplicacyon*, Fish calls his culprits 'rauinous wolues' and lists them in painstaking detail, filling in the broader categories that *A proper dyaloge* mentions. Included in his 'idell rauinous sort' are 'Bisshoppes, Abbottes, Priours, Deacons, Archedeacons, Suffraganes, Prestes, Monkes, Chanons, Freres, Pardoners and Somners' (412, 17–21).

The second book of More's response to Fish's *Supplicacyon* focuses on Fish's frontal attack on purgatory, a subject which gets extensive treatment in Fish's pamphlet relative to the size of the work as a whole. For Fish, as for the gentleman and husbandman, purgatory is the pernicious church doctrine which allows clerics of all stripes to put the financial squeeze on Christians foolish, hopeful, or fearful enough to believe in their hollow promises. Addressing himself to the king, Fish states: 'this purgatory and the Popes pardons is all the cause of translacion of your kingdome so fast into their hondes' (419–20, 31–1); and a few lines later he adds: 'Here may your grace well perceyue that except ye suffer theyre ypochrisie to be disclosed all is like to runne ynto theire hondes and as long as it is couered so long shall it seme to euery man to be a greate ympiete not to gyue theim' (420, 13–16).

Fish's sentiments on purgatory are reflected in the gentleman's monologue near the beginning of *A proper dyaloge*, where he complains at length about his lost lands and the theft of his patrimony because of the donations given by his ancestors to the clergy. And it is clear from the refrain, 'Sayenge that they wold for their soules praye' – repeated with slight variation thirteen times in this section of the work – that the device which allowed the clerics to rob him of his lands was the church doctrine of purgatory. And lest the point be missed, both husbandman and gentleman repeat it time and again once the dialogue itself begins and each makes his complaints felt against the clergy. Both works imply that if the practice is not exposed for what it truly is the country will fall into economic ruin. Fish claims that if clerical hypocrisy on the subject of purgatory is not disclosed 'all is like to runne ynto their hondes,' a sentiment expressed somewhat more ironically by the husbandman when he says 'yf they pray longe thus so god me mende / They shall make the lande worsse than nought' (265–6).

Throughout his commentary, the gentleman blames his 'aunceteres' (109) for their thoughtless generosity. Fish, in his turn, refers to the 'predecessours' (420, 24) of the present generation of 'loordes knightes squirs gentilmen and yemen in englond' (420, 19) who gave 'to the spiritualte' (420, 23) so that they might eventually be released from the torments of purgatory.

Whereas the husbandman speaks of a country robbed 'round aboute' (245) by a clergy that malevolently affects both 'comones and estates none excepte' (246) and further mentions that the land has been brought 'to beggery' (248), Fish refers to a new and oppressed category of beggar on whose behalf he speaks to the king; futhermore, he fleshes out *A proper dyaloge*'s general comments on the state of the nation. Fish's graphic description could not but have impressed the authors of *A proper dyaloge*, whose two speakers now find themselves rapidly approaching membership in the following unenviable fellowship:

> Most lamentably compleyneth theyre wofull mysery vnto youre highnes youre poore daily bedemen the wretched hidous monstres ... the foule vnhappy sorte of lepres, and other sore people, nedy, impotent, blinde, lame, and sike, that live onely by almesse, howe that theyre nombre is daily so sore encreased that all the almesse of all the weldisposed people of this youre realme is not half ynough for to susteine theim, but that for verey constreint they die for hunger. And this most pestilent mischief is comen vppon youre saide poore beedmen by the reason that there is yn the tymes of youre noble predecessours passed craftily crept ynto this your realme an other sort ... of strong puissaunt and counterfeit holy, and ydell beggers and vacabundes. ... (412, 1–14).

The 'ydell beggers and vacabundes' to whom Fish refers are, of course, the clergy, whose increasing numbers over the years are a cause of worry to him. He tells Henry that they are 'nowe encreased vnder your sight not onely into a great nombre, but also ynto a kingdome' (412, 16–17) The gentleman expresses the same concern (377–85):

> For whye with in thes .iiij. hundred yere
> Thorough oute christendome was not a freer
>   Of thes / whom we mendicantes call.
> And syth that tyme dyuers facciones
> Of collegianes / monkes and chanones
>   Haue spred this region ouer all.

> Also of prestes / were not the tenthe parte
> Which as they saye / haue none other arte
>> But for vs worldly people to praye.

Despite this increase in the number of clerics (there being, for instance, ten times as many priests as previously)

> ... the worlde is nowe farre worsse
> As euery man felyth in his poorsse
>> Than it was at that tyme I dare saye. (386–8)

Statistics also play a part in assessing the degree of power and wealth the clerics have amassed through their deceitful doctrine of purgatory. The gentleman claims that the clergy has appropriated so much that 'halfe the realme is their owne' (311). Fish at one point states that 'they haue gotten ynto theyre hondes more then the therd part of all youre Realme' (412, 23), and argues later that their possessions 'drawe nighe vnto the half of the hole substaunce of the realme' (414, 27–8).

Both works mention how the clergy tops up its wealth in all sorts of questionable ways by impoverishing those who subscribe to its fraudulent rituals and obey its demands for money. In addition to paying exorbitant rents for their farms, farmers and others are susceptible to 'other contentes of brybery' (298–302)

> As payenge of tythes / open and preuy
>> And for herynge of confession.
> Also prestes dueties and clerkes wages
> Byenge of perdones and freres quarterages
>> With chirches and aultares reparacion.

Fish feels the same way (413, 4ff): 'Whate money get they by mortuaries, by hearing of confessions (and yet they wil kepe therof no counceyle) by halowing of churches, altares, superaltares, chapelles, and belles, by cursing of men and absoluing theim agein for money?'

We have already seen that the gentleman and husbandman criticize the clergy for not coming to the support of the prince. Fish also makes the same point by stating that the clerics, with all their money, 'exempt theim silues from thobedience of your grace' (415, 5). In addition they actively work to subvert the king when their own best interests are threatened. Authors of both works allude to King

John's difficulties with the spiritual orders and depict him as the victim of their treachery and deceit (*A proper dyaloge* 1213ff; *A Supplicacyon* 415, 10ff).

The extent to which the clergy is directly involved in the political life of the country is indicated by its prominent place in the parliament of England. The gentleman, sceptical of any good that might come from presenting their legitimate claims before parliament, tells the husbandman 'that in the parlament / The chefe of the clergye are resident / In a maruelous great multitude' (519–21). And Fish, emphasizing the power of the clergy in high places, tells the king: 'Are they not stronger in your owne parliament house then your silfe? Whate a nombre of Bisshopes, abbotes, and priours are lordes of your parliament? (417, 27–9).

And finally, like *A proper dyaloge*, Fish's work mentions reasons for the church's reluctance to allow the Bible in the vernacular. Fish tells us that the church wants the truth of the Bible to be kept hidden so that the laity will not recognize the deceitful ways of clerics. But Fish, as is his wont throughout the tract, treats this subject by piling one example on top of another and making use of the popular medieval rhetorical device known as amplification (420, 5–13):

> This is the great scabbe why they will not let the newe testament go a brode yn your moder tong lest men shulde espie that they by theyre cloked ypochrisi do translate thus fast your kingdome into theyre hondes, that they are not obedient vnto your highe power, that they are cruell, vnclene, vnmerciful, and ypochrites, that thei seke not the honour of Christ but their owne, that remission of sinnes are not giuen by the popes pardon, but by Christ, for the sure feith and trust that we haue in him.

It is clear then, I think, that whatever distant sources or ideas *A proper dyaloge* may have drawn on, it was certainly indebted as well to the swirl of a limited number of contemporary critical views circulating about the traditional church, ideas captured – and given birth – in such works as *Rede Me and Be Nott Wrothe* and *A Supplicacyon for the Beggers*.

The Tradition of Complaint:
A Sampler of Texts

According to John Peter, the themes of complaint literature in the medieval period fall into 'four rough categories' (60). For the purposes of this brief survey, the category of complaint against the professions is central, especially complaint against the clergy, which Peter calls 'far and away the most important' (80) profession under attack during the period. Clearly, no summary of this nature can do justice to the complexity and plenitude of complaint literature, which attacks various manifestations of actual or perceived corruption within the church, nor is such literature necessarily an altogether disinterested and unbiased picture of the state and health of the medieval church. However, the fact that complaint literature was abundant – if often boringly repetitive – suggests that the *literati* of the period, such as they were, recognized the importance of the church in the life of their culture and were concerned about deviations from an ethical norm which derived either from the Bible, the Church Fathers, or simple tradition itself.

The two best-known authors of medieval literature critical of the church are Geoffrey Chaucer (c 1343–1400) and William Langland (c 1332–c 1399). In the *General Prologue* to *The Canterbury Tales* and in the *Tales* themselves, Chaucer exposes members of the clergy to public scrutiny even as the frame of the tales calls into question the efficacy of pilgrimages, a subject made forever memorable by Erasmus in his colloquy *Peregrinatio Religionis Ergo* ('A pilgrimage for religion's sake'). Chaucer's worldly monk, who is addicted to hunting, and his money-hungry mendicant called Huberd are masterpieces of understated portraiture, and the complex relationship between Chaucer the narrator and Chaucer the pilgrim makes the complaint nature of the work indirect and ironic (Donaldson 1–13).

Chaucer's focus on a clergy single-mindedly devoted to affairs of the world such as pleasure and the accumulation of wealth is reiterated throughout the literature of the period. Indeed, the piling up of wealth in all of its various manifestations and sexual immorality amongst the clergy are the two themes which, according to my survey at least, receive the most detailed treatment in early complaint literature directed against the church.

Despite the allegorical veil, there is no difficulty in determining the narrator's attitude towards his subjects in *Piers the Plowman* (1360–99). As the extensive notes to Skeat's edition make clear, Langland's attacks on the clergy, monks, friars, and the church hierarchy in general are extensive and thorough. Langland attacks simony, all four orders of friars, worldly prelates, monetary abuses associated with confession, papal authority, undue clerical involvement in temporal matters, and clerical immorality. Not himself associated with Lollardy or Wycliffe, Langland nevertheless, as is clear even from this summary of his targets, had much to say about the church that would have appealed to and reflected Lollard views. Milman, speaking on behalf of the author's doctrinal orthodoxy, states: 'The Visionary is no disciple, no precursor of Wycliffe in his broader religious views ... he acquiesces seemingly with unquestioned faith in the Creed and in the usages of the Church. He is not profane but reverent as to the Virgin and the Saints. Pilgrimages, penances, oblations on the altar, absolution, he does not reject, though they are nought in comparison with holiness and charity' (Langland 2 l–li). And Whitaker speaks in a similar vein when he claims that Langland's ploughman carried 'too many remnants of his old faith ... incumbrances with which the Lollards of his own, or the Protestants of a later age, would not willingly have received him as a proselyte' (Langland 2 xliii).

Another major figure in the complaint tradition is John Gower (1330–1408). In two of his works in particular he is critical of certain clerical and/or church practices. In *Confessio Amantis* (1390), for instance, he states that the church gets involved in war 'For worldes good' (8 line 249); in addition, he attacks priestly arrogance, and claims that clerical avarice and benefice-hunting 'causeth forto bringe / This newe Secte of Lollardie' (11 lines 348–9), a clear indication of his own orthodoxy. The result of the church's unseemly involvement in the world is confusion for Christ's flock:

Lo, thus tobroke is Cristes folde,
Wherof the flock withoute guide

Devoured is on every side,
In lacke of hem that ben unware
Schepherdes, whiche her wit beware
Upon the world in other halve. (12 lines 390–5)

It is, however, in his Latin work *Vox Clamantis* (c 1382) that Gower presents his most detailed and outspoken opposition to abuses that he perceives in his church. The headings to certain chapters in Book III give good illustrations of Gower's major concerns. Chapter 5, for instance, concerns 'churchmen who possess the world's temporal goods and neglect the spiritual' (*The Major Latin Works* 124); chapter 9 'discusses the fact that just as it is not right for temporal lords to usurp control in spiritual matters, so it is not right for prelates of the clergy to undertake wars and temporal matters of that kind, which worldly pride and avarice bring about' (130). Chapter 11 deals with 'churchmen who adopt a holy name for themselves, but nevertheless lay hold of earthly possessions,' a major theme of *A proper dyaloge* (137), and chapter 19 concerns 'rectors who live in parishes, but nevertheless neglect the care of souls.' They buy and sell 'all kinds of temporal goods from day to day, just like lay merchants [and] they amass worldly wealth' (150). Chapters 1–15 of Book IV focus on monastic orders, their accumulation of wealth and 'temporal goods' (165), and the second half of the book criticizes that perennial subject of complaint amongst authors, the friars.

Much shorter, lesser-known works of literature, usually consigned to the dusty corners of history, also express interesting, and sometimes amusing, critical comments on perceived abuses within the church. A number of medieval lyrics are cruelly outspoken about church offences. One stanza from a fourteenth-century lyric attacking 'Frer Minours' (*Medieval English Lyrics* 141) is enough to suggest the tone of anger in some of these works, a tone which finds its sixteenth-century counterpart in Fish's *A Supplicacyon for the Beggers*:

A cart was made all of fire as it shuld be:
A gray frer I sawe therinne that best liked me.
Wele I wote thay shall be brent, by my leaute!
God graunt me that grace that I may it se!
With an O and an I, brent be thay all,
And all that helpes therto, faire mot befall. (142)

Another lyric of slightly later date (*Medieval English Lyrics* 162–3) humorously portrays a seducer priest, Jankin, who impregnates the poem's speaker, Alison. The poet juxtaposes the sanctity associated with various parts of the mass with Jankin's sexual attraction to Alison, whose name, conveniently, rhymes with the poem's refrain 'Kyrieleyson,' one of the mass's prayers. In its blasphemous juxtaposition of sacred and profane, the poem is reminiscent of Skelton's similar technique in *Phyllyp Sparowe*, and even of Barlowe and Roye's in *Rede Me and Be Nott Wrothe* (337–46).

John Audelay's poem of the early fifteenth century ('It is the best, early and late'; *Medieval English Lyrics* 171–2), exhorts the four estates to maintain their proper order and degree. Two of the eight stanzas are directed at members of the church hierarchy. The exhortation in the poem to proper living suggests that a good deal of improper living was the order of the day:

> A prest shuld shew uche more mekeness,
> And leve in love and charity:
> Throgh his grace and his goodness
> Set all other in unity,
> I say algate.

> A frere shuld love all holiness,
> Prayers, penans and poverty:
> Religious men, Christ hem ches
> To forsake pride and vainglory,
> I say algate.

An anonymous lyric of the later fifteenth century focuses in part on clerical greed and spiritual blackmail. A young man will have his misdemeanours overlooked if the bishop who pursues him is bought off by the offender:

> If thou be a yong man, in lust thy life to lace,
> About chirch and market the bishop will thee chace:
> And if thou mayst be get thou getes nouther grace,
> But thou have the peny redy to tak to.
>
> (*Medieval English Lyrics* 225)

A particularly interesting poem for the purposes of this edition is one that Davies dates around 1500 (265–6). It is a two-pronged attack directed against friars and those who oppose a vernacular Bible. Because of its association with one of the main themes of *A proper dyaloge*, it is worth quoting in full:

Alas! what shul we freres do,
Now lewed men cun Holy Writ?
Alle aboute where I go
They aposen me of it.

Then wondreth me that it is so,
How lewed men cun alle wit.
Sertely, we be undo
But if we mo amende it.

I trowe the devil brought it aboute,
To write the Gospel in Englishe,
For lewed men ben nowe so stout
That they yeven us neither fleshe ne fishe.

When I come into a shope
For to say, 'in principio,'
They bidene me, 'Go forth, lewed "Pope",'
And worche and win my silver so.

If I say it longeth not
For prestes to worche whether they go,
They leggen for them Holy Writ,
And seyn that Seint Polle did so.

Than they loken on my habite
And seyn, 'Forsothe, withouten othes,
Whether it be russet, black or white,
It is worthe alle oure weringe clothes!'

I seye I bidde not for me
Bot for them that have none:
They seyn, 'Thou havest to or thre!
Yeven them that nedeth therof one.'

Thus oure disceites bene aspiede,
In this maner, and many moo,

Fewe men bedden us abide,
But hey fast, that we were go.

If it go forthe in this maner
It wole doen is miche gile.
Men shul finde unnethe a frere
In Englonde within a while.

Two anonymous complaint ballads written possibly in the 1520s are worth brief consideration. The first, a poem entitled *Now a Dayes*, is a complaint about the present sorry economic state in England and harks back, as *A proper dyaloge* does, to a happier period before the greed and self-interest of a few began to destroy the fabric of society by impoverishing the many. In his poem, the author does not take specific aim at one particular segment of society but is prepared to indict all who work on their own behalf without regard for the common good. Only sixteen lines of this 280-line poem are directed against the church, but they are worth mentioning in any case, since they focus on the perennial theme of greed associated with church officials, a notion altogether in harmony with *A proper dyaloge*'s complaint (*Ballads from Manuscript* vol 2):

The spirituall church, their myslevyng,
to the temporall, evell ensample gevyng;
and thus, ether others works reprovyng,
    thei lyve in bate and stryfe.
The lay men say that preestes Iett,
alle ys ffysshe that commyth to the nett;
thei spare none that they can gett,
    Whether she be mayd or wyfe.

men say that priors and abbottes be
Grete grosyers in this countre;
they vse bying and sellyng openlye;
    the church hath the name.
Thei are nott content with ther possession,
But gapyng ever for promotion,
and thus withdrawyng mens Devotion,
vnto the landes grete shame.

Like the author of *Now a Dayes*, the author of *The Ruyn' of a Ream'*, a 259-line ballad, complains about his 'natyfe Contre' (2), which is plagued by 'Manyfolde vycis' (3) and 'fallyng in decay' (4) (*Ballads from Manuscript* vol 2). Like *Now a Dayes* as well, to which it might be indebted, or vice versa, *The Ruyn' of a Ream'* recalls with longing better days when the country was sounder economically, more just and more generally caring for its population. The author reminds his readers of the fall of the Roman Empire and implies that England might suffer the same fate unless it mends its ways (43–9).

Since at least one-third of the poem is given over to an attack on 'The spyrytualte' (73), it is clear that the author regards the church as the major culprit in the country's decline. Prelates are 'destytute of prudens' (80), 'Clothyd in Ryche Araye (88), in possession of 'Covetous myndis enfecte with Symony' (96), 'Rootyd so sore in pryde' (116), and accustomed to living 'lyke dukis and Erlys of the temporalte' (123). They avoid preaching, thereby turning their backs on the example set by 'Ierom and Ambrose' (136). Their 'Chefe delyte' is 'to bere A Rule / In grete mennus howsys of hye Autoryte' (143–4). Their pride in their own positions is such 'that noman with them they thynke may compare' (178–9) as they ride alone looking 'so solemly / as gargelles in A wall, whyche gryn and stare' (178–9). These complaints, of course, are not new, since they reflect concerns about the spiritual estate which, as we have seen, stretch well back in history; however, what is new is the two-stanza segment referring to a devoted member of the clergy, called by the author 'A famus devyne.' Unlike others of his calling, this divine 'wyll not enclyne' to the vices in which his colleagues indulge. He 'laboreth, studyethe, and preschythe daylye, / fedyng menus Sowlys with swete devyne syence, / and evry mannus fawtis declaryng playnly, / Aleggyng scrypture for every sentence: / this profounde man of lernyng and sapyens / Shewith to the prelatis their grete Abusyon; / Therfor Among them he ys had in derision' (106–12). Although this figure has never been definitely identified, Furnivall offers three names: Cuthbert Tunstal, bishop of Durham and London, the Franciscan friar Henry Standish and, interestingly, William Tyndale (154–5). It is difficult to believe that either Tunstal or Standish, sworn enemies to Tyndale, would have ever been held 'in derision,' and their names in a list along with Tyndale's seem anomalous. However, if the poem was written earlier than the 1520s, perhaps even in the reign of Henry VII, as Furnivall also suggests, then all three candidates are probably out of the running and the devoted cleric mentioned with approval in the poem must be consigned to oblivion.

One of the most interesting and, in some ways, perplexing works of complaint of this period is the anonymous *The Plowman's Tale* (reprinted in *Supplement to the Works of Geoffrey Chaucer* 147–90). Andrew Wawn's study of this 1380-line poem has done much to clear up its authorial and bibliographical mysteries. Often associated with Chaucer's *Canterbury Tales* in order to give it an authority it might not otherwise possess, it was first included in the Chaucer canon in 1542 in William Thynne's second edition of Chaucer's *Works* (Wawn 'The Genesis' 2). Skeat accords it a place in the Chaucer apocrypha and Wawn dates the majority of its composition from around the beginning of the fifteenth century. Wawn's historical and linguistic analysis of the poem demonstrates beyond a doubt that Henry Bradley's claim made in 1897 that the poem 'is essentially a product of the sixteenth century and represents a massive expansion and recasting of a fourteenth-century poem of which only fragments remain' is in error ('The Genesis' 22). For Wawn, the majority of the poem was written at the beginning of the fifteenth century by someone attuned to Lollard views; its debate section was revised and expanded by another Lollard sympathizer soon after the preparation; and its fifty-two-line 'Prologue' and three eight-line stanzas attacking the pope (lines 205–28) were added in the sixteenth century to make it more suitable as a propaganda piece for Henrician Reformation politics (Wawn 'The Genesis' and 'Chaucer').

The majority of *The Plowman's Tale* is in the form of a dialogue between two birds, a 'Pellican' and a 'Griffon,' the former speaking on behalf of its Lollard author, the latter on behalf of the Catholic church. However, a glance at the division of the speeches between the two birds shows that the poem is a dialogue in theory only: the loquacious Pelican monopolizes the poem, fulminating against the church for about 1121 lines, while the Griffon manages only about 98 lines in total. The remainder of the poem's lines are spoken by the narrator-pilgrim.

The Lollard-Pelican is relentless in his attacks on the church: the various orders of the clergy being 'Peters successours' (102) should be 'of low degree, / And usen none erthly honours' (103–4). Many of the clergy 'willeth to be kinges peres' (125). They ride on horses and are ostentatiously clothed in golden attire. They tell lies to the common people (147) and accumulate enough wealth to fill many bags (145). They intimidate 'Christes people' (165) with meaningless curses and serve Antichrist's purposes (190) despite supposing that they are 'Christes ministers' (189). They lust after honours and wealth and the pleasures of the flesh, and their cruelty surpasses even the cruellest pagan rulers: 'There was more mercy in Maximien / And in Nero, that never was good / Than [there] is now in some of hem' (293–5). Their tithes are unfair: they take from the poor and give to the rich in order to receive favours from those in a position to grant them. The pope in particular claims succession from Peter but abuses his authority to increase his wealth (365ff). This shamelessly repetitive screed uttered by a Pelican with logorrhea pauses only long enough for the 'Grifon' to ask the Pelican what it can say 'ayenst chanons / That men clepen seculere?' (717–18). The Pelican needs no more encouragement and is off again, striking out in all directions against canons and secular clergy. A little more than two hundred lines later the slow-learning Griffon asks about 'monkes' (990). After the Pelican's further attack the Griffon defends his church by counter-attacking the Pelican's call for complete reform. This part of the poem is the first and only genuine example of dialogue in the entire work. The Griffon argues that dismantling the church would leave the faithful defenceless in the face of its enemies; he claims that the Pelican's attacks against the church's wealth are motivated largely by envy; and he exhorts his interlocutor to mind his own affairs and let others live according to their conscience. Warming to the attack, the Griffon grasps the nettle and demands that the Pelican recant his pernicious views. When he refuses to do so, the Griffon gathers together his feathered allies – 'Ravins, rokes, crowes, and pye, / [and] Gray foules' (1334–5) – to attack the Pelican. However, the Pelican is defended by 'the Phenix' (1343), who 'slew hem down without mercy' (1349).

The Plowman's Tale is an important example of complaint literature for a number of reasons: the fact that it survived into the sixteenth century and was revived, slightly altered by a person or persons unknown, and published by Thomas Godfray in 1536 to support reform and the Henrician agenda suggests the strong continuity of Lollardy in the Reformation period and its essential compatibility with and, in some senses, inseparability from Lutheran views and English reformist positions. It is also an important work because of the influence it may have had on other English Reformation tracts, in particular, I feel, Rede Me and Be Nott Wrothe. Although The Plowman's Tale was not published until 1536, Wawn gives evidence to suggest that the work was known in some form before its publication ('Chaucer'), and it may well be that it served as a source of inspiration for early English Protestant writers. Certainly its tone, its breathless complaints, some of its language, and the disingenuous, straight-man questions the Griffon asks the Pelican remind me of aspects of Barlowe and Roye's no-holds-barred, scatter-gun approach to attack in *Rede Me*. Finally, as Lane points out, it is part of a tradition which privileges the ploughman or shepherd as social critic and spokesman for the common people against the forces of corruption and immorality at loose in society (74–88), a tradition which culminates in Spenser's *Shepheardes Calendar* and which perhaps has its origins in Langland's great poem and in the anonymous *The Plowman's Tale*. The fact that *A proper dyaloge* uses a husbandman or farmer as one of its two speakers may indicate that its authors were aware of the tradition in which they were working. The further fact that *A proper dyaloge* was called 'A Dyalog betwixt the gentylman and the plowman' in a list of proscribed books issued by the government in 1531 (list reprinted in *Political, Religious and Love Poems* 62–3) may also suggest that the figure of the ploughman was closely associated with Lollard and radical reformist thought in general – a not altogether preposterous conclusion, given the popularity of residual Lollard belief in England amongst the lower orders of society that both Dickens and Thomson demonstrate.

Another important figure who is central to the complaint tradition is John Skelton (1460?–1529), Henry's VIII's tutor and poet laureate. Although it is not always easy to distinguish precisely between satire and complaint, as Peter has demonstrated (1–13), Skelton seems to be best known as a satirist, perhaps because his most famous attacks against the church are delivered full in the face of Thomas Cardinal Wolsey, Henry's lord chancellor. Wolsey is the particular focus of Skelton's anger in three of his major poems: 'Speke Parott,' 'Collyn Clout,' and 'Why Come Ye Nat to Courte?' (Skelton 230–46, 246–78, 278–311 respectively), and his attacks on the cardinal, as I have shown elsewhere, serve as probable sources for Wolsey's further excoriation in Barlowe and Roye's *Rede Me and Be Nott Wrothe* (Barlowe and Roye, Commentary *passim*). But Skelton also turned his talents for complaint against more generalized abuses that he detected in the church, especially in his poem 'Collyn Clout.' The narrator, a vagabond, acknowledges that his 'ryme is ragged, / Tattered and jagged, / Rudely rayne-beaten, / Rusty and mothe eaten' (53–6), but also claims that 'It hath in it some pyth' (58). The pith is abuses within the Catholic church, especially amongst its various spiritual orders. Bishops are attacked for meddling in the law, for being lazy, for insinuating themselves into rich men's houses and 'kynges halles' (127), and for sumptuous living. Religious are accused of abandoning the rules of their founders, clerics of living in accordance with worldly standards rather than spiritual ones. Near the end of this long exposé of misdemeanours, the vagabond utters the following apology in order to defend himself against the charge of indiscriminate and bilious complaint (1095–1106):

> Of no good bysshop speke I,
> Nor good preest I escrye,
> Good frere, nor good chanon,
> Good nonne, nor good clerke,
> Nor of no good werke;
> But my recountynge is
> Of them that do amys
> In spekynge and rebellynge
> In hyndrynge and dysavaylynge
> Holy churche our mother,
> One agayne another.

Finally, three other works of complaint which use the ploughman motif to good effect against the church are worthy of note. The first, *Pierce the Ploughmans Crede*, was composed, according to Skeat, between 1394 and 1399 (xi), and first published in 1553, possibly to capitalize on the popularity of *The Vision of Piers Plowman* printed in 1550 by Robert Crowley. *Pierce* is an 855-line attack on the four orders of friars. An unnamed speaker, who already knows his '*paternoster*' (6) and '*Aue-marie*' (7), seeks someone to help him learn the Creed. The speaker begins by asking various friars for help. They seem more interested in denigrating their colleagues than in giving spiritual guidance. The speaker encounters a Minorite or gray friar and asks him whether he thinks a Carmelite might help him learn the Creed. According to the Minorite, Carmelites are 'but jugulers and iapers' (43) who 'wymmen bi-traieth' (50). After numerous abusive comments about Carmelites, the Minorite claims that he can help the speaker learn the Creed if he makes a financial donation. The speaker recalls the gospels of Matthew and Luke, where covetousness is condemned and people are exhorted to judge others by their fruits; as a result, he escapes the clutches of the Minorite and seeks out the Dominicans. Ingenuous to the end, the speaker seems impressed by the Dominicans' convent, its ostentatious wealth and its well-dressed inhabitants. Innocently mentioning to a Dominican that an Augustinian friar told him that the Austin friars were the first order founded, he listens to the Dominican praise his own order at the expense of the Augustinians: '*And* we ben proued the prijs. of popes of Rome / *And* of gretest degre. as godspelles telleth' (256–7). Recalling that Christ never spoke this way in the gospels, the speaker moves on until he confronts an Augustinian friar, who immediately begins to berate the Minorites. And so it goes. The speaker meets representatives from all four orders of friars and the author takes the opportunity to focus on their worldliness, wealth, lechery, jealousy, and, most important, their malicious slandering of each other.

Continuing his journey, the narrator meets the poem's only true Christian, Piers the Ploughman. Piers, representing a clear Wycliffite position, exposes the friars directly as they have earlier indicted themselves by indirection. The ploughman cites the spiritual works of mercy and shows how the friars ignore all of them. Monks are also briefly mentioned as being not much better than friars; however, friars are the major source of complaint in this poem, as Piers makes clear when he states that friars have misled monks. As the poem draws to a close the speaker finally gets his initial wish: Piers the simple ploughman teaches him the Creed.

Another poem in the ploughman tradition is *God spede the plough*, a ninety-six-line anonymous poem composed, according to Skeat, near the beginning of the sixteenth century ('*Pierce the Ploughmans Crede*' 73). The poem is a complaint spoken by a husbandman who rues the hard life he and his fellow farmers are forced to lead. Although the husbandman does not direct charges of abuse solely at the church, the main thrust of his attack seems to be in that direction, if one can judge from the amount of time he devotes to it. Husbandmen are deprived of the fruits of their labour by 'graye Freres' (49), 'white Freres' (51), 'freres Augustynes' (53), 'the poore obseruauntes' (58), 'the Sompner' (65), 'prestis' (73) and 'clerkys of Oxford' (75). Like the husbandman in *A proper dyaloge*, this husbandman, speaking on behalf of his colleagues, feels the financial pinch because of parasitical and greedy church officials. It is for this reason that each stanza ends with the refrain 'I praye to God, spede with the plough,' for without an efficient plough and his own hard work, the farmer could not maintain his obligations to those who drain his resources.

The final work examined in this brief survey of complaint literature is entitled *The prayer and complaynt of the Ploweman vnto Christ: written not longe after the yere of our Lorde. M. and thre hundred* (*STC* 20036). This Lollard or Lollard-inspired tract was published by Martinus de Keyser of Antwerp, probably around 1531, and includes a preface which some have argued was written by William Tyndale but which Hume claims came from the pen of George Joye (*English Protestant Books Printed Abroad* 1078–9). The contemporary preface sets out to establish the relevance of the old tract for its new reformist audience by attacking in a general way the behaviour of clerics and scandalous church practices. For its part, the tract itself, spoken by the ubiquitous ploughman, is critical of auricular confession, absolution in return for financial payment, the mass, clerical celibacy, tithing practices, and the doctrine of purgatory. The humble ploughman, here as elsewhere speaking wisely despite his modest lifestyle and lack of education, exhorts God to hear his prayers nothwithstanding his poverty and occupation: 'And so lorde our hope is / thou wylt as sone yhere a plowmans prayer and he kepe thyne hestes / as thou wylt do a mannes of relygion / though that the plowman ne may haue so moche syluer for his prayer as men of relygion' (B7r). The implication is that all men, regardless of rank or wealth, have ready access to God's ear. Those who appropriate wisdom to themselves do so in order to line their own pockets by claiming a fraudlent mediating power between suppliant and God. As in *A proper dyaloge*, the ploughman here sets out to expose church abuse by focusing on its unconscionable worldliness.

The Tradition of Complaint:
Themes in *A proper dyaloge*

Clerical Wealth and Possessions

Near the conclusion of the first part of the dialogue section of *A proper dyaloge*, the husbandman tells the gentleman that the clergy, about whose various manifestations of 'ambicion' and 'greed' both men have been complaining, writes off these complaints and accusations as the intemperate ravings of 'a secte newe fangled' (647), dismissively called 'thes heretikes Lutheranes' (646), whose sole intent is to bring about the 'chirches perdicion' (649).[40] It remains now to consider briefly the validity of the church's charge of newfangledness by examining the historical context out of which the complaints of the husbandman and gentleman grow. In part, of course, they do this themselves on two occasions, first when they draw upon 'an olde treatyse made about the tyme of kinge Rycharde the seconde' (685–7), which proves after its own fashion that the church has no right to worldly power, especially as manifested in temporal possessions such as land and property, and secondly when they invoke 'a compendious olde treatyse' to show that a vernacular Bible has validity, if only from the argument based on historical precedent.

The first Lollard prose document cited by the dialogue's speakers is an unrelenting exposé of arguments based on scriptural, patristic, and contemporary documents to demonstrate that 'lordlynes and worldly dominion' (688–9) are neither appropriate to nor possible for those who truly wish to follow 'Christes lyuynge and his doctrine' (692). Effectively, in their various complaints brought against the clergy, especially the one focusing on clerical wealth as manifested in property holdings, both the dialogue and the first Lollard tract are suggesting that the church render to Caesar the things that are Caesar's, and to God the things that are God's. That is, the dialogue and the tract call for a complete jurisdictional separation between church and state which would allow the church and its clergy to tend the spiritual needs of its constituents, and the state to tend to everything that pertains to 'worldly dominion,' be that political decision-making, possession and distribution of property, or the general economic welfare of the commonwealth. That this position mirrors a clear Wycliffite-Lollard view cannot be doubted if the sixth conclusion of the *Twelve Conclusions of the Lollards*, reportedly attached to the doors of Westminster Hall during a session of parliament in 1395, is anything to go by. It states (Hudson *Selections from English Wycliffite Writings* 26):

> The sexte conclusiun that mayntenith michil pride is that a kyng and a bisschop al in o persone, a prelat and a iustice in temperel cause, a curat and an officer in wordly seruise, makin euery reme out of god reule. This conclusiun is opinly schewid, for temperelte and spirituelte ben to partys of holi chirche, and therfor he that hath takin him to the ton schulde nout medlin him with the tothir, *quia nemo potest duobus dominis seruire.* Us thinkith that hermofodrita or ambidexter were a god name to sich manere of men of duble astate. The correlari is that we, procuratouris of God in this cause, pursue to this parlement that alle manere of curatis bothe heye and lowe ben fulli excusid of temperel office, and occupie hem with her cure and bout ellis.

A similar sentiment rings out clearly in the pages of Tyndale's *Obedience of a Christian Man*, and it is also the principle that Fish invokes in his impassioned plea to Henry VIII to take back his country into his own hands.[41]

This call for the separation of church and state is everywhere apparent in the writings of the early reformers and Lollards. According to Hudson, the first condemnatory bull issued by Gregory XI against Wycliffe in 1377 listed nineteen errors, many of which directed attention to Wycliffe's attacks on the church's excessive concern with temporal powers. In summing up the characteristic Lollard position (*Selections from English Wycliffite Writings* 5) she states:

> Christ and the early apostles had taught that Christians should be subject to temporal powers, that the clergy's business was with spiritual matters and that they should neither possess

more earthly goods than were necessary for their immediate survival, nor wield power of any kind over secular authorities. The contemporary church, with all its wealth and property and with its claims to exemption from many of the usual laws and taxes imposed by the secular ruler, was consequently corrupted from the evangelical ideal propounded in the gospels.

The origin of this radical view of the division of authority and the subordination of the spiritual to the temporal order is not entirely clear, nor is it necessarily attributable to one person. One name and one work, however, continue to appear in the literature which deals with this subject, and that is Marsilius (Marsiglio) of Padua and his *Defensor Pacis*.[42] Hudson points out that in Gregory XI's bull of 1377 condemning many of Wycliffe's teachings, the pope mentions Marsilius and the lesser-known John of Jandun as Wycliffe's mentors (*Selections from English Wycliffite Writings* 4); Hudson herself claims that 'almost all the elements of Wyclif's heresy are traceable to earlier thinkers, to Marsilius of Padua, to Bradwardine, to FitzRalph, to Berengar amongst others' (*Lollards and Their Books* 142). And Dickens (*The English Reformation* 106–7), speaking more authoritatively than most on the tricky question of sources, does little to raise doubts about Marsilius's influence on reformist thought and thinkers during this period. He states:

> When the powerful states of Renaissance Europe sought various forms of control over the churches within their power, they could find in medieval theory a plenitude of justificatory arguments. In Dante, in the publicists who espoused the cause of Philip IV of France against the popes, in Marsiglio of Padua and in Wycliffe, there abounded Erastian notions drawn from biblical, theological, philosophical and historical sources.

> Wycliffe was neither the greatest nor the most original of the medieval Erastians; moreover it can clearly be shown that he was not the one who provided the main fund of these ideas to the defenders of Henrician Reformation in England. All these distinctions may be claimed with some confidence for Marsiglio, the most portentous of medieval rebels.

Dickens, who sees Marsilius as a source for Wycliffe, also claims that Wycliffe 'elaborated' (108) Marsilius's ideas in the next century, although, given the elaborateness of Marsilius's ideas as they appear in *Defensor Pacis*, it might be more realistic to claim that Wycliffe applied Marsilius's theory to the practical situation in much the same way as Wycliffe's own followers, the Lollards, applied his theoretical, if revolutionary, statements, made initially by a dedicated schoolman within the context of a university, to the real world.[43]

Called 'the most able, audacious and elaborate attack ever made upon the pretensions of the medieval Church' by Dickens (107), and logically ruthless by Knowles (*Religious Orders* 2 65), the *Defensor Pacis* appeared in 1324 and provoked a papal condemnation issued in 1326 which forced Marsilius to flee Paris and seek safety in Nuremberg in the court of Ludwig of Bavaria (*Marsilius* ed Gerwith xix). *Defensor* is a long and complicated work, but the essence of its profound and shocking message to the papacy and church is clear in some of the practical 'Conclusions' it draws based upon the theoretical and philosophical tenets it expresses in the first two 'Discourses.' A sampler of these 'Conclusions' indicates the revolutionary message that Marsilius is sending to both church and state. Number 7, for instance, puts paid to the notion of papal authority and undercuts the church doctrine of purgatory, a view that adumbrates Luther's own position on purgatory and foreshadows by two centuries the view of purgatory expressed in the dialogue section of *A proper dyaloge*:

> 7. The decretals or decrees of the Roman or any other pontiffs, collectively or distributively, made without the grant of the human legislator bind no one to temporal pain or punishment. ... (427)[44]

Other 'Conclusions,' which are consistent with what we have seen as the Wycliffe or Lollard position on church authority, are also generally in agreement with the complaints brought against the church by the gentleman and husbandman and by the authors of the first Lollard tract included in *A proper dyaloge*:

> 22. Only the ruler in accordance with the laws of the believers has the authority to regulate the number of churches or temples, and of the priests, deacons, and other officials who are to minister therein. ... (428)

And 'Conclusions' 13 and 14 disenfranchise the spiritual orders from authority in the secular realm, leaving all decisions in the hands of the temporal power:[45]

> No ruler, and still less any partial group or individual person of whatever status, has plenitude of control or power over the individual or civil acts of other persons without the determination of the mortal legislator. ...
> A bishop or priest, as such, has no rulership or coercive jurisdiction over any clergyman or layman, even if the latter be a heretic. ... (427)

Putting Marsilius's theory, as mediated by Wycliffe and his followers, into practice would effectively, and in general terms, respond to the charges brought against the church in *A proper dyaloge*. It would also, of course, emasculate the church hierarchy from top to bottom. It would render all priestly threats – especially the threat of purgatory – ineffectual, it would disenfranchise political prelates, it would turf out abbots and bishops from parliament, and, most devastating of all, it would allow the clergy spiritual jurisdiction only in so far as such jurisdiction was validated by what Marsilius calls on numerous occasions 'the faithful legislator.' As for the specific charge of 'lordlynes' and worldliness brought against the clerics at the beginning of the first Lollard tract and in the text itself of *A proper dyaloge*, Marsilius's theory would force these clerics to reassess their present life in accordance with 'the doctrine or the lyfe of Iesu Christe' and his apostles as found in the New Testament. The church would inevitably be transformed from formidable political force to humble and largely ineffectual provider of spiritual care and would, of course, regard this as a monstrous undermining of its ideology and legitimate jurisdictional right. It is no surprise that Marsilius, Wycliffe, and the early English reformers, including the authors of *A proper dyaloge*, were all condemned by the church. The implications of their revolutionary positions would effectively reduce the church to a powerless non-entity, a structure without content.

The reformist literature of this entire period, running from Marsilius's own time to the early days of the English Reformation, is sufficiently clear on the question and extent of church power to render redundant any detailed analysis here.[46] But perhaps one example – albeit a notorious one – will suffice to demonstrate the extent to which unbridled clerical authority and power in all of their various manifestations could dominate the spiritual function of the clergy and serve to render sceptical even the most ardent believer in the validity of the traditional church as a legitimate teaching institution. The example is Cardinal Thomas Wolsey, Henry VIII's chancellor until his fall in 1529. His enormous and ruinous power, wealth, and corruption are the subject of attack in a number of contemporary works, including anonymous ballads, some of the poems of John Skelton, Barlowe and Roye's *Rede Me and Be Nott Wrothe*, and various Tyndale works.[47] One cannot help feeling that Wolsey's reputation is not far from the memories of the authors of *A proper dyaloge*, since he was the subject of a blistering attack in *Rede Me* and is also alluded to without name in the closing lines of Fish's *A Supplicacyon* (421). In signing off his work, Fish upbraids the king for not taking action against 'one of the offenders of this croked and peruers generacyon' of clerics. He continues:

> And this by the reason that the chief instrument of youre lawe ye the chief of your counsell and he whiche hath youre swerde in his honde to whome also all the other instrumentes are obedient is alweys a spirituell man whiche hath euer suche an inordinate loue vnto his owne kingdome that he will mainteyn that, though all the temporall kingdoms and comon welth of the worlde shulde therfore vtterly be vndone.

The extent to which Wolsey strove to maintain his 'owne kingdome' and those he felt resided within it is evident in the way he abused his *legate a latere* title. A notorious pluralist in his own right, Wolsey feathered his illegitimate son's nest with a number of ecclesiastical sinecures. Dickens (62) states that Thomas Wynter, Wolsey's son, 'while still a schoolboy was dean of Wells, provost of Beverly, archdeacon of York, archdeacon of Richmond, chancellor of Salisbury, prebendary of Wells, York, Salisbury, Lincoln and Southwell, rector of Rudby in Yorkshire and of St. Matthew's, Ipswich.' Although clearly indebted to a long written tradition of complaint about clerical wealth and power, the authors of *A proper dyaloge* did not need to ransack history for examples to validate their claims.[48] Indeed, one of their own contemporaries, recently fallen from power, would have served as the *locus classicus* of the abuses they were attacking in their own work.[49]

The specific manifestation of clerical power and involvement in the affairs of this world criticized in *A proper dyaloge* and shown to be unscriptural by any measure in the first Lollard tract is the inordinate wealth of the clergy based largely on land and property holdings. Both gentleman and husbandman complain about their loss of income and consequent decline in standard of living because of the church's appropriation of their property and that of their colleagues. The gentleman regularly blames his present situation on his ancestors, who gave their land – and his patrimony – in 'perpetuall allmes' to clerics in return for the clerics' fraudulent promise to pray for their souls and those of their loved ones so as to loose them from or reduce their time in purgatory. For his part, the husbandman blames the gentleman, and by extension the gentleman's ancestors, for his impoverished state: had the gentleman not had his land claims snatched from his hands on the strength of a worthless promise, the husbandman would still be able to farm his land; however, by giving over his property to the clerics, the gentleman has forced the farmer from his land. In addition, the clergy has combined many small farms into single large ones; consequently the farmer can no longer afford the exorbitant rent in order to work a piece of land. And the gentleman, hitherto a landowner in his own right, is now in the position previously held by the farmer: ironically he has become a tenant on property that he once owned.

The gentleman's complaint that his ancestors are to blame for his present situation, plus the inclusion of a fourteenth-century Lollard tract in *A proper dyaloge* to prove that clerical temporal possessions are inappropriate, lead one to conclude that this issue is not peculiar to the sixteenth century, even though it is a recurrent theme in the major English works of this early period of reform in the 1520s. It appears not only in *A proper dyaloge*, but, as we have seen, also in *Rede Me and Be Nott Wrothe*, in Fish's *A Supplicacyon*, where it is the major theme, and in various Tyndale writings. The reformist literature of the entire Wycliffe-Lollard period also indicates that the evils of clerical temporal possessions were very much on the minds of the reformist forerunners of the sixteenth-century authors. Aston, for instance, states that 'if Wycliffe was consistent in anything, it was in his insistence upon the evils of ecclesiastical endowment and the ability and duty of secular powers to remove temporalities from a habitually offending church' (*Lollards* 267). Knowles cites Wycliffe's arguments against clerical temporalities by drawing on comments from some of his Latin works.[50] In *De nova praevaricantia mandatorum* Wycliffe claims that monks (possessioners, as opposed to mendicant friars subject to the vow of poverty) violate their own monastic rule when they collect rents and take the funds from parish churches situated on their properties. In *Determinacio ad argumenta Johannis Outredi*, he argues that if goods donated for spiritual uses are not put to these purposes, such goods should be returned to the donors by the 'spiritual authorities.' If they choose not to do this, the heirs of the donors should reclaim their right to such goods (Knowles *Religious Orders* 2 99–100), which would no doubt bring enormous relief to our gentleman-complainant in *A proper dyaloge*. Knowles also points out that a claim arguing that private property, even property belonging to the church, might revert to the government 'for the public defence' was brought before parliament in 1371. He adds that

> The claim was resisted by the representatives of the great monasteries, but it was upheld by a group of mendicants ... who petitioned Parliament that all possessions of the clergy should be regarded as national assets in all cases on necessity. No direct notice was taken of the petition ... but the corporate rights of the 'possessioners' ... had been publicly challenged, and for the next forty years the monks were to be the object of a number of attacks, public and private. (2 97–8)

It is interesting to note that in this particular instance the Lollard cause was advanced by the mendicants, normally a most unlikely source of support, but in this case entirely understandable, given the animosity between friars and monks over the question of possessions during this period (see Knowles *passim*).

Lollard attacks in general – as opposed to direct broadsides from Wycliffe – on clerical temporalities were frequent prior to their appearance in the works of the early English Lutherans. In a document dated from the late fourteenth century entitled 'Sixteen Points on which the Bishops accuse Lollards' (Hudson *Selections from English Wycliffite Writings* 19), the ninth point reads as follows: 'it is agens the lawe of God that bischopis and other prelatis of the chirche schulden haue temperal possessions, for by Goddis lawe, thei schulden go oon fote preching the worde of God.' In this case the Lollard response to the bishops' summary of their position is a model of tolerance and moderation by comparison to many other comments uttered by the Lollards on temporalities, although one can argue that the qualifying statement in the first sentence is ironic, since the Lollards knew from experience that its proviso was being violated with reckless abandon:

> Also we granten that bischoppis acordyngly with Goddis lawe mown haue temperal goodis and possessiouns in resunable mesure, so that thei spenden hem as Goddis awmyneris, and not holding hem as wordely lordes.

And then follow the inevitable scriptural citations that are familiar to us from the first Lollard tract in *A proper dyaloge*:

> For Crist seith in the gospel, 'Ye schullen not haue lordschipis, as lordes and kyngis of the puple.' And seint Peter seith, 'Be ye not hauynge lordschipe in the clergye', and so, though b[i]schoppis ride or go so they do wel ther office, thei ben excused. (22)

A less subtle and measured statement of Lollard claims against clerical temporal possessions is found in 'The Lollard Disendowment Bill' presented to parliament possibly in 1410, although many of its recommendations seem to have been current some years prior to this date. Among other things, it is interesting for the precise details it provides about the possible long-term economic benefits of clerical disendowment, a practical concern on which Fish was to focus some years later in his *A Supplicacyon*. In addition, it gives a contemporary – if not altogether valid – picture of the state of the kingdom and the wealth of the church in specific terms through biased Lollard eyes. Finally, it takes the argument for clerical disendowment in a rather new direction from the one we have seen to date: rather than simply emphasizing the unscriptural nature of clerical temporalities, it attempts to show the material benefits accruing to a country wise enough to disendow its all-too-rich clergy, a ploy no doubt meant to appeal to those whose belief in Mammon was at least as strong as their belief in God.

> To the moste excellent redoubte lorde the Kyng, and to alle the noble lordes of this present parlement, shewen mekely alle the trewe comynes seyynge this sothely: oure liege lorde the Kyng may have of the temperaltees by bisshopes, abbotes and priours, yoccupyed and wasted provdely withinne the rewme xv erles and mvc knyhtes, vi mcc squyers and c houses of almesse mo thanne he hath now at this tyme, well mayntened and trevly by londes and tenementz susteyned. And euermore whanne alle this is perfourmed, oure lorde the Kyng may have

euery yeer in clere to his tresour for defence of his rewme xx m
libri and more, as hit may be trevly prevyd.

Then follows a lengthy explanation of how the above proposal might
be accomplished by taking back the properties and the monetary val-
ues attached thereto from various bishops and abbeys. The bill mentions clerical and monastic properties found in the jurisdictions of
the archbishop of Canterbury, the bishop of Durham, the archbishop
of York, the bishops of Winchester, Lincoln, Ely, Bath, Worcester,
Chester, London, St David, Salisbury and Exeter, and Norwich. After
proposing this sweeping decimation of clerical temporalities, the bill
concludes with a final justification of its thesis:

> And therfor alle the trewe comeners desireth to the worship
> of God and profyte of the rewme that thes worldly clerkes, biss-
> hopes, abbotes and priours that arun so worldly lordes, that they
> be putte to leven by here spiritualtes, for they lyven nat now ne
> done the office of trewe curates other [as] prelates shulden ne
> they helpe nat the pore comens with here lordeshippes as that
> trewe sekulers lordes shulden, ne they lyve nat in penaunce ne in
> bodely travaylle as trewe religious shulden by here p[ro]fession.
> But of euery estate they take luste and ese and putte fro hem the
> travaylle and takyth profytes that shulden kome to trewe men,
> the which lyf and evyll ensample of hem hath be so longe vicious
> that alle the comen peple, bothe lordes and symple comvnes,
> beth now so vicious and enfecte thurh boldeship of here synne
> that vnneth eny man dredith God ne the devyll. (Hudson *Selec-
> tions from English Wycliffite Writings* 135–7)[51]

And finally, another Lollard tract on clerical disendowment is
interesting as much for its form as for its content. Like all we have
seen thus far, this document emphasizes clerical greed as manifested
in the unseemly amount of property held by the church. However,
the form in which these claims are expressed is ironic: Hudson calls
the document an 'anti-clerical satire' (182) in which Satan addresses
his colleagues, the clergy, in a letter. In this *'Epistola Sathanae ad
Cleros'* Satan begins his address by pointing out how the simple and
unpretentious life of Christ and his apostles as narrated in the New
Testament left the clergy of an earlier time in an almost impoverished state until it was canny enough to reverse this trend by paying
attention to its own material welfare:

And then we, seyng the myschef that we were browght to by Crist and his disciples and preastis lyvyng aftur in word and ded, ordenyd a generall cowncell of all our dukis, princis and barons and comouns of all our cursyd cumpeny, of our religwijs and lordschipe of hell, to sett remedy in that case, or that we were fully distroyd. ... Therfore seing that all our myschef came by in cause of poore, mek and lowly lyvyng, that was in preastis aftur Crist and his disciples, we tawght that ouur remedy and welfare must come by in riches, by pride and hyer beryng of themself, wich was contrary to Crist and his lyvyng. Werfore we ordeynyd to make preatis of all degrys that ther myght be great plenty of them, to withstand lordis of the world, and to ouergo kyngis and other temporall lordis that ought to haue lordschipis, and so to make them subiectis to our preastis. And, for to come the bettur to our purpose, whan we had aspied that Constantyn the emperour was healyd of his leper thorow grace of our enmy Crist, he thowght he wold do wyrschipe to God for his health, knowing not how he myght bettur do it than, aftur our entysement, to gyf his lordschipe to Cristis vycar here on erthe; than this Constantyn, thorow our entysyng, by color of almes gaf to Syluester, that than was pope, half his empyre with all the wirschipe and lordschipe that longith therto. And we entysed hym to tak it, for so he schuld best mantane holie churche, and thus thorow our assent he tok yt. And so he and his successors euer syns, with other prelattis of the churche, gaderyd more and more tyll thei were well nye as ryche as kyngis and other lordis. And so thei were tangled with the venyme of wordly riches, that the churche was well nie in schort tyme turnyd to our lordschipe. (Hudson *Selections from English Wycliffite Writings* 90–1)

Apart from its imaginative re-creation of past events stretching back to biblical times, what is intriguing about this document is that it mentions the Donation of Constantine, which, until Lorenzo Valla's time, was universally regarded as valid and a legitimate historical happening. However, this document, claiming that the Roman emperor Constantine (280–337) had given an enormous portion of his kingdom to Pope Sylvester I, thereby justifying the papacy's right – and by extension the clergy's right – to hold and accumulate property, was questioned and proven false by the great Italian humanist Lorenzo Valla (1407–57) in his *Declamatio* (1440) (Valla 89–114).

Lollards writing earlier than Valla and those opposed in principle to church temporalities doubtless would have been delighted to know that the document on which the validity of the donation was based was in fact a forgery since it would have strengthened their case about the questionable practice of acquiring temporalities.[52]

Although it is not necessary or possible to examine all of the Lollard or Lollard-inspired texts which speak out against clerical possessions to see that the issue was a crucial one for early reformers, it is, nevertheless, appropriate to mention that this concern was not solely confined to a war of words between committed polemicists on both sides of the issue.[53] Aston points out that the issue of temporalities had played a 'prominent part' in the Peasants' Revolt of 1381 (*Lollards* 10),[54] and again in the seditious uprising of 1431.[55] It is also clear that the desire to disendow clergy might not have sprung in every case from the purest motives. Aston states that the knights in 1385 who were encouraging Richard II to disendow clerics were themselves aware of what part they might play in the disposition of the property and how they might benefit from it (20). And in the abortive Oldcastle uprising of 1414, the record shows that there were at least a few participants who saw plenty of opportunity to feather their own nests if their cause was successful. Aston concludes that those whose motives were mixed 'helped to make the cause resemble a treasonable scramble for property and preferment' (26).[56]

It is no easier to determine the origin of these complaints against clerical temporalities or to find a single archetype from which all subsequent attacks derive than it was in the case of the attacks on clerical wealth and power in general. Knowles mentions the general criticisms brought against clerical wealth, as manifested in land grabs, by the twelfth-century writers Gerald of Wales and Walter Map, calling them the 'two outstanding figures in a whole army of contemporary satirists' (*The Monastic Orders in England* 677). But more prominent than 'an army of contemporary satirists' and the clearest philosophical explicator of arguments against clerical temporalities is once again Marsilius of Padua and his *Defensor Pacis*.[57] In certain of his 'Conclusions' Marsilius insists in his forceful Erastian way that the control of a country's land rests solely with 'the faithful legislator,' who has total jurisdictional authority over his country's resources. Conclusion 23, for example, contains the interesting catch-all phrase 'other things,' which implies that 'the faithful legislator' has authority over anything 'established for religious purposes.' Such phraseology would serve as a great comfort for our disenfranchised gentleman left without resources because of his ancestors' donations to the clergy. It reads:

> Only by the authority of the faithful legislator can and should separable church offices be bestowed and taken away, and similarly benefices and other things established for religious purposes ... (428)

Similarly, conclusions 27 and 28 emphasize the temporal rulers authority when it comes to the disposition of 'Ecclesiastic temporal goods' and 'temporal goods ... set aside for religious purposes':

> Ecclesiastic temporal goods which remain over and above the needs of priests and other gospel ministers and of the helpless poor, and which are not needed for divine worship, can lawfully, in accordance with divine law, be used in whole or in part by the legislator for the common or public welfare or defense. ... (429)

> All temporal goods which have been set aside for religious purposes or for deeds of mercy ... are to be distributed only by the ruler in accordance with the designation of the legislator and the intention of the donor. ... (429)

It remains to consider briefly the justice of the complaints brought against the church hierarchy concerning its temporal possessions and temporalities and to determine, to some extent at least, whether the accusations made in *A proper dyaloge* and the proposals for disendowment articulated in the passages quoted above have any validity.

In both *A Supplicacyon for the Beggers* and *A proper dyaloge*, references are made to the extent to which clerics have appropriated the 'lordshippes, maners, londes, and territories' (More 7 412) of England. Fish informs the king that the various clerical orders 'haue gotten ynto there hondes more than the third part of all your Realme' (412), and several lines later he states that if one adds what they gain from tithes and other forms of spiritual extortion to the land in their possession, one could conclude that their possessions 'drawe nighe vnto half of the hole substaunce of the realme' (414). In *A proper dyaloge*, the gentleman complains to the husbandman that 'halfe the realme' (311) belongs to the spiritual orders and later adds that over a period of four hundred years not only have the mendicant orders sprung up, but also priests have increased tenfold and 'collegianes / monkes and chanons Haue spred this region ouer all' (381–2), a statement which elaborates on Fish's claim that the clerics have 'encreased ... ynto a kingdome' (412).

As for valid numbers, it is notoriously difficult to be precise, to say nothing of how one determines what Fish means by a 'kingdome.' Pantin points out that there were seventeen English bishoprics in 1300 (15) and that between 1215 and 1272 there were seventy-eight bishops who ruled in England in various capacities. Heath adds that there were about nine thousand parish churches in medieval England, 'Barely enough to satisfy the innumerable clerics of that time' (27). Priests seemed to fall into three categories: 'those who held parochial benefices' in a non-resident capacity (27), beneficed clergy who were resident, and what Pantin calls 'a very large clerical proletariate of priests working for a salary' (28).

As for the numbers of religious, our best source for these details is Knowles. Wycliffe's claim that the English friars numbered four thousand in his day is countered by Knowles, who argues that Wycliffe's number would be 'roughly correct for 1348' (*Religious Orders* 2 103)[58] but should be halved for 1380, probably because of the ravages of the Black Death, which swept through the country in the middle of the century. He further adds that Wycliffe's estimate of twenty thousand friars in the country cited in one of his sermons is a 'fantastic overstatement' (2 104). There is, however, some evidence to show that the church itself was concerned, if not with the number of friars, at least with the number of orders which were springing up. Some attempt to put an end to this came out of the Second Council of Lyons, which on 17 July 1274 issued a decree suppressing all but the four major orders of friars.

Concerning the number of monks and their declining numbers after the arrival of the friars on the scene, Knowles (2 256) has the following to say:

> In the centuries from 1066 to 1540 certain broad tendencies can be discovered. Thus ... the numbers of monks and regular canons rose steeply from the Conquest for more than a century. At the death of Edward the Confessor there were only 850 monks in England, distributed over some 50 houses; by 1150 their numbers had risen to 5500 in 290 houses, and by 1216 to 6200 in 340 houses. Within the same period the number of regular canons of all kinds had risen from zero to 3800 in 220

houses, and those of nuns and canonesses from 200 in twelve
nunneries to 3000 in 140. Thus the total number of religious
men and women in England ... had reached the astonishingly
high total of 13,000. This total for the orders concerned, was
never exceeded. The great age of monasticism had passed, and a
stabilization, if not a decline, of numbers was to be expected,
but it was undoubtedly hastened by the arrival of the friars, who
drew off at least some of the potential recruits from the abbeys,
and who in the first century of their existence in England
founded some 200 houses with a population of 5000 friars.

He concludes that 'in the early decades of the fourteenth century the
population of religious men and women in England reached an abso-
lute maximum of some 17,500' (2 256). And McFarlane, commenting
on the number of clergy in England around Wycliffe's time, claims
that they 'probably numbered rather more than 2 per cent of the total
population; that is to say, from fifty to sixty thousand souls' (John
Wycliffe and the Beginnings of English Nonconformity 42). Based on
these statistics, and even taking into account Knowles's comment
that at a certain point in the history of its development the monastic
movement in England had reached the astonishing total of thirteen
thousand participants, Fish's comment that the total number of clerics in England had reached a point where he could call it a 'kingdome' seems hyperbolic, a statement written within a polemical
work to win an argument rather than present the facts as they
existed.

The amount of land held by clerics, claimed by both A Supplicacyon
and A proper dyaloge to be approaching half the kingdom, also seems
excessive. Certainly as far as secular priests are concerned a vast
majority – what Pantin calls 'a very large clerical proletariate' (28) –
were unbeneficed and worked for a salary. As for beneficed secular
priests, not all were pluralists, nor were pluralists necessarily in possession of enormous and wealthy properties. Indeed, even those holding more than one benefice may simply have been able to eke out a
living, since the income deriving from certain benefices was minimal.
Members of the higher clerical orders, such as bishops, were clearly in
better positions to do well financially from patronage and benefices,
but it would be a mistake to think that all were in the same financial
category as Thomas Wolsey, although there were some extraordinarily
wealthy prelates before his time, such as William of Wykeham, who
held the archdeaconry of Durham and ten prebends and was Keeper of

the Privy Seal, or David of Wollore, who held one hospital, seven prebends, and one parish church (Pantin 36–7).[59]

The clearest general summary of the wealth of the monk possessioners comes to us from Knowles's monumental study of the various orders. On the strength of what he says about monastic land wealth, added to the comments made by Pantin on the potential wealth of some other members of the clerical establishment, one might conclude that Fish's and Barlowe and Roye's claim that the clergy in general held one-half of the lands of the realm, although excessive, might not be outrageously so. Knowles's brief snapshot indicates enormous wealth concentrated in real estate (*The Monastic Orders in England* 680):

> The possessions of the monasteries in land and in every kind of wealth and influence were even greater than their numbers might seem to warrant. Already at the Conquest ... the black monks owned roughly one-sixth of the cultivated land and actual rents of England south of the Humber and Mersey. After the Conquest their possessions ... steadily increased, and although the total wealth of the country was also everywhere increased, by the reduction of waste to cultivation, by the development of sheep farming and by the growth of trade, the share of the monks in the whole was without doubt greater in 1170 than in 1066, and perhaps amounted to as much as one quarter of the total wealth of the country in lands, rents and dues. Above all, they had grown in wealth and influence in ecclesiastical property, and were the owners or patrons of perhaps a quarter of the churches of England. To this must be added the ownership of so many great fabrics and groups of buildings stored, at least where the black monks were masters, with precious objects of all kinds and housing almost all the artistic treasures and books of the land.

Whatever else might be said about the relationship between Lollard thought and early English Protestant ideas or about the continuity between the two, certainly the pre-Lollard and Lollard positions on clerical temporalities served the early English church well by providing a historical precedent not only for works critical of such possessions, but also for actions of questionable motivation, such as the ravaging of monastic lands and houses during the Dissolution period of the mid and late 1530s.[60]

The Vernacular Bible

If clerical temporalities are a major concern of *A proper dyaloge*, the question of a vernacular Bible shares centre stage with them. Even prior to the addition of the second prose tract in the second edition of *A proper dyaloge*, where the focus is on the notion of biblical translations into the vernacular, the two speakers allude to the attempts of the traditional church to keep the Bible out of the hands of the laity. About two-thirds of the way through the dialogue section, for instance, the husbandman claims that if the Bible were generally available in English, people would be able to see what Christ's life was truly like, and recognize by comparison how inappropriate the present clergy's life-style is (409–19). And about 150 lines later the gentleman alludes to Cuthbert Tunstal's burning of Tyndale's New Testament in 1526 as another attempt on the part of the church to hide the truth from those who might profit and learn from it (569–77). Clearly for both gentleman and husbandman – as for all genuine reformers – the truth of Christianity was housed in the Bible, and deviations from the word of God or byzantine additions to it to justify corrupt practices such as clerical temporalities were of no worth and had nothing to do with its simple message of the faith.

Following the conclusion of the dialogue section proper in the second edition of *A proper dyaloge* comes the 'compendious olde treatyse / shewynge / howe that we ought to haue the scripture in Englysshe,' the early fifteenth-century prose tract which works to establish historical justification for biblical translations, and, as such, well serves the purposes of the sixteenth-century reformers as articulated in the dialogue through the words of the husbandman and gentleman. Whether the work is by the Lollard John Purvey, as Deanesly and others claim, or the orthodox Richard Ullerston, as Hudson argues, is of little moment here, since what is important for our purposes is the fact that the authors of *A proper dyaloge* were aware of a tradition of dispute over biblical translation which mirrored a similar dispute in their own time and which served to justify the claim that their complaints were part of a history of literature calling for various manifestations of reform within the traditional church. I have already summarized the contents of this revised tract as it appears in *A proper dyaloge* (see Contents and Structure) and shown how it differs from the original Deanesly/Bühler version (see Authors). What now remains is to make clear in a general way how this work called – 'perhaps the most interesting' 'Lollard' [sic] tract 'from an historical as well as from a cultural point of view' (Bühler 167) – was part of the early literature of dispute over a vernacular Bible. The fullest summary of the latter in is Deanesly, to whose work my own comments are largely indebted.

If the early English reformers of the sixteenth century had any feeling for history whatsoever, they must have been impressed by the similarities between their own struggles for a vernacular Bible and those of their Lollard predecessors.[61] Archbishop Thomas Arundel's seventh constitution, promulgated at the Oxford synod of 1408 and directed against vernacular translation of the Bible and more specifically against the two Wycliffe versions, could not but have struck the sixteenth-century English reformers as remarkably similar in direction and spirit to Cuthbert Tunstal's October 1526 prohibition against William Tyndale's version of the New Testament.[62] Moreover, Tyndale's defence of his own writings – and more specifically his frequent apologies for his biblical translation – against the attacks of Thomas More, amongst others, must have seemed to echo the earlier Lollard written defences of biblical translation against the strong attacks of the traditional church, particularly in the period between Wycliffe's death (1384) and the Oxford Constitutions (1408). Deanesly, for instance, points out that between these two dates five treatises, that we know of, on the subject of biblical translation appeared, three of which were Lollard-inspired and spoke out on behalf of vernacular Bibles, and two of which, written by friars – the main opponents of biblical translations – argued against them (131ff).[63]

The arguments found in the running titles (provided by Deanesly) of the 'Determinations' attributed to friars William Butler and Thomas Palmer are not unfamiliar to those aware of the sixteenth-century traditionalists' opposition to the vernacular Bible. We read that lay people should not read the Bible because the human intellect is insufficient to deal with its complexities; that the Mosaic law was not written; that the Bible is too subtle except for those specifically trained to interpret it; that the literal sense is useless and requires allegorical exegesis to make it meaningful; that it is impossible to translate the Bible, even the literal sense.[64] In addition – and what is often most perplexing to students of the polemical literature of the Reformation period – both friars call upon the Fathers of the Church and biblical citations to support their claims, a corroborative technique not foreign to those who opposed their views, as 'A compendious olde treatyse' itself demonstrates. Clearly, the issue of biblical translation, a matter of considerable import both before and after the production of the so-called Wycliffe Bible, must have struck a common reformist chord for the sixteenth-century reformers, since they employed the tract in their own struggle with those who opposed their view.

The written historical proofs called up by 'A compendious olde treatyse' and tracts like it to justify a vernacular Bible might not have had much value from a practical point of view. Many of them probably represented no real threat to the traditional church position on vernacular scriptures, although, despite their status as fragments or ephemera, they could still be used to give some weight to the historical argument. Deanesly claims that the significance of these various references allows us to determine which were important and which were 'quite unknown, and without influence.' She adds that 'It enables us to see what archbishop Arundel meant, when he said in 1408 that translations made before Wycliffe's day should remain lawful: because the translations of which he was thinking were not those which might be "alleged" by a modern specialist in English literature' (132). For instance, as Deanesly claims, the generally accepted fourteenth-century view that Bede and Alfred translated large sections of the Bible is incorrect (132) (see, however, the Commentary to lines 1457–61 for Bately's view), and the earliest surviving gospel translations worthy of the name were the West Saxon gospels 'of an otherwise unknown Aelfric, monk of Bath, who wrote about 900' (136) and whose work seems to have been for the benefit of monks rather than the common man. She calls Richard Rolle's Psalter mentioned in 'A compendious olde treatyse' 'the earliest biblical book to be translated into English prose after the conquest' (144) and mentions a number of verse translations of biblical texts which play no part in even 'A compendious olde treatyse''s sometimes arcane range of reference. She also states 'that there was no important biblical translation, whole or partial, made in the fourteenth century before the days of Wycliffe's influence' (15). If we can accept Deanesly's views about the rarity of legitimate and extended Bible translation into English prior to the Wycliffe Bible, we must call into question 'A compendious olde treatyse''s claims on behalf of the prevalence of translation. We are, however, on safe ground accepting its statements about the *value* of vernacular translations uttered by various worthies over the centuries, even though such translations were nowhere near as frequent, complete, valuable, or generally accessible as the treatise suggests. Before condemning the original author of 'a compendious olde treatyse' for playing fast and loose with the truth by fabricating a tradition of legitimate and valued biblical translation in English, we must at least consider the possibility that the error or exaggeration was unintentional, especially in light of Thomas More's similar mistake. In the opening chapter of her book, Deanesly points out that More himself erred in his *A Dialogue Concerning Heresies* by assuming that there were English translations of the Bible produced before the appearance of the Wycliffe version and its final condemnation by Arundel at the Oxford Constitution of 1408. The versions which More claimed he saw were probably none other than the Wycliffe version printed without glosses, and not pre-existing non-Wycliffe English translations that More claimed did not fall under Arundel's prohibition. If a scholar with the reputation of Thomas More could believe that a complete version of the English Bible existed before Wycliffe's version, it is not inconceivable that a lesser light might make the same mistake about the general availability of English translations or partial translations prior to his own time, especially when contemporary sources such as William of Malmesbury's *Gesta Regum Anglorum* vouched for their existence (Deanesly 136).

The call for a vernacular version of the Bible as expressed through historical precedent in 'A compendious olde treatyse' was echoed in similar calls found in the works of the early English reformers of the sixteenth century aware of both Luther's and Tyndale's versions of the sacred text and the negative reaction to them on the part of the church. Naturally the need for an English translation and semi-tendentious explanations of why the church opposed it are found everywhere in Tyndale's works. But the demand for an English Bible echoes throughout the English polemical writing of the period up to 1530, the year of the appearance of *A proper dyaloge*. We have already made reference to it in Barlowe and Roye's *Rede Me and Be Nott Wrothe* and in Fish's *A Supplicacyon for the Beggers*. As might be expected, it plays a large part in Roye's English translation of Erasmus's *Paraclesis* and Luther's *Das Siebend Capitel S. Pauil zu den Chorinthern*, which appeared in 1529 under the title *An exhortacyon to the dylygent study of scripture* (STC 10493). Not only is this tract famous for its Erasmian call for a vernacular Bible which would allow ploughman, weaver, and wayfaring man to read the scriptures, but also, in its introduction, Roye himself underlines his own commitment to a vernacular Bible and his opposition to those who stand in its way: 'And truely I do greatly dyssent from those men, whiche wolde not that the scrypture of Chryst shulde be translated into al tonges / that it myght be redde dylygentlye of the pryuate and seculer men and women' (b1r and b1v).

In his *The Revelation of Antichrist* (STC 11394), published in 1529, John Frith, a close associate of William Tyndale, explains why the church refuses to allow the Bible in English. Frith's reasons are ones that we have heard innumerable times already in the works of his reformist colleagues. In exposing the worldliness and deceit of the clerical order he states:

> By theyr workes shall you know them / laye their workes to the scripture / and ye shuld lamente their abhominable lyvinge. But alas you can not / for they will not suffer you to have it / they kepe the metyard from you that you shulde rule al thinges with all. They burne the gospel of god yee and very Christ himself / for he is nothing but his word as he testifieth him silfe. ... And why do they hyed this word of light from you? No doute be cause their workes are evill. for every man that doth evill hateth the light / nether cometh to the light / lest his workes shuld be reproved / but he that worketh the verite / cometh to te [sic] light / that his wordes may be openly sene because they are done of God. They pretend to kepe it from you for pure love / because you shuld take no hurte of it / nether falle in to heresye / but they are gelyous over you amysse / yee they wold clene exclude you from Christ and make you folowe them. (A8v and B1r)

And finally, in a work entitled *The summe of the holye scripture and ordinarye of the Christen teachyng* (STC 3036), usually attributed to Simon Fish, we read of biblical precedents for vernacular texts and some curious conclusions about the prevalence of Latin even amongst Africans. The author states that the Jews had their laws in Hebrew (B8v) and that after the conversion of Italy and Africa the Bible was translated into Latin for their further edification (C1r). Fish mentions several holy women who understood the Bible, amongst whom are Paula and Eustochia and Demetrias, familiar to us from references to them in *A proper dyaloge* (1624–5; 1634). During this period as well, when Latin was the lingua franca, 'comune housholders redde the bible in theyre houses with theyre children' (C1r). Fish's conclusion is that in light of these precedents it is 'nowe of greate necessite that the holy scripture be translated into all langages / or that all the children lerne the latyn tongue' (C1r).

In conclusion, it seems clear that the Lollard focus on clerical temporalities and a vernacular scripture played a large part in shaping the early English Protestant response to these two vital subjects by providing sixteenth-century reformers with historical precedents for their own positions. Although Lollardy may not have been well organized or doctrinally homogeneous enough to act as a major threat to the conventional religious ideology, there is no doubt that it paved the way for the movers and shakers of religious reform in the early sixteenth century to assert their own positions, certain that they were working within a tradition which, at its most idealistic, was eager to present to all who would accept it a scriptural Christianity cleansed of the impurities that had accumulated around it over the years. And *A proper dyaloge betwene a Gentillman and an Husbandman* is a fine example of how what Dickens calls 'the Lollard survival' came to the aid of the movement that would eventually truly challenge the prevailing version of Christian truth.

Interrelation of Editions

This text is an old-spelling critical edition of the 1530 edition of *A proper dyaloge / betwene a gentillman and an Husbandman / eche complaynynge to other their miserable calamite / through the ambicion of the clergye* published in Antwerp by Hans Luft (ie, Johannes Hoochstraten) as part of what Anthea Hume calls the '"Marburg" series' ('English Protestant Books Printed Abroad'). The single copy of this text, and consequently my sole choice for both copy and control text, is held at the British Library (STC 1462.5). There is no indication of author(s) of this work. The text is made up of three parts: the dialogue itself (1–684; 1043–56; 1145–1291), 'an olde treatyse made aboute the tyme of kinge Rycharde the seconde' (685–1042; 1057–1144), and 'A compendious olde treatyse / shewynge / howe that we ought to haue the scripture in Englysshe' (1292–1678).

I have collated my copy text with the 1871 Arber reprint (*English Reprints* viii 129–84) and with three other documents which contain only parts of my text, but which, in and of themselves, were published as complete tracts. The first of these is the Bodleian Library copy (STC 1462.3) published by Hans Luft (but without imprint) probably in 1529, which does not contain 'A compendious olde treatyse'; the second is the Huntington Library copy of a separate edition of 'A compendious olde treatyse' published in 1530 by Luft (STC 3021); and the third is another edition of 'A compendyous Olde treatyse' published probably around 1538 by 'Rycharde Banckes, dwellynge in gracious strete, besyde the cundyte' (STC 3022; see Ames *Typographical Antiquities* 3 257–8). All of these editions have been collated for substantive variants and the results are recorded in 'Emendations' or 'Variants.'

I have also examined John Foxe's reprint of 'A compendious olde treatyse' (IV 670–6), and reprinted in appendix B Margaret Deanesly's own reprint of the original English text upon which 'A compendious olde treatyse' seems to be based. In appendix A, I have collated my version of 'an olde treatyse made aboute the tyme of kinge Rychard the seconde' with the text as it appears in Matthew's *The English Works of Wyclif Hitherto Unpublished* under the title 'The Clergy May Not Hold Property' (359–404).

Although the British Library copy of *A proper dyaloge* is my copy text, it is so largely because of its complete state and not necessarily because of its consistently better readings than the other 'incomplete' editions. Arber's complete text follows the British Library copy, and when it detects errors it indicates them by placing corrections in brackets in the text. The Bodleian copy has some better readings in that section of its text where it corresponds to the complete text, namely in the dialogue section and in the first prose addition entitled 'an olde treatyse ... Rycharde the seconde.' As the 'Emendations' show, I have chosen about thirty of its readings over the British Library's; two-thirds of these are preferred readings in punctuation, capitalization, or line indentation; the rest are word, spelling, and phraseology preferences. Similarly, I have chosen nine readings of Huntington's version of 'A compendious olde treatyse' over the British Library's; all of these are improvements to punctuation. As I argued above, my view of the order of publication is as follows: the Bodleian text was published first, probably in late 1529; the Huntington text next in 1530; and finally, the British Library complete *A proper dyaloge* – an amalgam of Bodleian and Huntington – sometime in 1530, definitely after the appearance of Huntington, upon which, I believe, it relies.

Wherever possible I have retained the original punctuation throughout the tract, emending when necessary and wherever possible with 'correct' punctuation from one of the other contemporary partial editions, namely Bodleian or Huntington. In general, the punctuation of the British Library edition, especially in the opening and dialogue section, is in tune with our own punctuation practices, if not our punctuation marks: the virgule is regularly used instead of the comma. In the corresponding section of the Bodleian copy the virgule is over-used within individual lines, at least to our present way of thinking. There are certain patterns of punctuation early in the treatise which are worthy of note. In the opening acrostic poem ('An A.B.C. to the spiritualte') made up of three rime-royal stanzas, the end-line punctuation of full stops falls on all *b* lines and the last *c* line of each stanza; and internal virgule punctuation is used throughout, sometimes in accord with our own practice (7–8):

> A wake ye gostely persones / awake / awake
> Bothe preste / pope / bisshoppe and Cardinall.

and sometimes not (16–17):

> Kynges and Emperoures / ye have depryued
> Lewedly vsurpynge / their chefe possessiones.

Once the initial three-stanza poems ends, however, the rest of the stanzas break the punctuation pattern: occasionally one will repeat it, but more often than not subsequent stanzas go their own way, even to the point where some need to be emended so that a full stop appears at the end of the final line of the stanza.

When the dialogue between gentleman and husbandman begins, the stanzas work in six-line units rhyming *a a b c c b* with a full stop, or in some cases a question mark, normally at the end of the third and sixth lines. Furthermore, lines 3 and 6 of each unit are indented. Sometimes this punctuation pattern interferes with the meaning of the lines themselves. When this happens I either gloss the lines in the 'Commentary' or alert the reader to the problem, rather than emending the punctuation. The pattern of rhyme and punctuation is followed even when normal line units of three or six are broken between two speakers (see, for example 397ff).

As for the two extended prose passages in *A proper dyaloge*, there is, as one might expect, no detectable punctuation pattern. However, occasionally full stops are omitted at the ends of sentences. When it is clear that this has happened, I emend such sentence endings by adding full stops. Similarly, if a sentence begins with a word that is not capitalized, I emend and capitalize.

In general I have followed the paragraphing of the British Library edition in its two prose passages. I have silently expanded all ampersands and normalized long *s*s. Black-letter type of the sixteenth century appears here as roman. I have not tried to reproduce original type size, nor have I included pilcrows which appear in the original printed text.

Bibliographical Descriptions

1529 *STC* 1462.3

Title-Page: A proper dyalo= / I ge / betwene a Gentillman and an Hufband mā / I eche complaynenge to other theyr my fe= I rable calamyte / through the am=I bicion of the clergye. ℂ An A.B.C. to the fpiritualte. [three-stanza acrostic]
    Collation: 8°, A–C ($4)–B3, B4, C4; C3 missigned C4; 48 unnumbered leaves
    Contents: A1r title page; ℂ An A.B.C. to the fpiritualte. A2v ℂ Herefoloweth the dyaloge / the I Gentyllman begynynge I firft hys complaynte: B4r ℂ Here foloweth an olde treaty fe ma= I de aboute the tyme of kinge Ry=charde the fecounde. C8v AMEN.
This edition has no colophon, running titles, or catch-words.
Copy Collated: Bodleian Library, the only known copy.

1530 *STC* 1462.5

Title-Page: A proper dyalo= I ge / betwene a Gentillman and a hu fbandmā / eche complaynynge to other their mi fe=I rable calamite / through the am= I bicion of the clergye. ℂ An A.B.C. to the fpiritualte. [three-stanza acrostic]
    Collation: 8°, A–D ($2) 64 unnumbered leaves
    Contents: A1r title page; ℂ An A.B.C. to the fpiritualte. A2v ℂ Here foloweth the Dialoge / the Gen I tillmā begīnīge firft his cōplaynte. B4r ℂ Here foloweth an olde treaty fe ma=I de aboute the tyme of kynge Ry=I charde the feconde. [The initial 'W' on the first word of this treatise is ornamented] C8r A compēdious [the first two words 'a compedious' are about triple the size of the blackletter used

elsewhere] olde treaty ſe / ſhewynge / howe that we ought to haue the
ſcripture in Engly ſſhe. ⸿ The excuſacyon of ẙ treaty ſe ⸿ Vnto the
Reader. D8r Amen. Emprented at Marborow in the lan=l de of Heſſen /
by me Hans Luft / l in the yere of owre lorde.M. CCCCC.and. XXX.
This edition has no colophon, running titles, or catch-words.
Copy Collated: British Library, the only known copy.

1530 *STC* 3021

Title-Page: A compendious l olde treaty ſe / ſhewynge / howe that we l
ought to haue ẙ ſcripture in En=l gly ſſhe / ⸿ The excuſacyon of ẙ
treaty ſe [two-stanza poem followed by a border at the foot of the page
of the three Graces and Minos(?) Orestes(?)] The Greek word in the
border is χαριτες, the word for Charities or Graces][65]

   Collation: 8°, A ($2) 16 unnumbered leaves
   Contents: A1r title page; ⸿ The excuſacyon of ẙ treaty ſe A1v ⸿
Vnto the Reader. A2r Amen. A8v Amen. ⸿ Emprented at Marlborow in
the lãde of Heſ =l ſen / be my Hans Luft / in the yere of owre lorde l
M.CCCCC.and.XXX.
This edition has no colophon, running titles, or catch-words.
Copy Collated: Huntington Library.

STC 3022

Title-Page: ⸿ A compendyous Olde l treaty ſe ſhewynge / howe that /
we ought to haue the Scrip l ture in E ngly ſhe with l the Auctours. ⸿
Cum priuilegio. l ⸿ The excuſacyõ of the treaty ſe. [one stanza of a
two-stanza poem enclosed in a decorative border of vines and joined
hexagonal shapes]

   Collation: 12° A–C ($2–C2) 37 unnumbered pages (page numbers
   totalling 37 have been added by hand; page 37 is a printer's design)
   Contents: A1r title page; ⸿ The excuſacyõ of the treaty ſe. A1v ⸿
Unto the reder. A2v amen. C1v ⸿ Amen. ⸿ Finis. ⸿ Impryntɇd by me
Rycharde l Banckes / dwellynge in gra l cious ſtrete / beſyde the
cundyte. c2r [A design: in the background Christ in the Garden of
Gethsamine praying before a chalice. In the foreground three sleeping
figures, probably two apostles on either side of a female figure. The
Garden is enclosed by a fence with a tree in the background on the
right-hand side] C3r [printer's device: two unicorns on their hind legs
holding a shield with their front legs. On the shield near the base a
snail; near the middle, two ornamental B's. At the top of the shield

but outside of it, a haloed figure, possibly St John or Christ himself]
This edition has no colophon or running titles.
Catch-words: A2r–A2v lay ſour A8v–B1r preached B6v–B7r ℂ Al ſo B8v–
B8r ged [god]
Copy Collated: British Library. This is an imperfect copy. Signatures
A4 and A5 have been added by hand.

Notes

1 Despite the fact that what I am calling the first edition of this work appeared without any indication of publisher, Hume claims that it is linked to the 'Marburg' series, ie, those English works published by Hans Luft between 1528 and 1530, by its *schwabacher* type (Hume 'English Protestant Books Printed Abroad,' More 7 1076). Luft's place of publication appears in the imprint to the second edition as 'Marborow' and in the separate edition of 'A compendious olde treatyse' (see Hume 1076–7 and below) as 'Marlborow.'

2 In mentioning the distinctly English quality of this dialogue, Herford states that 'The fundamental situation would hardly have seemed plausible elsewhere. To represent peasant and knight fraternising over their common misfortunes, would probably have occurred to no German pasquillist whatever. Both classes might indeed be sufficiently hostile to the old ecclesiastical order, but they fought in different camps [and] they wanted different things. ... A strong government, like that of Wolsey [sic], might have forced them to make common cause, like the "Gentleman" and the "Husbandman" of the English dialogue' (46).

3 Dickens states: 'Our sources afford much information on the social status of the Lollards. All save a few belonged to the common people – weavers, wheelwrights, smiths, carpenters, shoemakers, tailors and other tradesmen, "of whom", writes Foxe, "few or none were learned, being simple labourers and artificers, but as it pleased the Lord to work in them knowledge and understanding by reading a few English books, such as they could get in corners"' (*The English Reformation* 53). I am not suggesting that this sixteenth-century husbandman is a Lollard *per se*, but rather that he is in a line of descent from them and influenced by their writings.

4 Burke says essentially the same thing when he states that 'its immediacy made the dialogue an appropriate medium for the presentation of contro-

versial issues; issues which were certainly far from lacking in the sixteenth century, from the *questione della lingua* to the Reformation' (8).

5 Roger Deakins has the same notion in mind when he says: '"Dialogue" is
discussion that is "philosophical" (in the root sense of "loving wisdom")
but which nonetheless rejects the technical languages of professional aca-
demic philosophy in favor of language which is (in some sense) "ordi-
nary" or "natural"' (5).

6 Hutten's character as summarized by Smith would seem to be consistent
with one who delighted in personal attack and vilification: 'More than to
any other one person Erasmus's final break with the Reformation was due
to Ulrich von Hutten, the brilliant but unstable Alcibiades hitherto sit-
ting at the feet of the Dutch Socrates in an attitude of worshipful respect.
The character and fate of this wandering knight might make the subject
of a Shakespearean tragedy, for the hero, not without a genuine spark of
nobility in his turbulent nature, precipitated himself through his own
fault into an abyss of utter ruin. The ardor with which he apparently
embraced Luther's cause spent itself in such futile ragings against the
Romanists that they began to laugh at him as one whose bark was worse
than his bite' (332)

7 Although Herford focuses on the early dialogues in Germany and
England, Burke claims that the form was popular in Italy, France, Portugal, Spain, and the Netherlands (2). He states that 'in Italy alone, scarcely
a year of the sixteenth century went past without some dialogue of
importance being published' (5). See, for example, Bernardino Ochino
Seven Dialogues.

8 Spurgeon's (*Tudor Translations*) facsimile edition of number of Tudor
translations of Erasmus's *Colloquies* (*A dialogue or communications of
two persons* c 1536; *A very pleasaunt and fruitful Diologe called the Epi-
cure* 1545; *Two dyaloges wrytten in latin ... one called Polyphemus or the
gospeller / the other dysposyng of thynges and names ...* c 1549; *A mery
Dialogue, declaringe the propertyes of shrowde shrewes, and honest
wyues* 1557; *One dialogue or Colloquy, Inns* 1566; *A Modest Mean to
Marriage* 1568; *Of the yong man and the euill disposed woman* 1568; *The
discouerie of witchcraft* 1584) attests to the popularity of the anti-genre
dialogue in England throughout the sixteenth century. The fact that many
of them humorously exposed and attacked abuses in the church lends
support to the view that they would have been of interest to reformers.

9 It is almost certain that Barlowe and Roye would have known Erasmus's
Colloquies in some form and may have taken his irreverence towards
ecclesiastical abuses as a model for their own more strident attacks.

10 It is Clebsch who surmises that the 'A.B.C. against the clergy' title refers

to *A proper dyaloge*. He also thinks that a reference to a work called 'A.B.C. to the Prelacy,' condemned in an undated list of heretical books found in a manuscript in the British Museum, is probably yet another title for *A proper dyaloge* (265, 268).

11 Rupp claims that Bayfield was 'one of the most active agents of the society' called the Christian Brethren. He adds that this organization 'subsidized scholars, ordered the translation and arranged the printing, transportation and sale of forbidden books and employed agents in an adventurous traffic which passed to and from the Rhine and the ports of the Low Countries to the ports of London, Lynn and Bristol, and from there to the Universities and to certain large religious houses like Reading and Bury St Edmunds' (198). It was this organization which doubtless was responsible for getting *A proper dyaloge* into England. The fact that Bayfield admitted that he had read it suggests that he knew it well and may have been the one involved in smuggling it into England.

12 Rupp has no patience with those who refer to *The Burying of the Mass* under its other title. He states that 'it is high time this title "Rede me and be nott wrothe" went the way of Senlac Hill and other misnomers' (55). In the revised first edition of *The English Reformation*, A.G. Dickens refers to those who use the title 'Rede me and be not [sic] wrothe' as 'misguided' (469). However, in the second edition he seems to have had a change of heart and omits the word 'misguided' (404). I chose the title *Rede Me and Be Nott Wrothe* for my critical edition and gave reasons for doing so (4–5).

13 It may be that the editor who made this mistake is less culpable than at first appears, since in Bishop Stokesly's sermon preached at Paul's Cross in 1531, at which the bishop named thirty heretical books, two works, *Dialogue of the Gentleman and Plowman* and 'A.B.C. against the Clergy,' are mentioned as if they are two separate works (cited in Clebsch 266–7).

14 This title may have been used deliberately to confuse this work with the anonymous but popular *The Plowman's Tale*, which, although not published until 1536 by Thomas Godfray, was probably available in some form.

15 In a more recent study, McLean makes a case for both sides of the argument: he marshals evidence to show that Bishop William Barlowe and Jerome were two separate individuals and then shows how an argument can be made for seeing them as the same individual. *The Works of William Barlowe Including Bishop Barlowe's Dialogue on the Lutheran Factions* 169–94.

16 What little we know of Roye's and Barlowe's lives has been outlined in my edition of *Rede Me and Be Nott Wrothe* and in the studies of Hume, Clebsch, Rupp, and Arber. Comments on the men by their own contem-

poraries or near-contemporaries can be found in *The Complete Works of St. Thomas More passim* and Foxe *passim*. The most famous contemporary comment on William Roye is William Tyndale's, found in his 'Preface' to the *Parable of the Wicked Mammon* (*Doctrinal Treatises* 37ff).

17 Aston's comment leaves the door open to a number of possibilities. 'Working for' Roye could mean that Roye hired Barlowe to write the work for him, or that Barlowe served as Roye's amanuensis, and that Roye himself was responsible for the work. More logically, perhaps, it could mean that both men worked together on the tract. The same problem of determining parts played in the composition of a work is evident in the critical commentary surrounding Tyndale's New Testament. Critics know that William Roye worked with Tyndale on the New Testament, but no one seems able to agree on the part Roye played or the nature of his contribution. Tyndale's own comments on Roye's contribution in the 'Preface' to the *Parable of the Wicked Mammon* are subject to various interpretations (*Doctrinal Treatises* 37–8).

18 I have noted examples of historical distortion when they appear in *A proper dyaloge* in the Commentary. Distortions in *Rede Me and Be Nott Wrothe* can be found in the Commentary to my critical edition of that text.

19 In *Lollards and Their Books* (233–4), Hudson questions whether the Lambeth manuscript version of this text, reprinted in Matthew, is the actual source for *A proper dyaloge*'s version. Having studied a number of medieval manuscripts of the text she concludes 'that the print derives from a manuscript very close to Lambeth but not identical with it.'

20 In *Selections from English Wycliffite Writings* Hudson is even more outspoken in her criticism of Deanesly's attribution of the work to Purvey. She claims that the work was by the orthodox Richard Ullerston 'and has nothing whatever to do with Purvey' (145). David Norton seems to accept Hudson's view in his brief reference to the Oxford debate. He mentions the friar Thomas Palmer as the spokesman for the conservative side opposed to a vernacular tranlsation of the Bible and mentions 'A Latin tract by Richard Ullerston and an anonymous English tract [which] take the opposite view' (*A History of the Bible as Literature* vol 1 62).

21 In order to avoid confusing the issue of authorship in this part of the introduction, I will refer to the Latin text simply as 'the Latin text' and to the earliest English translation, edited separately by Deanesly and Bühler, as Deanesly/Bühler. Bühler's edition, based on seven extant manuscripts, is essentially identical to Deanesly's, except for two substantive variants: 'enmeye' in Deanesly is 'enueye' in Bühler (line 264) and 'last' in

Deanesly is '[b]est' in Bühler (line 305). There are, of course, spelling, punctuation, and capitalization differences between the two editions.

22 Bühler states, as I here argue, that Foxe based his version on Luft's edition, although he is prepared to state that Foxe used the 1530 edition that was published as a separate entity (167).

23 The dates of Fleming's consecration to bishop and his death as given in Arber – 1520 and 1531 respectively – are clearly wrong by one hundred years in each case; the wrong dates are probably undetected editorial errors.

24 Both Bühler (169) and Hudson ('The Debate on Bible Translation' 2) suggest that the 1530 editions were based on a fifteenth-century revision and not on the Deanesly/Bühler version. Although this is possible, they give no evidence for this claim. Deanesly does not appear to subscribe to this view.

25 In his comments to the reader in the *Parable of the Wicked Mammon*, Tyndale refers to Roye as 'a man somewhat crafty' (37) and accuses him of winning over Jerome Barlowe 'to make rhymes' (39), a reference, I think, to *Rede Me and Be Nott Wrothe* (*Doctrinal Treatises and Introductions to Different Portions of the Holy Scriptures*).

26 Compare Tyndale's use of Robin Hood with Robert Barnes's: 'O lorde god where arte thou why slepist thou? why sufferst thou this blasphemy? Thou hast defended thy prophetes with wilde fier from heven And wylte thou suffer thy wonly son and thy heuynly worde / thus to be dyspysyd? and to be rekenyd but as a story of Robyn hoode?' *A supplicatyon made by Robert Barnes vnto henrye the eyght* 1531 N6r fol. c.ij (*STC* 1470). Barnes alludes to Robin Hood in a section of the tract devoted to the Bible in the vernacular. Robin Hood allusions in the context of Bible study are evident into the seventeenth century. Thomas points out that 'in 1606 Nicholas Bownd observed that [the people] certainly knew more about Robin Hood than they did about the stories of the Bible, which were "as strange to them as any news that you can tell them"' (*Religion and the Decline of Magic* 195).

27 John King examines the use of the Robin Hood reference in his book *English Reformation Literature* 84, 212–13, 250, 383. All of his references, however, post-date Tyndale's. Interestingly, Barlowe and Roye, those two erstwhile reformist companions of Tyndale, make use of the Robin Hood reference in *Rede Me and Be Nott Wrothe* in a context which suggests that the traditional church has less objection to the faithful reading such profane tales than the Bible in the vernacular: 'Their frantyke foly is so pevishhe, / That they contempne in Englisshe, / To have the newe Testament. / But as for tales of Robyn hode, / With wother iestes

nether honest nor goode, / They have none impediment' (1427–32). And in a Lollard tract which Deanesly entitles the 'dialogue between a wise man and a fool,' the author refers to the tales of Robin Hood as well as those of Guy of Warwick and Bevis of Hampton to point out that some faint-hearted individuals chose to read escapist romance rather than follow the true path of Christianity (274).

28 The expression appears in John Frith's *Antithesis*, published by Hans Luft in 1529 (STC 11394): 'The pope and Bisshopes saye that the frute maketh the tre good / clene contrarye to all scripture and reason / And thus tvrne they the trees and the rootes vpwarde while they affirme that faith springeth and is made good of workes' (N4r Fo. c missigned xcij). Since Frith and Tyndale were close friends, it is possible that Frith may have borrowed the expression from Tyndale's *Obedience of a Christian Man*.

29 As regards this reference to Nicholas de Lyra in his *Answer to Sir Thomas More's Dialogue*, Anne O'Donnell claims that Tyndale is echoing a passage in Erasmus's *Praise of Folly* (CWE 27) where Erasmus pokes fun at the 'medieval exegete' (O'Donnell 'Scripture Versus Church' 125).

30 Daniell issues a warning about Mombert's text, claiming that he frequently supplies 'spurious marginal notes ... in imitation of old spelling, so that, at a glance, it may be difficult to sort out which are notes by Tyndale, and which glosses by Mombert' (*Tyndale's Old Testament* ed Daniell xxix).

31 In light of the number of alterations to Deanesly/Bühler that I have touched on, I find it hard to agree with Hudson when she states that 'the amount of modification in the sixteenth century, apart from modernization of the language, was probably slight' ('The Debate on Bible Translation, Oxford 1401' 2 note 6).

32 The attraction that Tyndale might have felt for Lollard themes in general, an attraction which would make his involvement in this work comprehensible, has been discussed in detail by Smeeton *passim*.

33 In lines 473–8 the husbandman refers to the so-called Reformation Parliament, whose first session was held on 3 November 1529 (S.E. Lehmberg *The Reformation Parliament*). It is my view that the first edition of *A proper dyaloge* was published either late in 1529 or early in 1530. Since the textual reference to this parliament does not allude to any decisions coming from it, but rather suggests that the presentation of a petition to it would probably not bear fruit (485ff), it seems that the authors have no clear idea of any definite decisions made by this first session. This leads me to conclude that this edition of *A proper dyaloge* was published early in the life of this parliament before any recommendations were forthcoming.

34 Howard Cole makes some keen observations on the notion of creative imitation and borrowing in his perceptive book *A Quest of Inquirie*. And speaking of Tyndale's derivativeness Dick states that 'it would be anachronistic and inaccurate to call Tyndale a plagiarist, since Romantic concepts of authorial originality and the legal definition of copyright are wholly alien to the intellectual climate of the early sixteenth century' ('"To Dig the Wells of Abraham"' 40).

35 Dick supports the view I am asserting here in his comment on Tyndale's writings: 'The ideas in his texts can be drawn only from the narrow range available in the contemporary ideology and can find expression only within a relatively limited vocabulary' ('"To Dig the Wells of Abraham"' 39).

36 All subsequent references to Fish's *A Supplicacyon* are taken from the reprint of the first edition, complete with John Foxe's side-notes, published in More 7 appendix B 412–22. Reference to Fish's work are to page and line numbers.

37 Apparently Fish's work won favour with Henry VIII as Tyndale's *Obedience of a Christian Man* had earlier, and essentially for the same reason: the work's strong anti-clerical stand and its exhortation to the king to take back the secular power and lands stolen from him and his ancestors by the clergy struck a responsive chord in Henry, who at this time was at loggerheads with the papacy over the question of his divorce and papal authority. The editors of More 7 also claim that with Wolsey's fall from power in 1529 a new attempt to curb clerical power began to be felt in the kingdom. They mention the 'Darcy memorandum,' a document deriving from the alliance of the dukes of Norfolk and Suffolk, which in part emphasized the need 'to view what of all temporal lands the spiritual men hath, and by what titles, and for what purposes and whether it be followed or no' (lxvii). In light of this revival of concern over clerical power and possessions as witnessed in such statements and in Tyndale's *Obedience* and Fish's *Supplicacyon*, 'We can see ... why Thomas More's answer to Fish's *Supplication* turned out to be more than ten times as long as Fish's incendiary pamphlet of barely sixteen pages. More is not answering one pamphlet; he is aiming ... to stem a widespread movement headed by a now powerful faction with direct and intimate access to the king' (lxviii). Henry VIII's keen interest in Fish's *Supplicacyon* is narrated in Foxe's biography of Fish ('The Story of M. Symon Fish'), our best source of knowledge on Fish's life and activities (published in More 7 appendix D 439–44).

38 Much like *Rede Me and Be Nott Wrothe*, Fish's *Supplicacyon* made it onto a number of proscription lists. It appears on the addition to William

Warham's mandate issued probably sometime in 1529 (Clebsch 262; More 7 409) as well as on the list issued by Henry's ecclesiastical commission in May 1530. The fact that it does not appear on a list issued in late 1530 or early 1531 leads Clebsch to wonder whether Fish had abjured at this point or whether Henry VIII, who liked the work, requested that it be stricken from the list. It appears on Stokesley's list issued on 3 December 1531, and Clebsch speculates that the royal protection may no longer have covered the work after Fish's death (Clebsch 262–7).

39 In their summary of the debate surrounding the doctrine of purgatory, the editors of More 7 make clear that this issue did not begin with Tyndale and Fish, although these two were largely responsible for disseminating negative views on the subject current at the time. The editors mention Luther's 'inconclusive "conclusions"' on purgatory, expressed in 1520, which would lead to his complete denial of its existence in the *Repeal of Purgatory* published in 1530. They mention as well Oecolampadius's translation of St John of Damascus on 'How Much the Good Works of the Living Profit the Dead,' and Henry VIII's attack on Luther's 'denial' of purgatory that the King issued in his *Assertio Septem Sacramentorum*, published in 1521. More continued the attack on Luther's views in his 1523 *Responsio ad Lutherum* and John Eck defended the traditional position in 1523 in *De purgatorio contra Ludderum*. Zwingli questioned the efficacy of the doctrine in 1523. Another English reformer, John Frith, defended Luther's position in *The Revelation of Antichrist* (1529), and in 1533 Frith produced *A disputacion of purgatorye* (STC 11387), which attacked three pro-purgatory works: John Fisher's *Assertionis Lutheranae confutatio* published in 1523, More's response to Fish in his *The supplycacyon of soulys*, and John Rastell's *A New Boke of Purgatory*.

40 The fact that the speakers of this dialogue and, by extension, the authors of this tract can state that they are dismissed as Lutherans by the traditional church and, just a few lines later, can call upon a Lollard tract to justify their own criticisms against the church is proof positive of the continuity of thought between Lollards and Lutherans. It also seems to suggest that there is not a lot to be gained by trying to decide whether a particular criticism made by these early English reformers has a Lutheran or Lollard ancestry. Chances are good that these reformers did not think of their indebtedness – if they thought of it at all – in quite this bifurcated way.

41 Tyndale states: 'Kings were ordained, then, as I before said, and the sword put in their hands, to take vengeance of evil-doers, that others might fear; and were not ordained to fight one against another, or to rise against the emperor to defend the false authority of the pope, that very antichrist.

Bishops, they only can minister the temporal sword; their office, the preaching of God's word, laid apart, which they will neither do, nor suffer any man to do, but slay with the temporal sword, which they have gotten out of the hand of all princes, them that would. The preaching of God's word is hateful and contrary unto them' (*Doctrinal Treatises* 185). And about the spiritual estates Fish says: 'And whate do al these gredy sort of sturdy idell holy theues with these yerely exactions that they take of the people? Truely nothing but exempt theim silues from thobedience of your grace. Nothing but translate all rule power lordishippe auctorite obedience and dignite from your grace vnto theim. Nothing but that all your subiectes shulde fall ynto disobedience and rebellion ageinst your grace and be vnder theym' (*A Supplicacyon for the Beggers* More 7 415)

42 Although the majority of my discussion focuses on Marsilius's influence on early Reformation thought, it would be unwise entirely to discount William of Ockham's (c 1285–1347) contribution, especially in the area of authority. O'Donovan's summary of Ockham's theories is cogent and helpful (13–20), but she, like others, acknowledges Marsilius's *perceived* predominance as a source for the reformers: 'Marsilius was far too devoted to a rigorously consistent and unambiguous theological-political project to have any use for Ockham's subtle dialectics of moderation. The architectonic boldness of the *Defender of the Peace* partly accounts for its serving the Roman Church as a measure of heretical deflection with which each generation of heretics was associated in papal accusations' (20).

43 Unlike Dickens and others, Pantin seems to doubt whether Wycliffe knew Marsilius (180).

44 In the second discourse, Marsilius is even clearer on the church's fraudulent claims to be able to bind and loose souls: 'God alone removes the guilt and the debt of eternal damnation from the truly penitent sinner, without any prior or concomitant action on the part of the priest' (146)

45 It is interesting to note that, in the same year as *A proper dyaloge* appeared, a debate on the question of the secular authority's right to involve itself in spiritual affairs was underway in Nürnberg. The titles of some of the tracts indicate the nature of the dispute: *Whether Secular Government Has the Right to Wield the Sword in Matters of Faith; An Answer to the Memorandum That Deals With This Question: Whether Secular Government Has the Right to Wield the Sword in Matters of Faith; Whether a Secular Government May Regulate Spiritual Matters, Restrain False Teaching, and Put Down Ungodly Abuses; Whether Secular Christian Government Has the Power to Ban False Preachers or Erring Sects and to Establish Order in Ecclesiastical Affairs*. See *Whether Secular Government* ... trans James M. Estes.

46 A fine summary of clerical power as it resided in the bishops can be found in W.A. Pantin *The English Church in the Fourteenth Century*, especially the chapters entitled 'The Social Structure of the English Church' and 'Patronage and the Use of Benefices' (9–46).

47 See, for instance, *Ballads from Manuscript* 360; Skelton's 'Speke Parott,' 'Collyn Clout,' and 'Why Come Ye Nat to Courte' (*The Complete English Poems*); Tyndale's *The Practice of Prelates* (in *Expositions*) *passim*.

48 To suggest that all members of the church hierarchy were involved in worldly affairs and keen to earn wealth and power would be stretching the truth to make my point and accepting the word of tendentious polemicists with scores to settle. For a more balanced view than one receives from either the sixteenth-century English reformers or their Lollard predecessors, see Peter Heath *The English Parish Clergy on the Eve of the Reformation*.

49 For various views of Wolsey's life and activities, see the following studies: Neville Williams *The Cardinal and the Secretary*; Peter Gwyn *The Rise and Fall of Cardinal Wolsey*; Charles Ferguson *Naked to Mine Enemies: The Life of Cardinal Wolsey*; George Cavendish *Thomas Wolsey, Late Cardinal. His Life and Death Written by George Cavendish his Gentleman-Usher* ed Roger Lockyer; J.J. Scarisbrick *Henry VIII*.

50 Sporadic references to Wycliffe throughout do not do justice to the complexity of his thought or to the historical context in which it is set. For a fine summary of both of these elements see K.B. McFarlane *John Wycliffe and the Beginnings of English Nonconformity*.

51 About this proposal McFarlane states: 'the arithmetic was faulty, but it was unacceptable for other reasons. The King for one utterly repudiated its anti-clericalism: his trusted servant John Norbury delighted the monasteries by urging [Bishop] Arundel to crush these heretics; and the Prince of Wales was hostile. Even that part of the Lollards' programme most calculated to tempt the avarice of laymen could no longer be relied upon to earn them a hearing. The house of Lancaster was not receptive to those notions which had temporarily beguiled John of Gaunt' (155).

52 A document exposing the forgery was published in 1534, at a time when Henry VIII was asserting his own claims for authority in both temporal and spiritual realms. See *A treatyse of the donation gyuen vnto Syluester pope of Rhome, by Constantyne emperour of Rome* STC 5641. Langland refers pejoratively to the Donation in *Piers Plowman* passus XV 519–23. A modern English rendering of these lines is as follows: 'For when Constantine endowed the Church so generously, and gave it lands and vassals, estates and incomes, an angel was heard to cry in the air over the city of Rome, saying: "This day the wealth of the Church is poisoned, and those

who have Peter's power have drunk venom"' (*Piers the Ploughman* trans Goodridge 232–3).

53 It is also important to understand that there were traditionalists writing in support of clerical temporalities. Pantin mentions three of them who wrote and flourished in the fourteenth century: Uthred of Boldon (1315/ 25–97), Adam Easton (d 1397), and Thomas Brunton (1320–99) (166–85).

54 A contemporary, if idiosyncratic, summary of this rebellion involving Wat Tyler, Jack Straw, and John Ball is in *Froissart's 'Chronicles'* II 238ff.

55 About this uprising Thomson states: 'Although the motive force behind the 1431 rising is described as Lollardy ... it should be noted that it was very much a political kind of Lollardy. ... None of the indictments contain any charges of doctrinal unorthodoxy or even of the possession of heretical books. The programme of the rebels, as far as can be seen, was one for church disendowment, the land of the Church being taken over for the endowment of earls, knights, squires, and almshouses' (*The Later Lollards* 61).

56 McFarlane has also shown that economic considerations were as least as important as moral ones on the question of clerical disendowment, especially of alien priories belonging to the French king but situated in England. He states 'An interesting feature of the land-acquisitions of the [Lollard] knights is the extent to which they invested in monastic lands. ... Taken into the king's hands for the duration of the war [with France], these offered, in a period notable for the scarcity of good land in the market, an opportunity for investors well enough placed to secure them by their influence at court. The first step was to obtain their custody for the duration of the war from the king at an artificially low rent; the second to negotiate with the mother-house in Normandy or elsewhere to buy out its interest; since the French saw no prospect of recovering possession ... they were willing to take a small price as the value of their reversion and be glad to get anything at all.' McFarlane concludes: 'To argue that all owners of alien priory lands were Lollards would be as absurd as to assert that all sixteenth-century purchasers of monastic property were Protestants; but at least each had something substantial to lose by reaction. These courtiers had a vested interest in disendowment at a time when Lollard petitions were recommending the government to use the lands of the possessioners for the creation of new soldiers' fiefs. They had incidentally also ... a vested interest in the prolongation of the war. Lollards or not, they were compelled to endure a conflict between interest and creed' (*Lancastrian Kings and Lollard Knights* 190–2).

57 William of Ockham, a near-contemporary of Marsilius, also undermined the traditional church's position on temporalities in his work *An rex*

Angliae pro succursu guerrae possit recipere bona ecclesiarum. For a overview of Ockham's thought and his effect on English reformist thought see the various essays in *From Ockham to Wyclif.* Knowles provides a fine summary of the conflict between those who supported the church's position on temporalities and those who attacked it in *The Religious Orders in England* vol 2. He also discusses the related notion of Dominion and Grace, the internecine struggle between friars and possessioners over ownership, and the influence that this subject had on the development of Wycliffe's own views on clerical temporalities.

58 Knowles gives the approximate totals for 1320 as: Preachers 1760; Minors 1700; Carmelites 800; Austin Friars 600 (*Religious Orders* 2 258).

59 McFarlane acknowledges the significant wealth of certain members of the clerical orders. He claims that although they made up slightly more than two per cent of the population, 'they possessed huge endowments which they owed to the past generosity of pious laymen and which had been increased in value by the good management of successions of clerical landlords. Their property, which may have yielded an income three times that of the king, was not at all evenly divided among them. While the majority of churchmen were little better off than the peasants they lived among, a few ... enjoyed large revenues and kept great state' (*John Wycliffe and the Beginnings of English Nonconformity* 42).

60 Dickens provides a fine summary of the survival of Lollardy in the sixteenth century. He states that the inspiration for the heresy in early Tudor England was 'overwhelmingly Wycliffe, at least until about 1530' (50). Thomson, if less categorical than Dickens, nevertheless feels that a relationship between Lollardy and Lutheranism in England in the early sixteenth century was a distinct possibility. He states: 'How far Lollard ideas provided a fertile soil for Lutheranism is hard to say, but the speed with which the latter spread ... suggests that the ground may well have been prepared for it' (*The Later Lollards* 138). Thomson, who took up the study of Lollardy where McFarlane left off, indicates through his study of heresy prosecutions that Lollardy and Lollard thought flourished during the early part of the sixteenth century: between 1506 and 1521 in various districts of the country there were 23 burnings and 221 abjurations, compared to 10 deaths by burning or execution, 142 abjurations, 30 arrests, 30 accusations, and 15 purgations in the much longer period between 1414 and 1499.

61 Aston has little doubt about the sixteenth-century reformers' awareness of tradition to support their own causes, and she comments on the sometimes unscrupulous efforts made to rewrite texts in order to make them support issues of current importance. She states that with certain texts from the past 'the work of recovery was openly acknowledged. Antiquity,

since it was valuable, was avowed. But other Reformation editors pro-
ceeded on different principles. It was one thing to publish a text, more or
less as it stood, archaisms and all, to prove that new reformers were but
old reformers writ large, with the right of precedent on their side. It was
another to take over an old text, and rewrite it (without acknowledge-
ment) to serve a new purpose, or alter it sufficiently to obscure its origin'
(*Lollards and Reformers* 227). In the case of *A proper dyaloge* it was to the
authors' advantage to acknowledge the ancestry of the prose additions in
order to call history to their support, although, in the case of the second
prose text on biblical translation, this did not prevent them from altering
the original to update its message.

62 Arundel's seventh constitution reads as follows: 'Also, since it is dangerous, as S. Jerome witnesses, to translate the text of holy scripture from
one language into another, because in such translations the same meaning is not easily retained in all particulars: even as S. Jerome, although he
was inspired, confessed that he had often erred in this matter: therefore
we decree and ordain that no one shall in future translate on his own
authority any text of holy scripture into the English tongue or into any
other tongue, by way of book, booklet, or treatise. Nor shall any man read
this kind of book, booklet or treatise, now recently composed in the time
of the said John Wycliffe, or later, or any that shall be composed in future,
in whole or part, publicly or secretly, under penalty of the greater excommunication, until that translation shall be recognised and approved by
the diocesan of the place, or if the matter demand in, by a provincial
council. Whoever disobeys this, let him be punished after the same fashion ... as an abettor of heresy and error' (cited in Deanesly 296). It is interesting to note that here and elsewhere both sides call upon identical
'allies' to support their opposite views. Here, for instance, Arundel
invokes St Jerome. In *A proper dyaloge* (1597ff) Jerome comes to the support of those who defend biblical translations. Tunstal's monition to his
archbishops against biblical translations reads as follows: 'Monicio ad tra-
dendum libros novi testamenti in idiomate vulgare, translatos per fratrem
Martinum Lutherum et eius ministrum Willumum Tyndall alias Hochyn
et fratrem Willmum Roy' (cited in Sturge 132).

63 One of the three so-called Lollard treatises that Deanesly claims were
written in this period is our own 'A compendious olde treatyse.' As I have
already stated (note 20, above), Hudson ('The Debate on Bible Translations') denies that this is a Lollard tract and argues that it was written by
the orthodox Richard Ullerston.

64 Not an uncommon sentiment throughout the history of biblical translation as Norton eloquently traces it in his two-volume study.

65 This border is clearly one that Luft made good use of. The complete border is found in Tyndale's *Obedience of a Christian Man* (STC 24446), in John Frith's *A Pistle to the Christian Reader* 1529 (STC 11394), and in Roye's *An exhortation to the diligent studye of scripture. ...* (STC 10493), all published by Luft.

A proper dyaloge
betwene a Gentillman
and an Husbandman

A proper dyalo= [A1r]
ge / betwene a Gentillman and an husbandman /
eche complaynynge to other their mise=
rable calamite / through the am=
bicion of the clergye. 5

An A.B.C. to the spiritualte.

A wake ye gostely persones / awake / awake
Bothe preste / pope / bisshoppe and Cardinall.
Considre wisely / what wayes that ye take
Daungerously beynge lyke to haue a fall. 10
Every where / the mischefe of you all.
Ferre and nere / breaketh oute very fast
Godde will nedes be revenged at the last.
  Howe longe haue ye the worlde captiued
In sore bondage / of mennes tradiciones? 15
Kynges and Emperoures / ye have depryued
Lewedly vsurpynge / their chefe possessiones.
Muche misery ye make / in all regiones.
Nowe youre fraudes / almoste at the latter cast
Of godde sore to be revenged at the last. 20
  Poore people to oppresse / ye haue no shame
Qwakynge for feare / of your double tyranny.
Rightfull iustice ye haue put oute of frame
Sekynge the lust / of youre godde / the belly.
Therfore I dare you boldely certefye. 25
Very litle though ye be therof a gast
Yet god will be revenged at the last.

O Christen reder / from rashnes refraine [A1v]
Of hastye iudgement / and lyght sentence.

Though sum recken it frowardnes of brayne   30
Thus to detecte / the clergyes inconuenience.
Vnto christes wordes geue / thou aduertence
Which saieth nothinge to be done so secretly
But it shall be knowen manifestly.

Where as men discerne no grefe of darcknes   35
Full litle is desyred the confortable lyght.
The daye is restrayned to shewe his clerenes
Tyll the clowdes be expelled of the night
As longe as we perceyue not wronge from right
Nether holynes from false hypocrisye   40
The truthe can not be knowen manifestly.

Cursed they are / as Esaye dothe expresse
Which presume the euyll for good to commende
Sayenge that swete is soure / and light darcknes
As nowe in the clergye / we may perpende.   45
Whos disguysed madnes in the later ende
As seynt Paule to Timothe did prophesye
Shall be knowen to all men manifestly.

Example of twayne he dothe there recyte
Whos names were called Iannes and Iambres   50
Which by enchauntments / through deuels might
Strongely resisted the prophete Moyses.
Doynge lyke merueyles and wonderfulnes
So that none could the very trouth espye
Tyll theyr Iugglynge was knowen manifestly.   55

Christe / like wise / with his predicacion   [A2r]
The phariseyes shewynge outwarde holynes
Was a counted of small reputacion
Vyce cloked vnder shyne of vertuousnes.
Vntill at the last their furiousnes   60
Accusyng the woman taken in aduoutery
They sawe their fautes detecte manifestly.

Their vyces opened / they could not abyde
Shame drevynge them to confusyon
Which afore season through pope holy pryde   65
They bolstred out vnder abusyon
It is the practyse of their collusyon.
Zele of rightuousnes to fayne outwardly
Tyll their fautes be detecte manyfestly.

Which in oure clergye is evidently sene   70
Fayned godlynes falsly pretendynge
Wherby moste parte of people do wene
That they seke goddes honour in all thinge
How beit / men shuld se that their sekynge
Is to confounde christes gospell vtterly   75
Were their fautes detecte manyfestly.

What greater despyte can they ymagine /
Agaynst god his hye honour to deface
Than to vsurpe on them his power diuine
Abhominably sittinge in holy place?   80
Which hath continued longe tyme and space
And shall with outragious blasphemy
Till their fautes be detecte manifestly.

Scripture vnto them was first proferyd   [A2v]
Mekely withoute any prouocacion.   85
Which to receyue when it was offeryd
They refused with indignacion.
Wherfore touchinge their reformacion.
Litle trust is to be had certaynly
Tyll their fautes be detecte manifestly.   90

Thus to conclude / o christen reder
Vnto pacience / I the exhorte.
Aduertesynge / howe and in what maner
Christe rebuked this pharisaycall sorte.
Whom as Mathew in the .xxiij. doth reporte.   95

With fearefull sentence he cursed ernestly
Their wicked fautes detectynge manifestly.

Nihil est opertum quod non reueletur. Math .x.

Here foloweth the Dialoge / the Gen
tillman beginninge first his complaynte.   100

Gentillman.
With soroufull harte / maye I complayne
Concerninge the chaunce / of my misery
Although parauenture it is but vayne
Trueth oppressyd / with open tyranny.   105
My enheritaunce and patrimony.
Agaynst right / from me they kepe awaye
Which saye / for my frendes soules they praye.

Myne aunceteres of worthy progeny   [A3r]
With rentes and lyuelood largely endued   110
Mayntayned their estates honorably
Aydynge the poore / indigence to exclude.
Tyll at the last / the clergy to them sued.
Pretendinge godlynes / vnder a fals waye
Sayenge they wold for their soules praye.   115

Stoutely they alleged before their syght
Howe after this lyfe is a purgatory.
Wherin their soules both daye and nyght
Shuld be tormented with out memory
Excepte of their substaunce transitory.   120
Vnto theyr seactes / they wold some what paye
Sayenge that they wold for their soules praye.

They bare them in hande that they had myght
Synners to bynde and loose at their owne plesure
Takynge vpon them to leade theym a right   125

Vnto ioye / that euer shuld endure.
Of popes pardones they boosted the treasure.
Chalengynge of heuene and hell the kaye
Sayenge / that they wold for their soules praye.

To trust wife or children / they did disswade   130
Eyther any frendes or persones temporall.
Affermynge / that oure loue shuld a way vade
Without any memory of them at all
Onely to hope in their seactes spirituall.
They entyced / with persuasiones gaye   135
Sayenge that they wold for their soules praye.

Thus with wylines and argumentes vayne   [A3v]
Myne aunceters brought in to perplexite
Partely thorough feare of eternall payne
And partely for desyre of felicite.   140
They consented makynge no difficulte
To graunte their requestes without delaye
Sayenge that they wold for their soules praye.

Their chefe lordshippes and londes principall
With commodytes of their possessyon   145
Vnto the clergye they gaue forthe with all
Dysheretinge their right successyon.
Which to receiue without excepcion
The couetous clergy made no denay
Sayenge that they wold for their soules praye.   150

By the meanes wherof / I and suche other
Suffrynge the extremyte of indigence
Are occasioned to theft or mourder
Fallynge in to moche inconuenience.
Because the clergye agaynst conscience   155
Deuoureth oure possessiones nighte and daye
Sayeng that for oure frendes soules they praye.

I haue wife and children vpon my hande

Wantinge substaunce / their lifes to sustayne
Wherfore to the clergy that haue my lande   160
Sometyme I come and pituously complayne
Whos statelines / to helpe me hauynge disdayne
With oute any comforte to me they saye
That for my frendes soules they dayly praye.

Shuld I and my houshold for houngre dye   [A4r]   165
They wold not an halfe peny with vs parte
So that they lyue in welthe aboundantly
Full litle they regarde oure woofull smerte.
To waste oure goodes they nothinge aduerte
In vicious lustes and pompous araye   170
Sayenge that for our frendes soules they praye.

They take vpon them apostles auctorite
But they folowe nothinge their profession
Often tymes they preache of christes pouerte
Howe be it towarde it they haue no affeccion.   175
Yf so be they pleate ones in possession
Harde it is to get ought fro them awaye
Sayenge / that for oure frendes soules they praye.

Thus must we beare their oppression
Whiles to complayne there is no remedye   180
The worlde they haue brought in subiection
Vnder their ambicious tyranny.
No respecte they haue to the mysery
Of vs poore gentillmen that be laye
Sayenge that for our frendes soules they praye.   185

Alas / is it not a myserable case
To se ydle persones voyde of pyte
Occupyenge the landes before oure face
Which shuld pertayne vnto vs of duete.
They haue richesse / and we calamyte   190
Their honour encreaced / oures must dekaye
Sayenge that for oure frendes soules they praye.

The husbandman. [A4v]

Syr / god geue you good morowe
I perceiue the cause of youre sorowe   195
 And most lamentable calamyte.
Is for the oppression intollerable
Of thes monstres so vncharitable
 Whom men call the spiritualte.
Trouthe it is / ye poore gentillmen are   200
By their craftynes made nedy and bare
 Your landes with holdinge by violence
How be it we husbandmen euery where
Are nowe in worsse condicion ferre
 As it may be marked by experience.   205

Gentillman.

In worse caas? nay / that can not be so
For loke ouer the hoole worlde to and fro
 Namely here in oure owne region.
And thou shalt fynde that in their handes   210
Remayneth the chefe lordeshippes and landes
 Of poore gentillmens possession.
They haue oure aunceters lyuelood and rentes
Their principall fearmes and teneamentes
 With temporall fredomes and libertees.   215
They haue gotten vnto their kingdomes
Many noble baronries and erldomes
 With esquyres landes and knightes fees.

Husbondeman.

Notwithstondinge yet they saye precysely   220
That your Aunceters gaue to theym freely
 Soche worldly dominion and lyuelood.

Gentillman.

Freely quod a? nay / that is but fayned
For they ware certeynly therto constreyned   [A5r]   225
 By their couetous disceite and falshod.

Husbondman.
Howe dyd they youre aunceteres compell?

Gentillman.
Mary in threatnynge the paynes of hell   230
   And sharpe punishment of purgatorye.
Wher to brenne / they made them beleue
Excepte they wolde vnto theym geue
   Parte of their substaunce and patrimony.

Husbondeman.   235
But howe wold they delyuer them fro thence?

Gentillman.
As they saide by their prayers assistence
   Which with boostynge wordes they dyd alowe.

Husbondman.   240
Prayer? god geue her a shamefull represe
For it is the moost briberynge thefe
   That euer was / I make god a vowe.
For by her the clergy withoute dowte
Robbeth the hole countre rounde aboute   245
   Bothe comones and estates none excepte.
I wote they haue prayed so longe all redy
That they haue brought the lande to beggery
   And all thryftynes clene a waye swepte.
What soeuer we get with sweate and labour   250
That prolle they awaye with their prayour
   Sayenge they praye for oure soules allwaye.
But is their prayer not more avaylynge
To the deade soules / than to the lyuynge
   So it is not worthe a rotten aye.   255

Gentillman.
To the soules departed it is not profitable   [A5v]
For whye / thos that are in case dampnable
   No assistence of prayour can attayne.
And as for purgatory ther is none   260

All though there be clerkes many one
   Which to seke it take moche payne.

   Husbondman.
Than I wold their prayenge were at an ende
For yf they pray longe thus so god me mende   265
   They shall make the lande worsse than nought.
But nowe I will rehearce seriously
Howe we husbandemen full pituously
   Vnto miserable wrechednes are brought.
Fyrst whan englonde was in his floures   270
Ordred by the temporall gouernoures
   Knowenge no spirituall iurisdiccion.
Than was ther in eche state and degre
Haboundance and plentuous prosperite
   Pessable welthe without affliccion.   275
Noblenes of blood / was had in price
Vertuousnes avaunced / hated was vyce
   Princes obeyd / with due reuerence.
Artificers and men of occupacion
Quietly wanne their sustentacion   280
   Without any grefe of nedy indigence.
We husband men lyke wise prosperously
Occupyenge the feates of husbandry
   Hyerd fearmes of pryce competent.
Wherby oure lyuinge honestly we wanne   285
And had ynough to paye every manne
   Helpinge other that were indigent.
Tyll at the last the rauenous clergye
Through their craftynes and hypocrisye   [A6r]
   Gatt to theym worldly dominacion.   290
Than were we ouercharged very sore
Our fearmes set vp dayly more and more
   With shamefull pryce in soche a fasshyon.
That we paye more nowe by halfe the sume
Than a fore tymes we dyd of custome   295
   Holdinge ought of their possession.
Besyde this / other contentes of brybery

As payenge of tythes / open and preuy
   And for herynge of confession.
Also prestes dueties and clerkes wages   300
Byenge of perdones and freres quarterages
   With chirches and aultares reparacion.
All oure charges can not be nombred
Wherwith we are greatly acombred
   Ouer whelmyd with desolacion.   305
We tourmoyle oure selfes nyght and daye
And are fayne to dryncke whygge and whaye
   For to maynteyne the clargyes facciones.

     Gentillman.
This were a great shame to be knowen   310
Seynge halfe the realme is their owne
   That they charge you with soche exaccions.
Me thyncketh so to do is no small cryme
For they kepte as good houses a fore tyme
   Whiles theyr fearme hyers was ferre lesse.   315

     Husbandman.
Ye / more plentuous houses a great deale
How be yt in hyndrynge the comone weale
   They vse also this practyse doutles.
Where as poore husbandmen afore season   320
Accordinge vnto equite and reason   [A6v]
   House or lande to fearme dyd desyre.
Without any difficulte they might it get
And yet no hygher price was ther vp set
   Than good conscience did require.   325
But nowe their ambicious suttlete
Makyth one fearme of two or thre
   Ye some tyme they bringe .vi. to one.
Which to gentillmen they let in farmage
Or elles to ryche marchauntes for avauntage   330
   To the vndoynge of husbandemen echone.
Wherby the comones sufferinge damage
The hole lande is brought in to rerage

As by experience ye may well see.
Thus is the wealth of village and towne 335
With the fame of honorable renowne
   Fallen in to myserable pouerte.
Plentuous housholdes hereby ar dekayde
Relefe of poore people is awaye strayde
   Allmes exyled with hospitalyte. 340
By soche meanes / all thinge waxeth dere
Complaynte of subiectes cryenge ferre and nere
   Oppressed with greuous calamyte.

    Gentillman.
Truely thou shewest the very abuse 345
Neuerthelesse concernynge oure excuse
   Why we gentillmen fearmes occupye.
The principall occasion is onely this
That oure patrimony geuen awaye is
   Vnto thes wolffes of the clergye. 350
By whos oppression we are so beggeryd
That necessite hath vs compellyd
   With fearmes soche shyft to make. [A7r]
For as ye husbandemen can well vnderstande
Touchinge expences and charges of the lande 355
   They disdayne any parte with vs to take.

    Husbandman.
Ye by saynte Marye / I you warrante
In soche cases / their ayde is very scant
   Makinge curtesye to do any goode. 360
Let the realme go what waye it wull
They hauynge ease / and their belyes full
   Regarde litle the comone weale by throode.
Yf princes demaunde their succour or ayde
This answere of them is comonely saide 365
   We are pore bedemen of youre grace.
We praye for your disceaced auncetryes
For whom we synge masses and dirigees
   To soccour their soules in nedefull cace.

Gentillman.   370
Oh / they afoorde prayers good cheape
Sayenge rather many masses by heape
   Than to geue a poore man his dyner.
Wherfore as thou saydest / so god helpe me
I se of their prayenge no comodyte   375
   Nether avauntage in any maner.
For whye with in thes .iiij. hundred yere
Thorough oute christendome was not a freer
   Of thes / whom we mendicantes call.
And syth that tyme dyuers facciones   380
Of collegianes / monkes and chanones
   Haue spred this region ouer all.
Also of prestes / were not the tenthe parte
Which as they saye / haue none other arte
   But for vs worldly people to praye.   [A7v]   385
And yet the worlde is nowe farre worsse
As euery man felyth in his poorsse
   Than it was at that tyme I dare saye.
Wherfore the trueth openly to be tryde
I wolde they shuld laye their prayenge a syde   390
   And geue theym selfes to labour bodely.

Husbandman.
It were harde to bringe theym therto
Vtterly refusynge any labour to do
   Because they are people gostely.   395

Gentillman.
Were not the apostles gostely also?

Husbandman.
Yes syr / but it is so longe ago
   That their lyuynge is oute of memorye.   400

Gentillman.
We fynde it well in the newe testament.

Husbandman.
The clargye saye / it is not conuenyent
  For laye men therwith to be busye.   405

Gentillman.
Wotest thou wherfore they do that?

 Husbondman.
In fayth syr I coniecture some what
  And I suppose I do not moche erre.   410
Might men the scripture in Englishe rede
We secular people shuld than se in dede
  What Christ and the apostles lyves were.
Which I dout nothinge are contrarye
Vnto the lyuynge of oure clargye   415
  Geuyn to pompous ydlenes euery where.
Whos abhominacion ones knowen   [A8r]
Their pryde shuld be sone ouer throwen
  And fewe wold their statelynes for beare.

 Gentyllman.   420
Thou hyttest the nayle vpon the heed
For that is the thinge that they dreed
  Least scripture shuld come vnto light.
God commaundyd man in the begynnynge
With sweat of vysage to wynne his lyuynge   425
  As Moses in his fyrst boke dothe wryte.
And as Marcke sayeth in the .vi. chapter
Christe herevpon erthe was a carpenter
  Not dysdayninge an occupacion.
Also the disciples vniuersally   430
With their handes laboured busyly
  Exchewynge ydle conuersacion.

 Husbandman.
Oure clargye lyue nothynge after their rate

Gentillman. 435
No / they seke ydelly to auaunce their estate
   And to be had in reputacyon.

Husbondman.
Are they worldly or gostely to saye the trothe?

Gentyllman. 440
So god helpe me I trowe none of bothe
   As it apperyth by their fasshion.
For in matters of worldly busynes
The clergye haue moche more entresse
   Than temporall men I ensue the. 445
The landes of lordes and dukes to possesse
Thei abasshe not a whit the seculernes
   Chalengynge tytles of worldly honour.
But is the realme in any necessyte [A8v]
Where as they shuld condescend of duete 450
   To stande by their prince with soccour
Than to be of the world they denye
Sayenge that their helpe is spiritually
   From the worlde makinge a separacion.

Husbandman. 455
Whiles they vse soche craftynes to contryue
The temporalte ought theym to depryue
   Of their worldly dominacyon.
And euen as they saye that they are gostely
So without any assistence worldly 460
   To lyue gostely they shuld haue no let.

Gentillman.
That were an expedyent medicyne
Accordinge vnto saynt Paules doctryne
   Qui non laborat / non manducet. 465
Notwithstonding their power is so stronge
That whether they do ryght or wronge

They haue their owne will without fayle.
Their enormytees so ferre out breaketh
That all the worlde agaynst theym speaket   470
   But alas man what dothe it avayle?

   Husbondman.
The remedy that I can ymagyne
Were best that we together determyne
   To get vs to london incontynent.   475
Where as it is here for a surete tolde
The kinge with his nobles dothe holde
   A generall counsell or parlament

   Gentillman.
What woldest thou that we shuld do there?   480

   Husbondman.   [B1r]
The constraynte of oure myserye to declare
   Vnder a meke forme of lamentacion.

   Gentillman.
So shuld we be sure of soche answeres   485
As were made vnto the poore beggers
   For thir pituous supplicacyon.
Against whom the clergyes resons nought worthe
The soules of purgatory they brought forthe
   The beggers complaynte to discomfyte.   490
Wherfore against oure peticion I the tell
They wold bringe out all the deuells in hell
   For to do vs some shamefull despyte.

   Husbondman.
And was ther none other waye at all   495
But the soules of purgatory to call
   In ayde and assistence of the clergye.

   Gentillman.
It was the suerest waye by seynt Ihone

For had they to playne scripture gone 500
    I wousse they hadde be taken tardye.
The beggers complaynte was so grounded
That the clargye hadde be confounded
    Had they not to purgatory hasted.

    Husbondman. 505
Where sayd they purgatorye shuld be?

    Gentillman.
By scripture they shewed no certente
    Albeit with stowte wordes they it faced.
Euen like vnto the man / which went 510
A certeyne straunge ylonde to inuent
    But whan he sawe / he could it not fynde.
Least his wit and travaile shuld seme in vayne [B1v]
Reporte of other men he beganne to fayne
    The symplicite of rude people to blynde. 515
But touchinge oure communicacion
Ther is a nother consideracion
    Which somewhat more troubleth my mynde.
Thou knowest that in the parlament
The chefe of the clergye are resident 520
    In a maruelous great multitude.
Whos fearce displeasure is so terrible
That I iudge it were not possible
    Any cause against them to conclude.
As for this ones we shall not be herde 525
And great men I tell the are a ferde
    With them to haue any doynge.
Whosoeuer will agaynst them contende
Shall be sure of a mischefe in the ende
    Is he gentillman lorde or kynge. 530
And that vnto kynge Ihon I me reporte
With other princes and lordes a great sorte
    Whom the cronycles expresse by name.
Whiles they were a lyue they did them trouble
And after their deathe with cruelnes double 535

They ceased not their honour to diffame.
Dyd not they so longe striue and wrastle
Against the good knyght syr Ihon oldecastle
   Other wise called lorde of Cobham.
That from hyghe heresye vnto treasone   540
They brought him to fynall destruction
   With other many a noble man.
Moreouer at seynt Edmundes bury some saye
That the famous prince duke Humfray
   By them of his lyfe was abreuiate.   [B2r] 545
Sythe that tyme I coulde recken mo
Whom they caused to be dispatched so
   Parauenture some of no lowe estate.

    Husbondman.
Their tyranny is great without fayle   550
Neuerthelesse yf we wold them assayle
   With argumentes of the holy gospell.
They shuld not be ones able to resiste
For the wordes of oure sauiour christe
   Shuld stoppe them were they neuer so fell. 555
Who in the .xxiij. chapter of seynt Luke
To their great confusyon and rebuke
   Forbydeth secular ambicion.
Wherin he himselfe example gaue
Contempnynge worldly honour to haue   560
   Of this world claymynge no kingdome.
Also when his disciples forthe he sent
He commaunded them to be content
   With foode and apparayle necessary.
Wherto saint Paules doctrine accordinge 565
Saieth: hauynge meate drinke and clothinge
   We shuld no thinge couet superfluously.

    Gentillman.
Yf the holy gospell allege we shuld
As stronge heretikes take vs they would   570
   Vnto their churche disobedient.

For why they haue commaunded straytely
That none vnder great payne be so hardye
  To haue in englishe the testament.
Which as thou knowest at London   575
The bisshop makinge ther a sermon
  With shamefull blasphemy was brent.   [B2v]

    Husbondeman.
Alas that cruelte goeth to my hert
Wherfor I feare me we shall all smert   580
  At lengthe with bitter punishment.

    Gentillman.
Vndouted it is greatly to be fearyd
Least the hole region shalbe plagyd
  For their outragious blasphemy.   585
In kinge Henryes dayes of the name the fyft
The clergye their pride aboue to lyft
  Persecuted christen brothers haynously.
The gospell of Christ a syde to cast
Which at that tyme prospered fast   590
  With all their puysaunce they dyd conspyre.
Euery where they threwe theym in presones
In sharpe gayles / and horrible doungeones
  Causynge many to be brent in fyre.
Their furious malice neuer stentyd   595
Tyll they had the light oute quenchyd
  Of the gospell and holy scripture.
Wher of all bokes that they could get
They caused on a fayre fyre to be set
  To expell goddes worde doynge their cure.   600
But consyder what ther of did chaunce
Moste terrible plages of fearfull vengeaunce
  And endles sorowe to oure nacion.
For within shorte season after they lost
Which many a mans lyfe dyd cost   605
  In fraunce their dominacion.
Amonge theym selfes moste hatefull mourdre

Many stronge batayles / one after a nother
    With great effusyon of englisshe bloode.   [B3r]
Frende against frende / brother against brother.   610
Euery man at variaunce with other
    The realme longe season in myschefe stoode.

    Husbondman.
This is nowe a dayes clene oute of mynde

    Gentillman.   615
I praye god / hereafter we do not fynde
    The same vengeaunce for like offence.
For as it is in the byble playnely red
God left neuer lande yet vnpunished
    Which agaynst his worde made resistence.   620

    Husbondeman.
Well syr / yf scrypture ye forthe bringe
I beseche you / what is their answeringe
    Are they so bolde goddes worde to denye?

    Gentillman.   625
Naye but after their ymaginacion
They make there of an interpretacion
    Vnto the texte clene contrary.
They allege the popes auctorite
Customes of auncyent antiquite   630
    With diuers counseiles approbacion.
Also the holynes of religious fathers
With the bloode sheadinge of marters
    For their chirches preservacion.
Besyde that contynuaunce of yeres   635
Myracles of bishoppes / monkes and freres
    Whom for speciall patrones they holde.
And fynally to make a conclusion
In fortefyenge their abusion
    Other practyses they vse manyfolde.   640
They resorte to lordes and great estates   [B3v]

With whom they are dayly checke mates
. Ye to saye the trouthe their soueraynes.
Where amonge other communicacion
They admonishe them with protestacion   645
   To beware of thes heretikes Lutheranes.
Whom they saye is a secte new fangled
With execrable heresyes entangled
   Sekinge the chirches perdicion.
Which oure fore fathers as wise as we   650
Were contente with humble simplicite
   To honour / obeynge their tuycion.
Also none presumed till nowe a late
Against the clergye to beare any hate
   Or grudged at their possession.   655

    Husbondman.
By seynt mary syr / that is a starcke lye
I can shewe you a worcke by and by
   Against that poynte makinge obiection.
Which of warantyse I dare be bolde   660
That it is aboue an hundred yere olde
   As the englishe selfe dothe testifye.
Wherin the auctour with argumentes
Speaketh against the lordshippes and rentes
   Of the clergye possessed wrongfully.   665

    Gentillman.
Is it so olde as thou doest here expresse
Reprouynge their pompous lordlynes
   So is it than no newe found heresy.

    Husbondman.   670
No / but alas / halfe the boke we want
Hauynge no more left than a remenant
   From the begynnynge of the .vi. chapter verely.   [B4r]

    Gentillman.
As for that it maketh no matter   675

Begynne hardely at the sixte chapter
  Redynge forthe to the ende seriously.
For though old writinges apere to be rude
Yet notwithstandinge they do include
  The pithe of a matter most fructuously.   680

Husbondman.
To rede it I shall be diligent
Though the style be nothinge eloquent
  With ornate speache set out curiously.

Here foloweth an olde treatyse ma=   685
de aboute the tyme of kinge Ry=
charde the seconde.

Where as the clergy perceyueth that lordlynes and worldly
dominion can not be borne out bi scripture / then flie they to
argumentes of mennes persuasyon sayenge after thys maner Seynt Huge   690
and seynt Swithune were thus lordes / and in this they ensued
Christes lyuyng and his doctrine / therfore we may be laufully thus
lordes. But I wote well that Gabriel shall blowe his horne or they
haue proued the minor. That is / that thes sayntes or patrones in
this sued the doctrine or the lyfe of Iesu Christe. And of this   695
thou mayst se that soch argumentes that ar not clothed with
Christes lyuynge or his teachinge / be right nought worthe all
though the clerkes blynde with them moch folke in the world. But
here haue I no leyser to tell though I coulde / [B4v] what
chefesaunce and costes the churche maketh and what werres they hold   700
to contynue this symony and heresy so vnavisely brought in to the
chirche. And yet they seke all the wayes therto that they can. Ye
in so moch that they go openly armyd in to the felde to kyll
christen men / for to get and holde soche lordshippe. And
notwithstondynge seynt Peter was so pore that he had nether golde   705
nor syluer as he saieth in the Actes of the apostles.[1] And his
other worldly good he left / whan he beganne to sue Christe. And as
towchynge the tytle of worldly lawe that he had to soch worldly

---

1 *side-note* Act.iij.

goodes / he made neuer cleyme ne neuer resceyued after any worldly
710 lordshippe. And yet they call all their hole kingdom seynt Peters
grounde or lordshippe. And therfor seynt Bernarde writeth to
Eugenie the pope sayenge. Yf thou wilt be a lorde / seke by a
nother waye to attayne it / but not by thys apostles ryght.[2] For he
may not geue the that he had not / that he had he gaue / the whiche
715 was busynes vpon chirches. Whether he gaue lordshippe or no / here
what he saieth. Be ye not lordes in the clergy / but be ye made
forme and example off Christes flocke.[3] And least ye trowe thys be
not sayde of trothe take kepe what Christe saieth in the gospell.
The kinges of hethen haue lordshippe vpon theym / for sothe ye not
720 so. Se howe playnly lordshippe is forboden to all apostles / for yf
thou be a lorde howe darest thou take vpon the apostleshyp / or yf
thou be a bysshoppe / howe darest thou take vpon the lordship?
Pleynly thou [B5r] art forboden bothe. And yf thou wylt haue bothe
together thou shalt lese bothe / and be of the nomber / of whych
725 god pleineth by the prophete Osee sayenge. They reygnyd but not by
me sayeth god. And yf we holde that / that is forboden / here we
that is boden of Chryste. He that is greatest of you se that he be
made as younger in symplenes / and he that is a fore goere loke he
be as a seruaunt. Thys is the forme of apostles lyfe / lordshyppes
730 forboden and seruys is boden thys sayeth saynt Bernerde there. And
therfor no man may put a nother grounde besydes that that is put
whych is Christe Iesu.

But yet I wote well that clarkes and relygyous folcke that loue
vnkyndly these lordlynes wyll glose here and saye / that they
735 occupye not soche lordshyppes in proper as secular lordes doo / but
in comone / lyke as the apostles and perfyte people dyde in the
beginnynge of Christes chirche / as wryteth Saynct Luke in the
fourthe chaptre of the Actes of the apostles / the whyche had all
thynges in comone / lyke as soche clarkes and religyous saye they
740 haue nowe. In tokeninge wherof no man sayde of any thinge at that
tyme / thys is myne / so oure clarkes and namely relygyous people
whan they wyll speake in termes of their religyon. A pryuate person
wyll not saye this or thys is myne / but in parsone of all his

---

2 *side-note* Libro.ij
3 *side-note* i.Petri.

bretheren he wyll saye / this is oures. And ouer thys they saye
more suttelly that they occupye not this by tytle of secular lordshyppe / 745
but by tytle of perpetuall allmes. But what euer thys
[B5v] people saye here / we mote take hede to the rule of prefe
that fayleth not. The whiche rule Christe teacheth vs in the
gospell in dyuers places / where he sayeth / beleue ye the workes.
For why by their workes ye shall knowe theim. And thys rule is   750
wonder nedefull to a man that hath a do with any man of the
Pharyseys condycyones. For as Christe sayeth Math.xxiij. They saye
but they do not. And so as Christes workes bere witnesse of hym as
he hym selfe sayeth / and sheweth what he was and howe he lyued /
so the dedes and maner of lyuinge / or the thynge in it selfe   755
bearyth wytnesse wythout fayle howe it stondyth amonge theym in
thys poynte. And yf we take hede thus by thys rule we shall se at
oure eye howe the clargye sayeth other wyse than it is in dede.
For in some place in pryuate parsone / and in some place in comone
or parsone aggregate / whiche is all one as saynct Austyne sayeth   760
vppon the psalter / the clargy occupyeth the secular lordshyppe
secularly / and so in propere. For in the same maner wyse as the Barone
/ or the knyghte occupyeth and gouuernyth hys baronrye or
hys knyghtes fe / so after the amortesyenge occupyeth the clarcke
/ the Monke / or Chanon / the College or Conuente / the same   765
lordshippe and gouerneth it by the same lawes in iudgement and
punishinge as presonnynge and hangynge with soche other worldly
turmentyng the which some tyme belongyd to the secular arme of the
chirche. Ye oft tymes we may se howe they busye theym selfes to be
kinges in their [B6r] owne / and reioyce them full moche in that   770
ciuilyte or secularite yf they may get it. And this is an euidence
that they wold gladly be kynges of all the realme or the world. For
where their londes and secular mennes fraunchyse ar to gether they
striue who shall haue the galowes / or other maner tourmentes for
felaunes. They kepe also vnder bondage their tenauntes and their   775
yssue with their londes. And this is the moste ciuilite or secular
lordshyppinge that any kynge or lorde hath on his tenauntes. And
therfore we maye se howe they cleyme in their goodes a maner of
proper possessyon contrarye to the comonnynge of the comone goodes
in tyme of the perfyte men in the begynnynge of Christes chirche.   780
And so what so ever the clergy sayeth the dede sheweth well that

they haue not their goodes in comone lyke as Christe with his
apostles and perfyte men had in the begynnynge of christes chirche.
For in holdynge or hauynge of their goodes / is properte of
785 possessyon and secular lordshippinge. The which stondith not with
the plente of christes perfeccyon in prestes as it sueth of this
processe and of that / that is declared before. And as for that
other glose that clerkes haue here / where they saye that they
holde thes lordshyppes by tytle of perpetuall almes. But here ye
790 shall vnderstande that mercy or almes[4] is a will of releuinge of
some wretche oute of his mysese as Lyncolniensis sayeth in the
begynnynge of his dictis.[5] So that yf a man shuld effectually do
almesse he must loke to whom he shulde do [B6v] almesse to / were
in mysease and had nede to be releuyd. In tokeninge wherof / christ
795 onely assigneth almesse to thos / in whom he marketh mysease. And
so here of this it will sue / that yf a man will releue one wretche
and make a nother or mo / he dothe none almesse / but rather maketh
mysease. And moche more he dothe none almesse yf he make riche
thos persones that haue no nede. For as moche as they be sufficient to
800 theym selfes / this hath no coloure of almesse. For this may be
better called a woodnes or a wastynge of goddes goodes. And ouer
this yf a man take thos goodes / the which god in the best wyse
euen and with oute erroures hath assygned to the state of secular
lordes / and geue thos goodes to another people that hath no nede
805 of theym / ye to the which people soche goodes are forfendid. This
shuld be called no almesse / but peruertinge of goddes ordinaunce
/ and the destruction of the state of secular lordes the which god
hath approued in his chirche. For as saynt Paule sayeth. Almesse
dede shuld be ruled so that it were releuinge to thos that receiue
810 it. And moch rather it shuld not be vndoynge of thos that do it.[6]
And therfore Christ teachith in the gospell to do almes of tho
thinges that be nedeles or superfluite.[7] And in this dede a man
shuld haue regarde to the nede of him that he dothe almes to and to
the charge of his owne house. What allmes was it then I praye you

---

4 *side-note* Almes
5 *side-note* Dicto.ij.
6 *side-note* ij.Cori.viij.
7 *side-note* Quod superest date elemosinam. Luce.xiij.

/ to vndo the state of the Emperoure / and to make the clarkes   815
riche with his lordshippes / namely syth Christ con= [B7r] firmyd
to the Emperour his state / with tho thinges that longe therto /
notwithstonding at that tyme the emperoure was hethen. And he hath
forfendyd expresly hys clergy in worde and in example soche
lordshyppe. And as thys was no allmes / so we mote saye of other   820
kynges / dukes and erles / barones and knyghtes that are vndone
hereby / and the clerkes made ryche and worldly lordes with theyr
goodes. And though it had be so that the clergy myght haue occupyed
thus worldly lordshyppe / and also though it hadde be no
destruccion nor appeyrynge of any other state / yet it hadde be no   825
allmes for to geue to theym soche goodes / wherfor it may be
ryghtfully sayde. No man may put a nother grounde besydes that is
put / which is Christe Iesu.

Here we may se by the grounde of the gospel and by the
ordynaunce of christe / that the clergye was sufficiently purueyd   830
for lyuelood. For god is so perfyte in all hys werckynge / that he
may ordeyne no state in hys chirche but yf he ordeyne sufficient
lyuelood to the same state. And this is open in goddes lawe who so
takyth hede / and that vnder euery lawe of god / as vnder the lawe
of innocencye and of kynde / vnder the lawe geuen by Moyses and   835
also vnder the lawe geuen by christe. In the tyme of the state of
innocencye we knowe well by beleue that god hadde so ordeyned for
mankynde that it shuld haue hadde lyuelood ynough withoute any
tedious laboure. And of the lawe of kynde / christ speakyth in the
gospell sayenge thus All thynges that ye wyll that other men do   840
[B7v] to you / do ye to theym.[8] And yf thys lawe hadde be kepte
ther shuld no man haue bene myscheuously nedy. And in the tyme of
the lawe geuen by Moyses / god made a full and a sufficient
ordynaunce for all hys people howe and wher by they shuld lyue. For
he dealyd the londe amonge the laye people and he assygned the   845
fyrst frutes and tythes to the prestes and deakenes. And all though
that he wold that ther shuld be all waye poore men in the lande of
ysraell / yet he made an ordinaunce agaynst myscheuous nede.[9] And
comandyd all the people that ther shuld be in no wyse a nedye man

---

8 *side-note* Mat.vij
9 *side-note* Deute.xv.

850 and a begger amonge them as it is wrytten. And so in thys lawe he
ordeyned sufficiently ynough for hys people. And in the tyme of the
newe lawe christe assigned the seculer lordshyppes to temporall
lordes as it is taught before / and alowed the comonte her lyuelood
gotten by true marchaundyse and husboundrye and other craftys. And

855 in worde and ensaumple he taught hys prestes to be proctoures for
nedye people and poore at the ryche men / and specifyed thes poore
/ and taught howe they that were myghty / shuld make a purueaunce
for soche poore folke that they were not constrayned by nede for to
begge / as great clerkes marcke vpon thes wordes of the gospell

860 where chryste sayeth thus. Whan thou makest thy feast / that is of
allmes / call poore people / feble / lame and blynde.[10] He sayeth
not lett soche poore men call vpon thee / but call thou vpon theym
meanynge in that / that thou shuldest make a purueaunce for soche
people / that they be not myscheuously fau [B8r] tye. And for the

865 clergy he ordeined sufficiently / teching theym in worde and
ensample howe they shuld holde theym appayde with lyuelood and
hylynge mynistred to theym / for theyr true laboure in the gospell
as it is written before. Of thys than thou mayst se howe god in all
hys lawes hath sufficiently ordeyned for all the states that be

870 founded and approuyd. And howe it is agaynst the goodnes and wysdom
of god / to ordeyne any state / but yf he ordeyned sufficient
lyuelood therto. Syth than thys ordenaunce of god was sufficient as
well for the clergye as for other men it semeth a foule presumpcion
to brynge in a newe and a contrarye ordinaunce of lyuelood for

875 clerckes vpon the ordinaunce that Criste hath made for theym
before. Of the whiche ordynaunce / the clergye full many yeres
after the begynnynge of Chrystes chyrche / whan it was best
gouuernyd / held theym well a payde. For thys meaneth that Christes
ordynaunce was insufficient / and worthy to be vndone. And yf we

880 take good hede / they hadde no more nede to pleyne theym of thys
ordynaunce / than hadde the other two states of hys chyrche / which
vnto this daye holde theym a payde with thys ordynaunce of chryst
/ were it fully kepte. And more sekirnes and ensuraunce maye no man
make of any thinge than chryst hath of hys lyuelood to the clergye.

885 For chryst not onely affermyth to the people that he wyll not fayle

---

10 *side-note* Luce.xiiij.

theym in lyuelood and hylinge / but also prouyth thys by argumentes
that may not be assoyled. So that they be true seruauntes [B8v] to
him. For Chryste meanyth thus in his arguynge there. Syth god
fayleth not bryddes and lyles and grasse that groweth in the felde
/ nether hethen men. Howe moche rather shall he not fayle his true
seruauntes? And so this purueaunce of perpetuall almes that oure
clerkes speake of / meanyth faute of beleue and despeyre of the
gracious gouernaunce of god. Syth than as it is sayde before / it
is no allmes to releue one wretche and to make another or moo / and
to make theim ryche wyth temporall lordshippe / the whiche bene
forfendyd to soche people and namely yf soche almes geuynge be
destroyenge or appeyringe of any state approuyd by God in his
chirche / it will sue that the endowynge of the clargye with
worldly lordshippe / ought not to be called almesse / but rather
all a mysse / or wastynge of goddes goodes or destroyenge of his
ordinaunce / for as moche as the clergye was sufficiently ordeyned
by Christe. For why / this almes that clerckes speake of here /
made many wretches and it was geuen to theym that had no nede. And
thus it is empeyringe not only of one estate of the chyrche / but
of all thre of the which I spake in the begynnynge. And so this
almes geuynge hath made all oure realme nedy / ye and as I suppose
full nygh all christendom full poore and nedy and mischeuous ouer
that it shulde haue bene yf the clargye had held theym a payde with
christes ordinaunce. But nowe thourough this perpetuall all a mysse
/ that the clarkes call almes / christes ordinaunceys vndon in some
landes holly and [C1r] in Englonde for the more party and it is
lykely to be all vndone in processe of tyme. For by a mortesyenge
of lordshippes / the lordes be vndone in great party. And many
noble men because they lacke their owne parte through folishe gifte
of their aunceters be full nedy. Forthermore it may be vnderstonde
of this processe / that withdrawyng of this lordshippes from the
clergy and restoringe againe of them to the states that god hathe
assigned them to / shuld not be called robbery of holy chirche as
oure clerkes saye / but rather rightwise restitucion of good
wrongfully and theefly withold. And therfore ther may none othe or
vowe binde any man to maytayne this theft and destruccion of goddes
ordinaunce / and this great harmynge of Christes chirche. As the
vowe of Iepte shuld not haue bound him to kill and sacrifice his

890

895

900

905

910

915

920

owne doughter. Ne the othe of Herode shuld not haue bounde him to
925 kill innocent Ihon. But as Iepte shuld a broken his othe or vowe
and haue offered a nother thinge that had bene pleasynge to god and
accordinge with his lawe: As saynt Austyne sayeth vpon the same
storye. So Herode shuld haue broken his othe and a saued innocent
blood and sore a repented him for his vnavysed swerynge. And so
930 shuld lordes nowe a dayes breake theyr othes that they haue
vnavysely and without counseyle of holy scripture sworne to
maynteine this theefte / ye heresy and symony as it is proued
before / the which oure clerkes call perpetuall allmes. And not sue
theire folishe dedes and othes that they haue made to maynteyne
935 this mischeuous per= [C1v] uertynge of christes ordinaunce. For as
the state of the clergye hath no power or leaue / to make the
people or lordes to synne deadly or to destroye gods ordinaunce in
his chirche. So they haue no leaue or power of god to counceile or
to constrayne in any case the lordes or the people to swere for to
940 maynteyne this endowenge of the clerkes and religious folke /[11]
which is full great thefte heresy and symony / and wounder
harmefull to christes chirche as it is shewed in this processe and
in other writen before. But the lordes specially shuld se here /
what were pleasynge not to these clerkes / but to god / and that
945 shuld they do. For hereto they be bounde by vertue of their office
vpon peyne of dampnacion. And there may no man dispence with them
of that bound stondinge her state. For no man shuld put a nother
grounde besydes that / that is put which is christ Iesu.
   And therfore men deme it a great synne to geue londe entayled by
950 mennes lawe from the parsone or kynred that it is entayled to / ye
although it be so that the parsone or kynred that soche lande is
geuen to be nedye and haue leaue by goddes lawe to occupye soche
maner londe or lordshippe. And this is demyd full great synne among
the people not onely to the geuer but also to the taker. For both
955 they do dampnable wronge to him that it is entayled to / as the
people demyth ye although it be geuen for good and true seruyce
that the receyuer hath done to the geuer before / or elles by waye
of almes of releuynge of the persone or kinred that it is geuen to.
How [C2r] moche rather than I praye you with out comparison is it

---

11 *side-note* Loke well apon this reason

a greater synne / as well to the reaceyuers as to the geuers / to   960
take the lordeshippes / the whiche god that hath full lordshippe
vpon all the world hathe geuen by perpetuall lawe or right to the
state of secular lordes/ and geue this from the state to the whiche
god entayled this lordshippe to a nother straunge people off a
nother lyne / the which hadde neuer neade / ne leaue of god to   965
occupye it. And yf prestes cleyme tythes because god graunted them
to the kynred of leuy / yet ther argument is voide. For christe
came of the lynage of Iuda / to whiche lyne was no tythes graunted
and so as men suppose this entayle was not confermyd by christe and
his apostles to the priestes in the newe lawe.   970

For Gregory the tenthe ordeyned first tythes to be payed to
curates only.[12] And yet they cleyme so ferforthe tythes that no man
maye lawefully with holde theym or ministre them saue they. Ne they
maye be turned or geuen to any other state or kynred saue onely to
theym. Allthough men wolde do that vnder coloure or by tytle off   975
perpetuall allmes. For this shulde be demyd of the clergye a
dampnable synne and destroyenge of holy chirche and sacrilege. How
moche rather is it then an hydeous and dampnable synne / to geue or
to take a waye the seculer lordshippes from the state of secular
lordes / the whiche god had geuen and entayled to them by the same   980
lawe and right / by the whiche he hadde geuen the tithes to the
prestes in the olde lawe.

[C2v] And this entayle was neuer interrupt nor broken vnto christes
tyme and his holy apostles. And than they confermed this entayle by
lawe so stronge to the seculer parte that no man (saue Antichriste   985
and his disciples) may openly impungne this entayle as is shewed
before. And so as no man shulde presume to withdrawe with holde or
turne the tithes from the state of presthod / as they saye / so
moche rather should no man presume by geuynge or takinge to aliene
the temperall lordshippes from the state of seculer lordes. And   990
thus clerkes haue not so moche coloure to saye that the lordes and
the laye people robbe them for as moche as they take theyr
temperalteis fro theym. And thys takynge of ther temperalties in
to the handes of the clergye hath neuer the lesse malyce in hit
selfe. For as moche as it is done by simulacion of holynes / the   995

---

12 *side-note* Policro. Lib.vij.

whiche is double wickednes. For thus Lucifer robbed Adam both of
goodes of fortune / of kinde and of grace /[13] as the clergye hath
robbed and yet dothe the chirche of thes thre maner goodes. For
right as lucifer dyd this harme to Adam and Eue vnder coloure of
1000 loue and frendshippe and helpinge of them: so do nowe his angells
/ those ypocrites that tranfigure them selfes into angells of light
/ and deceyue the people by false beheste of heuenly helpe that
they will procure to theym for their goodes as they saye / and yf
a bishope and his college or an abbate and his conuent maye not
1005 aliene fro them any of the temporalties that they haue / nor geue
to their founder any of thos possessions that he hath geuen them /
what nede that euer he haue / bounde onely by a posityfe lawe or
a tradicion that they them selfe haue made. And yf any soche lord
[C3r] shippes be withdrawen aliened / or taken fro them by
1010 rechelesnes of their predecessoures / they ought on all wise / ye
to the deathe laboure to get the possessiones in to their hondes
agayne as they saye. Howe moche more than shuld not a secular lorde
or a laye aliene from him and his yssue or fro the state of secular
lordes / the secular lordshippes the whiche god hath lymyted to
1015 that state / syth he is bounde by the lawe of kynde to ordeyne for
his children. And ouer this he is bounde by godes lawe to susteyne
the state of secular lordes / the whiche is auctorysed in the
chirche by chryste and his apostles. Of this processe than yf a man
take hede he shall perceyue the falsenes of this glose / whan oure
1020 clerckes and religious folke saye that they hold these lordshippes
onely by title of perpetuall allmes. For certis syth these tythes
and offerynges the which as I suppose counteruayle the secular
lordes rentes of the realme or elles passe as it is full lykely
/ for though they be lesse in one chirche they passe in a nother and
1025 be sufficient for all the prestes in christendome yf they were euen
dealed. Than it were no nede to amorteyse secular lordshippes to
the state of the clergye. The which amortesyenge is vndoynge of
lordes / and apostasye of the clergye. And yf this amortesyenge
were not nedefull / then were it no allmes as it is declared. And
1030 ouer the tythes and offerynges that be nowe off certeynte / the
clerckes haue many great and small perquysytis / the whiche smacke

---

13 *side-note* Gene.iij

of symonye and extorcion. As the fyrst frutes of vacante bene=
[C3v] fyces / prouynge of testamentes and money for halowenge of
chapelles / chirches / chauncelles and other ornamentes of the
chirche / and for sacryng of ordres / and full many mo that for   1035
multitude may not well be numbred. For well nigh all theire
blessynges be set to sale and to priis / in to chrystenynge and
confirmacion. Wherfore I may nowe saye as I sayde at the
begynninge. No man may put a nother grounde besydes that / that is
put / the whiche is Christe Iesu. The which grounde of lyuynge   1040
christe graunte vs to kepe that we maye escape the euerlastinge
peynes of hell. AMEN

     The husbandman.
Loo / nowe by this treatyse may ye well se
That aforetymes against the spiritualte   1045
    Men dyd invey / shewinge their vyces.
Also here after this auctour dothe tell
What great Ieoparde it is and perell
    For prestes to be in secular offices.
Ye / and to lordes / which against right   1050
Suffre theym therein or therto excyte
    Prouynge it by their oune doctours and lawes.

     Gentillman.
I beseche the rede forthe the processe
That the people may se their vnhappynesse   1055
    Which make all the worlde foles and dawes.

Saynt Cipriane sayeth that by the counceile of bisshops ther is
made a statute /[14] that all that bene charged with priesthode and
ordeyned in the seruys of clerkes / shuld not serue but to the
aulter and to ministre the sacramentes / to preache gods   1060
wor [C4r] de / and to take hede to prayers and orysones. It is for
sothe writen. No man bering his knighthod to god: entryketh him

---

14 *side-note* hist.xxi. .iij. ca.Cipriane

with secular nedes. The which oure bisshops and oure predecessours
beholdinge religiously and purueynge holsomly / deme that whosoeuer
1065 taketh ministres of the chirche / from spirituall office to secular
/ that ther be none offrynge done for him / ne any sacrifice
holowed for his sepulture. For they deserue not to be
named before the aulter of god in the prayer off priestes / the
which will clepe awaye priestes and ministres of the chirche from
1070 the aulter. Thus sayeth seynt Cipriane. Here men maye se how
perelous it is to the kyng and secular lordes to withholde any
prieste of christ in secular busynes. This is proued thus. For
euery secular lorde by the lawe of the gospell is gods bayly. But
yf any bayly hyred a worckman with his lordes good and put him to
1075 his owne seruys / he must be vntrewe to his owne lorde. Right so is
any secular lorde to oure lorde Christ Iesu / but yf he amende hym
/ that taketh a prieste and putteth him in his secular office
breakinge the heest of his lorde god that commaundeth / thou shalt
coueyet none other mannes servaunte. And he withdraweth hym fro the
1080 seruys of god and fro the kepinge of christen mennes soules / the
which he hath taken charge of / for which soules oure lorde Iesu
Christe toke flesche and bloude and suffered hard dethe / and
shedde his owne harte bloode. This parelous doynge of secular
lordes is bothe against goddes lawe and mannes. It is ageinst gods
1085 lawe [C4v] for as seynt Paule saieth. No man that is a perfyte
knight of god / as euery priest shuld be by his ordre /
entremedleth him with worldly deades and busynes.[15] And for this
ende that he may so please that lorde to whose seruyce he hathe put
him selfe / and that is good. For soche worldly busynes in clerkes
1090 is against their ordre. And therfore the apostles said as it is
writen in the dedes of the apostles /[16] it is not euen / vs to leue
the worde of god and ministre to boordes of poore folke. And yf it
was vnequite as the apostles saide in their comone decree / them
for to leaue the preachinge of goddes worde / and ministre to the
1095 boordes of poore folke: Howe moche more vnequite and wronge to god
and man is it / preastes to leaue contemplacion / studye / prayer
and preachinge of goddes worde and ministrynge to poore folke for

---

15 *side-note* ij.Thi.ij
16 *side-note* Acto.vi

the servyce of a secular lorde? It is also agaynst the Popes lawe
/ for he speaketh to a bisshoppe[17] and byddeth hym that he warne
preastes and clerckes / that they be not occupyed in secular   1100
offices ne procurators of secular lordes deades and her goodes. And
yf prestes and clerckes be so bolde to occupye theym in soche
busynes and if they fall after by losse of lordes goodes / then
sayeth the lawe it is not worthy that they be holpen and socoured
of holy chirche / sythe through theim holy chirche is sclaundred.   1105
And saynct Gregorye wrote to the defensoure of Rome in this maner.
It is tolde to vs that oure moste reuerente brother Basyle the
bysshoppe is occupyed in secular causes and kepith vnproffitable
moote halles. Which [C5r] thinge makyth him foule and destroyeth
the reuerence of presthood / therfore anone as thou hast reaceiued   1110
this mandement / compell him with sharppe execucion to turne
agayne. So that it be not lefull to the by no excusacion to tarye
fyue dayes / lest in any maner thou suffre hym any longer to tarye
there in / thou be culpable with hym agaynst vs. And so bysshoppes
and other prestes be bounde to teache and enforme lordes / to   1115
withdrawe theym fro this synne and sharpely to reproue prestes and
curates vnder them that they occupye no secular office. This is
proued thus by the holy prophet Ezechiell sayenge.[18] Yf the wayte
or the watcheman se enemies come / and yf the people be not warned
and kepe not them selues but enemies come and sle the people / then   1120
sayeth god that the people is taken in their wickednes. And of the
wayte that shulde haue blowen his horne god will axe acountes and
rekeninge of the bloode and of the deathe of the people. But nowe
to gostely vnderstandinge / euery bisshoppe shuld be a wayte or a
watch man / to tell and warne before to all the people by his good   1125
lyuinge and teachinge the perell of synne / and this is the reason
why bisshopes and other prelates and prestes shuld not be occupyed
with worldly deades and causes. For soche occupacions and charges
make prestes slepinge and slombringe in synne. And therfore it is
great perell to make ouer them gostly waytes and watchemen / as   1130
bisshopes / parsones / vicaries / that be slepers in lustes of the
flesshe and in slomebernes / and blinded with pouder of couetyse of

---

17 *side-note* Linn.iij. decre.in fine
18 *side-note* Ezechie.xxxiij.

worldly deades that they nether can ne maye kepe them selfes [C5v]
ne no nother man. For of this perell and soche other / a prelate
1135 that hath witte and cunninge shuld sharpely reproue and warne all
maner men to the shedinge of his oune bloode as christ did. And yf
he so leaue and blame not then he assentyth to their trespases and
synneth deadly. For as sayeth Malach.[19] Prestes lippes kepe
cunninge and the people shall aske the lawe of god of his mouth /
1140 for he is the Angell of god / yf he kepe well the ordre and degre
of presthood. And therfor it is not lefull to any man to drawe to
seculer offices and busynes the messangeres of christe / that hath
so vtterly forfendyd theym bothe in worde and deade secular offices
in presthood. etc.

> Husbandman. 1145
> Syr howe lyke ye nowe this olde treatyse
> Yf so be noble men wold it aduertyse
>   Puttynge a parte pryuate affeccion.
> Shuld they not perceyue here euydently
> That the clergye dothe theym great iniury 1150
>   Retaynynge thus temporall possessyon?
>
> Gentyllman.
> Nowe I promyse the after my iudgement
> I haue not hard of soche an olde fragment
>   Better groundyd on reason with scripture. 1155
> Yf soche auncyent thynges myght come to lyght
> That noble men hadde ones of theym a syght
>   The world yet wolde chaunge perauenture.
> For here agaynst the clergye can not bercke
> Sayenge as they do / thys is a newe wercke 1160
>   Of heretykes contryued lately.
> And by thys treatyse it apperyth playne
> That before oure dayes men dyd compleyne [C6r]
>   Agaynst clerkes ambycyon so stately.

---

19 *side-note* Mala.ij

Husbandman. 1165
Concernynge thys treatyse and lyke matters
I haue hard saye of my forefathers
 Howe in kynge henry the .v. raygne.
What tyme as ye dyd specyfye
The clergye persecutyd the gospell fercely 1170
 Causynge moche chrysten people to be slayne.
The kynge at the last hauynge informacyon
Thourough seryous consyderacyon
 Of soche proper matters as thys is.
Beganne to note the clergyes tyranny 1175
And what temporaltees / they dyd occupye
 Their spirituall state ferre a mysse.
Wherfore he determyned certeynly
To depryue theym temporally
 Of all theyr worldly gouuernaunce. 1180
Whos pretence / as sone as they perceyued
Amonge theym selfes they Imagyned
 To get the kynge ouer in to fraunce.
That whyles he conqueryd ther his ryght
In england do what they lyst they myght 1185
 Theyr froward tyranny to fulfyll.
Which counseil / thus brought to passe
The kynge euer after so busyed wasse
 That he could not performe hys sayde wyll.

Gentyllman. 1190
So moote I the / it was happye for the kynge
That by soche a colour they could hym brynge
 From medlynge with that case any more.
For hadde he it ones ernestly begonne
They had put hym to a confusyon [c6v] 1195
 Euene as they dyd other kynges before.

Husbandman.
What suppose ye they wold haue done?

Gentyllman.

Mary / fyrst with a fayre interdyccion   1200
   To coursse the lande as blacke as pytche.
Than to inhybyt sayenge and syngynge
Of mattyns / masse / and belles ryngynge
   With christen buryall of poore and ryche.
Besyde that precheres euery where   1205
Shuld haue brought men in soche fere
   By theyr threatnynge exclamacyon.
That their malycyous partye to take
Subgettes shuld theyr prynce forsake
   Contrary to goddes ordynacyon.   1210
Euene as they dyd in hygh Germany
To the Emperour lewes of Bauerye
   Whom Pope Ihone sought to confounde.
And so dyd the clergy as I vnderstande
Vnto kynge Ihon here in Englande   1215
   To kynge Steuen / and henry the secounde.

Husbandman.

They saye kynge Ihone was poysoned
Because an halfe peny lofe of breed
   He sayde / he wold make worthe .xij. pence.   1220

Gentillman.

Tushe that is a cast of theyr comon gyse
Soche infamy of prynces to deuyse
   To cloke theyr oune tyrannous vyolence.
For hadde not kynge Ihone gone aboute   1225
From their temporaltees to put theym owt
   He hadde ben longe after a lyues man.   [c7r]
But murder they neuer so shamefully
They can geue it a cloke full craftely
   Sayenge / nobis non licet occidere quenquam.   1230
Whan they brennyd the newe testament
They pretendyd a zele very feruent
   To maynteyne onely goddes honour.
Which they sayde with protestacyon

Was obscured by translacyon   1235
   In englysshe / causynge moche errour.
But the trueth playnly to be sayde
Thys was the cause why they were a frayde
   Least laye men shuld knowe theyr iniquite.
Which through goddes worde is so vttred   1240
That it were not possyble to be suffred
   Yf to rede scripture men had lyberte.
Also after the same maner a fasshyon
Subtelly to colour theyr abhomynacyon
   They destroyed cronicles not longe a gone.   1245
Which for certeyne poyntes vnreuerently
Soundynge agaynst the kynges auncetrye
   As they saye / were brent euerychone.
But for all that / they shulde haue been spared
From burnynge: had they not so declared   1250
   The clergyes abhomynable excesse.

   Husbandman.
I suppose then / that they vse the same wayes
In burnynge of heretykes nowe a dayes
   Whom they pursue with great furyousnes.   1255

   Gentillman.
No fayle / they perswade temporall menne
Thes heretykes (as they saye) to brenne
   Least other good christians they shuld infecte.   [c7v]
But the cause why they wolde haue theim rydde   1260
Is onely that theyr vnhappynes nowe hydde
   They dreede least they shuld openly detecte.

   Husbandman.
By my trouth it is nothinge vnlickly
For let one lyue neuer so wyckedly   1265
   In abhominable scandalisacion.
As longe as he will their church obaye
Not refusynge his tithes duely to paye
   They shall make of him no accusacion.

Howbeyt let him ones begynne to pynche 1270
Or withdrawe their tithinge an ynche
   For an heretike they will him ascite.
Wherfore I wonder moche of the temporalte
That in performynge the clargyes cruelte
   To burne soche parsones they haue delyte. 1275

   Gentillman.
It is no merueil yf thou marcke well
The clargye sayenge that it is goddes quarrell
   Their mischeuous murdre to execute.

   Husbandman. 1280
So they are not a knowen by their wyll
That it is their cause christen men to kyll
   But the faute vnto other they impute.

   Gentyllman.
Touchinge that / another tyme at leyser 1285
I shall shewe the more of their maner
   But nowe I can not tary verely.

   Husbandman.
Well syr / yf ye may no longer abyde
Oure lorde be your continuall gyde 1290
   Grauntinge the trouth to be knowen openly.

A compendious [c8r]
olde treatyse / shewynge / howe that we
ought to haue the scripture in
Englysshe. 1295

   Thexcusacyon of the treatyse

Though I am olde / clothed in barbarous wede
Nothynge garnysshed with gaye eloquency
Yet I tell the trouth / yf ye lyst to take hede

Agaynst theyr frowarde / furious frenesy   1300
Which recken it for a great heresy
And vnto laye people greuous outrage
To haue goddes worde in their natyfe langage.

Enemyes I shall haue / many a shoren crowne
With forked cappes and gaye croosys of golde   1305
Which to maynteyne ther ambicious renowne
Are glad laye people in ignorance to holde
Yet to shewe the verite / one maye be bolde
All though it be a prouerbe daylye spoken
Who that tellyth trouth / his head shalbe broken.   1310

Vnto the Reader

Grace and peace: not that the worlde geuyth / but from god the
father and oure sauioure Iesu Christ with increace of the holy
spryt be with the and all that thurste the truthe. Amen.
Consyderynge the malyciousnes [C8v] of our prelatz and theyr   1315
adherentes whiche so furiously barke ageynst the worde of God / and
specially the new testament translatyd and set forthe by Master
William Tyndale / which they falsely pretende to be sore corrupte.
That ye may knowe that yt is only the inwarde malyce whiche they
haue euer had ageynst the worde of God. I haue here put in prynte   1320
a tretyse wrytten aboute the yere of oure lorde a thousande foure
hundryd. By which thou shalte playnly perceyue / that they wolde
yet neuer from the begynnynge admytte any translacion to the laye
people / so that it is not the corrupte translacion that they
withstonde. For yf that were true the ydle bellyes wolde haue had   1325
leyser Inough to put forth a nother well translated. But yt is
theyr owne myscheuous lyuynge that mouith them accordyng as Christe
sayd Ihonn.iij. Euery man that workyth euyll hatyth the lyght / ner
comyth to the lyght lest hys workes shulde be reproued. etc. Thus
mayst thou se that bycause their workes are nought and not bycause   1330
yt is euill translatyd / they so furiously resyste the worde of god
whiche is the trew lyght. For yet was ther neuer none translatyd
but other with falshed or tyranny they put yt downe. Wherfore I
exhorte the reder not to consydre and note the wordes but the
matter. And praye to god to sende the rulers hartes to vnderstonde   1335

the trewth and further the same and the god of all comforte be with
the AMEN

Thys treatyse more than an .C. yere olde
Declareth howe owre prelatis do ferre a mysse
1340 Which of frowarde presumpcion are so bolde   [D1r]
To forbede the worde of god in englishe
For as the prophete saieth blessed he is
That exercyseth him selfe diligently[20]
In scripture night and daye continually.

1345 For to make vpon antichrist I take figure of king Antioche of
whome gods lawe speaketh in the boke of Machabeijs / for right as
kinge Antioche came in the ende well nygh of the olde lawe / and
brent the bokes of gods lawe / and compelled the people to do
maumentry. So now Antichrist the kinge off clergy that lyuen worse
1350 then hethen prestes / brenneth nowe nygh thende of the new lawe
theuangely of Christe that is nyghe the ende of the world / to
deceyue wellnygh all the worlde / and to proue the seruauntes of
god. For nowe god shall knowe who will stande by his lawe / for
Sathanas as prophetes saye is nowe vnbounde and hathe ben .CCCC.
1355 yeres and more for to inhabit oure clergye / as he did the clergye
of the olde lawe / but now with moche more malyce. For as they
dampned Christ so now oure bisshopes dampne and bren goddes lawe /
for bycause it is drawen into our mother tounge.[21] But it ought to
be (and we saued shuld be) as we shall proue by open evidence
1360 thorowe goddes helpe. First we take witnesse of Boetius de
disciplia scolarium / that saythe that childerne shulde be taught
in the bokes off Seneke. And Bede expoundeth this sayenge / [D1v]
and saythe that childerne in vertues shulde be taught. For the
bokes of Seneke ben moralles and for they be not taught thus in
1365 there youthe they contynue still euyll maneryd and be vnable to
conceyue the subtyle science of trouthe sayng / the wise man is as
a cleane myrror new pullisshed. Wisdome shall not enter into a
wicked soule. And moche is herof the sentence of Bede. And Algasell

---

20 *side-note* Psal.i

21 *side-note* Ye may se it is no nouelteis that the bishoppes burne the gospell.

in his logyke saieth / the soule of man is a cleane myrror newe
pulished in which is seyn lightly the ymage of vertue.[22] And for   1370
the people haue not cunnynge in youthe they haue darke soules and
blinde with ignorance / so that they profyt not in vertue but in
falsnes and malice and other vices / and moche is therof the
matter. Sythen hethen philosophers wolden the people to profyt in
naturall science / howe moche more shuld christen clerckes will the   1375
people to profyt in science of vertues / for so wold god. For when
the lawe was geuen to Moses in the mount of Sinai / god gaue it to
his people in ther mother tonge of Ebrue / that all the people
shuld vnderstande it / and commaunded Moses to reade it to them
vntyll they vnderstode it / and so he did / as it is playne Deute.   1380
xxxi. And Esdras also redde it in theire mother tonge / fro morowe
vntyll none as it is playne in the first boke of Esdras Ca.viij.
And he redde it apertly in the streate and the eares of the people
were intently geuen therto / in so moche that the people fell into
greate weping for the miskeping of the lawe. Also gods lawe saith   1385
Deutero.xxxij. that fathers shuld make the lawe knowen to [D2r]
their sonnes / and the sonnes that shulde be borne of them shuld
ryse and teache these thinges to ther sonnes. And the holy apostle
seynt Peter in the fourth chapter of his first boke speaketh after
this manner / sayenge. Whosoeuer speake / speake he as the worde of   1390
god: and euery man as he hath taken grace of knowinge / so ministre
he forth to other men. It is wrytten playnly in the boke of
noumbres Chapter.xi. When the prophet Moses hadde chosen seuenty
eldermen / and the sprite of god rested on them and they
prophesyed. Two men besydes them / Eldad and Medad / prophesyed in 1395
the tentes / and Iosue the ministre of Moses said to Moses / forbyd
thou them. And Moses sayde / what enviest thou for me? Who shall
let that all the people prophesye / yf god gyue them his spirite?[23]
Also it is redde in the gospell[24] that saynct Ihon euangelist said
vnto Christ / lorde we shall forbid one that casteth out spirites   1400
in thy name / which foloweth not vs. And Christ said do not forbid
for who so is not against vs is with vs. And vnto the same agreyth

---

22 *side-note* Reade robyn hode / saye oure masters.
23 *side-note* moses letted no man to prophesye.
24 *side-note* Luce.ix.

well the prophesy of Iohell whiche seynct Petre preachinge to the
Iewes strongly alleged as Luke recyteth in the seconde chapter of
1405 the actes of the apostles sayenge after this maner. That god nowe
in the laste dayes shall shede out his spirite vpon euery flesch.
For god sayeth your sonnes and doughters shuld prophesy / and your
yong men shall se visyons.[25] And vpon whit sonday god gaue knowlege
of his lawe to diuerse nacions without any excepcions in ther
1410 mother tonge / by the vnderstanding [D2v] of one tounge. And of
this it is notabyll sithen the laye people in the olde lawe had
their lawe in ther mother tounge / that the lay englishe people in
the newe lawe haue it as all other nacions haue / syns Christ
bought vs as he did other and hath geuen to vs the same grace as to
1415 other.
     For saynt Peter .Actu.xi. was reproued for he had baptysed
Cornelij and his felows that were hethen men. And Peter answered
and sayde Yf god haue gevyn the same grace to them that he hath to
vs / who am I that may forbyd god? As who saythe it lyeth not in
1420 the power of men. Than who art thou that forbiddest the people to
haue gods lawe in ther mother tounge? we saye that thou art
Antichrist himself. For Paule saieth .i.Corin.x. I will euery man
to speake with tounges / more forsothe to prophesy / also he saith
howe shall he saye Amen vpon thy blessynge that woteth not what
1425 thou sayst. Vpon this saith doctor Lyre. Yf the people vnderstonde
the prayer of the priest it shall the better be ledde vnto god /
and the more deuoutly answere Amen.[26] Also Paule saith in the same
chapter. I will rather fyue wordes to be spoken to the
vnderstanding of men / then ten thousand that they vnderstand not.
1430 And .lxx. doctours with other mo before the incarnacion of christe
translated the bible out of Ebrue into Greke. And after the
ascension many translated all the bible in diuerse langages / as
into spanysh tonge / frenshe tunge / almanye / and italy / and by
many yeres haue had it. It was hard of a worthy man of Almaynye
1435 that the same tyme was a flemmyng [D3r] whose name was Iames
Merland which translated all the bible into flemysh. For whiche
dede he was somonned before the Pope of great malyce. And the boke
was taken to examinacion. And truely he approued it. And then it

---

25 *side-note* But they saye only master doctor can vnderstande the scripture.
26 *side-note* Here youre owne master Lire yf ye wil not here Paul.

was delyuered to him agayn vnto confusion of all his enemyes.
Worshupfull Bede in his first booke called de gestis Anglorum   1440
.chapter. iij. telleth that saynt Oswolde the Kyng of
Northumberlande asked of the skottes an holy bisshoppe Aidan to
preache to his people / and the kyng him selfe interpreted it in
englishe to the people. Sythen this blessed deade of this Kynge is
alowed of all holy churche / whye not nowe ought it as well to be   1445
alowed / a man to reade the gospell in Englishe to the people /
sythen that seynt Paule saith yf oure gospell be hidde / it is
hidde in them that shall be dampned.[27] And he saith also he that
knoweth not shall not be knowen of gode. And therfore venerabilis
Bede ledde by the spirite of god translated a greate parte of the   1450
bible into Englishe / whose originalles ben in many Abbeyes in
England. And Cisterciensis .libro v. chaptre .xxiiij. saythe that
the Euangely off Ihon was drawen into Englishe by the forsayde Bede
whiche Euangelye off Ihon and other Gospels ben yet in many places
of so olde englishe that skant can anye englishe man reade them.   1455
For this Bede reygned in the yere off oure lorde god .vij. hundred
and .xxxij. Also Cistercien .libro. vi. chaptre .i. saythe that
kyng Alfred ordyned open scoles of diuerse artes in Ox= [D3v] forde
and he turned the best lawes in to his mother tounge and the
Psalter also / he reygned in the yere of oure lorde god .viij.   1460
hundred .lxxiij. And saynt thomas sayth super librum politicorum
expounding this worde / barbarus / that barbarus is he that
vnderstondyth not that he readeth in his mother tonge. Wherfore the
apostle saith If I knowe not the vertue of the voice to whome I
speake I shalbe to him barbarus / that is to saye / he   1465
vnderstandeth not what I saye / nor I what he saith. And so all the
prestes that vnderstonde not what they readyn by ther mother tonge
be called barbarus / and therfore Bede did drawe into englishe
liberall artes leste englishemen shuld be come barbarus / hec
Thomas. Also Lincoln sayeth in a sermon that begynnith / Scriptum   1470
est de leuitis. Yf any prieste saye he can not preache / one
remedye is / resigne he vppe his benefyce.[28] Another remedy yf he
will not thus / recorde he in the weke the naked texte of the

---

27 *side-note* A fearefull sayenge.
28 *side-note* Resygne in no wise but apon a good pensyon.

sondaye gospell that he haue the grosse storye and tell it to the
1475 people / that is yf he vnderstonde latyn / and do he this euery
weke in the yere he shall profyt moch. For thus preched oure lorde
sayenge Ihon .vi. The wordes that I speake to you be spirit and
lyfe. Yf he do not vnderstonde latyn go he to one of his
neighboures that vnderstondeth / which will charitably expoune it
1480 to him / and thus edifye he his flocke. Vpon this argueth a great
clerke and saithe /yf it be laufull to preache the naked texte to
the people / it is also lefull to write and read it to them. Also
sir Wil= [D4r] liam Thorisby archebishop of Yorke did do draw a
treatyse in englishe by a worshipfull clercke / whose name was
1485 Gatryke / in the whiche were conteyned the articles of beleue / the
seuen dedly synnes / the seuen workes of mercy / the .x.
commaundmentes.[29] And sent them in small pagines to the commyn
people to learne it and to knowe it / of which yet many a copye be
in england. Also Richard the heremyte of Hampole drewe into
1490 englishe the Psalter with a glose and the lessons of dirige and
many other treatices / by the whiche many engleshe men haue ben
greatly edifyed. And they ben cursed of god that wolden let the
people to be lewder then they ben. But many men nowe be lyke vnto
the frendes of Hiob / that whiles they enforced to defende god
1495 they offended in him greuously. And though suche as be slayne do
myracles / neuertheles they ben stynkynge marters. This saieth
Richerd the heremyt expouning this verse / Ne auferas de ore meo
verbum veritatis vsquequaque. And Christ saieth that men shulde
deame them self to do great plesaunt seruice to god in killing of
1500 his people.[30] Arbitretur se obsequium prestare deo. etc. Also a man
of london whose name was Wyrynge had a bible in english of northen
speache whiche was seyne of many men and it semyd to be .CC. yeres
old. Also it is knowen to many men in the tyme of king Richerd the
.ii. that into a parlement was put a bible by thassent of .ii.
1505 archbisshops and of the clergy to adnulle the bible that tyme
translated into Englishe with other Englishe bookes of thexposicion
off the gospells whiche [D4v] when it was harde and seyn of lordes

---

29 *side-note* The same treatise is in the chirch over againste London stone at this
hourE.
30 *side-note* This prophesye of christ must be fulfilled take hede

and of the comones. The duke of Lancaster Ihon answered thereto
ryght sharpely sayenge this sentence / we will not be refuse of all
other nacions.　　　　　　　　　　　　　　　　　　　　　　1510
　For sythen they haue goddes lawe whiche is the lawe of oure
belefe in there owne langage / we will haue oures in Englishe
whosoeuer say naye. And this he affermyd with a greate othe. Also
Thomas Arundell Archebisshoppe off Canterbury[31] sayde in a sermon
at westmester / at the buryenge of Quiene Anne / that it was more　　1515
ioye of here than of any woman that euer he knewe. For she an alien
borne hadde in englishe all the .iiij. gospels with the doctours
vpon them. And he said that she had sent them to him to examen /
and he saide that they were good and trewe. And he blamyd in that
sermon sharpely the negligence of the prelates and other men.　　1520
　In so moche that he saide that he wold leaue vp the office of
Chaunceler and forsake worldly busynes / and gyue him to fulfyll
his pastorall offyce / for that he had seyn / and redde in tho
bokes. And after this promyse he became the moste cruell enemye
that mighte be againste englishe bokes.[32] And therfore as many men　　1525
sayne God smote him with a cruell dethe as he didde also Richard
flemyng bisshoppe of Lincolne. And yet oure bisshops ben so
indurate and so ferre strayed from god that they haue no grace one
to beware of a nother / but proudely against all reasons and
euidence of gods lawes / and doctours sentences / they brenne gods　　1530
worde the whiche ha= [D5r] the brought thys realme to vndoynge for
euer but if godes grace be the more / for thys cruell deade is
cause of pestilence / hungers / warres / and that also this realme
shalbe conqueryd in short tyme /[33] as saynct Edward the kyng and
confessor prophesyethe in his booke that beginnith thus / Sanctus　　1535
Edwardus rex vidit spiritualibus oculis. And therfore it were good
to the Kyng and to other lordes to make some remedy agaynst this
constitucion of Antechrist that saythe it is vnlawfull to vs
englyshe men to haue in englyshe goddes lawe / and therfore he
brennythe and sleythe them that maynteyne this goode deade / and　　1540
that is for default that the kyng and lordes knowen not ne wyll not

---

31 *side-note* Ypocrisy is the nature of all bishoppes.

32 *side-note* Neuer trust bishop as longe as he kepeth hys possessions.

33 *side-note* Wher is the auncient blode that was in england in these dayes.

knowe ther owne office in maintenance of god and his lawe.[34] For as
sainct Austen saithe the Kyng with his knyghtes representyn the
godhede of Christe / and prestes the manhode of Christe / Rex est
1545   vicarius diuinitatis / et sacerdos est vicarius Christi
humanitatis / hec Augustinus in de questionibus veteris et noue
legis .ca.xci. And if the kyng desyer to knowe perfytly his offyce
/ he maye fynde men to shewe to hym bookes that truely and perfytly
shall enforme hym to doo his office to the plesaunce of god. But
1550   this can not be lerne of Byshoppys for they enforme hym after
Antichristes lawe and ordenaunce for his lawes nowe reignen. Yet
agaynst them that sayn the gospell in englyshe wold make men to
erre / wote they well that we fynde in latyn langage more heretykes
then of all other langages[35] for the decre. saythe.xxiiij.xciij.
1555   Quidam autem [D5v] heretici / that there be founden syxty laten
heretykes. And yf men shuld hate any langage for heresy then must
they hate laten. But god forbede that any langage shuld be hated
for heresy sythen manye heretykes wer of the disciples of the
apostles. For sainct Ihonn saithe they haue gonn owt of vs but they
1560   were not of vs. And Paule saithe it behouyth heresys to be / and
antichrist makythe many mo heretykes then there shuld be for he
stoppythe so the knowyng of gods lawe /[36] and punysheth so them
that he knowyth that haue it / that they dare not comen therof
openly to haue trewe informacion / and thys makyth layemen that
1565   desyren and louen to knowe gods law to goo to gyther in pryuyte and
conceyuen by theyr owne wyttes many tymes heresys the whiche
heresies in short tyme shuld be destroyed / yf men myght haue free
comenyng openly / and but if this maye be had moche of the people
shall dye in heresy / for it lyethe neuer in Antichristes power to
1570   destroye all englyshe bookes for as fast as he brennethe / other
men shale drawe / and thus the cause of heresy and of the people
that dyeth in heresy is the frowardnes of byshoppes that wyll not
suffer men to haue opyn comoning and fre in the lawe of god and
therfore they be cowntable of as many sowlys as dyen in thys
1575   default / and are traytors to god in stoppynge of his lawe the

---

34 *side-note* Et nunc reges intelligite erudimini qui iudicatis terram.
35 *side-note* Bisshops will not teache against their god their bely.
36 *side-note* How Antichrist is cause of al heresyes.

whiche was made in saluacion of the people. And nowe they turne his
lawe by ther cruell constitucyons into dampnacion[37] of the people
as it shalbe prouyd apon them at the dayte of dome for gods lawe
saithe / <u>Stabunt iusti in magna constan</u> [D6r] <u>tia aduersus eos qui
se angustiauerunt, & qui abstulerunt labores eorum. etc.</u>[38] For
that the other men laboren they brennen / and yf owre clergy wold
study well this lessen of sapience to the ende / they shuld mowe
rede therin theyr oune dampnacion / but yf they amend this defaulte
with other defaultes. Saithe not the holy man Ardemakan in the
booke of questions that the wurshupfull sacrament of the alter maye
be made in eche comen langage. For he saithe so diden the apostles.
But we couet not thys / but that Antechrist geue vs leaue to haue
the lawe of ower beleue in englishe. Also they that haue comonyd
moche with the Iewes / saye that they haue in euery lande that they
be borne in / the byble in ther mother tounge / that is Ebrewe. And
they be more practyse therin than annye men / ye as well the lewde
men as the prestes. But it is redde in her synagoges amongest the
people of ther prestes to fulfyll ther prestes office and to the
edificacion of the poraile / that for worldly busynes and slewthe
maye not studye it. Also the .iiij. euangelistes wrote the gospell
in diuerse langages / as Mathewe in Iurye / Marke in Italy / Luke
in Achaie / and Ihon in Asie. And all these wrotte in the langages
of the same contreys / also Tobye saithe Chap.xiij. that god
disperged / sprede / or scaterid the Iewes abrode among the hethen
people that they tellynge vnto theym the merueylles of godde: they
shuld knowe that there were none other god / but god of Israell.
And god ordyned his people to beleue his lawe wrytten among them in
ther mother tounge / vt patet [D6v] Ge.xvij. and Exo.xiij. In so
moche the boke of Iudithe is wrytten in Calde speche / vt patet per
Hieronimum in prologo eiusdem. Also the bookes of Daniel / and of
Esdre ben written in Calde / vt patet per Hieroni. in prologis
eorundem / also the booke of Iohel is in Arabyke and Syre speche /
vt patet per Hieroni. in prologo eiusdem. Also Ezechiell the
prophet prophesyed in Babylon / and lefte his prophesye vnder the
mother tounge of Babylon / vt patet per Hieronimum in prologo
eiusdem. Also the prophesye of Isaie is translated in to the tounge

1580
1585
1590
1595
1600
1605
1610

---

37 *side-note* Is not this turninge the rotys of the tres vpward
38 *side-note* Reade Sapien vi.&.vij

of Ethiope / as Hie. concludyth in primo prologo Gene. Then sythen
the darke prophesyes were translated amonges the hethen people that
they myght haue knowlege of god and of the incarnacion of Christ /
1615 moche more it ought to be translatyd to englyshe people that haue
receiuyd the faythe and bounden them selfe to kepe it vpon payne of
dampnacion / sythen Christ commaunded his apostles to preache his
gospell vnto all the worlde and exceptyd no people nor langage.[39]
Also Origen translated the bybble owt of Ebrewe into Greke with
1620 helpe of other in the yere of owre lorde god CC.xxxiiij. Also
Aquila translated it in the tyme of Adrian the emperoure in the
yere of oure lorde. C.xxiiij. Also Theodosion translated it in the
tyme of themperowre Comede.liiij. yere after Aquila / also Simacus
translated it in the tyme of themperowre Serene.xxx. yere after
1625 Theodosion.viij. yere after Simacus it was translated the auctor
vnknowen yn the tyme of Alexander the em= [D7r] perowre. And Ierome
translated it into latyn / vt in cronicis Cistercien.li.ij.
ca.xxxij. And after that Ierom had translated it into laten / he
translated to women moche of the bible. And to the maydens
1630 Eustochia and Paula / he translated the bookes of Iosue of Iudicum
and Ruth and Hester / and Ecclesiastes / Jeremy / Isaie and Daniell
/ and the .xij. prophetes / and the .vij. canonyke epystylles / vt
patet in prologo eorundem. And so all men maye se here by Ierom /
that it was neuer his entent to bynde the lawe of god vnder his
1635 translacion of laten but by his owne dede geuythe leaue to
translate it into euery speche / for Ierom wrytythe in his
.lxxviij. epystle to this man Atleta / that he shuld enforme his
daughter in the bookes of the olde lawe and the newe. Also in his
.lxxv. epistle he wrytythe to the virgin Demetriadis / that she
1640 shuld for to encrease her selfe in vertue rede nowe vpon one booke
/ and nowe vpon another. And he specifiethe vnto her that she also
reade the gospell / and the epistylles of the Apostles. And thus
Thenglyshemen desyre to haue the lawe of god in englyshe / sythen
it is called the lawe vndefyled conuertyng sowlys in to clennes /
1645 lex domini immaculata conuertens animas / but Antechrist saithe
that it is corrupte with the litterall lettre[40] that sleyth sowlys

---

39 *side-note* Mathei.xxviij.

40 *side-note* But my lordes say that it maketh men heretikes and peruerteth soules.

takyng his auctorite of Paule / that saithe / litera occidit
spiritus autem viuificat. That is the letre of the ceremonies of
the olde lawe sleyth the Iewes / and them that nowe vsen them / but
the spirite of the newe lawe quykenethe trewe [D7v] Christen men /   1650
sythen Christ saythe my wordes ben spritte and lyffe. Also we take
ensample of holy virgyns to loue to reade the gospell as they diden
/ as Katheryn / Cecyle / Lucye / Agnes / Margaret / whiche alegyd
the holy gospell to the infidels / that slewe them for the keping
therof. Of these foresaid auctorites it is prouyd laufull / that   1655
both men and women laufully may reade and wryte gods lawe in their
mother tonge / and they that forfenden this they shewe them selfes
heyers and sonnes of the first tormentors / and werse / for they
shewen them selfes the veraye disciples of Antichrist / whiche
hathe and shall passe all the malyce of tyrauntes that haue ben   1660
before in stoppyng and peruertynge of gods lawe whiche deade
engendrythe the great vengeaunce to fall in this realme / but yf
it be amendid for Paule saithe Roma.i. The wrathe of god is shewyd
from heuyn vpon cruelnes and vnryghtfulnes of these men that with
holden the trowthe of god in vnryght wysnes / Reuelatur enim ira   1665
dei super omnem impietatem et iniusticiam hominum eorum qui
veritatem dei in iniustitia detinent. Now god of hys mercy geue
vnto ower kyng / and to ower lordes grace of trewe vnderstandyng to
amende this default principally and all other / then shall we mowe
easely to be amendid. For vntyll it be amendid there shall neuer be   1670
rest and peace in thys realme. Who that fyndythe or redythe this
lettre put it furthe in examinacyon and suffer it not to be hydde
or destroyed / but multyplyed for no man knoweth what proffyt maye
come therof. For he that compiled it / purposyth with goddes helpe
to mayntayne it vnto the deathe / yf neade be. And therfore all   1675
christen men and women / praye that the worde of god maye be
vnbounde / and deliuered from the power of Antichrist / and renne
amonge his people. Amen.

Emprented at Marborow in the lan=
de of Hessen / by me Hans Luft /   1680
in the yere of owre lorde.M.
CCCCC.and.XXX.

Commentary

All New Testament references in the commentary are taken from *Tyndale's New Testament, Translated by William Tyndale: A Modern Spelling Edition of the 1534 Translation* intro David Daniell (New Haven and London: Yale University Press 1989). RSV chapter and verse numbers are given in parentheses after New Testament citations. All Old Testament citations are from the RSV edition of the Bible. Biblical citations in the text which do not appear in RSV are taken from the English translation of the Vulgate text. All old and middle English alphabet letters have been silently normalized in this commentary.

1 *dyaloge* Two other dialogues were written within three years of *A proper dyaloge* by the proposed author(s) of this work. The first is *Rede Me and Be Nott Wrothe* 1528 (STC 21427; Barlowe and Roye), a work called 'an abridged Who's Who of the reformation struggle of the 1520s' (More 8 III 1177). The second is *A Brefe Dialoge bitwene a Christen Father and his stobborne Sonne* 1527 (More 8 II 1069; Hume 'William Roye's *Brefe Dialoge*'; STC 24223.3).

6 The twenty-one-line poem which follows is an acrostic. STC lists eleven ABCs published in English between 1535 and 1584, the majority on religious subjects. OED 3 defines an ABC as the most 'elementary part' or 'simplest rudiments' of a subject. Here we are supposed to recognize the irony as the author(s) feel the need to draw to the attention of the 'spiritualte' their pernicious ways by using a method normally reserved for children or the uninitiated.

8 The four major categories of the Roman Catholic hierarchy. The suggestion is that corruption within the 'spiritualte' runs the gamut from top to bottom.

10 In *Rede Me* the authors predict the same fate for Cardinal Wolsey as they here see for the 'spiritualte' in general: 'With confusion thou shalt have a fall' (6, 51). *Rede Me* was published in 1528 and Wolsey fell in 1529.

11 The pattern of punctuation in these seven-line rime-royal stanzas sometimes stands in the way of the meaning. Here, for instance, in accordance with contemporary punctuation conventions, we would not put a full stop at the end of line 11, since 11–12 should be seen as one unit of meaning. The two lines mean that clerical evil is manifest everywhere; cf *Rede Me*: 'Their blynde affeccion ... / Wherby all the worlde both farre and near / Hath bene combred with longe continuance' (35–7, 58).

14–15 How long have you kept the world in bondage by invoking traditions created by men (as opposed to God's law)? 'Traditions' is used in the same sense in *Rede Me*, where the authors refer to 'the vnrightousnes of mans lawes and tradicions' (125–6, 55). Cf Tyndale in *Prologue Upon the Epistles to the Romans*: 'we should beware of the traditions and doctrine of men, which beguile the simple with sophistry and learning that is not after the gospel' (*Doctrinal Treatises* 508). Cf Mark 7, where Christ chastises the Pharisees for their outward holy appearance: 'And he said unto them: well, ye cast aside the commandment of God, to maintain your own traditions.' RSV (Mark 7:8) seems closer to this text: 'You leave the commandment of God, and hold fast the tradition of men.'

16–17 Not an uncommon complaint of the period; cf Simon Fish *A Supplicacyon for the Beggers* 1529, a work addressed to Henry VIII. Fish tries to draw the king's attention to the damage the clergy is doing to Henry's various 'possessiones': 'Dyd not dyuers of your noble progenitours seynge theyre crowne and dignite runne ynto ruyne and to be thus craftely translated ynto the hondes of this myscheuous generacyon make dyuers statutes for the reformacyon therof. ... But whate avayled it? Haue they not gotten ynto theyre hondes more londes sins then eny duke yn ynglond hath, the statute notwithstonding? Ye haue they not for all that translated ynto theyre hondes from your grace half your kyngdome thoroughly? ... O howe all the substaunce of your Realme forthwith, your swerde, power, crowne, dignite, and obedience of your people, rynneth hedlong ynto the insaciabill whyrlepole of these gredi goulafres to be swalowed and devoured' (More 7 418–19 15–4). The work of the Reformation period which best details the history of the conflict between civil and spiritual authority is Tyndale's *The Practice of Prelates* 1530. Tyndale sets the theme of the work early by pointing out the appropriate duties of the 'spiritualite': 'if Christ's kingdom be not of this world, nor any of his disciples may be otherwise than he was; then Christ's vicars, which minister his kingdom here in his bodily absence, and have the oversight of his flock, may be none emperors, kings, dukes, lords, knights, temporal judges, or any temporal officer, or under false names have any such dominion, or minister any such office as requireth violence' (*Exposition and Notes* 247).

22 *double tyranny* Refers to their spiritual powers which they abuse and the temporal powers they have appropriated; cf Fish 'of one kyngdome [they have] made tweyne: the spirituall kyngdome (as they call it) for they wyll be named first, and your temporall kingdome' (More 7 418).

24 Cf *Rede Me* 3665, 155: 'their god which is their belly.' The word 'belly' or its plural 'bellies' occurs five times in *Rede Me* to emphasize the gross sensuality of the clergy. The authors also make use of the colourful phrase 'bely beast' (90, 54), a synonym for 'glutton,' to hammer home the point. See also Tyndale *The Obedience of a Christian Man*: 'The belly is a god, and cause of all unto our spirituality' (*Doctrinal Treatises* 299 side-note).

25–7 Therefore boldly I dare to inform you, even though you may not be very frightened, that God will finally take vengeance on you.

28–31 Compare this statement, asking readers to believe what follows and not to judge the sentiments expressed too quickly or too harshly, with the following similar comments in *Rede Me*. In the exchange between the treatise and author, the treatise expresses its reservations about telling the truth:

> Yf I presume to make relacion
>> Of secret matters that be vncertayne
> They will count it for diffamacion
>> Or thinges contryved of a frowarde brayne
> To descrybe their faultes it is but vayne (56–62)

And again in the prefatory letter to *Rede Me*: 'I hoape that the reder what ever he be, will nott take this worke as a thynge convicious, or a principle of hatred and debate' (107–9). See also 'The Plowman's Prologue' to *The Plowman's Tale* (*Supplement to the Works of Geoffrey Chaucer* 148 lines 51–2):

> I pray you that no man me reproche
> Whyl that I am my tale telling.

32–4 Luke 8: 'Nothing is in secret, that shall not come abroad: Neither any thing hid, that shall not be known, and come to light.' RSV 8:17 is closer to the text: 'For nothing is hid that shall not be made manifest, nor anything secret that shall not be known and come to light.'

35–41 A difficult stanza: as long as we cannot distinguish hypocrisy from holiness we will not know the truth, just as we do not miss the benefits of light (truth) if we don't know it and continue to live in darkness (ignorance). The author(s) feel that it is their job to expel the clouds of ignorance and allow the light of truth to shine forth. They will do this by exposing the hypocrisy and deceit of the clergy. Cf *Rede Me*: 'I therfore consyderynge the worlde thus to be wrapped in mysery and blindnes (and now in these latter dayes becom an hole or denne of falce foxy hipocrites ...) have iudged it a thynge moste convenient to sett this smale treatous as a glas or myroure most cleare before all mens eyes' (78–86). See also Tyndale: 'Christ here teacheth his disciples, and them that should be the light and salt in living and doctrine, to shine in the weak and feeble eyes of the world, diseased with the megrim, and accustomed to darkness, that without great pain they can behold no light' (*Exposition of Matthew v.vi.vii.* in *Expositions and Notes* 67–8).

42–4 Isaiah 5:20: 'Woe to those who call evil good and good evil, who put darkness for light and light for darkness, who put bitter for sweet and sweet for bitter!'

46ff Paul, 2 Timothy 3: 'As Jannes and Jambres withstood Moses, even so do these resist the truth, men they are of corrupt minds, and lewd as concerning the faith: but they shall prevail no longer. For their madness shall be uttered unto all men as theirs was' (RSV 2 Timothy 3:8–9). The reference to Jannes and Jambres comes from Exodus 7–8, where Pharaoh's magicians are mentioned in several verses. The following excerpt from Exodus provides the context for the reference and helps elucidate 51–5: 'And the Lord said to Moses and Aaron "When Pharaoh says to you, 'Prove yourselves by working a miracle' then you shall say to Aaron 'Take your rod and cast it down before Pharaoh, that it may become a serpent.' So Moses and Aaron went to Pharaoh and did as the Lord commanded; Aaron cast down his rod before Pharaoh and his servants, and it became a serpent. Then Pharaoh summoned the wise men and the sorcerers; and they also, the magicians of Egypt, did the same by their secret arts. For every man cast down his rod, and they became serpents. But Aaron's rod swallowed up their rods"' (Exodus 7:8–13).

56–62 John 8: 'And Jesus went unto mount Olivet and early in the morning came again into the temple and all the people came unto him, and he sat down and taught them. And the scribes and the Pharisees brought unto him a woman taken in advoutry, and set her in the midst and said unto him: Master, this woman was taken in advoutry, even as the deed was a-doing. Moses in the law commanded us that such should be stoned. What sayest thou therefore? And this they said to tempt him: that they might have whereof to accuse him. Jesus stooped down, and with his finger wrote on the ground. And while they continued asking him, he lifted himself up, and said unto them: let him that is among you without sin cast the first stone at her' (RSV 7:53). The sense of the stanza seems to be that Christ's discourses were not regarded as important by the Pharisees, whose outward holiness and glitter of virtue cloaked or hid inner vice. However, Christ's response to their foolish accusations against the adulteress drew their evil into the open.

65 *pope holy pryde* An interesting anachronism, since the biblical Pharisees

pre-dated the papacy. However, here and throughout the literature of the
period, the Roman Catholic church is regularly referred to as if it were in a
direct line of descent from the Pharisees. Tyndale, for instance, in the 'Preface' to *The Practice of Prelates*, makes a number of connections between the
Pharisees' behaviour in the Bible and present-day members of the Catholic
hierarchy. He refers to the latter as 'our scribes and Pharisees' (*Exposition
and Notes* 242). Tyndale uses the expression 'pope holy' in his *Prologue to
the Prophet Jonas*: 'Wickliffe preached repentance unto our fathers not long
since. They repented not; for their hearts were indurate, and their eyes
blinded with their own pope-holy righteousness' (*Doctrinal Treatises* 458).
See also Higden *Polychronicon* (Rolls 41 vol 5 book iv 165): 'this Iulianus ...
bycam a monk, and made hym ful papholy under monkes wede.'

70ff Compare this view that the clergy fool the people with their 'Fayned
godlynes' to a similar sentiment expressed more dramatically in *Rede Me*.
The naïve Watkyn, one of the dialogue's speakers, is taken in by the monks'
and friars' apparent holiness. His more knowledgeable interlocutor, Ieffraye,
disabuses him of his naïveté; referring to the life of the religious Watkyn
says:

> They have man the worlde forsaken,
> And a spretuall lyfe taken,
>> Consistynge in gostly busynes.

Ief. What call ye the worlde I praye?

Wat. Welthy ryches and pleasurs gaye,
And occasions of synfulnes.

Ief. Then are they in the worlde still,
For they have all that they will,
With ryches and possessions ...

Wat. Yett Ieffrye thou errest so god me save,
For the fryers no possessions have,
But lyve only by pure almes.

Ief. Fryers? nowe they are worst of all,
Ruffian wretches and rascall,
Lodesmen of all knavisshnes. (1681–1700)

77–80 The clergy usurp God's power and attack his honour by employing
what the text has earlier referred to as 'mennes tradiciones.'

84–7 The sense seems to be that the Roman Catholic hierarchy refuses to
accept scripture's message in order to maintain their own non-scriptural
authority. The lines may also anticipate later references to the refusal of the
Catholic church to allow a vernacular Bible.

88 *reformacion* The word here means simply improvement or correction of
life or morals rather than being a reference to the religious movement of the

1520s and 1530s. According to OED, the word was not used in this latter sense until 1563. Fish uses it in the same sense as *A proper dyaloge* in *Supplicacyon* (More 7 418). Lines 88–90 are more comprehensible if the full stop at the end of 88 is ignored and the three lines are read as one unit of meaning.

92 The exhortation to patience echoes the sentiments expressed earlier in 28–31.

93ff The reference here is to Christ's repetition of the phrase 'Woe be unto you scribes and Pharisees, hypocrites ...' in Matthew 23.

98 Matthew 10: 'There is nothing so close, that shall not be opened, and nothing so hid, that shall not be known' (RSV 10: 26).

106 contemporary punctuation practice would omit the full stop after 'patrimony'; lines 106–7 are one unit of meaning.

109–15 In *The Practice of Prelates* Tyndale claims that in the primitive church 'the love of God being yet hot in the hearts of men, the rich that had the substance of this world's goods brought of their abundance great plenty unto the sustentation of the poor' (*Expositions and Notes* 253). It is difficult to determine from the sources available exactly when the reformers thought that clerical greed began to destroy the social fabric, although later in the tract (1351–3) the Conquest is established as a possible approximate date. Certainly the Lollards, followers of Wycliffe, were writing against 'temporalties' and arguing for the disendowment of the clergy in the latter part of the fourteenth century (Aston *Lollards* 10). And if F.D. Matthew is correct in placing a date of between 1365 and 1375 on the 'olde treatyse' which makes up about 440 lines of this present tract, we can be certain that the concern about clerical possession of large tracts of land is much older than these dates. Tyndale's 'history' suggests that clerical greed, as seen in the appropriation of goods and lands, was very old indeed, and he outlines its development, after his fashion, in *The Practice of Prelates*. Laying all corruption at the feet of the papacy, he traces the gradual appropriation of lands and temporal power from the time of Pope Boniface III (AD 607) down to his own despised and worldly Cardinal Thomas Wolsey (*Expositions and Notes* 258ff). For his part, Fish seems to think that England at least began to suffer the effects of clerical greed in the reign of King John (1167–1216). In referring to the clergy's actions against the king, Fish in *A Supplicacyon* states: 'Was not all to gither by theyre polycy translated from this good king vnto theim. Ye and what do they more? Truely nothing but applie theym silues by all the sleyghtes they may to haue to do with euery mannes wife, ... that theyre bastardes might enherite the possessions of euery man to put the right begotten children clere beside theire inheritaunce yn subuersion of all estates and godly ordre' (More 7 416). Finally it is doubtful that the author(s) of *A proper dyaloge* have any specific period of time in mind; they are probably merely trying to suggest that the clerical appropriation of temporal possessions has a long and ignominious pedigree. Probably as well they are invoking the myth of 'the good old days' and suggesting in a general way that the pristine purity of the primitive church is now, regrettably, a part of the past. Barlowe and Roye in *Rede Me* hold the same general view of present-day corruption. They claim that the world 'in these latter dayes' has 'becom an hole or denne of falce foxy hipocrites and a mancion for all ravenynge wolves disgysed in lambes skynnes, which hate all love, and with oute drede of god wander but for theire praye' (80–4, 54).

117 *purgatory* For a helpful discussion of the official church position on purgatory and the reformers' reaction to it, see More 7 lxxxvii and Jacques Le Goff *The Birth of Purgatory*. The author(s) argue, through the gentleman's complaint, that the fears of the fire of purgatory and the clergy's promise to reduce the time spent in purgatory account, in large measure, for the loss of 'rentes and lyuelood' and for the transfer of this real estate to the hands of the clergy. In *The Supplycacyon of Soulys* (1529) Thomas More argues at length against Fish's unflattering portrait of purgatory in his own *Supplicacyon*. Here Fish states: 'Nether haue they [the clergy] eny other coloure to gather these yerely exaccions ynto theyre hondes but that they say they pray for vs to God to delyuer our soules out of the paynes of purgatori without whose prayer they sey or at lest without the popes pardon we coude neuer be deliuered thens, whiche if it be true then is it good reason that we gyue theim all these thinges all were it C times as moche. But there be many men of greate litterature and iudgement that for the love they haue vnto the trouth and vnto the comen welth haue not feared to put theim silf ynto the greatest infamie that may be, in abiection of all the world, ye yn perill of deth to declare theyre oppinion in this matter, whiche is that there is no purgatory but that it is a thing inuented by the couitousnesse of the spiritualtie onely to translate all kingdomes from other princes vnto theim and that there is not one word spoken of hit in al holy scripture' (More 7 419 5–18). Tyndale makes the same point somewhat more humorously in *The Obedience of a Christian Man*: 'They [the clergy] fear them with purgatory, and promise to pray perpetually, lest the lands should ever return home again unto the right heirs. What hast thou bought with robbing thy heirs, or with giving the hypocrites that which thou robbest of other men? Perpetual prayer? Yea, perpetual pain: for they appoint thee no time of deliverance, their prayers are so mighty. The pope for money can empty purgatory when he will. It is, verily, purgatory; for it purgeth and maketh clean riddance: yea, it is hell; for it devoureth all things' (*Doctrinal Treatises* 244). The most sustained, and possibly the most scholarly attack on purgatory during this period is John Frith's *A disputacion of purgatorye made by Iohan Frith which is deuided in to thre* *bokes* (*STC* 11386.5), printed in Antwerp probably in 1531. In this work the scholarly and generally even-tempered Frith responds to three stalwart defenders of the doctrine of purgatory: More in *The supplycacyon of soulys* (1529), John Fisher in *Assertionis Lutheranae confutatio* (1523), and John Rastell in *A New Boke of Purgatory* (1530). For the context of Frith's *disputacion* see Clebsch 88ff.

121 *seactes* The orders and divisions of the spirituality within the Catholic church, including the various orders of monks, friars, etc. In *The Parable of the Wicked Mammon*, Tyndale helps define the term by quoting Peter's second epistle and glossing one of its key words: '"There were false prophets among the people (meaning of the Jews), even as there shall be false teachers or doctors among you, which privily shall bring in sects damnable" (sects is part-taking as one holdeth of Francis, another of Dominic' (*Doctrinal Treatises* 124). Part iv of the ballad 'The Image of Ypocrisye (1533) lists many of the sects within the traditional church. In *Tractatus De Pseudo-Freris*, a work attributed to Wycliffe by Matthew, Wycliffe defines a sect as 'a new ordre bi newe patroun and newe lawe ... and if benet or dominic or fraunciss or bernard or angel of heuene make a newe secte upon cristis secte, he is herfore worthy to be blamed; and this secte shulde be despisid and cristis secte shulde be holde clene' (*The English Works of Wyclif* 301).

123–9 This stanza is based on what the author(s) regard as a perversion of Matthew 16: 'When Jesus came into coasts of the city which is called Cesarea Philippi, he asked his disciples saying: whom do men say that I the son of man am? They said, some say that thou are John the Baptist, some Elias, some Jeremias, or one of the prophets. He said unto them: but whom say ye that I am? Simon Peter answered and said: Thou art Christ the son of the living God. And Jesus answered and said to him: happy art thou Simon the son of Jonas, for flesh and blood hath not opened unto thee that, but my father which is in heaven. And I say also unto thee, that thou art Peter: and upon this rock I will build my congregation. And the gates of hell shall not prevail against it. And I will give unto thee, the keys of the kingdom of heaven: and whatsoever thou bindest upon earth, shall be bound in heaven: and whatsoever thou loosest on earth, shall be loosed in heaven' (RSV 16:13–19). With a view to attacking the church's position that it alone possesses binding and loosing authority because of its exclusive ownership of the 'keys,' Tyndale writes in *The Obedience of a Christian Man*: 'The keys, whereof they so greatly boast themselves, are no carnal things, but spiritual; and nothing else save knowledge of the law, and of the promises or gospel.' 'As Peter answered in the name of all, so Christ promised him the keys in the person of all' (Matthew 16) (*Doctrinal Treatises* 205). And again: 'And instead of God's law, they bind with their own law: and instead of God's promises, they loose and justify with pardons and ceremonies, which they themselves have imagined for their own profit' (*Doctrinal Treatises* 243). 'He [the pope] bindeth where God looseth, and looseth where God bindeth. He blesseth where God curseth, and curseth where God blesseth. He taketh authority also to bind and loose in purgatory. That permit I unto him; for it is a creature of his own making. He also bindeth the angels: for we read of popes that have commanded the angels to fet divers out of purgatory. Howbeit I am not yet certified whether they obeyed or no' (*Doctrinal Treatises* 268–9). One of the 'Articles collected out of Wickliff's Sermons' is 'That the pope of Rome hath no more in the keys of the church, than hath any other within the order of priesthood' (Foxe III 4).

130ff Throughout his writings Tyndale shows how the traditional church perniciously works to destroy the core of society, the family. In *The Practice of Prelates* we hear how the church threatens marriages and works to break up families (*Expositions and Notes* 258, 264). Elsewhere, he attacks the immorality of priests and religious who satisfy their sexual desires by seducing and corrupting wives and daughters (*Expositions and Notes* 123, 275). In *The Exposition of the First Epistle of St. John* the church is accused of stealing from parishes, thereby impoverishing families (*Expositions and Notes* 173). In *The Obedience of a Christian Man* the church prevents families from learning about God's word by forbidding the scriptures in the vernacular; families find no true guidance from priests in their parishes; women who pay too much attention to the power of saints are led to disobey their husbands; and the church has spies in 'every great man's house' (*Doctrinal Treatises* 141, 147–8, 171, 191).

136 The refrain stated here – 'Sayenge that they wold for their soules praye' – and repeated with slight variation in the twelve other stanzas in the gentleman's complaint, is meant to serve as an ironic reminder of the perverse and idiosyncratic meaning the Roman Catholic clergy give to the word 'pray.' Tyndale sets the church's meaning of the word beside what he regards as its true meaning in this excerpt from *The Exposition of Matthew v.vi.vii.*: 'with prayer they get praise ... and pray therto, and rob widows' houses. ... With their prayers they exclude all true prayers, and make it impossible that there should be any among them. For prayer is either a longing for the honour and name of God, that all men should fear him, and keep his precepts, and believe in him; and contrary to that, they seek their own honour, that men should fear them and keep their ordinances, and believe in their sweet blessings, prayers, pardons, and whatsoever they promise. ... Either prayer is a complaining and a shewing of thine own misery and necessity, or of thy neighbour's before God; desiring him, with all the power of thine heart, to have compassion and to succour. Contrary to this, they have excluded with their prayers all necessity and misery from among them' (*Expositions and Notes* 78). The repetition of the refrain also suggests that it is a stock, almost automatic, response of the clergy to the various complaints of the layman.

137–42 My ancestors, confused by the untrue and vain arguments of the clergy, and fearing the pains of purgatory and desirous of happiness, consented to the clergy's request to take their lands. Cf Tyndale in *The Obedience of a Christian Man*: The papists claim that, if a man repent, 'God ... forgiveth the offence only, and not the pain also, say they, save turneth the everlasting pain unto a temporal pain; and appointeth seven years in purgatory for every deadly sin. But the pope for money forgiveth both, and hath more power than God, and is more merciful than God' (*Doctrinal Treatises* 271).

144–6 Cf Fish's *Supplicacyon*: 'The goodliest lordshippes, maners, londes, and territories are theyrs' (More 7 412 23–4).

151–84 Compare this litany of complaints about the gentleman's impoverished life with Fish's opening in the *Supplicacyon*: 'Most lamentably compleyneth theyre wofull mysery vnto youre highnes youre poore daily bedemen the wretched hidous monstres (on whome scarcely for horror any yie dare loke) the foule vnhappy sorte of lepres, and other sore people, nedy, impotent, blinde, lame, and sike, that live onely by almesse, howe that theyre nombre is daily so sore encreased that all the almesse of all the weldisposed people of this youre realme is not half ynough for to susteine theim, but that for verey constreint they die for hunger. And this most pestilent mischief is comen vppon youre saide poore beedmen by the reason that there is yn the tymes of youre noble predecessours passed craftily crept ynto this your realme an other sort (not of impotent but) of strong puissaunt and counterfeit holy, and ydell beggers and vacabundes whiche syns the tyme of theyre first entre by all the craft and wilinesse of Satan are nowe encreased vnder your sight not onely into a great nombre, but also ynto a kingdome. These are ... the Bisshoppes, Abbottes, Priours, Deacons, Archedeacons, Suffraganes, Prestes, Monkes, Chanons, Freres, Pardoners, and Somners. And who is abill to nombre this idell rauinous sort whiche ... haue begged so importunatly that they haue gotten ynto theyre hondes more than the therd part of all youre Realme' (More 7 412 1–23). The whole question of church endowments, which is the subject of this long passage, is dealt with in detail in Wycliffe's (?) *Of Dominion*. Among other things, what this tract shows is that the question of endowments has an ancestry stretching back at least to Wycliffe's time, if not before (*The English Works of Wyclif* 284–93).

161–4 Sometimes I complain piteously for help to the stately clergy. They disdain my appeal and give me no comfort but claim that they will pray for my friends' souls.

166 They would not part with a half-penny to help us.

193ff The entrance of 'The husbandman' marks the beginning of the dialogue proper. Although agreeing with the gentleman that the latter's plight is serious, regrettable, and caused by the 'spiritualte' (199), the husbandman will argue that his situation is worse than his interlocutor's. This position allows both husbandman and gentleman to expatiate on their respective plights and thereby expose the clergy in a more dramatic and 'natural' way than can a simple monologue or litany of complaints. The fact that both gentleman and husbandman suffer under clerical rule indicates that the detrimental actions of the church affect all of society, high and low members alike.

201 *their* ie, the clergy's.

220–3 The husbandman's statement that the gentleman and his ancestors freely gave their lands to the clergy allows the gentleman once again to claim that his ancestors were hoodwinked by clerical promises of spiritual benefit and gain. In *The Obedience of a Christian Man* Tyndale supports the gentleman's claim that his land should be returned to him: 'Yea, the king ought to look in the chronicles, what the popes have done to kings in time past, and make them restore it also; and ought to take away from them their lands which they have gotten with their false prayers, and restore it unto the right heirs again' (*Doctrinal Treatises* 335).

270ff A harking back to the good old days prior to the Conquest (1066). Fish makes the comparison as well: 'The danes nether the saxons yn the time of the auncient Britons shulde neuer haue ben abill to haue brought theire armies from so farre hither ynto your lond to haue conquered it if they had had at that time suche a sort of idell glotons to finde at home. The nobill king Arthur had neuer ben abill to haue caried his armie to the fote of the mountaines to resist the coming downe of lucius the Emperoure if suche yerely exactions had ben taken of his people' (*Supplicacyon*, More 7 414 12–19).

284 *Hyerd fearmes* Rent paid to work a certain portion of land.

294–6 We pay more by half than we previously did before they took charge of the property.

297–302 Cf Fish's *Supplicacyon*: 'What money pull they yn by probates of testamentes, priuy tithes, and by mennes offeringes to theyre pilgremages, and at theyre first masses? Euery man and childe that is buried must pay sumwhat for masses and diriges to be song for him or elles they will accuse the dedes frendes and executours of heresie. Whate money get they by mortuaries, by hearing of confessions ... by halowing of churches, altares, superaltares, chapelles and belles, by cursing of men and absoluing theim agein for money? What a multitude of money gather the pardoners in a yere?' (More 7 412–13 31–8).

306–8 Cf *Rede Me:*
> Pover cilly shepperdes they gett,
> Whome into their farmes they sett,
>> Lyvynge on mylke, whyg, and whey. (2812–14, 132)

311 It is possible that the author(s) used Fish as their source for this calcula-
tion: 'And who is abill to nombre this idell rauinous sort whiche ... haue
begged so importunatly that they haue gotten ynto theyre hondes more than
the therd part of all youre Realme' (More 7 412). After then listing the
clergy's gains from tithes, offerings, pilgrimages, charges for confessions, probating of wills, and the like, Fish concludes: 'Ley then these sommes to the
forseid therd part of the possessions of the realme that ye may se whether it
drawe nighe vnto the half of the hole substaunce of the realme or not, so
shall ye finde that it draweth ferre aboue' (*Supplicacyon,* More 7 414 25–9).
320–2 Whereas farmers in previous times paid rent for house and land based
on fairness and reason.
326–34 Cf *Rede Me:*
> A newe waye they do invent.
>> Lettynge a dosen farmes vnder one.
> Whiche one or two ryche francklynges,
> Occupyinge a dosen mens lyvynges,
>> Take all in their owne hondes a lone. (2789–93, 132)

And a few lines later the authors of *Rede Me* state that 'by farmage [they]
Brynge the londe into a rearage' (2863–4, 134). Pollard cites Bishop Langland's
letter to Cardinal Wolsey, 30 September 1528, where the practice of placing
many farms in the hands of one man is mentioned: 'If your Grace did, at the
eyes, see as I have now seen, your heart would mourn to see the towns, villages, hamlets, manor places, in ruin and decay, the people gone, the ploughs
laid down, the living of many honest husbandmen in one man's hand ... the
commons in many places taken away from the poor people, whereby they are
compelled to forsake their houses, and so wearied out that they wot not
where to live, and so maketh their lamentation' (85–6, note 4 cited in *Rede
Me* 202). See also *Ballads from Manuscript,* where the text of a petition
entitled 'Petition to Henry VIII, against the Engrossing of Many Small Farms
into One Man's Hands, and the Consequent Neglect of Tillage for Pasture,
Loss of Corn, Poultry etc., Decay of Houses and Churches, Ploughs and Men'
is cited. In the ballad 'Now a Dayes' (97) one reads (as cited in *Rede Me* 202):
> men say that priors and abbottes be
> Grete grosyers in this countrie;
> they vse bying and sellyng openlye;
> the church hath the name.

345ff In an attempt to justify the action of his gentlemenly class against husbandmen, the gentleman points out that he and his ilk are now forced to lease lands from the clergy (land previously rented by husbandmen from gentlemen at a just price) because the class of gentlemen lost its patrimony when it was given away by ancestors in response to empty clerical threats and promises, which the gentleman has already discussed at length (102–92). Compare with the Lollard tract *Of Dominion*: 'that lordis reuersen the ordeynaunce of crist, and thus for lordis fooly fallen many harmes bothe to lordis, clerkis and comunes. Lordis ben maked pore and eke fewe in noumbre, and ofte tymes thei ben nedid to spoyle here tenauntis, and bi grucching ageyn they disturblyn the pees; and this nedid not to falle if lordis of this world hadden al this lordschipe of this world in here hond and ordeyned wel therfore' (*The English Works of Wyclif* 285).

350 *wolffes of the clergye* Cf Fish's 'rauinous wolues' (*Supplicacyon*, More 7 417).

358 *saynte Marye* An oath by the Virgin Mary.

364–9 Cf *Rede Me*:

> Wher as the religious sectes,
> Vnto no lawes are subiectes,
>> Obeyinge nether god nor kynge.
> Yf the kynge will their service vse,
> Forthwith they laye for an excuse,
>> That they must do goddes busines. (2488–93)

See Knowles (*Religious Orders* 2 298–9) for a discussion of clerical avoidance of military duty. Monks, for example, were not exempt from military duty but ignored 'writs of summons to fulfill military obligations' (299). Coulton refers to Charles the Great's concern about religious who 'take the vows not so much for devotion's sake as to escape from the army or some other royal obligation' (Coulton 3 336).

373 A reference to the duty of hospitality. Woodward states that 'The offering of shelter and food to travellers was a duty which devolved upon others besides monks ... yet it was chiefly to the monasteries that the traveller turned, and we know from the ruins which survive that even the humblest convent had its *hospitium* or guest house where the passerby could secure a meal and a place to sleep' (Woodward 20). Despite what the author(s) say here, Woodward claims that 'On the whole the tradition of hospitality seems to have been well maintained by the monks, and the fear was expressed at the time of dissolution that a "decay of hospitality" would ensue' (21).

378 *freer* ie, friar; a member of the mendicant orders founded in the thirteenth century and afterwards. The friars represented a departure from the previous monastic tradition in so far as they lacked corporate possessions.

They possessed a greater mobility because they were not confined to a single monastery or abbey. During the thirteenth century there was a remarkable growth in the number of mendicant orders, until the Second Council of Lyons issued a decree on 17 July 1274 directed at the suppression of all but the four major orders: Dominican or Black Friars (founded 1215–16; came to England 1221); Franciscan or Grey Friars (Friars Minor) (founded 1223; came to England 1224); Carmelites or White Friars (1226; given status as mendicants in 1245); Augustinian or Austen Friars (1256) (*New Catholic Encyclopedia*; More 7 331). The authors' statement that 'with in this .iiij. hundred yere / Thorough oute christendome ... mendicantes call' seems to be out by about a hundred years if *A proper dyaloge* was published in 1530. For the Lollard position on the pernicious practices of friars, see *The Rule and Testament of St. Francis* (*The English Works of Wyclif* 39–51), *Jack Upland* (*Jack Upland, Friar Daw's Reply and Upland's Rejoinder* 54–72), and 'Fifty Heresies and Errors of Friars' (*Select English Works of John Wyclif*).

380ff Cf Fish's *Supplicacyon*: 'there is yn the tymes of youre noble predecessours passed craftily crept ynto this your realme an other sort ... of strong puissaunt and counterfeit holy, and ydell beggers and vacabundes whiche syns the tyme of theyre first entre ... are nowe encreased vnder your sight not onely into a great nombre, but also ynto a kingdome' (More 7 412 11–17). And here is Tyndale on the same subject: 'The spirituality increaseth daily. More prelates, more priests, more monks, friars, canons, nuns, and more heretics ... with like draff. Set before thee the increase of St Francis's disciples in so few years. Reckon how many thousands, yea, how many twenty thousands, not disciples only, but whole cloisters, are sprung out of hell of them in so little space' (*Obedience of a Christian Man, Doctrinal Treatises* 302).

391–5 Cf Fish's *Supplicacyon*: 'Set these sturdy lobies a brode in the world to get theim wiues of theire owne, to get theire liuing with their laboure in the swete of theire faces according to the commaundement of god' (More 7 422 12–15). See also *Rede Me*'s condemnation of the monks' idle lives:

> O Lorde god what goode dayes,
> Thes monkes have in abbeyes,
>   And do nether swett nor swyncke.
> Thei live in welthynes and ease,
> Havynge what soever they please,
>   With delicate meate and dryncke.
> Wher with they farce their bellies so full,
> That to all goodnes they are dull,
>   Makynge mery with gill and Ioan.
> They sitt slepynge in a corner,
> Or momblynge their pater noster,

> Their mynde nothynge ther apon.
> Be they never so stronge or starcke,
> They will exercyse no maner warcke,
>   Nor laboure boddily. (1621–35)

402ff *the newe testament* A reference to the church's refusal to allow the Bible in the vernacular. This is a criticism of the church that appears in almost every reformation text of the period. See, for example, Tyndale in the 'Preface' to *The Obedience of a Christian Man*, where he spends much time arguing for the Bible in English. Prior to giving several reasons for its translation he states: 'That thou mayst perceive how that the scriptures ought to be in the mother tongue, and that the reasons which our spirits make for the contrary, are but sophistry and false wiles to fear them from the light, that thou mightest follow them blindfold, and be their captive to honour their ceremonies and to offer to their belly' (*Doctrinal Treatises* 144). See also Tyndale's *A Pathway into the Holy Scripture, passim* (*Doctrinal Treatises*). *A proper dyaloge* turns its full attention to a vernacular Bible when it appends its prose defence of the translation of the Bible to the end of the work. For a good analysis of the issues surrounding a vernacular Bible in both Europe and England, see Deanesly. The first edition of Tyndale's New Testament was ordered destroyed by Cuthbert Tunstal, bishop of London, and publicly burned at Paul's Cross in October 1526 (Mozley, Demaus, Sturge). Cf *Rede Me*:

> Ief. They sett nott by the gospel a flye,
>   Diddest thou not heare whatt villany,
>   They did vnto the gospell?
> Wat. Why, did they agaynst hym conspyre?
> Ief. By my trothe they sett hym a fyre,
>   Openly in London cite.
> Wat. Who caused it so to be done?
> Ief. In sothe the Bisshoppe of London,
>   With the Cardinalles authorite.
>   Which at Paules crosse ernestly,
>   Denounced it to be heresy,
>   That the gospell shuld come to lyght.
>   Callynge theym heretikes excecrable,
>   Whiche caused the gospell venerable,
>   To come vnto laye mens syght. (707–20)

421 *OED* gives the first recorded use of this saying to *A proper dyaloge*, although Tilley gives 1508 Stanbridge *Vulgaria* p 18 as an earlier source (N16 488).

424–6 Genesis 3:19: 'In the sweat of your face you shall eat bread till you return to the ground, for out of it you were taken.'

427–9 Mark 6: 'Is not this that carpenter, Mary's son, the brother of James and Joses and of Juda and Simon? and are not his sisters here with us?' (RSV 6:3).

443–8 Cf *Rede Me*:

> There be monkes of soche statlynes,
> That scant will soffer at their messe,
>> A lorde of bludde with theym to sitt.
> Whose prowde service to beholde,
> In plate of silver and golde,
>> It passeth a mans witt.
> Knyghtes and squyers honorable,
> Are fayne to serve at their table,
>> As vnto Dukes excellent.
> Divers of theym have the degre,
> Of worthy Erles in dignite,
>> And are lordes of the parlement. (2527–38)

449–54 See 364–9.

465 2 Thessalonians 3: 'For when we were with you, this we warned you of, that if there were any which would not work, that the same should not eat' (RSV 2 Thessalonians 3:10). This entire section on the appropriation of property by the spirituality should be read with the important Lollard tract *Of Clerks Possessions* in mind. This work establishes the Lollard ancestry of the complaints articulated in *A proper dyaloge* (*The English Works of Wyclif* 116–40).

475ff The reference is to the so-called 'Reformation Parliament which met in seven sessions during the years 1529–36' and which 'was clearly one of the most important assemblies ever to gather in England' (Lehmberg vii). Lehmberg claims that largely because of Thomas Wolsey's management style as chancellor, parliament had not met for six years (1). However, with Wolsey's fall in 1529, Henry VIII, who had, effectively, placed the running of government in Wolsey's hands, may have now turned to parliament for guidance as to how to best manage state affairs. Whatever reasons Henry had for reconvening parliament – and Lehmberg makes clear that there may have been many – certainly one concerned the general discontent with clerical abuse and power, an obvious theme of *A proper dyaloge*. Members of the parliament itself had their own reasons for welcoming the session. They must have shared the general animus against the fallen cardinal, but for them hatred of the over-mighty churchman was but one aspect of the anti-clerical sentiment which was present throughout the country. Fabyan's *Chronicle* sums up their intentions neatly in its succinct entry under 1529, 'A Parliament for enormities of the cleargy' (Lehmberg 5). Since *A proper dyaloge* was published on the continent in 1530 and the second session of the Reformation Parliament was not held until 1531, the author(s) could only have known about the first session, the one that Lehmberg refers to as 'the anticlerical commons' (76). Hall sums up the principal concerns of this first parliament, concerns which the author(s) of this tract would doubtless have shared:

> When the commons were assembled in the nether house, thei began to common of their grefes wherwith the spiritualtie had before tyme greuously oppressed them, both contrarie to the lawe of the realme, and contrarie to all righte, and in especial thei were sore moued with six greate causes.
>
> The first for the excesse fynes, which the ordinaries toke for probat of Testamentes, insomuche that Sir henry Guilford knight of the garter and comptroller of the kinges house, declared in the open Parliament on his fidelitie that he and other beyng executors to Sir William Compton knight paied for the probate of his wil to the Cardinal and the Archbishop of Cauntorburie a thousand Marke sterlyng: after this declaracion were shewed so many extorcions done by ordinaries for probates of willes, that it were to muche to rehearse.
>
> The second cause was the great polling and extreme exaccion, which the spirituall men vsed in takyng of corps presentes or mortuaries, for the children of the defunct should al dye for hunger and go a beggyng rather than thei would of charite geue to them the sely kow which the dead man ought if he had but only one, such was the charitie then.
>
> The third cause was, that priestes beyng ... stuardes and officers to Bishoppes, Abbotes, and other spirituall heddes, had and occupied Fermes, Graunges, and grasing in euery contrey, so that the poore husbandmen coulde haue nothyng but of them, and yet for that they should pay derely.
>
> The fourth cause was that Abbotes Priors and spiritual men kept Tanne houses and bought and soulde woll, clothe and all maner of marchaundise as other temporall marchauntes did.
>
> The fift cause, was because that spiritual persones promoted to great benefices, and hauyng there liuyng of ther flocke, were liyng in the courte of lordes houses, and toke al of the parishoners, and nothing spent on them at al, so that for lack of residence both the poore of the parish lacked refreshyng, and vniuersally all the parishoners lacked preaching, and true instruccion of Gods worde, to the greate perell of there soules.
>
> The sixt cause was to se one priest beyng litle learned to haue tenne

or twelue benefices and to be resident on none, and to know many well
learned scholers in the vniversite which wer able to preche and teache,
to haue nether benefice nor exhibicion. (765; see also Holinshed 744–5).
For a revisionist view of the prevalence of anti-clericalism in the reign of
Henry VIII see *The English Reformation Revisited*, passim.
483 A classic ironic lamentation can be found in *Rede Me* (111–348, 60–6),
where a priest laments the death of the mass.
485ff The references are to Simon Fish's *A Supplicacyon for the Beggers* and
Thomas More's response *The supplycacyon of soulys* (1529). The author(s)
here claim that Fish's complaints against clerical greed were answered by
More not on their own terms but through references to the unscriptural doctrine of purgatory. Almost all of the second book of More's response (pp 170–
228) is devoted to his defence of purgatory against Fish's brief but vitriolic
attack on it.
499 *seynt Ihone* An oath by the Evangelist.
500–1 In fact More does invoke scripture to support his view on the existence and validity of purgatory; he refers to Kings, Zechariah, Machabees,
John, Revelation, Acts, and Corinthians (More 7 179–87). In this entire section the author(s) refer to the defence of purgatory by the clergy in general. In
fact, what they probably mean is that More spoke on their behalf in his
answer to Frith.
510–15 I am assuming that the reference here is to Sir John Mandeville's
Travels, a work written originally in French probably by Jean d'Outremeuse
in the 1360s. Hamelius states that 'All the elements of [d'Outremeuse's]
romancing are prosaic and vulgar. But he puts them together with brazen
audacity, disfigures or invents proper names, alters numbers and circum-
stances, to the despair of those honest commentators who have traced him to
his sources. ... Whether his motives were purely mercenary, or whether he
obeyed an original impulse, his chief aim was to entertain while pretending
to impart solid historical or geographical information' (*Mandeville's Travels*
10). Mandeville's *Travels* seems an appropriate choice for the author(s) of *A
proper dyaloge*, since, as well as being fiction in the guise of fact, it is also a
decidely Lollard, anti-papal tract (15).
519–21 Cf Fish *A Supplicacyon*: 'Are they not stronger in your owne parliament house then your silfe? Whate a nombre of Bisshopes, abbotes, and
priours are lordes of your parliament? are not all the lerned men in your
realme in fee with theim to speake yn your parliament house for theim
ageinst your crowne, dignite, and comon welth of your realme, a feawe of
youre owne lerned counsell onely excepted? Whate lawe can be made ageinst
theim that may be aduaylable? Who is he (though he be greued never so sore)
for the murdre of his auncestre, rauisshement of his wyfe, of his doughter,

robbery, trespas, maiheme, dette, or eny other offence dare ley it to theyre charge by any wey of accion, and if he do then is he by and by by theyre wily-nesse accused of heresie' (More 7 417–18, 27–2). More responds: 'Thys beg-gars proctour wold fayn shew hym self a man of great experyence / and one that had great knowlege of the maner and order vsed in the kyngys parlya-mentys. But than he speketh so sauourly therof: that yt well apperyth of hys wyse wordes he neyther canneth eny skyll therof / nor neuer cam in the house. For as for the hygher house furst the kynges own ryall parson alone more than counterpaysyth all the lordys spyrytuall present wyth hym and the temporyll to. And ouer thys the spyrytual lordys can neuer in nomber excede the lordys temporall / but must nedys be farre vnderneth them yf yt please the kyng. For hys hyghnes may call thyder by hys wryt many mo tem-porall lordys at hys own pleasure. And beyng as they be / there was neuer yet sene that the spyrytuall lordes bendyd them selfe there as a partye agaynst the temporall lordes. ... And therfor in the hygher house the spyrytuall parte neuer apperyd yet so strong / that they myght ouer matche that temporall lordes. ... Now where he sayth that in the comen house all the lerned men of the realme ar feed to speke for the clergy except the kynges lerned counsell: there be .ii. foyles at ones. For neyther be all the lernyd men of the realme knyghtes or burgeyses in the comen house / and the kyngys lerned councell ys not there at all. ... And for the ferther profe that the kynges hyghnes ys not so weke and vnable in hys owne parlyament as thys beggers proctour so pre-sumptuously telleth hym / hys grace well knowyth and all hys people to / that is theyr own conuocacyons hys grace neuer deuysed nor desyred any thyng in hys lyfe / that euer was denyed hym. And therfore thys gay innuen-cyon of thys beggers protour / that he fayneth the kynges hyghnes to be in hys hygh courte of parlyament more weke and feble than the clergye / ys a very feble deuyce' (More 7 140–1). Woodward states that in the sixteenth cen-tury 'the heads of the thirty important abbeys and priories were Lords of Par-liament and were accustomed to receive individual writs of summons whenever parliament met. ... Together with the twenty-one English and Welsh bishops the parliamentary abbots made up the number of the Lords Spiritual, who had they all been present, could have formed a very substan-tial group, indeed an actual majority, in the upper house, for at the beginning of the reign of Henry VIII there were only about forty lay peers. However, it is interesting to notice that whatever the historical origins of the representa-tion of the clergy in the parliament, the judges of 1515 declared that the Lords Spiritual "have no place in the Parliament-chamber by reason of their spirituality, but only by reason of their temporal possessions." In other words it was their estates, their social position and not their ecclesiastical which secured for the bishops and abbots their entry to parliament and once there they did not form a separate estate or house, but remained on a par with the Lords Temporal, their fellow landlords' (6). Lehmberg gives the composition of the Upper House during the Reformation Parliament. The House was made up of 107 members, broken down in the following manner: first, Lords spiritual: archbishops, bishops, and custodians of spiritualities 21; abbots and priors 29; Total 50. Second, Lords temporal: dukes 3; marquises 2; earls 13; viscounts 1; barons 38; total 57 (37).

528–9 Cf Hall: 'These thinges [clerical misdemeanours] before this time [ie, the Reformation Parliament] might in nowise be towched nor yet talked of by no man except he would be made an heretike, or lese al that he had, for the bishops were chauncelors, and had all the rule about the kyng, so that no man durst once presume to attempt any thing contrary to their proffit, or commoditie' (765).

530 *Is he gentillman lorde or kynge* Contemporary English calls for the subjunctive 'be' to replace the text's 'Is.'

531–6 the author(s) may have Fish's narrative of King John (1199–1216) in mind here:

> And whate do al these gredy sort of sturdy idell holy theues with these yerely exactions that they take of the people? Truely nothing but exempt theim silues from thobedience of your grace. Nothing but translate all rule power lordishippe auctorite obedience and dignite from your grace vnto theim. Nothing but that all your subiectes shulde fall ynto disobedience and rebellion ageinst your grace and be vnder theym. As they did vnto your nobill predecessour king Iohn: whiche forbicause that he wolde haue punisshed certeyn trayt ours that had conspired with the frenche king to haue deposed him from his crowne and dignite (emong the whiche a clerke called Stephen whome afterward ageinst the kinges will the Pope made Bisshoppe of Caunterbury was one) enterdited his Lond. For the whiche mater your most nobill realme wrongfully ... hath stond tributary (not vnto any kind temporall prince, but vnto a cruell deuelisshe bloudsupper dronken in the bloude of the sayntes and marters of christ) euersins. Here were an holy sort of prelates that thus cruelly coude punisshe suche a rightuous kinge, all his realme, and succession for doing right.
>
> Here were a charitable sort of holy men that coude thus enterdite an hole realme, and plucke awey thobedience of the people from theyre naturall liege lorde and kinge, for none other cause but for his rightuousnesse. Here were a blissed sort not of meke herdes but of bloudsuppers that coude set the frenche king vppon suche a rightuous prince to cause hym to lose his crowne and dignite, to make effusion of the bloude of his people, oneles this good and blissed king of greate com-

passion ... had submitted him silf vnto theym. O case most horrible that euer so nobill a king, Realme, and succession shulde thus be made to stoupe to suche a sort of bloudsuppers. (More 7 415 3–32)

More responds:

But thys man agaynst the clergye fetcheth forth old farne years and ron-neth vp to kyng Iohans days / spendyng mych labour about the prayse and commendacyon of the good gracyous kyng and cryeng out vppon the pope that then was and the clergye of England / and all the lordys and all the comens of the realme / because kynge Iohan as he sayth made the realm trybutary to the pope / wherin he meaneth peraduen-ture the peter pense. But surely therin ys all hys hote accusacyon a very colde tale when the trouth ys knowen. For so ys yt in dede that albe it there be wrytars that say the peter pense were graunted by kyng Iohan for the release of the interdyccyon: yet were they payed in dede ere euer kyng Iohans grete graundfather was borne / and therof ys there profe ynough. Now yf he say as in dede some wryters say / that kynge Iohan made Englande and Irland trybutary to the pope and the see apos-tolyque by the graunt of a thowsand markys: we dare surely say agayn that yt ys vntrew / and that all Rome neyther can shew suche a graunt nor neuer could / and if they could yt were right nought worth. For neuer coulde eny kyng of England geue away the realm to the pope / or make the lande tributary though he wolde / nor no such money ys there payed nor neuer was. ... (More 7 128–9)

536–9 Sir John Oldcastle (d 1417), referred to by Thomas More in *The Sup-plycacyon of Soulys* as 'a captayn of heretykes in Englande in the dayes of kynge Henry the fyft (More 7 149). See Holinshed (62–3): 'In this same yere [1413] the lord Cobham called Sir John Oldcastel was dampned for a lollard and an heredyke by all holy chirche and commytted to the Toure of london where he brake a wey withynne fewe days. And anone after he and his com-plices conjecteden and conspireden not oonly the deeth of the kyng and of his brethern But also the destruccion of all holy Chirche For they purposed hem to haue assembeled to gedirs be nyght in Seynt Gyles felde a myle oute of the Cite for to have perfourmed here false ententes. But the kyng and his lordes havyng knowlege of here false purpose toke the felde rather than they awayt-ing upon here comyng And so they toke mony of here preestes and Clerkes and other lewde men that wern of the same secte of diverse coostes of Englond wenyng to have found there sir John Oldecastell. But they were foule bygyled For anone after ther was drawen and hanged of hem xxxix up on a day upon newe galowes made for hem upon the high way faste beside the same felde where they thought to have assembled. Of the which com-panye vij of the grettest lollardes wern brent bother they and the galowes

that they henge upon' (cited in More 7 345–6). Foxe has an extended, if
biased, narrative of Oldcastle's life in III 320ff. Oldcastle's intents are clear
from the judicial proceedings that have come down to us. His objectives were
'wholly to annul the royal estate as well as the estate and office of prelates
and religious orders in England, and to kill the king, his brothers ... the prelates and other magnates of the kingdom, and to turn men of religion, after
they had abandoned divine worship and religious observances, to secular
occupations: totally to despoil cathedrals and other churches and religious
houses of their relics and other ecclesiastical goods, and to level them completely to the ground' (quoted in Aston *Lollards* 25).

543–5 The reference is to Humphrey, duke of Gloucester, and the story is
told in Hall (208–9), Foxe (III 709ff), and Holinshed (146ff). Hall focuses on
Gloucester's conflict with Henry VI's queen and only incidentally mentions
Henry Beaufort, bishop of Winchester, and his part in Gloucester's downfall.
Foxe and Holinshed, however, emphasize Gloucester's running controversy
with Winchester and it is this aspect of Gloucester's life that the author(s) of
A proper dyaloge want to focus on: it is another example of the church's
malevolence directed against the innocent and truly God-fearing. Holinshed
prefaces the narrative with the following comments emphasizing either Winchester's jealousy of Gloucester or Gloucester's disdain of the bishop's pomp
and riches as possible motives for the dispute: 'Somewhat before this season
fell a great diuision in the realme of England, which of a sparkle was like to
haue grown to a great flame. For whether the bishop of Winchester called
Henrie Beaufort, sonne to Iohn duke of Lancaster by his third wife, enuied
the authoritie of Humfrie duke of Glocester, protectour of the realme; or
whether the duke disdained at the riches and pompous estate of the bishop:
sure it is that the whole realme was troubled with them and their partakers:
so that the citizens of London were faine to keepe dailie and nightlie
watches, and to shut vp their shops for feare of that which was doubted to
haue insued of their assembling of people about them' (III 146). Tyndale
leaves no doubt who the guilt party was: 'And in king Harry the sixth's days,
how raged they [the clergy] as fierce lions against good duke Humphry of
Glocester, the king's uncle, and protector of the realm in the king's youth
and childhood, because that for him they might not slay whom they would,
and make what chevisance they lusted! Would not the bishop of Winchester
have fallen upon him and oppressed him openly with might and power in the
city of London, had not the citizens come to his help?' (*The Practice of Prelates, Expositions and Notes* 297). After being imprisoned in St Edmund Bury,
the duke was found dead. Polydore claims he was 'stranguled' (*Three Books*
73), but Hall is less certain: 'The duke the night after his emprisonement,
was found dedde in his bed, and his body shewed to the lordes and commons,

as though he had died of a palsey or empostome: but all in different persons well knewe, that he died of no natural death but of some violent force: some iudged hym to be strangled: some affirme that a hote spitte was put in at his foundement; other write, that he was stiffeled or smoldered betwene twoo fetherbeddes' (209).

556–8 Luke 23: The reference is possibly to Christ standing humbly before both Pilate and Herod and finally allowing himself to be crucified (RSV 23:33–6). But compare with John 18: 'Then Pilate entered into the judgement hall again, and called Jesus, and said unto him: art thou the king of the Jews? Jesus answered: sayest thou that of thyself, or did other tell it thee of me? Pilate answered: Am I a Jew? Thine own nation and high priests have delivered thee unto me. What hast thou done? Jesus answered: my kingdom is not of this world. If my kingdom were of this world, then would my ministers surely fight, that I should not be delivered to the Jews, but now is my kingdom not from hence' (RSV 18:33–6).

562–4 Perhaps Matthew 6: 'Therefore take no thought saying: what shall we eat, or what shall we drink, or wherewith shall we beclothed? After all these things seek the Gentiles. For your heavenly father knoweth that ye have need of all these things. But rather seek ye first the kingdom of heaven and the righteousness thereof, and all these things shall be ministered unto you' (RSV 6:31–3).

565–7 1 Timothy 6: 'When we have food and raiment, let us therewith be content. They that will be rich, fall into temptation and snares, and into many foolish and noisome lusts, which drown men in perdition and destruction' (RSV 1 Timothy 6:8–9).

569–71 If we should cite the gospel they would deem us heretics and claim that we were disobedient to their church.

575–7 See note to 402ff. The 'shamefull blasphemy' alluded to here may refer to what the author(s) regard as Tunstal's comments on the errors in Tyndale's translation. Sturge states that 'it is clear that Tunstal's opposition was based to a large extent on alleged incorrect renderings, two thousand of which he claimed to have found' (131). With characteristic hyperbole, *Rede Me* increases the number of errors that Tunstal found to three thousand (723–4, 77). And Tyndale in his 'Preface' to *The Five Books of Moses* states: 'And as for my translation, in which they affirm unto the lay-people (as I have heard say) to be I wot not how many thousand heresies, so that it cannot be mended or correct; they have yet taken so great pain to examine it, and to compare it unto that they would fain have it, and to their own imaginations and juggling terms, and to have somewhat to rail at, and under that cloak to blaspheme the truth' (*Doctrinal Treatises* 393).

586ff The reference is to the reign of Henry V (1413–22), during which the

Lollard heretic Sir John Oldcastle was defeated and condemned. Dickens provides a concise summary of the event which makes clear why the Lollard sympathizers who wrote *A proper dyaloge* are not kindly disposed to Henry's reign: 'The proletarian character of Lollardy developed rapidly during the earlier decades of the fifteenth century, when the movement was stripped of its political aspirations. From their advent the Lancastrian kings backed the bishops in a fresh campaign against heresy. In 1401 Purvey was forced to recant, William Sawtre burned and the Statute *De Heretico Comburendo* [quoted in *Documents Illustrative of English Church History* 133–7] passed through Parliament. These steps failed, however, to crush the Lollard parliamentarians, who produced bills nine years later to soften the laws against heresy and to distribute the surplus wealth of the Church between the King, a newly-created nobility and such useful institutions as hospitals. Then, in the early days of 1414, catastrophe intervened when Sir John Oldcastle, a leading convert imprisoned for heresy, escaped and planned a Lollard march upon London from all parts of the kingdom. Easily overthrown by Henry V at St Giles' Fields, this rash gathering resulted in numerous arrests of leaders and suspects. Deprived of influential backing the cause was obliged to move underground' (45). In a more general way Foxe adds: 'After that the true servant of Jesus Christ, John Wickliff, a man of very excellent life and learning, had, for the space of more than twenty-six years, most valiantly battled with the great Antichrist of Europe, or pope of Rome, and his diversely disguised host of anointed hypocrites, to restore the church again to the pure estate that Christ left her in at his ascension, he departed hence most christianly in the hands of God, the year of our Lord 1384 ... and was buried in his own parish church at Lutterworth, in Leicestershire. No small number of godly disciples left that good man behind him, to defend the lowliness of the gospel against the exceeding pride, ambition, simony, avarice, hypocrisy, whoredom, sacrilege, tyranny, idolatrous worshippings, and other filthy fruits, of those stiff-necked pharisees; against whom Thomas Arundel, the archbishop of Canterbury ... collected, in Paul's church in London, a universal synod of all the papistical clergy of England, in the year of our Lord 1413 ... to withstand their most godly enterprise. And this was the first year of king Henry v., whom they had then made fit for their hand' (III 320–1).

589–90 The reference is to the Wycliffe Bible (Forshall and Madden).

590 Aston states: 'There is no doubt that the Lollards were avid in their reading, and they derived plenty of errors from the Bible' (*Lollards* 14). She adds that 'Lollard enthusiasm for their English Bible translations lasted through the fifteenth century to assist the beginnings of the Reformation' (197).

591–4 Hall is in agreement with the author(s) where they suggest that many arrests and imprisonments for heresy were carried out during Henry's reign:

'After this tyme [ie, after Oldcastle's escape from prison in Wales] in a certain vnlawfull assemble was taken sir Robert Acton knight, a man of greate wit and possessions, Ihon Broune Esquire, Ihon Beuerly clarke and a greate numbre of other whiche were brought to the kynges presence, and to hym declared the cause of their commocion and risyng: and accusyng a greate numbre of their sort and societie. ... After this folishe acte, so many persones were apprehended that all the prisons in and about London wer replenished with people. The chief of them whiche wer .xxix. wer condempned by the clergie of heresy, and attainted of high treason as mouers of warre against their kyng by the temporal lawe in the Guyld hall the .xii. daie of December and adiudged for treason to be drawen and hanged, and for heresy to be consumed with fire gallowes and all: Which iudgemente was executed in Ianiuer folowyng on thesaied Robert Acton and the .xxviij. other' (48–9).

598–600 Aston reports a ceremonial burning of Lollard books in London in 1431 (*Lollards* 205). Doubtless there were other such events whose records have not come down to us.

604–6 The author(s) do not condone Henry's war with France as do Shakespeare and Hall, but rather condemn it as a ruse on the part of the bishops to turn Henry's attention away from England so that the clergy could pillage and control it. Cf Tyndale: 'the bishops sent king Henry the fifth out to conquer France. The cause was, saith the chronicles, that the king went about to take their temporalities from them; and therefore, to bring the king into another imagination, they monied him, and sent him into France' (*The Practice of Prelates, Expositions and Notes* 302–3). Again he states in the *Answer to Sir Thomas More's Dialogue*: 'the prelates, lest he should have had leisure to hearken unto the truth, sent [the king] into France, to occupy his mind in war, and led him at their will' (212).

607–12 Lollards, along with the author(s) of this tract, saw Richard II's overthrow at the hands of Henry IV as a pernicious and ungodly act the results of which were bloodshed and persecution of all God-fearing peoples. Aston states: 'Tyndale's exposition of the divine judgement manifested in fifteenth-century events was a variation of the theory which Polydore Vergil first published a few years later. But it was a theory with a difference, in that the fatal breach between Plantagenet and Lancaster was envisaged in strictly religious terms, and the deposition and death of Richard II were laid at the door of hypocritical prelates who were out to silence the prophetical voice of Wycliffe' (*Lollards* 285). Tyndale states: 'I ask whether his [Henry V's] father slew not his leige king and true inheritor unto the crown; and was therefore set up of the bishops, a false king, to maintain their falsehood? And I ask whether, after that wicked deed, followed not the destruction of the commonalty and quenching of all noble blood?' (*Answer to Sir Thomas More's Dialogue* 212).

'These hypocrites [the prelates] laid to Wicliffe's charge, and do yet, that his doctrine caused insurrection. But they, to quench the truth of his preaching, slew the right king, and set up three false kings a row: by which mischievous sedition they caused half England to be slain up, and brought the realm into ... ruin and desolation' (*Exposition of the First Epistle of St John, Expositions and Notes* 224–5). 'Let England look about them, and mark what hath chanced them, since they slew their right king whom God had anointed over them, king Richard the Second. Their people, towns, and villages are minished by the third part; and of their noble blood remaineth not the third, nor I believe the sixth, yea, and if I durst be bold, I wene I might safely swear that there remaineth not the sixteenth part' (*Exposition of Matthew v.vi.vii., Expositions and Notes* 53).

618–20 Perhaps a reference to the Book of Exodus and the various punishments called down on Egypt by God for its refusal to release the chosen people.

629ff In this section of the *dyaloge* the author(s) are intent on showing the fraudulent antiquity of the church's authority and the devices it employs to maintain its claim to power and truth. Cf Tyndale *The Obedience of a Christian Man*: 'they allege for themselves the saying of Christ to Peter, Matt.xvi. "Whatsoever thou bindest on earth, it shall be bound; and whatsoever thou loosest," and so forth. "Lo, say they, whatsoever we bind, and whatsoever we loose, here is nothing excepted." And another text say they of Christ, in the last of Matthew: "All power is given to me," saith Christ. "in heaven and in earth: go therefore and preach," etc. Preaching leaveth the pope out: and saith, "Lo all power is given me in heaven and in earth;" and thereupon taketh upon him temporal power above king and emperor, and maketh laws and bindeth them' (*Doctrinal Treatises* 268).

632 *religious fathers* The Fathers of the Church; cf Tyndale's *Answer to Sir Thomas More's Dialogue*: 'They have corrupt the legend and lives almost of all saints. They have feigned false books, and put them forth; some in the name of St Jerome, some in the name of St Augustine, in the name of St Cyprian, St Dionyse and other holy men; which are proved none of theirs, partly by the style and Latin, and partly by authentic stories' (48). 'The fathers of the Jews and the bishops, which had as great authority over them as ours have over us, condemned Christ and his doctrine. If it be enough to say the fathers have condemned it, then are the Jews to be holden excused; yea, they are yet in the right way, and we in the false. But and if the Jews be bound to look in the scripture, and to see whether their fathers have done right or wrong; then are we likewise bound to look in the scripture, whether our fathers have done right or wrong, and ought to believe nothing without a reason of the scripture and authority of God's word' (*The Obedience of a Christian Man, Doctrinal Treatises* 329–30).

633 *the bloode sheadinge of marters* Cf Tyndale: 'We read in the works of St
Cyprian, that there were martyrs that suffered martyrdom for the name of
Christ all the year long, and were tormented and healed again, and then
brought forth afresh: which martyrs believed, as ye do, that the pain of their
martyrdom should be a deserving, and merit enough, not only to deserve
heaven for themselves, but to make satisfaction for the sins of other men
thereto; and gave pardons of their merits, after the ensample of the pope's
doctrine ... for which pride Cyprian wrote to them, and called them the
devil's martyrs, and not God's' (*Answer to Sir Thomas More's Dialogue* 199).
646–9 Cf Tyndale: 'Nothwithstanding because, as they be all shaven, they be
all shameless to affirm that they be the right church and cannot err, though
all the world seeth that not one of them is in the right way, and that they
have with utter defiance forsaken both the doctrine and living of Christ and
of all his apostles; let us see the sophistry wherewith they would persuade it.
One of their high reasons is this: The church, say they, was before the heretics; and the heretics came ever out of the church, and left it. And they were
before all them which they now call heretics and Lutherans, and the Lutherans came out of them etc. Wherefore they be the right church, and the other
heretics indeed, as they be called' (*Answer to Sir Thomas More's Dialogue*
42). See also More's 'Letter to Bugenhagen': 'But of course Wittenberg is innocent. It is simply the place where Luther pitched his camp – Luther, captain
of evildoing, architect and artificer of evil, leader of an army of savages. In
council with you and his other lieutenants he makes plans hour by hour,
devising nothing but how to incite rebellions, subvert the faith, uproot religion, profane holy things, corrupt morals, prostitute virgins, and destroy virtue' (More 7 25).
650–5 Our forefathers with humility and simplicity were content to obey
the church's (evil) teachings, and no one, until quite recently, presumed to
show their hatred of the clergy or complain about its temporal possessions.
656ff The gentleman's words that the church claims that no one until quite
recently complained about its various practices and vast holdings of land give
the husbandman the opportunity to introduce the Wycliffe tract to prove
that complaints against the clergy and their temporal possessions have a distinguished ancestry and that such complaints are not merely the creation of
the newfangled Lutheran sect.
661 *aboue an hundred yere olde* In his brief introduction to this work,
which he entitles 'The Clergy May Not Hold Property,' Matthew states that
it has similarities to the writings of Wycliffe, which date from between 1365
and 1375, even though he claims that 'No external evidence authorizes us to
attribute this tract to Wyclif' (*The English Works of Wyclif* 359). On 685ff the
author(s) claim that the 'olde treatyse' was 'made aboute the tyme of kinge

Rycharde the seconde.' Richard's reign extended from 1377 to 1399, and Aston claims that 'Internal evidence neither confirms nor contradicts the suggestion' that it was written during Richard's reign (Lollards 223). Probably the best guess as to the work's date is that it was written in the last quarter of the fourteenth century by a confirmed Wycliffite. Whatever the exact date, the fact that it is more than one hundred years old helps give the tradition of complaint against clerical possessions a legitimate pedigree, as the gentleman implies in 667–9.

662 The husbandman here claims that the style of the tract proves that it is old; cf 683–4.

671ff Even though the husbandman claims that he has 'no more left than a remenant,' Matthew reprints the entire tract copied from the Lambeth Manuscript.

676 In fact, the tract as reproduced here begins at the seventh chapter, not the sixth as stated.

688 The tract should be read with the Lollard piece *Of Clerks Possessioners* in mind (*The English Works of Wyclif* 116–40).

690 *A proper dyaloge*'s indebtedness to chapter 7 of the original begins with the reference to 'Seynt Huge.' In the original this section begins about half-way through the chapter.

690–1 *Seynt Huge and seynt Swithune* Of the three Hughs listed in *The Penguin Dictionary of Saints*, the two who best fit the description of a lord are Hugh of Cluny (1024–1109) and Hugh of Lincoln (1135–1200). The former is described as 'the eldest son of an important Burgundian nobleman.' He was made a monk of Cluny in Burgundy at a young age and appointed abbot when only twenty-five; 'during the sixty years of his abbacy Cluny reached the highest point of power and international influence in its long history' (174). Hugh of Lincoln is perhaps the more likely candidate, since he spent most of his life in England. When Henry II founded a Carthusian monastery at Witham in Somerset he sent to France for Hugh 'to take charge of it.' In 1186 he was made bishop of Lincoln, the largest diocese in England. He was responsible for beginning the rebuilding of Lincoln Cathedral. During his life he was admired and respected by both Henry II and Richard I and was not shy to correct or confront them when principles were at stake (175–6). *The Penguin Dictionary* states that St Hugh 'is one of the most attractive characters of medieval England' (176). Foxe mentions him in II 273 as a person 'who after his death is said to have done great miracles, and therefore was counted a saint.' Swithin (Swithun) (d 862), a man about whom very little seems to be known, 'was the trusted counsellor of the Wessex kings Egbert and Ethelwulf and was made bishop of Winchester in 852' (*The Penguin Dictionary of Saints* 316). Of St Swithun's miracles Foxe says, 'the miracles which are read in the church of Winchester, of this Swithin, them I leave to be read together with the Iliads of Homer, or the tales of Robin Hood' (II 15).

693 *Gabriel shall blowe his horne* A reference to the end of the world; cf Revelation 8ff. For the expression see Tilley G1 250. Matthew claims that 'One of the articles condemned at the Council of Constance as Wyclif's is – "Audacter prognostico omnibus istis sectis et suis complicibus, quod non defundunt fidelibus quod sacramentum sit accidens sine subjecto antequam Christus et tota triumphans ecclesia venerit equitans in finali judicio super flatum angeli Gabrielis"' (*The English Works of Wyclif* 528).

693 *or* ie, ere.

694 *the minor* The second term in a syllogism, the other two being the major and the conclusion. Syllogistic reasoning was a particular favourite of scholastic philosophers, and it may be that the author of this tract is parodying the form, although Wycliffe himself engaged in syllogistic dispute. In this instance the major premise is that Sts Hugh and Swithun were lords; the minor premise is that even as lords they followed Christ; the conclusion based on the 'logic' of the major and minor statements is that present-day clerics who follow Christ can also be lords, or perhaps present-day clerics who are lords can also follow Christ.

700 *chefesaunce* Matthew thinks the word means 'Payment made for a loan' (*The English Works of Wyclif* 528), but I think it means simply 'money' or 'funds' in general, at least in this context.

705–6 Acts 3: 'Then said Peter: Silver and gold have I none, such as I have, give I thee' (RSV Acts 3:6).

706–7 Luke 5: 'When Simon Peter saw that [ie, Christ performing a miracle by filling the apostles' nets with fish], he fell down at Jesus' knees saying: Lord go from me, for I am a sinful man. For he was utterly astonied and all that were with him, at the draught of fish which they took: and so was also James and John the sons of Zebedee which were partners with Simon. And Jesus said unto Simon: fear not, from henceforth thou shalt catch men. And they brought the ships to land, and forsook all, and followed him' (RSV 5:8–11).

707–9 After deciding to follow Christ, Peter never claimed or received worldly goods or land even though he may have had legal entitlement to such things.

710 *seynt Peters grounde* Cf Tyndale *The Obedience of a Christian Man* where Tyndale refers to 'St. Peter's patrimony' (*Doctrinal Treatises* 207).

711ff *seynt Bernarde* The reference is to Bernard of Clairvaux (1090–1153), founder of the Cistercian Order. 'In 1145 ... Eugenius III was elected pope. Bernard wrote for him a remarkable treatise on the duties of the papal office, in which he castigates the abuses of the Roman *curia* and expounds the religious mysteries which the pope should always keep before his eyes' (*The Penguin Dictionary of Saints* 66). This work, *De consideratione,* is what is cited here. A modern English rendering of 712–30 is as follows:

> You may claim these things on some other ground but not by apostolic right. For the Apostle could not give you what he did not have. What he had he gave: responsibility for the churches, as I have said. Did he give dominion? Listen to him, 'Not lording it over your charge but making yourself a pattern for the flock.' You should not think he was prompted to say this only by humility and not by truth, for the Lord says in the Gospel, 'The kings of the nations lord it over them and those who have power over them are called benefactors.' And he adds, 'But you are not like this.' It is clear: dominion is forbidden for Apostles.
>
> Therefore, go ahead and dare to usurp the apostolic office as a lord, or as pope usurp dominion. Clearly, you are forbidden to do either. If you want to have both of these at the same time, you will lose both. Moreover, you should not think that you are excluded from those about whom God complains, 'They have reigned but not by me; princes have arisen but I do not recognize them.' Now if it pleases you to reign without God, you have glory, but not before God. But if we believe this to be forbidden, let us listen to the decree which says, 'Let the one who is greater among you become lesser, and let the one who is the foremost become as a servant.' This is the precedent established by the Apostles: dominion is forbidden, ministry is imposed. (*Five Books on Consideration* II vi 10–11 pp 58–9)

See Luther's reference to this document in *Freedom of a Christian* 47 (*Martin Luther: Selections from His Writings*).

716–17 1 Peter 5: 'see that ye feed Christ's flock which is among you, taking the oversight of them, not as though ye were compelled thereto, but willingly: not for the desire of filthy lucre, but of a good mind: not as though ye were lords over the parishes: but that ye be an example of the flock' (RSV 1 Peter 5:2–3).

718–19 Matthew 20: 'You know that the lords of the gentiles have domination over them. And they that are great, exercise power over them. It shall not be so among you' (RSV 20:25). Luke 22: 'the kings of the gentiles reign over them, and they that bear rule over them, are called gracious lords. But ye shall not be so' (RSV 22:25).

725 Hosea 8:4: 'They made kings, but not through me. They set up princes, but without my knowledge.'

727–9 Matthew 23: 'He that is greatest among you, shall be your servant' (RSV 23:11). Matthew 20: 'But whosoever will be great among you, let him be your minister: and whosoever will be chief, let him be your servant' (RSV 20:27).

730–1 Cf 1 Timothy 3: 'These things write I unto thee, trusting to come shortly unto thee: but and if I tarry long, that then thou mayst yet have knowledge how thou oughtest to behave thyself in the house of God, which is the congregation of the living God, the pillar and ground of truth.' RSV (1 Timothy 3:15) is not close to the tract's language here. Since the author of this tract is speaking throughout against the clergy holding land that properly belongs to lay people, he may be playing here with two meanings of the word 'ground': No cleric may claim land (ie, ground) and put it beside Jesus Christ in whom he should be grounded.

737–9 Acts 4: 'And the multitude of them that believed, were of one heart, and of one soul. Also none of them said, that any of the things which he possessed, was his own: but had all things common' (RSV 4:32).

740–4 An attempt to show the deceit of the clergy. A few lines earlier the author stated that the clergy justifies its temporal holdings by claiming that it holds them in common, as the apostles and 'perfyte people' held all things at the formation of the church. Our present-day clergy thinks it can claim, like Christ's followers, never to say 'This is mine.' However – and here is the point – even a secular person of our own time when speaking of his own possessions uses the plural – 'this is oures' – since he speaks not only on his own behalf but on behalf of his other land-holding colleagues. Hence, to use the plural 'oures' rather than the singular 'myne' does not actually make any real difference.

744–6 Moreover, they subtly claim that they hold this land not by virtue of secular dominion or rule but rather by virtue of having received it as a gift of charity in perpetuity.

749–50 Matthew 5: 'Let your light so shine before men, that they may see your good works, and glorify your father which is in heaven' (RSV 5:16); Matthew 7: 'Beware of false prophets, which come to you in sheep's clothing but inwardly they are ravening wolves. Ye shall know them by their fruits' (RSV 7:16). See also James 2:18 and John 14:11.

752–3 Matthew 23: 'Then spake Jesus to the people, and to his disciples saying: The scribes and the Pharisees sit in Moses seat. All therefore whatsoever they bid you observe, that observe and do: but after their works do not: For they say and do not' (RSV 23:1–3).

753–4 John 5: 'For the works which the father hath given me to finish: the same works which I do, bear witness of me, that the father sent me. And the father himself which hath sent me, beareth witness of me' (RSV 5:36).

759–60 Augustine of Hippo (354–430), one of the greatest Latin doctors of the church and a prolific author of tracts which, among other things, defended the church against heresy. Augustine was also an indefatigable commentator on the Bible. Probably his two best-known works are the *Con-*

fessions and the *City of God*. The reference here is probably to Augustine's 'Second Discourse on Psalm 21': 'But you now, because you wish to hold your own goods in private and not in the general unity with Christ – for you wish to rule on earth, not to reign with Him in heaven – you possess your own establishments. And sometimes we have gone to these people to say to them: "Let us seek the truth and let us find it." And they answer: "Keep what you have: you have your sheep, I have mine; leave my sheep in peace as I leave yours." Good heavens! My sheep, his sheep – which did Christ purchase then? No; these sheep are neither mine nor thine; let them belong to Him who purchased them, Him who branded them. ... Why must I have mine and you yours. ... As far as possessions are concerned, let us kiss, brow and hands, and let there be an end of aliens' (*St. Augustine on the Psalms* v.31 226).

759–69 Whether held privately in some places or in common in others, the secular lands are managed by the clergy (since they once belonged to the laity) in a worldly fashion and, therefore, are held as private property. For in the same way as the baron or knight manages his estate, so once the property comes into the hands of the priest, monk, canon, or convent, these individuals manage their estates in accordance with the same laws of judgment and punishment. And these laws include imprisonment and hanging and other forms of torment which in former times used to be the responsibility of the secular branch of the church.

767 *presonnynge and hangynge* In his notes, Matthew states: 'The exercise of criminal jurisdiction by churchmen was felt to be a scandal, although the advantages and dignity attaching to it made it an object of ambition. Bishop Pecock ingeniously pleads that the steward or bailiff who held the court was, for that purpose, the King's officer. "Whatever man the bischop or abbot so chesith, the King therwith and theryn committith his power to the same person so chosun, and he ougte not but in an vnpropre maner of speche be clepid (namelich in maters of deeth) to be steward of the bischop or of the abbot, but of the King"' (from Pecock's *Repressor* cited by Matthew in *The English Works of Wyclif* 528–9).

774–5 Cf Matthew above: 'The exercise of criminal jurisdiction by churchmen was felt to be a scandal, although the advantages and dignity attaching to it made it an object of ambition.'

778–81 A summary statement coming at the end of a number of examples of the way in which the clergy behaves like lay lords in its management of land and property. Essentially the lines mean the following: therefore we can see how the clergy today behaves like private owners of property and goods and not according to the practice of those true Christians who shared with others during the early days of Christianity.

785-7 This kind of behaviour does not accord with the perfection of Christ which should reside in priests. Rather it reflects the reprehensible behaviour previously explained.

791-2 *Lyncolniensis* is Robert Grosseteste (1175–1253), 'English bishop of Lincoln from 1235 and influential scholar who introduced into the world of Latin Christendom Latin translations of Greek and Arab philosophical and scientific writings. His philosophical thinking – a somewhat eclectic blend of Aristotelian and Neoplatonic ideas – consistently searched for a rational scheme of things, both natural and divine' (*Britannica* 5 512; see also Stevenson). The reference here is to Grosseteste's *Dicta Theologica*: 'Compassion is the love or desire of relieving the sufferer of his suffering' (*Dicta Lincolniensis* 9). Matthew points out that in the Lambeth manuscript there is the following marginal note 'in later hand' at this point in the text: 'of lyncolne Robart grosted was bishope a 1253 before Wicklyf 120 yeres' (*The English Works of Wyclif* 385).

793-6 Cf Luke 14: 'When thou makest a dinner or a supper: call not thy friends, nor thy brethren neither thy kinsmen nor yet rich neighbours: lest they bid thee again, and a recompense be made thee. But when thou makest a feast, call the poor, the maimed, the lame and the blind, and thou shalt be happy, for they cannot recompense thee' (RSV 14:12–14).

799-801 Alms-giving is not true alms-giving if the gift is given to those who are already sufficently provided for.

806 The sense of this passage beginning at 801 is clearer if the full stop at 805 is replaced by a comma.

809-11 2 Corinthians 8: 'It is not my mind that others be set at ease, and ye brought into cumbrance: but that there be egalness now at this time, that your abundance succour their lack: that their abundance may supply your lack: that there may be equality' (RSV 2 Corinthians 8:13–14).

811-12 Not Luke 14 as the side-note states but rather Luke 11: 'Give alms of that ye have' (RSV 11:14). The authors here quote the Vulgate.

816-19 Cf Matthew 22: 'Give therefore to Caesar, that which is Caesar's' (RSV 22:21). See also RSV Luke 20:25.

823-6 Even if the clergy had been given possessions and even if the giving of these possessions had not resulted in the destruction or weakening of any other group or individual, nevertheless giving such possessions to the clergy would not be true alms-giving.

827-8 See 730–1.

833-6 And this [ie, that God gives to each estate enough to maintain itself] is evident in God's law to those who pay attention to it. One can see it clearly in the laws given to Adam and Eve, in the laws of nature, and in the laws of both Moses and Christ.

836–9 Genesis 1:27–30 'So God created man in his own image, in the image of God he created him; male and female he created them. And God blessed them, and God said to them, "Be fruitful and multiply, and fill the earth and subdue it; and have dominion over the fish of the sea and over the birds of the air and over every living thing that moves upon the earth." And God said, "Behold, I have given you every plant yielding seed which is upon the face of all the earth, and every tree with seed in its fruit; you shall have them for food. And to every beast of the earth, and to every bird of the air, and to everything that creeps on the earth, everything that has the breath of life, I have given every green plant for food."' However, following Adam and Eve's original sin, God states, 'In the sweat of your face you shall eat bread till you return to the ground, for out of it you were taken' (Genesis 3:19).

840–1 Matthew 7: 'Therefore whatsoever ye would that men should do to you, even so do ye to them' (RSV 7:12).

842–4 See Deuteronomy *passim*.

844–6 Deuteronomy 26:1–4 'When you come into the land which the Lord your God gives you for an inheritance, and have taken possession of it, and live in it, you shall take some of the first of all the fruit of the ground, which you harvest from your land that the Lord your God gives you, and you shall put it in a basket, and you shall go to the place which the Lord your God will choose, to make his name to dwell there. And you shall go to the priest who is in office at that time, and say to him "I declare this day to the Lord your God that I have come into the land which the Lord swore to our fathers to give us." Then the priest shall take the basket from your hand, and set it down before the altar of the Lord your God.'

846–50 Deuteronomy 15:7–11: 'If there is among you a poor man, one of your brethren, in any of your towns within your land which the Lord your God gives you, you shall not harden your heart or shut your hand against your poor brother, but you shall open your hand to him, and lend him sufficient for his need, whatever it may be. ... For the poor will never cease out of the land; therefore I command you, You shall open wide your hand to your brother, to the needy and to the poor, in the land.'

860–1 Luke 14: 'When thou makest a dinner or a supper: call not thy friends, nor thy brethren neither thy kinsmen nor yet rich neighbours: lest they bid thee again, and a recompens be made thee. But when thou makest a feast, call the poor, the maimed, the lame and the blind' (RSV 14:12–13).

869 *all the states* Cf Wycliffe: 'Ther ben in the Chirche thre statis that God hathe ordeyned; state of prestis, and state of knygtis, and the thridd is staat of comunys' ('state' *OED* 22).

883–4 There is nothing more secure or certain than Christ's promise to maintain a sufficient livelihood for his clergy.

887 The sense of the sentence beginning at 884 is clearer if the full stop at 887 is removed.

888–91 Matthew 6:

> Behold the fowls of the air: for they sow not, neither reap, nor yet carry into the barns: and yet your heavenly father feedeth them. Are ye not much better than they?
>
> Which of you (though he took thought therefore) could put one cubit unto his stature? And why care ye then for raiment? Consider the lilies of the field, how they grow. They labour not neither spin. And yet for all that I say unto you, that even Solomon in all his royalty was not arrayed like unto one of these.
>
> Wherefore if God so clothe the grass, which is today in the field, and tomorrow shall be cast into the furnace: shall he not much more do the same unto you, o ye of little faith? (RSV 6:26–30; see also Luke 12:22ff)

899–900 *almesse / but rather all a mysse* The author plays with the similar sounds of alms and a miss (alms pronounced al-mess) to indicate that giving alms to the clergy in perpetuity is not appropriate and indeed is counter to certain biblical injunctions. See also 909–10.

909–11 But now, as a result of these perpetual alms, Christ's ordinances are destroyed entirely in some countries and to a large extent in England, and eventually they will be destroyed completely in England as well.

912–15 Cf the gentleman's comments earlier in the opening section of the dialogue.

920 *ther* Refers to the preceding sentence where we are told that restoring property to its rightful owner(s) is appropriate restitution.

922–4 Judges 11:30ff: 'And Jephthah made a vow to the Lord, and said, "If thou wilt give the Ammonites into my hand, then whoever comes forth from the doors of my house to meet me, when I return victorious from the Ammonites, shall be the Lord's, and I will offer him up for a burnt offering." So Jephthah crossed over to the Ammonites to fight against them; and the Lord gave them into his hand ... Then Jephthah came to his home at Mizpah; and behold, his daughter came out to meet him with timbrels and with dances; she was his only child; beside her he had neither son nor daughter. And when he saw her, he rent his clothes, and said, "Alas my daughter! you have brought me very low, and you have become the cause of great trouble to me; for I have opened my mouth to the Lord, and I cannot take back my vow." And she said to him, "My father, if you have opened your mouth to the Lord, do to me according to what has gone forth from your mouth, now that the Lord has avenged you on your enemies, on the Ammonites." And she said to her father, "Let this thing be done for me; let me alone two months, that I may go wander on the mountains, and bewail my virginity, I and my companions" ... And at the end of two months, she returned to her father, who did with her according to his vow which he had made.'

924–5 Matthew 14:

> At that time Herod the tetrarch heard of the fame of Jesus, and said unto his servants: This is John the Baptist. He is risen again from death, and therefore are such miracles wrought by him. For Herod had taken John and bound him and put him in prison for Herodias' sake, his brother Philip's wife. For John said unto him: It is not lawful for thee to have her. And when he would have put him to death, he feared the people, because they counted him as a prophet.
>
> But when Herod's birthday was come, the daughter of Herodias danced before them, and pleased Herod. Wherefore he promised with an oath that he would give her whatsoever she would ask. And she being informed of her mother before, said 'give me here John Baptist's head in a platter.' And the king sorrowed. Nevertheless for his oath's sake, and for their sakes which sat also at the table, he commanded it to be given her: and sent and beheaded John in the prison, and his head was brought in a platter and given to the damsel, and she brought it to her mother. (RSV 14:1ff; see also Mark 6:14ff)

927–8 *As saynte Austyne sayeth* 'Nam Jephte homo facinorosus et improvidus, stulta devotione munus Deo promisit dicens, *Quidquid mihi redeunti a coede occurrerit ante ostia domus meae, hoc offeram Deo.* Numquid coactus devovit, aut numquid intellexit quomodo deberet votum facere? Quid enim si canis illi aut asinus occurrisset, quod Dominus offerri prohibuit; aut si filius alienus, aut si uxor, ut in dolore alieno exsultans redderet votum? Ideirco improvidae menti quod in alienam perniciem devoverat, in illum ipsum Judicio divino retortum est: et usque adeo insensatus fuit jephte, ut nec postea stulte se devovisse cognosceret, ut error ejus qui ab ipso coeperat, per ipsum emendaretur. Intelligere enim debuit Deum non tali sacrificio delectari, et rogare pro stultitia sua, et aliud offerre quod contra Legem non esset: sed fidelem se praestitit factus parricida, cum constet fidem stultam non solum minime prodesse, sed obesse. In causa itaque filiae suae ipse mactatus est, unde et Deus a tali sacrificio dissimulavit. Si enim hoc prohibuisset, aliud offerre sibi illum voluisse videretur, cum sciret ut indignum non debere illum offerre. Filia autem ejus lucrum fecit: quia enim innocens in malis patris mortua est, poena caruit inferi; quod diu forte vivendo adipisci nequisset' ('Quaestiones Veteris et Novi Testamenti' XLIII 2239–40; *Patrologiae Cursus Completus 35*). See also *Patrologiae Cursus Completus* 34 'Quaestionum S. Augustine in Heptateuchum' Book 7 XLIX 811. [For Jephta, a wicked man who lacked foresight, in a foolish act of piety promised God an offering, saying *I shall offer to God whatever meets me before the doors of my house as I* *return from battle.* Surely he did not vow under compulsion or not see in what way he ought to make the vow? For what if a dog or an ass had met him, which the Lord has said may not be offered, or if he had met another man's son or wife, so that in triumph he fulfilled his vow by means of another's grief. For that reason what he had vowed thoughtlessly for the destruction of another was turned against him himself by divine judgment. Jeptha was so irrational that he did not recognize even afterwards that he made his vow foolishly, so that the error which had begun with himself might have been remedied by himself. He ought to have perceived that God was not pleased by a sacrifice of this kind and that he ought to pray for forgiveness for his stupidity and to sacrifice something which was not against the Law. By becoming the murderer of one of his own family he showed himself faithful, even though it is agreed that a foolish faith is not only of little advantage but even a disadvantage. In the case of his daughter he was himself punished, since even God dissociated Himself from a sacrifice of such a kind. For if He had stopped this, He would seem to have wished him to offer Him something else, since he ought not sacrifice what was unworthy. Jeptha's daughter, however, benefited: because she died innocent in the wickedness of her father, she avoided the punishment of the lower world, which she would, perhaps, not have been able to achieve by living long.]

932 *heresy and symony* Cf 701 and 941; the author is not using the word 'heresy' in its strict sense as deviation from or opposition to a theological doctrine, but rather more loosely to suggest despicable practices such as the acceptance of perpetual alms or the accumulation of lordships.

938 the long sentence beginning at 935 and ending at 942 is clearer if the full stop at 938 is replaced by a comma.

942–3 *and in other writen before* Perhaps, for instance, such Lollard tracts as *Of Clerks Possessioners, The Order of Priesthood, Of Poor Preaching Priests* (*The English Works of Wyclif* 114–40; 164–79; 275–80).

945 *hereto* Refers to what the clergy should do, mentioned in the previous sentence.

946–7 A sentence that takes on the force of a refrain in this tract. See also 730–2, 827–8, 1039–40.

949–66 This long passage, based on a comparison, can be paraphrased as follows: men regard it as a sin to give land entailed to one person to another even though the latter may be in great need and the transfer might be seen as alms. Therefore, how much greater is the sin to givers as well as to receivers when the land given is taken from secular lords and transferred to clerics who are expressly forbidden by God's law to receive it.

959 *with out comparison* This seems a strange expression, since the sense of the passage (949–66) is based upon a comparison. What the authors probably mean is that the extent of the sin in the first action described in the first part of the comparison (944–58) is nothing compared to the sin described in the second part. Hence the latter is *with oute comparison* to the former.

966–7 Hebrews 7: 'Consider what a man this was [Melchisedec], unto whom the patriarch Abraham gave tithes of the spoils. And verily those children of Levi, which receive the office of the priests, have a commandment to take according to the law, tithes of the people, that is to say, of their brethren, yea though they sprang out of the loins of Abraham' (RSV 7:4–5). Cf *The Examination of William Thorpe* found in Foxe III 271.

967–8 Hebrews 7: 'For he of whom these things are spoken, pertaineth unto another tribe, of which never man served at the altar. For it is evident that our Lord sprang of the tribe of Juda, of which tribe spake Moses nothing concerning priesthood' (RSV 7:13–14).

971–2 'After Clement, the tenthe Gregory was pope foure yere. The thridde yere of his poperiche he made a counsaile at Londoun for profit of the Holy Lond, for he caste to wende thider in his owne persone. In that counseile were messangers of the Tartars and of the Grekes: the Grees byheet that they wolde come again to the unyte of holy cherche. There were sixe hondred bis-shoppes and a thowsand prelates, therfore oon seide: "Gregorius denus con-gregat omne genus." He wolde by this vers mene that the tenthe Gregory gadreth alle manere of men. Here was ordeyned that noble statute that was nevere i-herd toforehonde, that all persones with cure schulde be preostes after that tyme, and that after that tyme no men schulde have leve to assigne his tethynges as toforehande at his owne wille, but all tethynge schulde be payde to the moder chirche' (Higden *Polychronicon* Rolls 41 vol 8 book vii 257). Cf *The Examination of William Thorpe* found in Foxe III 270. Matthew's text wrongly has 'gregor the sexte' (*The English Works of Wyclif* 391).

971–82 Another comparison: Gregory X ordained that tithes should be paid only to priests, and priests have claimed this as their sole right and have deemed it unlawful for anyone to hold or minister tithes except them. And if someone should give tithes to people (other than priests) even as a 'perpetuall almes' gift, the clergy deem this a serious sin, a sacrilege, and a threat to the church itself. How much more sinful is it to take away secular lands and give them to clergy when God himself has given such lands to the seculars in accordance with the same laws as he gave tithes to the priests in the Old Testament.

985–6 *(saue Antichriste and his disciples)* ie, the pope and his clergy. Often identified with the seven-headed beast of Revelation 13, the word 'antichrist' is used throughout reformation literature to refer to the pope. The word appears in English in this sense as early as Wycliffe (OED), although King claims that the identification of Antichrist with the pope occurred in the

work of the twelfth-century writer Joachim de Fiore (198). Tyndale devotes
an entire section of *The Obedience of a Christian Man* to a definition of
Antichrist's various manifestations and deeds (*Doctrinal Treatises* 232–52).
See also the Wycliffe tract *Speculum de Antichristo* (*The English Works of
Wyclif* 109–13). A brief history of the term can be found in *Sacramentum
Verbi* vol 1 28–32.

990–3 Therefore the clergy does not have an excuse to say that secular people and the laity rob them when they (the priests) rob the laity by taking their
temporal holdings from them.

996–7 Genesis 3:16–19: 'To the woman he said "I will greatly multiply your
pain in childbearing; in pain you shall bring forth children, yet your desire
shall be for your husband, and he shall rule over you." And to Adam he said,
"Because you have listened to the voice of your wife, and have eaten of the
tree of which I commanded you, 'You shall not eat of it,' cursed is the ground
because of you; in toil you shall eat of it all the days of your life; thorns and
thistles it shall bring forth to you; and you shall eat the plants of the field. In
the sweat of your face you shall eat bread till you return to the ground for out
of it you were taken; you are dust and to dust you shall return."'

997 *goodes of fortune / of kinde and of grace /* In succumbing to Lucifer's
temptation, Adam lost various blessings and goods: prosperity, the ability to
pass on his good fortune to his descendants, and the divinely bestowed gifts
of God.

998–1018 A long and complex passage, the sense of which is as follows: just
as Adam lost prosperity, jeopardized the welfare of his descendants, and sac-
rificed the gifts of God by succumbing to the wiles of the ostensibly friendly
Lucifer, so do our laity lose the same things as Adam and Eve by succumbing
to the wiles of Lucifer's angels, namely the clergy. The laity loses its land,
with the result that it cannot care for or leave anything to its children; moreover the laity breaks God's law, which calls upon secular lords to maintain
each other.

1003–11 If religious figures cannot part with their own possessions or even
give them to their founder if he is in need because they are bound by a tradition that they themselves have created, and if they struggle to reclaim possessions that their predecessors may have given away, so 'Howe moche
more ...' (1012ff).

1007 *posityfe lawe* Arbitrarily or artificially instituted, or as 1007–8 says 'a
tradicion that they them selfe haue made.' Cf Gower *Confessio Amantis*
'Prologus' line 247, p 8.

1032–8 Cf Commentary 297–302.

1037 *priis* ie, price.

1046 *their vyces* ie, the vices of the spirituality.

1057ff *Saynt Cipriane* Cyprian, ie, Thascius Caecilius Cyprianus (c AD 200–
14 Sept 258), an early theologian and bishop of Carthage. He led the Christians of North Africa during the persecutions from Rome. He is the first
bishop-martyr of Africa. The reference here is to an letter entitled Epistula I,
'Cyprianus Presbyteris et Diaconibus et Plebi Furnis Consistentibus S.' in *S.
Thasci Caecili Cypriani Opera Omnia* ed Guilelmus Hartel. vol III pars II
30–1, part of the series *Corpus Scriptorum Ecclesiasticorum Latinorum*:
'cum iam pridem in concilio episcoporum statutum sit ne quis de clericis et
Dei ministris tutorem vel curatorum testamento suo constituat, quando sin-
guli divino sacerdotio honorati et in clerico ministerio constituti non nisi
altari et sacrificiis deservire et precibus adque orationibus vacare debeant.
s[sic]riptum est enim: nemo militans Deo obliget se molestiis saecularibus,
ut possit placere ei cui se probavit. q[sic]uod cum de omnibus dictum sit,
quanto magis molestiis et laqueis saecularibus obligari non debent qui divi-
nis rebus et spiritualibus occupati ab ecclesia recedere et ad terrenos se saec-
ulares actus vacare non possunt.' [although it has been resolved for a long
time already in the council of bishops that none of the clerics and ministers
of God may appoint in his will a guardian or a trustee, since each man
honoured with the sacred priesthood and established in clerical ministry
ought to serve the altar and the mass zealously and ought to devote himself
to petitions and prayers. For it is written: no one fighting on behalf of God
binds himself to secular concerns so that he can please Him to whom he has
recommended himself. Although this may be said about everyone, how
much more ought those who are occupied with divine and spiritual affairs
not be bound by worldly snares and concerns. They cannot withdraw from
the church and devote themselves to earthly and worldly acts].
1062–3 2 Timothy 2: 'No man that warreth, entangleth himself with worldly
business, and that because he would please him that hath chosen him to be a
soldier' (RSV 2 Timothy 2:4).
1072–5 Luke 16:
> There was a certain rich man, which had a steward, that was accused
> unto him, that he had wasted his goods. And he called him, and said
> unto him: How is it that I hear this of thee? Give accounts of thy stew-
> ardship: for thou mayest be no longer steward. The steward said within
> himself: what shall I do? for my master will take away from me the
> stewardship. I cannot dig, and to beg, I am ashamed. I wot what to do,
> that when I am put out of the stewardship, they may receive me into
> their houses.
>   Then called he all his master's debtors, and said unto the first: how
> much owest thou unto my master? And he said: an hundred tuns of oil.
> And he said to him: take thy bill, and sit down quickly, and write fifty.

Then said he to another: what owest thou? And he said: an hundred
quarters of wheat. He said to him: Take thy bill, and write fourscore.
(RSV 16:1ff)

This perplexing parable is the subject of one of Tyndale's major works, *The
Parable of the Wicked Mammon, Doctrinal Treatises* 37–126.

1078–9 Exodus 20:17: '"You shall not covet your neighbor's house; you shall
not covet your neighbor's wife, or his manservant, or his maidservant, or his
ox, or his ass, or anything that is your neighbor's."'

1079 *he* ie, the 'secular lorde' who puts a priest in a secular office.

1079 *hym* ie, the priest put in the secular office.

1085–7 See above 1062–3, 2 Timothy 2.

1090–2 Acts 6: 'it is not meet that we should leave the word of God and
serve at the tables' (RSV Acts 6:2).

1094 The sentence beginning on 1092 is clearer if the colon at 1095 is read as
if it were a semi-colon and the phrase beginning 'Howe moche' (1095) is read
as if it were an independent clause.

1098–1101 Possibly a reference to a decretal of Innocent III which I have not
been able to locate. Side-note 17 does little to clarify the matter.

1106ff The reference is probably to Gregory of Nazianzus (329–89), theologian and one of the four great Greek Doctors of the Church. I have been
unable to locate the letter here alluded to in Gregory's works (*Patrologia
Graeca* vols 35–8; *Patrologiae Cursus Completus* ed J.P. Migne). Certain of
Gregory's letters speak of a disagreement between him and St Basil as a result
of Basil's appointment of Gregory to the see of Sasima. Certainly the excerpt
published here indicates some degree of bad blood between the two. The
Latin text of this letter is found in Matthew 403–4 (*The English Works of
Wyclif*).

1117–23 Ezekiel 33:1–6: 'The word of the Lord came to me: "Son of man,
speak to your people and say to them, If I bring the sword upon a land, and
the people of the land take a man from among them, and make him their
watchman; and if he sees the sword coming upon the land and blows the
trumpet and warns the people; then if any one who hears the sound of the
trumpet does not take warning, and the sword comes and takes him away,
his blood shall be upon his own head. He heard the sound of the trumpet, and
did not take warning; his blood shall be upon himself. But if he had taken
warning, he would have saved his life. But if the watchman sees the sword
coming and does not blow the trumpet, so that the people are not warned,
and the sword comes, and takes away one of them; that man is taken away in
his iniquity, but his blood I will require at the watchman's hand."'

1123–4 *But nowe to gostely vnderstandinge* The author is going to apply the
lesson of Ezekiel to the contemporary situation.

1129 Cf Matthew 25, where the ten maidens sent out to meet the bridegroom 'all slumbered and slept' (RSV 25:5).

1138–41 Malachi 2:7: 'For the lips of a priest should guard knowledge, and men should seek instruction from his mouth, for he is the messenger of the Lord of hosts.'

1148 Remove the full stop at the end of this line for clearer meaning.

1155 There are thirty-one scriptural citations or allusions in the first part of 'thys olde treatyse.'

1159ff Cf 657–9.

1169–71 See 586ff. Thomas More himself corroborates the view that a number of people were slain during this period, but he, of course, regards such action as altogether appropriate for heretics: 'So happed yt then sone after that in the first yere of the kynges mooste noble progenytour kynge Henry the fyfte those heresyes secretely crepyng on styll among the people: a great nomber of theym had fyrst couertely conspyred and after openly gathred and assembled theym selfe / purposyng by open warre and batayle to destroy the kyng and hys nobles and subuerte the realme. Whose traytorouse malyce that good catholyque kynge preuented / wythstode / overthrew / and punyshed: by many of them taken in the feld / and after for theyr traytorouse heresyes bothe hanged and burned' (*The supplycacyon of soulys*, More 7 143).

1172–1210 See 604–6. Foxe adds: 'A bill was put in there again by the commons, against their [the clergy's] continual wasting of the temporalties, like as it had been twice before. ... Whereupon was grown all this malice afore specified; but this was then workmanly defeated by another proper practice of theirs: they put the king in remembrance to claim his right in France, and granted him thereunto a disme, with other great subsidy of money. Thus were Christ's people betrayed every way, and their lives bought and sold by these most cruel thieves. For, in the said parliament, the king made this most blasphemous and cruel act, to be as a law for ever: That whatsoever they were that should read the Scriptures in the mother tongue (which was then called Wickliff's learning), they should forfeit land, cattle, body, life, and goods, from their heirs forever, and so be condemned for heretics to God, enemies to the crown, and most arrant traitors to the land' (Foxe III 341). Although the author of this tract suggests that King Henry was hoodwinked by the clergy and would have acted on behalf of the persecuted had his attention not been diverted to France, Foxe seems to say that it was the king's act of parliament that brought down the wrath of the government against the reformers.

1196 See notes to 1212–14, 1215, 1216.

1212–14 *Emperour Iewes of Bauerye ... Pope Ihone* The reference is to the dispute between Louis of Bavaria and Pope John XXII (1316). Foxe highlights

the story of the dispute: 'After pope Clement V., by whose decease the Romish see stood vacant ... two years and three months, next was elected pope John XXII., a Cistercian monk, who sat in that papacy eighteen years. He was stout and inflexible, and given so much to the heaping up of riches, that he proclaimed them heretics who taught that Christ and his apostles had no possessions of their own in the world. At this time was emperor Louis of Bavaria, a worthy man, who, with this pope, and others that followed him, had no less contention than had Frederic ... in the time of king Henry III; insomuch that this contention and variance continued the space of four and twenty years. The cause and first origin of this tragical conflict, arose upon the constitution of Clement V., the predecessor to this pope; by whom it was ordained ... that emperors, by the German princes elected, might be called kings of the Romans, but might not enjoy the title or right of the empire to be nominated emperors, without their confirmation given by the pope. Wherefore this emperor, because he used the imperial dignity in Italy, before he was authorised by the pope, the said pope therefore excommunicated him. And notwithstanding the emperor oftentimes did proffer himself to make entreaty of peace and concord; yet the pope inflexible, would not bend. The writings on both parts be yet extant, wherein the said bishop doth make his vaunt, that he had full power to create and depose kings and emperors at his pleasure. In the same time were divers learned men, who seeing the matter, did greatly disallow the doings of the bishops of Rome; among whom was William Ocham, whose tractations were afterwards condemned by the pope, for writing against the temporal jurisdiction of the see; as did another, named Marsilius Patavinus, who wrote the book entitled "Defensor Pacis," which was given into the hands of the said emperor; wherein the controversy of the pope's unlawful jurisdiction in things temporal is largely disputed, and the usurped authority of that see set forth to the uttermost' (II 660–1).
1215 See 531–6.
1216 *kynge Steuen* Stephen of Blois, king of England (1135–54). Foxe is uncharacteristically vague about the dispute between church and crown in Stephen's reign. Citing Matthew Paris, Foxe states that 'Stephen, king of England, in these days reserved to himself the right and authority of bestowing spiritual livings, and investing prelates' (II 188). At another point, drawing on a different chronicle, he states that 'King Stephen, having many foes in divers quarters keeping their holds and castles against him, went to Oxford, and took the bishop of Salisbury, and put a rope about his neck, and so led him to the castle of Vies, that was his, and commanded them to render up the castle, or he would slay and hang their bishop. Which castle being given up, the king took the spoil thereof. The like also he did unto the bishop of Lincoln, named Alexander; whom in like manner he led in a rope to a cas-

tle of that bishop's, that was upon Trent, and bade them deliver up the castle, or else he would hang their lord before their gate' (II 184). Such irreverent treatment of ecclesiastical figures may have been responsible for the parliament in London in 1143 'to which all the bishops of the realm resorted, and there denounced the king accursed, and all those with him, who did any hurt to the church, or to any minister thereof' (II 186).

1216 *henry the secounde* A famous and complex story revolving around the relationship between Henry II (1133–89) and Thomas à Becket (1118–70). Foxe deals with it in some detail in II 196–262; his own view of this famous dispute between church and state is found in his preamble to the story: 'If the cause make a martyr, as is said, I see not why we should esteem Thomas Becket to die a martyr, more than any others whom the prince's sword doth here temporally punish for their temporal deserts. To die for the church I grant is a glorious matter. But the church, as it is a spiritual and not a temporal church, so it standeth upon causes spiritual ... and not upon things pertaining to this world, as possessions, liberties, exemptions, privileges, dignities, patrimonies, and superiorities. ... To contend with princes for the same, it is no matter, in my mind, material to make a martyr, but rather it is a rebellion against those to whom we owe subjection. Therefore, as I suppose Thomas Becket to be far from the cause and title of a martyr, neither can he be excused from the charge of being a plain rebel against his prince' (II 196–7). Foxe sums up what he calls 'the causes of variance recited between the king and the archbishop.' On the basis of these causes it is clear that the dispute centred on areas of authority and jurisdiction:

> when, according to the custom, the king's officers gathered of every one hide-money through the realm, for the defence of their own country, the king would have taken it to his coffers. But the bishop [ie, Becket] said, that which every man gave willingly, he should not count as his proper rent.
>
> Another cause was, that where a priest was accused of murder, and the king's officers and the friends of the dead accused the priest earnestly before the bishop of Salisbury, his diocesan, to whom he was sent, desiring justice to be done on him, the priest was put to his purgation. But when he was not able to defend himself, the bishop sent to the archbishop to ask what he should do. The archbishop commanded he should be deprived of all ecclesiastical benefices, and shut up in an abbey to do perpetual penance. After the same sort were divers clerks handled for like causes, but none put to death, nor lost joint, nor were they burned in the hand, or put to the like pain.
>
> The third cause was, that, where one Bruis, canon of Bedford, did revile the king's justices, the king was offended with the whole clergy.

For these and such like the archbishop, to pacify the king's anger, commanded the canon to be whipped and deprived of his benefices for certain years. But the king was not content with this gentle punishment, because it rather increased their boldness, and therefore he called the archbishop, bishops, and all the clergy, to assemble at Westminster. When they were assembled together, the king earnestly commanded that such wicked clerks should have no privilege of their clergy, but be delivered to the gaolers, because they passed so little of the spiritual correction; and this he said also their own canons and laws had decreed. (II 199–200)

1218–20 See Higden *Polychronicon* (Rolls 41 vol 8 book viii 197): 'Kyng Iohn deide at Newerk in the flux, a Seint Calixtis day the pope, the sevententhe yere of his kyngdom ... Bote the commun fame telleth that he was i-poysned at Swynesherde, in the abbay of white monkes. Me seith that he swore there at mete, that the loof that was tho [but] at an half peny schulde be worthe twelve pens with ynne that yere if he moste lyve.' Foxe lists the various theories regarding John's death: Caxton claims that he was poisoned by a Cistercian monk called Simon of Swineshead (II 340); Polydore 'that he died of sorrow and heaviness of heart' (II 341); Randulphus Niger that he died 'of surfeiting in the night' (II 341); Roger Hoveden that he succumbed 'of a bloody flux' (II 341); others that he died of 'a burning ague, some of a cold sweat, some of eating apples, some of eating pears, some of plums, etc' (II 341–2).

1225–7 Foxe quotes 'A Letter of King John, touching the Lands and Goods of such Clerks as refuse to celebrate Divine Service.':

'"The king to all clerks and lay people within the bishopric of Lincoln, greeting: Know ye that from Monday next before the feast of Easter, we have committed to William of Cornhill, archdeacon of Huntingdon, and to Joselin of Canvil, all the lands and goods of the abbots and priors, and of all the religious persons: and also of all clerks within the bishopric of Lincoln, which will not from that time celebrate divine service"' (II 322).

1228–36 Cf Tyndale *Parable of the Wicked Mammon:*

The old Antichrists brought Christ unto Pilate, saying, 'By our law he ought to die;' and when Pilate bade them judge him after their law, they answered, 'It is not lawful for us to kill any man:' ... They do all things of a good zeal, they say; they love you so well, that they had rather burn you, than that you should have fellowship with Christ. They are jealous over you amiss, as saith St Paul. They would divide you from Christ and his holy testament; and join you to the pope, to believe in his testament and promises.

Some man will ask, peradventure, Why I take the labour to make this work, inasmuch as they will burn it, seeing they burnt the gospel?

I answer, In burning the new Testament they did none other thing than that I looked for; no more shall they do, if they burn me also, if it be God's will it shall so be. (*Doctrinal Treatises* 43–4).

1230 *nobis non licet occidere quenquam* The reference is to John 18:31, where Christ is before Pilate. When Pilate claims that he can find no fault in Jesus and tells those who accuse him to judge him after their own law, they reply 'It is not lawful for us to put any man to death.'

1231–6 See 402 and 575–7.

1245 Aston records a public burning of Lollard books in London in the summer of 1432 (45–6). Clebsch states that in response to Leo x's bull *Exsurge Domine*, issued 5 June 1520, Thomas Wolsey organized a public burning of books Protestant tracts at Cambridge (11–12). Another public burning of books by Luther that had made their way into England took place on 12 May 1521 at Paul's Cross, at which event John Fisher preached against heresy (12). Wolsey held a burning of heretical books on 11 February 1526 at St Paul's Cathedral (27). And as has already been noted, Tyndale's English New Testament was burned at Paul's Cross in October 1525 under orders from Cuthbert Tunstal. Foxe tells the following story about Polydore Vergil burning English chronicles once he was through with them: 'when Polydore, being licensed by the king to view and search all libraries, had once accomplished his story by the help of such books as he had compiled out of libraries; in the end, when he had taken out what he would, like a true factor for the pope's own tooth, he piled his books together, and set them all on a light fire. For what cause he so did, I cannot certainly pronounce; but whoso considereth well his religion, may shrewdly suspect him' (v 279). Foxe also implies that the clergy was not reluctant to destroy sources ('rase out of libraries and churches') and documents which worked against their own best interests. The example he gives in v 278 concerns the vexed doctrine of transubstantiation.

1254–5 The most outstanding, complete, and entertaining record of the burning of heretics is Foxe's *The Acts and Monuments*.

1277–9 Thomas More's attitude to the punishment of heretics is not an uncommon sentiment among church authorities in general. In his *Confutation of Tyndale's Answer* he seems to argue for the inevitability of severe punishment for those who hold heretical views: 'And where he [Tyndale] layeth that the slaknesse of fedyng hath caused so many to be burned: I wyll not saye naye but that yt myght haue ben better with some, if there had ben vsed more dilygence in preachyng. But as for many such as haue ben burned / all the prechynge in the world wold not haue holpen theyr obstynacy. But sure yf the prelates had taken as good hede in tyme as they sholde haue done: there sholde peraduenture at length fewer haue ben burned therby. But there shold haue ben mo burned by a great many then there haue ben wythin this seuen yere laste passed. The lakke wherof I fere me will make mo burned within this seuen yere next commynge / then ellys sholde haue neded to haue ben burned in seuen score' (More 8 I 320–1). Later in the same tract, he is even more candid: 'And for heretikes as they be / the clergy dothe denounce them. And as they be well worthy, the temporaltie dothe burne them. And after the fire of Smythfelde, hell dothe receyue them / where the wretches burne for euer' (8 II 590).

1297–8 The treatise excuses itself for its linguistic clumsiness in the same way as the gentleman (678) and husbandman (683–4) apologize for similar traits in the 'olde treatyse.'

1296–1310 *Thexcusacyon of the treatyse* echoes a similar sentiment in *Rede me and Be Nott Wrothe*, where in the dialogue between author and treatise the work claims that it proposes to tell only the truth (57–60) and where it fears for those who tell the truth:

> Alas yett in their outragious furoure
>> They shall coursse and banne with cruel sentence
> All those whiche have to me eny favoure
>> Ether to my saynge geve credence ... (74–7)

1304 *shoren crowne* ie, the tonsure; cf. *Rede Me*: 'Come hither monkes: with brode shaven crounes / And all soche as are shoren above the ears' (134–5, 61).

1305 *With forked cappes and gaye croosys of golde* Cf *Rede Me*: 'A due forked mitres and crosses of golde' (164–5, 62).

1318 *William Tyndale* 1494–1536, England's most significant Protestant reformer, religious polemicist, and translator of the New Testament (1526, 1534) and parts of the Old. For the reference in 1318 see 402 and 575–7.

1321–2 For the date and authorship of this 'treatyse' see Introduction.

1325–6 Cf Tyndale, where he encourages others to correct what he has done or to issue their own translation; the following quotation refers to his work on the Pentateuch: 'Notwithstanding yet I submit this book, and all other that I have either made or translated ... unto all them that submit themselves unto the word of God, to be corrected of them; yea, and moreover to be disallowed and also burnt if it seem worthy, when they have examined it with the Hebrew, so that they first put forth of their own translating another that is more correct' (*Preface to the Five Books of Moses, Doctrinal Treatises* 396–7).

1328–9 John 3: 'For every man that evil doeth, hateth the light: neither cometh to light, lest his deeds should be reproved. But he that doth truth, cometh to the light, that his deeds might be known, how that they are wrought in God' (RSV 3:20–1).

1332–3 But note Thomas More's comments in *A Dialogue Concerning Here-*

sies: 'For ye shall understand that the great arch heretic, Wycliffe, whereas
the whole Bible was long before his days by virtuous and well learned men
translated into the English tongue and by good and godly people with devotion and soberness well and reverently read, took upon of a malicious purpose to translate it of new; ... it was ... at a council holden at Oxford, provided
upon great pain, that no man should from thenceforth translate [it] into the
English tongue, or any other language' (quoted in Deanesly 5–6). The council
at Oxford is a reference to the one held in 1408 which produced what Foxe
calls 'The cruel Constitution of Thomas Arundel, Archbishop, against the
Gospellers, or followers of God's Truth' (III 242–8). For More's misunder-
standing of apparent pre-Wycliffite approved vernacular Bibles see Deanesly
1–17.

1342–4 Psalm 1:1–2: 'Blessed is the man who walks not in the counsel of the
wicked, nor stands in the way of sinners, nor sits in the seat of scoffers; but
his delight is in the law of the Lord, and on his law he meditates day and
night.'

1346–9 1 Machabees 1:57–60: 'It was on the fifteenth of Casleu, in the hundred and forty-fifth year, that king Antiochus set up an idol to desecrate
God's altar; shrines there were in every township of Juda, offering of incense
and of victims before house doors and in the open street; never a copy of the
divine law but was torn up and burned; if any were found that kept the
sacred record, or obeyed the Lord's will, his life was forfeit to the king's
edict.' Two of the four books of Machabees are regarded as canonical by the
Roman Catholic church. All four books are regarded as apocryphal by Protestants. The author was doubtless using the Vulgate in his reference here.

1350ff There are frequent references in Foxe III to the confiscation of heretical
Lollard books, especially Wycliffe's, one of which was the Bible sometimes
attributed to him. Interestingly, John Hus in his 'Testimony and Judgment ...
touching Master John Wickliff' makes reference to the folly of burning Wycliffe's books. In the process he cites the same text from Machabees referred to
on 1346–9: 'it were too foolish a consequence to say, that because the multit-
ide of the prelates and clergy in the realms of England, France, and Bohemia,
do count Master John Wickliff for a heretic, that therefore Master John Wickliff is a heretic. For so Jesus were not God, because the Turks and the Jews so
judge etc. The like reasoning would apply to the burning of his books; for it is
written in the first book of Maccabees, the first chapter, that "They did burn
the books of the Lord, tearing them in pieces, and whosoever was found to
have kept any books of the Testament of the Lord, or which observed and kept
the law of the Lord, he was, by the king's commandment, put to death." If
then the burning of books by wicked men did argue or prove evil of the books,
then were the law of God evil and naught' (Foxe III 59).

1354 *Sathanas as prophetes saye is nowe vnbounde* Revelation 20: 'And I saw an angel come down from heaven, having the key of the bottomless pit, and a great chain in his hand. And he took the dragon that old serpent which is the devil and Satan, and he bound him a thousand years: and cast him into the bottomless pit, and he bound him, and set a seal on him, that he should deceive the people no more, till the thousand years were fulfilled. And after that he must be loosed for a little season' (RSV 20:1–3).

1354–6 The reference is to the period of the Norman Conquest. Foxe is extremely eloquent on the subject: 'Whereupon cometh the latter age of the church. Here now beginneth the fresh flowering blood of the church to faint, and strength to fail, oppressed with cold humours of worldly pomp, avarice, and tyranny; here now cometh in blind superstition, with cloaked hypocrisy, armed with rigorous laws, and cruel murdering of saints; here cometh in the order and name of cardinals, whose name was not heard of before the time of 1030 years after Christ, growing up in such excess and riches, that some of them now have two, some three hundred benefices at once. Here cometh in four orders of friars; here the supremacy of Rome raged in his ruff, which being once established in the consciences of men, the power of all other christian princes did quake and decay, for dread of the pope's interdict, suspense, and excommunication, which they feared no less than Christ's own sentence from heaven. Thus the Roman bishop, under the title of St. Peter, doing what he lusted, and princes not daring that which was right; in the mean while the people of Christ were miserably governed and abused, especially here in England and Scotland, as in this history, Christ so permitting, shall appear. For here then came in tyranny without mercy, pomp and ambition without measure, error and blindness without knowledge, articles and canons without number, avarice without end, impropriations, abalienations, reservations, vowsons, or expectations of benefices, translations of cathedral churches, contributions, annuities Petershots ... preventions of patronage, bulls, indulgences, and cases papal; with innumerable other grievances and proud proceedings of the Romish prelates, wherewith they brought all realms, with their princes, underneath their girdles; insomuch that the emperors, at length, could not take their crown but by the pope's grace and license. ... Then began corruption to enter and increase; then turned the gold and good metal into dross and filthiness; then quenched the clear light of the gospel ... then shepherds and watchmen became wicked wolves, Christ's friends changed into enemies. To be short, then came in the time that the Revelation speaketh of, when Satan, the old serpent, being tied up for a thousand years, was loosed for a certain space' (Foxe II 93–4). For Tyndale's negative view of the Conquest see *The Practice of Prelates, Expositions and Notes* 294. And near the conclusion of *Rede Me* one of the speakers, Ieffraye, paraphrases how the clergy might react if 'the gospell abroade be spred' (3539):

> For then with in a whyle after,
> Every plowe manne and carter,
>> Shall se what a lyfe we have led.
> Howe we have this five hondred yeres,
> Roffled theym amonge the bryres,
>> Of desperate infidelite.
> And howe we have the worlde brought,
> Vnto beggary worsse then nought,
>> Through oure chargeable vanite. (3540–8)

1360–1 *Boetius de disciplia scolarium* Deanesly states that this tract was often attributed to Boethius in the Middle Ages and refers the reader to *Patrologia Latina*, Migne 1844 vol 64 col 1223ff (439), and Bühler adds: 'The anonymous commentary to Boethius [Deventer: Jakob von Breda, 9 Oct,. 1490 – British Museum, [IA. 47809]: Item iuuenes primo instruentur in dictis Senecae, qui multas bonas compilauit epistolas, in quibus iuuenes exemplariter sunt instruendi' (179). [Likewise young men will be instructed in the sayings of Seneca, who composed many good letters in which young men are to be brought up by examples.]

1362 *Seneke* (c BC4–AD65): perhaps best known for his tragedies, the Roman Seneca is also renowned as a Stoic and moral philosopher. The titles of a number of his 'Dialogues' indicate some of his major concerns: 'On Anger,' 'On the Happy Life,' 'On Leisure,' 'On the Shortness of Life,' 'On Providence.' Hadas describes Seneca as 'The favorite pagan of the Latin Church' (*The Stoic Philosophy of Seneca* 1). Deanesly has nothing to say on the source of this reference to Bede found in 1359–65. As a result of my own investigation, I found three references in all of Bede to Wisdom 1:4 (1364): one in *Homeliarum L*, 'Liber Primus' I 12 125 (v 122); another in *In Lucae Evangelium Expositio* I 2566 (v 120), and a third in *In Cantica Canticorum* III 4 896–8 (v 119b). As far as I can tell there is only only reference to Seneca in all of Bede (Seneca's epistle xciv in *In Principium Genesis* I 96–107 v 118a), and it has nothing to do with what is being discussed here (*Bedae Venerabilis Opera* 6 vols in 10 in *Corpus Christianorum, Series Latina*, vols 118a, 119, 119a, 119b, 120, 121, 122, 123a, 123b, 123c).

1366–7 There appears to be an error here which confuses the sense of the passage. The expression 'is as a cleane myrror new pullisshed' does not appear in Deanesly/Bühler (see Appendix) and should be excised here so that the quotation from Wisdom (1367–8) follows immediately after 'the wise man' (1366). The expression 'is a cleane myrror newe pulished' is correctly placed in 1369–70 as a citation from Al-Ghazali.

1370 side-note 22 *robyn hode*: the suggestion is that the 'masters,' ie, the
clergy, encourage the people to read frivolous romances rather than the scriptures. Not an uncommon sentiment among the reformers:

> Their [the clerics'] frantyke foly is so pevisshe,
> That they contempne in Englisshe,
>   To have the newe Testament.
> But as for tales of Robyn hode,
> With wother iestes nether honest nor goode,
>   They have none impediment. (*Rede Me* 1427–32, 95)

Also not unlike part of the statement expressed by the nine doctors charged
with determining the legitimacy of the Brethren of Common Life's practices
attacked by the Inquisition in the Netherlands in 1398. The 'determination'
reads in part: 'there are many lay people to-day, who constantly read the *Song
of Roland* and the *Trojan War*, and other foolish and unprofitable fables: and
indeed it would be beneficial to them to expand that labour on reading and
understanding divine scriptures' (Deanesly 93). Here is Tyndale on the same
notion: 'that this threatening and forbidding the lay people to read the scripture is not for the love of your souls ... is evident, and clearer than the sun;
inasmuch as they permit and suffer you to read Robin Hood, and Bevis of
Hampton, Hercules, Hector and Troilus, with a thousand histories and fables
of love' (*The Obedience of a Christian Man, Doctrinal Treatises* 161).
In *Piers the Plowman* Sloth, a priest, knows rhymes about 'Robyn Hode' better than his *pater noster* (Langland vol 1 C. Passus VIII pp 167).

1368–70 *Algasell*. A reference to Al-Ghazali (Ghazzali), Muslim theologian
and mystic, b 1058, Tus, Iran; d 18 Dec. 1111, Tus. The reference here is to
Logica et philosophica Algazelis Arabis. Venice: P. Liechtensteyn 1506.
Capitulum secundum – De utilitate logice (fol A2v col 2): 'Anima ergo speculum est, nam et depinguntur in ea forme totius esse cum munda et tersa
fuerit a sordidis moribus; nec potest ipsa discernere vere inter mores hones-
tos et inhonestos nisi per scientiam' (Bühler 179). Interestingly, *Britannica*
states that more than four hundred works have been attributed to Al-
Ghazali, but that he probably didn't write this many; according to *Britannica*
fifty of his works are extant. See also *Algazel's Metaphysics: A Mediaeval
Translation*, in which the Muslim theologian devotes part of a chapter to a
discussion of the human soul (172–82). [The soul therefore is a mirror, for
there are reflected in it the forms of the whole that exists when it will be
pure and cleansed of foul habits; nor is it able to distinguish truly between
honest morals and dishonest except through knowledge.]

1376–8 The reference is to Exodus 20–32.

1380 Deuteronomy 31–2: 24–47: 'When Moses had finished writing the
words of this law in a book, to the very end, Moses commanded the Levites

who carried the ark of the covenant of the Lord, "Take this book of the law, and put it by the side of the ark of the covenant of the Lord your God, that it may be there for a witness against you. For I know how rebellious and stubborn you are; behold, while I am yet alive with you, today you have been rebellious against the Lord; how much more after my death! Assemble to me all the elders of your tribes, and your officers, that I may speak these words in their ears and call heaven and earth to witness against them. ..." Then Moses spoke the words of this song until they were finished, in the ears of all the assembly of Israel. ... And when Moses had finished speaking all these words to all Israel, he said to them, "Lay to heart all the words which I enjoin upon you this day, that you may command them to your children, that they may be careful to do all the words of this law."'

1381–5 2 Esdras 8:1–9 (ie, Nehemiah): 'And when the seventh month had come, the children of Israel were in their towns. And all the people gathered as one man into the square before the Water Gate; and they told Ezra the scribe to bring the book of the law of Moses which the Lord had given to Israel. And Ezra the priest brought the law before the assembly, both men and women and all who could hear with understanding, on the first day of the seventh month. And he read from it facing the square before the Water Gate from early morning until midday, in the presence of the men and the women and those who could understand; and the ears of all the people were attentive to the book of the law. ... And Ezra blessed the Lord, the great God; and all the people answered, "Amen, Amen," lifting up their hands; and they bowed their heads and worshiped the Lord with their faces to the ground. ... And Nehemiah, who was the governor, and Ezra the priest and scribe, and the Levites who taught the people said to all the people, "This day is Holy to the Lord your God; do not mourn or weep." For all the people wept when they heard the words of the law.'

1385–8 There is an error at this point in the text. The reference to Deuteronomy 32 is incorrect, since what follows is actually from Deuteronomy 4:9: 'Never let the memory of what thy own eyes have seen fade from thy heart, as long as thou livest; hand it on to thy sons, and thy sons' sons, the memory of that day when thou didst stand in the Lord's presence at mount Horeb' (Vulgate). The reason for the error is clear when one examines Deanesly/Bühler. In Deanesly/Bühler one reads, 'In Deut. 32 . c . it is writen: Aske thi fadris and thei schullen schewe to thee and thin eldris, and thei schulen sei to thee. Also the profete seith How many things he hath seid unto oure fadris: thei schul make hem knowen vn to her sonnes, and the sones that scholen be borne of hem schulen rise and schullen teche thes things, to her sonnes.' In the revised version the *citation* from Deuteronomy 32 has been omitted but the *reference* to Deuteronomy 32 is still there and the passage from Deuteronomy 4:9 follows directly after it. Hence it looks as if the citation actually from Deuteronomy 4:9 is from Deuteronomy 32.

1388–92 1 Peter 4: 'If any man speak, let him talk as though he spake the words of God. If any man minister, let him do it as of the ability which God ministreth unto him' (RSV 1 Peter 4:11).

1393–8 Numbers 11:24–9: 'So Moses went out and told the people the words of the Lord; and he gathered seventy men of the elders of the people, and placed them round about the tent. Then the Lord came down in the cloud and spoke to him, and took some of the spirit that was upon him and put it upon the seventy elders; and when the spirit rested upon them, they prophesied. ... Now two men remained in the camp, one named Eldad, and the other named Medad, and the spirit rested upon them. ... And a young man ran and told Moses, "Eldad and Medad are prophesying in the camp." And Joshua the son of Nun, the minister of Moses, one of his chosen men, said, "My lord Moses forbid them." But Moses said to him, "Are you jealous for my sake? Would that all the Lord's people were prophets, that the Lord would put his spirit upon them!"'

1399–1402 Luke 9: 'And John answered and said: Master, we saw one casting out devils in thy name, and we forbade him, because he does followeth not with us. And Jesus said unto him: forbid ye him not. For he that is not against us is with us' (RSV 9:49).

1402–8 Acts 2: 'But Peter stepped forth with the eleven, and lift up his voice, and said unto them: Ye men of Jewry, and all ye that inhabit Jerusalem: be this known unto you, and with your ears hear my words. These are not drunken, as ye suppose: for it is yet but the third hour of the day. But this is that which was spoken by the prophet Joel: It shall be in the last days saith God: of my spirit I will pour out upon all flesh. And your sons and your daughters shall prophesy, and your young men shall see visions' (RSV Acts 2:14–17).

1408–10 Acts 2: 'When the fiftieth day was come, they were all with one accord together in one place. And suddenly there came a sound from heaven, as it had been the coming of a mighty wind, and it filled all the house where they sat. And there appeared unto them cloven tongues, like as they had been fire, and it sat upon each of them: and they were all filled with the holy ghost, and began to speak with other tongues, even as the spirit gave them utterance. And there were dwelling at Jerusalem Jews, devout men, which were of all nations under heaven. When this was noised about, the multitude came together and were astonied, because that every man heard them speak his own tongue' (RSV Acts 2:1–6).

1416–19 Acts 11: 'Forasmuch then as God gave them like gifts, as he did unto us, when we believed in the Lord Jesus Christ: what was I that I should have withstood God' (RSV Acts 11:17). Cornelius is mentioned first in Acts 10 (RSV 10:1): 'There was a certain man in Cesarea called Cornelius, a captain of the soldiers of Italy. ...'

1422 *.i. Corin.x.* is incorrect; the biblical text is 1 Corinthians 14: 'I would that ye all spake with tongues: but rather that ye prophesied. For greater is he that prophesieth than he that speaketh with tongues, except he expound it also, that the congregation may have edifying' (RSV 1 Corinthians 14:5).

1424–5 1 Corinthians 14: 'how shall he that occupieth the room of the unlearned, say amen at thy giving of thanks, seeing he understandeth not what thou sayest?' (RSV 1 Corinthians 14:16).

1425–7 *doctor Lyre* Nicholas of Lyra (1270–1349). Deanesly states that 'The supreme value of the literal meaning [of scripture], first asserted by Bacon, was again and more clearly asserted by a Norman Minorite, Nicholas de Lyra, who died in 1340 [sic]. His postill, or commentary, on the Bible became the universal text-book for scholars in the fourteenth and fifteenth centuries, although, even within his own order, theologians hotly opposed his principles. His work is important as the chief link between Bacon's attitude to the Bible and that of the Lollards. ... They appealed to Lyra freely to justify their disregard for the secondary interpretations of the text, and Purvey translated and incorporated large portions of Lyra's prologue into his own work' (166). Tyndale is not especially complimentary to Nicholas. In *The Obedience of a Christian Man* he includes him with the scholastic theologians who render the Bible confusing and incomprehensible by their disputing and brawling (*Doctrinal Treatises* 149–51). And in his *Answer to Sir Thomas More's Dialogue* he states humorously and punningly that Nicolas de Lyra *delirat* (134). The reference here is to his '*Postilla super Biblia.* Venice: J. Herbort 1481. Vol. IV, fol. Dddr: "Si populus intelligat orationem seu benedictionem sacerdotis, melius reducitur in deum et deuotius respondet amen"' (Bühler 180–1). [If the people understand a priest's prayer and blessing, they are brought back to God better and reply 'amen' with more devotion.]

1427–9 1 Corinthians 14: 'Yet had I lever in the congregation, to speak five words with my mind to the information of others, rather than ten thousand words with the tongue' (RSV 1 Corinthians 14:19).

1430–1 'The pseudepigraphic *Letter of Aristeas* credits King Ptolemy II Philadelphus (285–246 B.C.) with having inaugurated the translation of the Pentateuch into Greek by seventy sages. ... It is still open to discussion whether this reputedly official undertaking is to be considered the first attempt at translating the Old Testament or parts of it into Greek and to have provided the impetus to further ventures of the same kind, or whether it should rather be viewed as an event which crowned a long series of previous diffuse attempts with a standardised version' (*The Cambridge History of the Bible* 1 167–8; see

also Worth 5–9). Cf Higden *Polychronicon* (Rolls 41 vol 4 book iii 39): 'Tofore the Incarnacioun of oure Lord thre hundred yere [and] fourty and oon, the seventy that tornede holy writt out of Hebrewe into Grewe were in here floures.'
1433 *spanysh tonge / frenshe tunge / almanye / and italy /* Spanish: 'Nothing is known from earlier than the 13th century when James I of Aragon in 1233 proscribed the possession of the Bible in "romance" (the Spanish vernacular) and ordered such to be burnt' (*Britannica* 14 770). 'Bonifatius Ferrer (d.1417) translated the whole Bible into Valencian Catalan but this was destroyed by the Inquisition' (*Britannica, The Cambridge History of the Bible* 2 467); French: 'The first complete Bible was produced in the 13th century at the University of Paris and towards the end of that century Guyart des Moulins executed his *Bible Historiale*' (*Britannica* 14 767); German: 'Nothing is known of the vernacular Scriptures ... prior to the 8th century when an idiomatic translation of Matthew from Latin into the Bavarian dialect was made. From Fulda (in Germany) c.830 came a more literal East Franconian German translation of the Gospel story. ... The first printed Bible (the Mentel Bible) appeared at Strassburg no later than 1466 and ran through 18 editions before 1522' (*Britannica* 14 768). Italy: 'The vernacular Scriptures made a relatively late appearance in Italy. Existing manuscripts of individual books derive from the 13th century and mainly consist of the Gospels and the Psalms. ... The first printed Italian Bible appeared in Venice in 1471 translated from the Latin Vulgate by Niccolo Malerni' (*Britannica* 14 768).
1435–6 *Iames Merland* (1225–91) A layman who in 1271 published *Rijmbijbel*. *Britannica* states that 'until the Reformation, Dutch Bible translations were largely free adaptations, paraphrases, or rhymed verse renderings of single books or parts thereof. A popular religious revival at the end of the 12th century accelerated the demand for the vernacular Scriptures. ... Best known of all rhymed versions is the *Rijmbijbel* of Jacob van Maerlant based on Peter Comestor's *Historia scholastica*' (14 767). *The Cambridge History of the Bible* 2 adds that van Maerlant 'came under ecclesiastical censure for his poem, according to his pupil Jan de Weert, because he thereby made the Bible available in the Dutch tongue' (430–1). Deanesly explains the ecclesiastical censure implied in lines 1432–5: 'Maerlant incurred ecclesiastical censure of some sort for his translation of the *Rijmbijbel*, and the tradition of this was sufficiently widely spread to be known to an English writer of the fourteenth century' (72). She cites van Maerlant's *Spiegel Historiael* 1 3 where he states, 'I have been subjected to attacks from the source [the papacy] because I have made known to the lay people secret things out of the Bible' (72).
1440 *his first booke* Actually the third book, chapter 3: 'As soon as he became King, Oswald greatly wished that the people whom he ruled should receive the Christian Faith, which had proved so great a support to him in his

struggles against the heathen. So he sent to the Scottish chiefs among whom he and his companions had received the sacrament of Baptism when in exile, asking them to send him a bishop who could bring the blessings of the Christian Faith to the English people, and administer the sacraments. His request was granted without delay, and they sent him Bishop Aidan, a man of outstanding gentleness, holiness, and moderation. ... And while the bishop, who was not yet fluent in the English language, preached the Gospel, it was most delightful to see the king himself interpreting the word of God to his thanes and leaders; for he himself had obtained perfect command of the Scottish tongue during his long exile' (Bede 141–2).

1447–8 2 Corinthians 4: 'If our gospel be yet hid, it is hid among them that are lost' (RSV 2 Corinthians 4:3).

1448–9 1 Corinthians 8: 'If any man think that he knoweth any thing, he knoweth nothing yet as he ought to know. But if any man love God the same is known of him' (RSV 1 Corinthians 8:2–3).

1449–52 side-note (Foxe 673): 'Bede translateth the Bible.'

1449–52 At the end of *A History of the English Church and People*, Bede mentions his work on the Bible. He states, 'From the time of my receiving the priesthood until my fifty-ninth year, I have worked, both for my own benefit and that of my brethren, to compile short extracts from the works of the venerable Fathers on holy scripture, and to comment on their meaning and interpretation. These books include *The Beginning of Genesis ... The First Part of Samuel ... Thirty Questions on the Book of Kings ... On the Proverbs of Solomon ... On the Song of Songs ... On Isaiah, Daniel, The Twelve Prophets, and part of Jeremiah ... On Ezra and Nehemiah ... On the Song of Habakkuk ... On the Book of the blessed father Tobias ... Chapters of Readings on the Pentateuch of Moses, Joshua, and Judges ... On the Books of Kings and Chronicles ... On the Book of the blessed father Job ... On Proverbs, Ecclesiastes, and the Song of Songs ... On the Prophets Isaiah, Ezra, and Nehemiah ... On the Gospel of Mark ... On the Gospel of Luke ... On the Apostle ... On the Acts of the Apostles ... On the Seven Catholic Epistles ... On the Apocalypse of Saint John'* (329–30). Higden *Polychronicon* (Rolls 41 vol 6 book v 221) states that Bede 'wroot threscore bookes and eyghtene.'

1451–2 *whose originalles ben in many Abbeyes in England.* **1454–5** *Gospels ben yet in many places of so olde englishe that skant can anye englishe man reade them.* Cf Cranmer's comments in the preface to the 1540 edition of the English Bible: 'It is not much above one hundred years ago since Scripture hath not been accustomed to be read in the vulgar tongue within this realm, and many hundred years before that it was translated and read in the Saxon tongue, which at that time was our mother tongue: whereof there remaineth yet divers copies found lately in old abbeys, of such antique manners of writ-

ing and speaking that few men now been able to read and understand them'
(quoted in Deanesly 12).

1452–5 *Cisterciensis .libro v.chaptre .xxiiij.* Higden, *Polychronicon* (Rolls 41
vol 6 book v 223–5): 'he sparede not the travayle of lettrure and of bookes,
bote evericle day, among the detty travaylle of service and of psalmes, he
taughte his disciples in lessouns and in questiouns, and he tornede Seynt
Iohn his gospel into Englisshe.' The emphasis in this section on Bede's biblical translation seems to be overstated. Bede did make a number of commen-
taries on biblical books, but his actual translations are minimal. According
to Deanesly, his deathbed work on the translation of St John's gospel probably did not extend to more than the first six chapters (134–5). The reference
to 'other Gospels ben yet in many places' (1454) and 'a greate parte of the
bible into Englishe / whose originalles ben in many Abbeyes' (1450–1) is
probably an allusion to the Saxon gospels that date from 1050–1100.
Deanesly states that 'the monasteries of Waltham, Durham, Burton, Canterbury, Bath and Exeter are the only known possessors of Saxon gospel books
about 1100 A.D.' (138).

1456–7 Bede's dates are AD 673–735; for a near-contemporary view of Bede's
life and activities, see Higden *Polychronicon* (Rolls 41 vol 6 book v 209–27).

1457–61 *Cistercien .libro. vi. chaptre .i.* Higden *Polychronicon* (Rolls 41 vol
6 book vi 355): 'He passed other men in craft of hontynge, and was a sotel
maister of buldynge and of other werkes; he gadrede psalmes and orisouns to
gedres in a litel book and cleped that book manual, that is an hond book; he
hadde the book with hym alwey. ... Therfore by counsail of Neotus the abbot,
whom he visited ful ofte, he was the firste that ordeyned comyn scole at
Oxenforde of dyverse artes and sciens, and procrede fredom and priveleges in
many articles to that citee; he suffrede no man to stye up to what manere
dignitee it were of holy chirche, but he were wel i-lettred.' Deanesly claims
that 'The only translations made by the command of king Alfred were those
chapters of the Bible he incorporated in the collection known as Alfred's
Dooms, or Alfred's Laws. He began this by an English rendering of Exodus,
chapters xx. to xxiii., – the civil code. This was followed by that passage from
Acts xv. which describes the enactment of the council of Jerusalem, and
gives the relation of Christianity to the Mosaic law. The other books which
Alfred actually selected for translation were not biblical, but such works as
Gregory's *Pastoral Rule* and Bede's *Ecclesiastical History*. ... Alfred died in
901: but though we possess twelve manuscripts of English glosses on the
psalter, some of them from the ninth century, there is nothing to connect
any of them with his name' (135–6). See Bately, however, who disagrees.

1461ff *saynt thomas sayth super librum politicorum* According to Deanesly,
1 Corinthians 14 (referred to in 1460–2) – 'Many kinds of voices are in the

world and none of them are without signification. If I know not what the voice meaneth, I shall be unto him that speaketh, an alien: and he that speaketh shall be an alien unto me' (RSV 1 Corinthians 14:10–11) – is quoted in a work attributed to Aquinas in the Parma 1867 edition *In octo libros Politicorum expositio* tom. xxi. 369. 'This work the 1882 editors reject as spurious' (Deanesly 442). Bühler, however, gives the source for this reference to Aquinas on the notion of 'barbarus' to Aquinas's commentary on Aristotle's *Politics* (181).

1470–6 *Lincoln* The reference is to Robert Grosseteste (see 790–2). About this sermon Deanesly states: 'This sermon of Grosseteste's ... has not been printed. There is no reason to doubt its authenticity, however, for his ordination sermons ... contain passages very similar in character' (141). Bühler quotes part of Grosseteste's sermon from the 'MS. Royal 6 E.V of the British Museum' (181–2).

1483–9 *William Thorisby* John de Thoresby, bishop of St David's 1347, of Worcester 1349, archbishop of York 1354–73 (Foxe VIII index; Arber VIII 176). Deanesly states that 'Thoresby issued a Latin catechism based on Peckham's canons of 1281 ... for his own province in 1357: and with it an expanded English version, made by John Gaytrik, a Benedictine of York, and known as the *Lay Folks Catechism*. ... This tract was copied into the bishop's register, and shows that a mediaeval bishop could issue a vernacular tract, when he wished, as an official publication. Forty days' indulgence was granted to those who should learn the tract by heart. The original *Catechism* was expanded later, in one case at least by a Lollard writer' (141). Gaytrik's version is found in *Religious Pieces in Prose and Verse*, where it is called 'Dan Jon Gaytrynge's [sic] Sermon' (1–15). In Wells (item 355) one reads of 'The Lay Folks' Catechism. ... Dan Jon Gaytryge's Sermon ... is the English rendering of Gaytrik in Thoresby's *Register* in York Minster' (970). However, in Simmons and Nolloth's edition of the tract the editors state that 'the English version ... was translated from the Latin by John de Taystek, a monk of St. Mary's Abbey at York: it was enrolled in the Archbishop's official Register' (*The Lay Folks' Catechism*). No mention is made of Gaytrik in this edition, although the English version in both Perry and Simmons/Nolloth is essentially the same. I am unable to account for this discrepancy.

1487 side-note 29 The church is probably S. Swithun's. Deanesly refers to one 'Roger Lyne, chantry priest in the church of S. Swithun, London Stone, who owned a collection of the Sunday epistles and gospels, unglossed, in the early Wycliffite text, either before or after 1408' (333).

1489ff *Richard the heremyte of Hampole* Richard Rolle de Hampole (c1300 Thornton, Yorkshire; d 1349 Hampole, Yorkshire). 'Rolle attended the University of Oxford but, dissatisfied with the subjects of study and the disputatiousness, left without a degree. He established himself as a hermit on the estate of John Dalton of Pickering, but later moved to other hermitages. ... He kept in touch with a number of religious communities in the north and seems to have become spiritual adviser to the nuns at Hampole in south Yorkshire, before his death there' (*Britannica* 10 146). Brown mentions that Rolle translated the Book of Psalms along with an English commentary 'into the Saxon dialect of North Yorkshire.' 'This Psalter ... appears to have been written for the benefit of Margaret Kirkby, a devout recluse at Anderby, and came to be held in high esteem by others, being widely diffused in the century after it was written' (16). Deanesly identifies the 'dirige' as Rolle's Latin *Novem lectiones mortuorum* (442) and calls his psalter 'the earliest biblical book to be translated into English prose after the conquest' (144). Aston claims that the Lollards produced their own versions of the works of Thoresby and Richard de Rolle by adding their own teaching as commentary to these orthodox texts, thereby turning them into essentially Lollard documents. Of Rolle's *Psalter* she states: 'while one group of texts adheres to the original, another was produced with many additions and alterations, which was a doctored version' (*Lollards* 209). And on Thoresby's *Catechism* she states: 'The manual of instructions which ... Archbishop Thoresby issued in 1357 and for which he had the same year obtained the approval of the convocation of York, likewise survives in two versions: orthodox and heretical' (210).

1493–5 See the Book of Job.

1495–8 The printed text of Rolle's translation and commentary on Psalm 118:43 is significantly different from the Latin. The English is as follows: 'And refe noght [ie, do not take away] fra my mouth worde of sothfastnes all out: for in thi domys [ie, judgment] .i. ouyre hopid.' 'Many ere rad and dare noght ay say the soth. forthi he prayes til god. that he be nan of thaim. bot that god suffire noght sothfastnes be reft fra. him. for life na for ded. for in thi domys, that is, in pynys, thorgh whilke thou chastis [ie, through which thou chastise us], .i. ouyrhopid. that is, that punyssynge refes me noght hope, bot ekis [ie, increases], it ouyre that it was bifore' (*The Psalter or Psalms of David*). In the gloss on this psalm one sees no reference to 'stynkynge marters,' as the text states. However, the Latin text as quoted in Bühler is closer to the version in our text: 'Et nota quod dicit verbum veritatis quia nonnulli sunt qui pro deo volunt sustinere verbum falsitatis scientioribus et sapientioribus nolentes credere. Similes amicis Job qui dominum deum defendere (? intendebant), offenderunt. Tales si occidantur quamuis miracula faciant, tamen vt vulgus dicit, sunt foetentes martires' (182).

1497–8 Psalm 119:43: 'And take not the word of truth utterly out of my mouth. ...'

1498–1500 John 16: 'the time shall come, that whosoever killeth you, will think that he doth God service' (RSV John 16:2).

1501–3 *Wyrynge* Not identified; Deanesly claims that the Bible referred to is 'some late Saxon manuscript of the gospels' (294).

1503–13 *the tyme of king Richerd the .ii.* (1307–1401) Isaacs suggests that this tract is the source of this anecdote, and I have been unable to find any earlier reference to it. Isaacs calls this tract 'A fascinating document concerning early translations and their vicissitudes' (*The Bible in Its Ancient and English Versions* 148). He adds: 'What Parliament would not sanction was done by the Provincial Council at Oxford in July 1408 at the instigation of Archbishop Arundel, and promulgated at St. Paul's in January 1409. The grim and comprehensive prohibition ordained "that no one henceforth on his own authority translate any text of Holy Scripture into the English or other language, by way of a book, pamphlet, or tract, and that no book, pamphlet, or tract of this kind be read, either already recently composed in the time of the said John Wyclif, or since then, or that may in future be composed, in part or in whole, publicly or privily, under pain of the greater excommunication, until the translation itself shall have been approved by the diocesan of the place or if need be by a provincial council"' (148–9).

1514ff Foxe tells the story in III 202ff, using many of the same words and expressions found here, which suggests that this tract was Foxe's source. Of Arundel's sermon praising Queen Anne, Foxe adds the following:

> The said virtuous Queen Anne, after she had lived with king Richard about eleven years, in the seventeenth year of his reign changed this mortal life, and was buried at Westminster; at whose funeral Thomas Arundel, then archbishop of York, and lord chancellor, made the sermon. ...
>
> In this sermon of Thomas Arundel, three points are to be considered: first, the laudable use of those old times received, to have the Scripture and doctors in our vulgar tongue. Secondly, the virtuous exercise and also example of this godly lady, who had these books out for a show hanging at her girdle; but also seemed, by this sermon, to be a studious occupier of the same. The third thing to be noted is, what fruit the said Thomas, archbishop, declared also himself to receive at the hearing and reading of the same books of hers in the English tongue. Notwithstanding, the same Thomas Arundel, after this sermon and promise made, became the most cruel enemy that might be against English books and the authors thereof; as followeth after in his story to be seen. For shortly after the death of queen Anne, the next year, the king being then in Ireland, this Thomas Arundel, archbishop of York, and Robert Braybrocke, bishop of London (whether sent by the archbishop of Can-

terbury and the clergy, or whether going of their own accord), crossed the seas to Ireland, to desire the king in all speedy wise to return and help the faith and church of Christ, against such as, holding Wickliff's teaching, went about, as they said, to subvert all their proceedings, and to destroy the canonical sanctions of their holy mother church. At his complaint the king hearing the one part speak, and not advising the other, was in such sort incensed, that incontinently leaving all his affairs incomplete, he sped his return toward England; having kept his Christmas at Dublin. The occasion of which complaint was, that in the beginning of that year, which was A.D. 1395, a parliament had been called at Westminster by the commandment of the king. In which parliament certain articles or conclusions were put up by them of the gospel's side, to the number of twelve; which conclusions moreover were fastened up upon the church-door of St. Paul's in London, and also at Westminster. ... (III 202–3)

The 'articles' referred to by Foxe are in III 203–6.

1517–18 Deanesly claims that 'all the .iiij. gospels with the doctours vpon them' was Purvey's English patristic glosses (445).

1526 *cruell dethe* Thomas Arundel, bishop of Ely 1374, archbishop of York 1388, archbishop of Canterbury 1396–1413. Concerning his death Foxe cites Thomas Gascoin's *Dictionario Theologico*: '"A.D. 1414, Thomas Arundel, archbishop of Canterbury, was so stricken in his tongue, that he could neither swallow nor speak for a certain space before his death, much like the example of the rich glutton; and so died upon the same. And this was thought of many to come upon him, for that he so bound the word of the Lord, that it should not be preached in his days."' Foxe feels compelled to add: 'Which if this be true, as it doth well here appear, these and such other horrible examples of God's wrath may be terrible spectacles for such as occupy their tongues and brains so busily to stop the cause of God's word, striving but against the stream' (Foxe III 404).

1526–7 *Richard flemyng bisshoppe of Lincolne* 1420–31; founder of Lincoln College, Oxford (1427). The institution was founded 'with a view to the extermination and destruction of the sects of heretics, who are growing more than is wont' (Deanesly 358). Fleming is named by Foxe as one of the 'inquisitors' who had been appointed in 1412 'to search out heretics, with all Wickliff's books' (III 321). He is also mentioned in 1416 in connection with the examination of one 'Master Robert' 'the parson of Heggeley in Lincolnshire' (III 538). But he is probably best remembered as the individual who saw to the exhumation and the burning of John Wycliffe's bones (Aston *Lollards* 75). I can find no reference to the specific details of Fleming's death. DNB makes no mention of it except to say that 'Fleming died at his palace at Sleaford on 25 Jan. 1430–1 and was buried in Lincoln Cathedral.'

1534–6 *Edward the kyng and confessor* Edward the Confessor (c 1003–1066, king of England from 1042 to 1066). The allusion here is perhaps to a story in *Polychronicon* (Rolls 41 vol 7 book vi 223–5): 'Also this yere, whanne Children masse day was i-halowed at Westmynstre, kyng Edward werthe sike. In his last siknes he sigh a sight, and tolde it to hem that stood aboute hym. "Tweie men of religioun," quod the kyng, "come to me that I knewe somtyme in Normandie, and seide that God hem hadde i-sent to warn me herof. For the rather dukes, bisshoppes, and abbottes of Engelond beeth nought Goddes children or servauntes, but the develes, God hath i-take the kyngdom into the enemyes hondes for twelve monthes and a day, and feendes schal walke and torne about in al this lond. I prayed and bysoughte that they moste, be my warnynge, do penaunce and be delyvered, by ensample of the men of Nineve."' The story is also told in *The Life of King Edward* 75ff.

1538–42 side-note 34 Taken from Psalms 2:10: 'Now therefore, O kings, be wise; be warned, O rulers of the earth.'

1542–5 side-note (Foxe 674): 'The king is the vicar of Christ.'

1543–4 *sainct Austen* Augustine *Quaestiones Veteris et Novi Testamenti* xci: 'Rex enim adoratur in terris quasi vicarius Dei. Christus autem post vicariam impletam dispensationem adoratur in coelis et in terra' (*Patrologiae Cursus Completus* 35 2284). [For a king is worshipped as a vicar of God on earth; Christ, on the other hand, after his stewardship as vicar had been fulfilled, is worshipped in the heavens and on earth.]

1553–6 *heretykes* The reference is to Gratian's *Decretum*, ie, *Decretum Gratiani*, or *Concordia Discordantium Canonum*, a 'collection of nearly 3,800 texts touching on all areas of church discipline and regulation compiled by the Benedictine monk Gratian about 1140. It soon became the basic text on which the masters of canon law lectured and commented in the universities' (*Britannica* 5 432; *New Catholic Encyclopedia* VI 706–8). For this textual reference see Causa XXIV: 'Quidam episcopus in heresim lapsus aliquos de sacerdotibus suis offitio priuauit, et sentencia excommunicationis notauit. Post mortem de heresi accusatus dampnatur, et sequaces eius cum omni familia sua' (Gratian's *Decretum* in *Corpus Iuris Canonici* vol I col 965). [A certain bishop lapsed into heresy and stripped some of his priests of their office and censured them with a sentence of excommunication. After his death, he and his followers together with all his household were accused of heresy and found guilty.] Quest. III c. xxxix: 'Quot sint sectae hereticorum. Quidam autem heretici qui de ecclesia recesserunt, ex nomine suorum auctorum nuncpantur; quidam vero ex causis, quas eligentes instituerint (*Corpus Juris Canonici* vol I col 1001). [How many sects of heretics are there? Some heretics who have parted from the church are known by the names of their founders, some in truth from the causes through choice of which they have established themselves.] In fact Quest. III c. xxxix lists seventy heretics, not sixty.

1559–60 1 John 2: 'Little children it is the last time, and as ye have heard how that Antichirst shall come: even now are there many antichrists come already. Whereby we know that it is the last time. They went out from us but they were not of us. For if they had been of us, they would no doubt, have continued with us' (RSV 1 John 2:18–19).

1560–1 1 Corinthians 11: 'For there must be sects among you, that they which are perfect among you, might be known' (RSV 1 Corinthians 11:19).

1561–77 A difficult passage: Antichrist is responsible for creating more heretics than there should be by preventing God's law from being openly known. As a result, men, fearing punishment, but desirous of God's word, work in private, and with their own wits come up with erroneous and heretical views, views which would not arise if men had free and open access to God's word. If this openness to God's word is not allowed, many people will die in heresy, since Antichrist cannot possibly burn all English books as fast as new opinions arise. Hence heresy, and those burnt for it, are the fault of the bishops who will not allow God's word and law to be openly seen or read. Therefore, these bishops are accountable for all the souls who die; they are, moreover, traitors to God for preventing the spread of his law, which was made for the salvation of the people.

1574–8 side-note 37: cf Tyndale's *The Obedience of a Christian Man*: 'If I must first believe the doctor, then is the doctor first true, and the truth of the scripture dependeth of his truth; and so the truth of God springeth of the truth of man. Thus antichrist turneth the roots of the trees upward' (*Doctrinal Treatises* 154). 'Our good deeds do but testify only that we are justified and beloved. For except we were beloved and had God's Spirit, we could neither do, nor yet consent unto any good deed. Antichrist turneth the roots of the trees upward. He maketh the goodness of God the branches, and our goodness the roots. We must be first good, after antichrist's doctrine, and move God, and compel him to be good again for our goodness' sake: so must God's goodness spring out of our goodness. Nay, verily; God's goodness is the root of all goodness; and our goodness, if we have any, springeth out of his goodness' (*Doctrinal Treatises* 295–6).

1579–80 Wisdom 5:1: 'How boldly, then, will the just man appear, to meet his old persecutors, that thwarted all his striving!' (Vulgate).

1584–97 *Ardemakan in the booke of questions* Richard FitzRalph, archbishop of Armagh and primate of Ireland (1347–61), called Armachanus. Foxe gives 'The Life and Story of Armachanus, Archbishop and Primate of Ireland' in II 749–66. Deanesly states that 'FitzRalph ... was much quoted by Wycliffe and the Lollards, as being a vigorous opponents of the friars. His *De Quaestionibus Armenorum* deals with many matters besides those connected with the Greek schism: the ninth book discusses "that question raised by the

Armenians according to holy scripture, whether, namely, any definite form of words is necessary for the consecration of the body and blood of Christ, and what that form is. ... No Christian doubts that the sacrament may be made as well in one tongue as in another, since the apostles did this, and since they handed on the tradition of doing this. For Matthew wrote the gospel in Hebrew, John in Greek, Mark in Italian, as did Paul the epistle to the Romans ... each without doubt taught that the consecration should be made in those tongues in which they wrote: wherefore it is clear, that consecration can take place in each language – nay more, for it appears that the gift of all tongues was for this reason conferred on the apostles, in order that they should believe that the form of consecration in this sacrament, as with the other documents of salvation, should be exercised to each nation in its own tongue"' (142). See also Pantin 151–64.

1595–7 Cf *The Cambridge History of the Bible* 1: 'It is a plausible hypothesis that behind each of the gospels stood an influential church responsible for its wide circulation and authoritative position. This, however, throws little light on the origins of the gospels, and attempts to be more precise, and to link Mark with Rome, Matthew with Antioch, Luke with Caesaria and John with Ephesus, rest to a greater or less degree on dubious external traditions or on disputable guesses from internal evidence' (269). A succinct analysis of the language of the New Testament can be found on 9–11 of *The Cambridge History of the Bible* 1.

1598–1600 Tobias 13:3–4: 'Sons of Israel, make his name known, publish it for all the Gentiles to hear; if he has dispersed you among heathen folk who know nothing of him, it was so that you might tell them the story of his great deeds, convince them that he, and no other, is God all-powerful' (Vulgate).

1603 *Ge.xvij. and Exo.xiij.* Genesis 17:7: 'And I will establish my covenant between me and you and your descendants after you throughout their generations for an everlasting covenant, to be God to you and to your descendants after you.' Exodus 13:9: 'And it shall be to you as a sign on your hand and as a memorial between your eyes, that the law of the Lord may be in your mouth; for with a strong hand the Lord has brought you out of Egypt. You shall therefore keep this ordinance at its appointed time from year to year.'

1603 *vt patet* here and at 1604, 1606, 1608, 1610, 1632 meaning essentially 'thus revealed.'

1605ff *Hieronimum* On Judith, Jerome says: 'Inasmuch as the Chaldee is closely allied to the Hebrew, I procured the help of the most skilful speaker of both languages I could find, and gave to the subject one day's hasty labour, my method being to explain in Latin, with the aid of a secretary, whatever an interpreter expressed to me in Hebrew words' (*A Select Library of Nicene* *and Post-Nicene Fathers of the Christian Church* 2nd series VI 494). On Daniel and Ezra, he says: 'The Septuagint version of Daniel the prophet is not read by the Churches of our Lord and Savior. They use Theodotion's version, but how this came to pass I cannot tell. Whether it be that the language is Chaldee, which differs in certain peculiarites from our speech, and the Seventy were unwilling to follow those deviations in a translation; or that the book was published in the name of the Seventy, by some one or other not familiar with Chaldee, or if there be some other reason, I know not; this one thing I can affirm – that it differs widely from the original, and is rightly rejected. For we must bear in mind that Daniel and Ezra, the former especially, were written in Hebrew letters, but in the Chaldee language, as was one section of Jeremiah; and further that Job has much affinity with Arabic' (*A Select Library* VI 492–3). Jerome's prefaces or summaries of them are in *A Select Library* VI 488–502 and *Patrologia Latina* 28–9.

1619–20 *Origen* (c 185–c 254), called by *Britannica* 'the most important theologian and biblical scholar of the early Greek Church' (8 997). *The Cambridge History of the Bible* 1 adds that 'He was the most versatile of all the scholars of the early Church; he was apologist and preacher, biblical commentator and philosophical theologian. In all these tasks his primary tool was the Bible' (454). Origen did not translate the Bible, as is here suggested, but he did do extensive comparative work on the entire Old Testament and produced a work known as *Hexapla*. 'It was set out in six parallel columns. The first contained the Hebrew text, the second a transliteration of that Hebrew text into Greek script; the other four contained different established Greek versions. ... The primary aim of the operation ... was to provide an improved version of the Septuagint text – one in which nothing would be lost and much would be gained. ... It has been estimated that the whole work must have covered about 6,500 pages' (458).

1619–26 See Eusebius on Origen: 'And so accurate was the examination that Origen brought to bear upon the divine books, that he even made a thorough study of the Hebrew tongue, and got into his own possession the original writings in the actual Hebrew characters, which were extant among the Jews. Thus too, he traced the editions of the other translators of the sacred writings besides the Seventy; and besides the beaten track of translations, that of Aquila and Symmachus and Theodotion, he discovered certain others, which were used in turn, which, after lying hidden for a long time, he traced and brought to light, I know not from what recesses. With regard to these, on account of their obscurity (not knowing whose in the world they were) he merely indicated this: that the one he found at Nicopolis near Actium, and the other in such another place. At any rate, in the Hexapla of the Psalms, after the four well-known editions, he placed beside them not only a fifth but also a sixth and a seventh translation; and in the case of one of these he has indicated again that it was found at Jericho in a jar in the time of Antoninus the son of Severus. All these he brought together, dividing them into clauses and placing them one over against the other, together with the actual Hebrew text; and so he left us the copies of the Hexapla, as it is called. He made a further separate arrangement of the edition of Aquila and Symmachus and Theodotion together with that of the Seventy, in the Tetrapla' (II 51, 53). In Higden's *Polychronicon* we read, 'Also, after the Ascencioun of oure Lord six score yere and foure, in Adrian the princes tyme, Aquila made a translacioun. Thanne, after thre and fifty yere, in Comodus the princes tyme, Theodocion was in his floures. Thanne after thritty yere, in Severus the princes tyme, Simachus made his translacioun. Thanne after eighte yere the fifte translacioun was i-founde at Ierusalem, and is i-cleped the comoun translacioun, ffor he that made it is unknowne. Thanne after eightene yere, in Alisaundre the princes tyme, Origenes made a translacioun with signes that beeth i-cleped astarisces and obelus, and afterward he made another translacioun with signes and merkes; and all these translated out of Hebrewe into Grewe. Many translated out of Grewe into Latyn; but at the laste Ierom translatede out of Hebrewe into Latyn, and his translacioun is i-holde nygh in every place out take in the Psawter' (Rolls 41 vol 4 book iii 39).

1621 *Aquila* 'About 130 Aquila, a convert to Judaism from Pontus in Asia Minor, translated the Hebrew Bible into Greek under the supervision of Rabbi Akiba. Executed with slavish literalness, it attempted to reproduce the most minute detail of the original, even to the extent of coining derivations from Greek roots to correspond to Hebrew usage' (*Britannica* 14 762; *The Cambridge History of the Bible* 1, 2 *passim*).

1622 *Theodosion* 'A second revision of the Greek text was made by Theodotion (of unknown origins) late in the 2nd century, though it is not entirely clear whether it was the Septuagint or some other Greek version that underlay his revision. The new rendering was characterized by a tendency toward verbal consistency and much transliteration of Hebrew words' (*Britannica* 14 762); *The Cambridge History of the Bible* 1 2).

1623 *Simachus* ie, Symmachus; 'Still another Greek translation was made toward the end of the same century [the second] by Symmachus, an otherwise unknown scholar, who made use of his predecessors. His influence was small despite the superior elegance of his work' (*Britannica* 14 762; *The Cambridge History of the Bible* 1 2 *passim*).

1623–5 side-note (Foxe 675): 'Argumentum doctum et irrefragabile.'

1626–7 Higden *Polychronicon* (Rolls 41 vol 5 book iv 183): 'Also by comfort of this pope [ie, Damasus] Ierom translated the bible out of Hebrewe in to Latyn, and amended also the sauter of the seventy that was thoo i-used wel nyh in alle chirches, and that psauter was eft appeyred, and he translated in newe agen.'

1629–33 See *A Select Library* VI 488–94. Paula and Eustochium, mother and daughter and close Roman friends of Jerome; see 'Prolegomena to Jerome' (*A Select Library* VI xviii).

1632 *.vij canonyke epystylles* The seven epistles of James, Peter, John, and Jude.

1637–8 I can find no reference to an Atleta in any of Jerome's letters including lxxviij., the one referred to here. Since the tract gets the letter numbering wrong in 1633 (see below), it is altogether possible that the author's memory of Jerome's works or the sources he was using for Jerome's letters were faulty. Despite this, the Atleta reference is puzzling. There is a Jerome letter which fits this particular reference but it is letter cxxviii not lxxviii and is addressed to Gaudentius not Atleta. In it Jerome states: 'She is now a child without truth and without ideas, but, as soon as she is seven years old ... she should until she is grown up commit to memory the psalter and the books of Solomon; the gospels, the apostles and the prophets should be the treasure of her heart' (*A Select Library* VI 259). Interestingly, there are two reference errors to Jerome in the version of the tract published in Deanesly/Bühler. All of Jerome's letters are in *Patrologia Latina* 30.

1638–42 The numbering of this letter is incorrect; the number is actually cxxx. In this extremely long letter to Demetrias, a wealthy Roman who had chosen virginity, Jerome writes, 'Love to occupy your mind with the reading of scripture' (*A Select Library* VI 265).

1645 *lex domini immaculata conuertens animas* Psalms 18:8 (Vulgate): 'The Lord's perfect law, how it brings the soul back to life.'

1646–7 2 Corinthians 3: 'but our ableness cometh from God, which hath made us able to minister the new testament, not of the letter, but of the spirit. For the letter killeth, but the spirit giveth life' (RSV 2 Corinthians 3:6).

1651 John 6: 'The words that I speak unto you, are spirit and life' (RSV 6:63).

1653 *Katheryn / Cecyle / Lucye / Agnes / Margaret* female martyrs of the church. Katherine of Alexandria, no date, feast date 25 November; Cecily or Cecilia, no date, feast date 22 November; Lucy, died c 304, feast date 13 December; Agnes, died c 304, feast date 21 January; Margaret, no date, feast date 20 July (*The Penguin Dictionary of Saints.*)

1662–7 Romans 1: 'For the wrath of God appeareth from heaven against all ungodliness and unrighteousness of men which withhold the truth in unrighteousness' (RSV Romans 1:18).

Glossary

Unless indicated otherwise, all definitions in this glossary are taken from the *Oxford English Dictionary*. Words with asterisks are OED antedatings or corrections. The spelling of all glossary entries is based on the first appearance of the word in the text.

abasshe (v) confound, discomfit 447
abreuiate (ppl a) shortened 545 (first recorded usage OED)
abuyson (n) deceit, deception 66, 639
acombred (v) oppressed, burdened 304
adnulle (v) destroy, declare invalid 1505
aduerte (v) pay attention, take heed 169
aduertence (n) notice, attention, consideration 32
Aduertesynge (ppl a) warning, informing 93
aduertyse (v) take note, heed 1147
aduoutery (n) adultery 61
affeccion (n) feeling as opposed to reason, passion, desire 1148
afoorde (v) perform 371
a gast (v) frightened 26
aggregate (adj) collected into one body 760
aliene (v) to transfer the property or ownership of anything; to make over to another owner 986, 1005, 1013; *aliened* (ppl a) 1009; someone from a foreign country 1516
allege (v) cite, quote, claim 569, 629, 1400
allmes (perpetuall) (n) tenure by almes 746, 789, 891, 909–10, 933, 976, 1021; see *almoign* (OED) perpetual tenure by free gift of charity
alowe (v) praise, commend 239
amorteyse (v) to convey property to a corporation, here to the church 1026; *amortesyenge* (vbl n) 764, 912, 1027, 1028

anone as (adv) as soon as 1110

apertly (adv) openly, publicly 1383

apostasye (n) abandonment of religious faith 102

appayde (v) satisfied 866, 878, 882

appeyrynge (vbl n) weakening, damaging 825, 897

Artificers (n) craftsmen 279

ascite (v) cite, summon 1272

assoyled (v) refuted 887

aye (n) ie, eye, obsolete form of 'egg' 255

bare in hande (v) maintain, assert, profess 123

baronries (n) the domain of a baron 217, 763

bayly (n) ie, bailiff; one charged with public administrative authority 1073, 1074

bedemen (n) those who pray for the spiritual welfare of others 366

beheste (n) promise 1002

behouyth (v) is necessary 1560

bering (ppl a) maintaining, holding 1062

boden (v) bid 726, 730

bolstred (*out*) (v) uphold, aid, abet 66

boordes (n) tables used for meals 1092, 1095

boosted (v) boast 127; *boostynge* (adj) 239

bound (n) ie, bond 947

briberynge (adj) thieving (redundant here); first recorded usage (*OED*) 242

busynes (n) care, attention 443, 714; business 1072, 1087, 1089, 1103, 1142, 1594

caas (n) situation, occurrence 207; *case* 186, 258, 1193; *cace* condition, state 369

cast (n) trick, contrivance 1222; *at the latter cast* near ruin or death 19

certente (n) certainty 508

certis (adv) certainly 1021

Chalengynge (ppl a) laying claim to 128

chanones (n) ie, canon, a clergyman living with others in a clergy-house and sharing characteristics of both monks and friars in that some were cloistered (as monks) whereas others were itinerant (as friars) 381

chaunce (n) occurrence; here an unfortunate one 103; happen 601

chauncelles (n) the eastern part of a church appropriated to the use of those who officiate in the performance of the services and separated from the other parts by a screen, railing, etc 1034

checke mates (n) equals in power or rank 642

chefesaunce (n) money, funds 699

ciuilyte (n) in a secular capacity 771, 776

clarkes (n) churchmen, clergymen 733, 741

clepe (n) call 1069

college (n) a body of religious colleagues 1004

collegianes (n) students, here probably those studying for the religious life 381

collusyon (n) deceit, fraud, trickery 67

coloure (n) appearance 800, 999; excuse 975, 991, 999, 1192; (v) cover over, hide 1244

comonnynge (vbl n) sharing and participating 779, 1568, 1573

comodyte (n) advantage, benefit 375

commodytes (n) goods, wares 145

communicacion (n) conversation 516, 644

comones (n) common people as opposed to noble or knightly ranks 246, 332

comonte (n) the body of the common people 853

comonyd (v) communicate, confer 1588

competent (adj) fair, appropriate 284

condescend (v) yield, agree (ironically) to sink to do something 450

coniecture (v) infer 409

constraynte (n) affliction, distress 482

Contempnynge (ppl a) scorning, despising 560

contentes (n) satisfactions (used ironically) or sum totals 297

contryue (v) plot, conspire with a view to deceiving 456, 1161

conuenyent (n) fitting, suitable 404

conuersacion (n) involvement in the world of business and commerce 432

counseiles (n) church councils convened for the regulation of doctrine or discipline 631

counteruayle (v) to be equal to 1022

cowntable (ppl a) ie, accountable 1574

culpable (adj) guilty 1114

cure (*doynge their*) (n) giving their care or attention to a task 600

curtesye (*Makinge*) (ppl a) making a show of ceremonious deprecation 360

cunninge (n) knowledge 1139, 1371

custome (n) habitually, customarily 295

darke (adj) mysterious, difficult 1613

dawes (n) sluggards 1056

deade (n) ie, deed 1661

dealyd (v) divide, distribute 844

deme (v) decide, determine 949, 953, 956, 976, 1064, 1499

deface (v) destroy, undermine 78

default (*for*) (n) for the want of 1541; lack, absence, want, fault 1575, 1583, 1584, 1669

dere (adj) costly, but also scarce 341

despyte (n) contempt, disdain 77; outrage, injury 493

detecte (v) uncover, expose 31, 62, 69, 76, 83, 90; *detectynge* (ppl a) 97

dirigees (n) songs sung to commemorate the dead 368

discomfyte (v) defeat, overthrow 490

disperged (v) ie, dispersed 1599

doutles (adv) undoubtedly, certainly 319

drevynge (ppl a) forcing, constraining 64

duete (n) that which is owing to anyone 189, 450

Dysheretinge (ppl a) depriving of an inheritance 147

echone (adj) everyone 331

effectually (adv) adequately, properly 793

effusyon (n) spilling, shedding 609

empeyringe (ppl a) making worse 904

endowenge (vbl n) to enrich with property 940

endued (v) ie, endowed 110

enforced (v) striven 1494

ensue (v) assure 445

ensued (v) followed 691

entayle (n) land settled on someone in succession so that it cannot be bequeathed at pleasure by any one successor 969, 983, 984, 986; (v) 949, 950, 955, 964, 980

entremedleth (v) to concern oneself with what is none of one's business 1086

entresse (n) interest 444

entryketh (v) entangle 1062

equite (n) fairness, even-handed dealing 321

erldomes (n) the domain or territory governed by an earl, a peer ranked just below a marquis and above a viscount 217

espye (v) detect, see 54

esquyres (n) members of the gentry ranked immediately below a knight 218

estate (n) condition, rank 436, 548, 641

estates (n) people of standing or rank 246

euen (n) just, appropriate 1091

evidently (adv) clearly, distinctly 70

Exchewynge (ppl a) avoiding 432

excusacion (n) the action of offering an excuse 1111, 1296

excyte (v) encourage 1051

expedyent (adj) fit, proper, suitable 463

facciones (n) behaviour, demeanour, ways 380

faced (v) brag, boast 509

fautes (n) lacks, deficiencies, faults 62, 69, 76, 83, 90, 97, 892, 1282

fautye (adj) guilty of wrongdoing 864

fayle (*No*) without doubt 1257

fayne (v) pretend 68; to be reluctant 307; to fashion fictitiously 514; (adj) pretended 71

fearme (v) to rent 7

feates (n) jobs 283

fees (*knightes*) estates belonging to knights 218, 764; More (7 345) defines 'knight's fee' as 'the amount of land for which the services of an armed knight were due to the sovereign; but neither the amount of land nor its value was clearly fixed.'

felaunes (n) ie, felons 775

fell (adj) ruthless 555

ferforthe (*so*) (adv) to such an extent 972

farmage (*in*) let on lease (first recorded usage in OED is *Rede Me*; the second is *A proper dyaloge*) 329

ferre lesse (n) ie, far less (than now) 315

floures (n) youth, but also by implication, better condition 270

for beare (v) endure, submit to 419

forboden (v) forbidden 720, 723, 726, 729

fore goere (n) leader 728

forfendid (v) forbid 806, 819, 896, 1657

forme (n) model, type 716, 729

fortefyenge (ppl a) strengthening 639

For whye (adv) because 258, 572, 750, 902

frame (*put oute of*) upset, altered 23

fraunchyse (n) territory, domain 773

frowardnes (n) perversity 30, 1567 *froward* 1186, 1300, 1340

fructuously (adv) beneficially, advantageously 680

fyrst frutes (n) a payment usually representing the amount of the first year's income formerly paid by each new holder of a feudal or ecclesiastical benefice to some superior. OED gives Wycliffe's work as the first recorded usage 845, 1032

Gatt (v) ie, got 290

gaye (adj) attractive, charming 135

gayles (n) obsolete form of 'jails' 543

glose (v) smooth and spurious talk 734; (n) 788, 1019

gostely (adj) belonging to an ecclesiastical order 7, 395; spiritual 397, 439, 459, 461, 1124

grace (*taken*) I have not been able to find this expression in OED; if my reading is correct, the expression may mean 'had the good fortune' or 'favoured' 1391

grounde (n) the portion of land forming the property of a person or occupied by one as a tenant 710, 731

grosse (adj) general 1474

grounded (v) resting upon a good basis 502, 1155

gyse (n) characteristic manner, custom, practice 1222

halowenge (vbl n) consecration, dedication 1033

hard (v) ie, heard 1434

hardely (adv) boldly 676

hardye (adj) bold, daring 573

hasted (v) hastened 504

haynously (adv) obsolete form of 'heinously' 588

heaue up (v) cast off 1521

heest (n) bidding, command 1077

hold (v) maintain 700

hospitalyte (n) the reception or entertainment of guests, strangers, visitors 340

Husbandman (n) farmer 2, 193, 219, 227, 235, 240, 263, 268, 282, 316, 320, 331, 354, 357, 392, 398, 403, 408, 433, 438, 455, 472, 481, 487, 494, 505, 549, 578, 613, 621, 656, 670, 681, 1145, 1165, 1197, 1217, 1252, 1263, 1280, 1288

husbandry (n) farm work of various sorts 283, 854

Hyerd (v) leased, rented 284; *hyers* (n) 315

hylynge (n) protection, perhaps here housing 866, 886

incontynent (adv) at once, immediately 475

inconuenyence (n) moral or ethical unsuitableness 31

indurate (ppl a) callous, stubborn 1528

interdyccion (n) the action of debarring a particular place or person from ecclesiastical functions and privileges 1200

inuent (v) discover 511

invey (v) denounce, condemn 1046

Iugglynge (n) trickery, deception 55

kaye (n) obsolete form of 'key' 128

kynde (n) nature, ie, after the fall 835, 839

lefull (n) permissible, lawful 1112, 1141

lese (v) ie, lose 724

let (n) hindrance 461; (v) hinder 1398

lewde (adj) lay 1591

Lewedly (adv) wickedly, evilly 17

leyser (n) freedom or opportunity 699, 1285, 1326

liberall artes (n) OED says 'Originally, the distinctive epithet of those "arts" or "sciences" that were considered "worthy of a free man"; opposed to *servile* or *mechanical*.'

lightly (adv) clearly 1370

longe (v) belong 818

lordlynes (n) the condition or state of a lord 688, 734

lordshippes (n) domains, estates, the lands belonging to lords 144, 211, 664, 704, 709, 711, 715, 719, 720, 722, 729, 735, 746, 761, 766, 789, 816, 820, 824, 852, 895, 899, 913, 916, 953, 961 (2), 964, 979, 990, 1008, 1014, 1020, 1026; *lordshyppinge* (vbl n) 777, 785

lyght (adj) unconsidered 29

lymyted (v) ie, limited 1014

lyuelood (n) means of living, maintenance 110, 213, 222, 831, 833, 838, 853, 866, 871, 874, 884, 886

lyst (v) please, care 1185, 1299

make ouer (v) to hand over, transfer 1130

make vpon (v) make open, reveal 1345

mandement (n) command, injunction 1111

marchaundyse (n) the action of buying and selling goods 854

marked (v) noted 205

maumentry (n) idolatry; the worship of images 1349

mende (*god me*) an asseveration 265

mendicantes (n) begging friars, those who live by alms 379

mischefe (n) danger, injury 11, 529; *mischeuous* (adj) 934, 1279, 1327; miserable 848, 907; (adv) miserably

moote halles (n) council chambers 1109

mote (v) might 747, 820, 1191

miskeping (vbl n) improper or faulty keeping or observance 1385

mysease (n) distress, affliction 796, 798

naturall science (n) worldly knowledge 1374–5

occasioned (v) impelled by circumstance 153

occupacions (n) things in which one takes an interest; *occupye* (v) to reside in as a tenant 347, 966; claim 745, 824, 1117; busy 1102, 1108, 1127; *Occupyenge* (ppl a) engaged in 283

ordeyne (v) provide for, equip 832(2), 837, 850, 864, 869, 871(2), 901, 1015; ordered 971, 1458, 1602; take holy orders 1059; *ordynacyon* (n) command 1208; *ordynaunce* (n) 830, 848, 872, 874, 875, 876, 878, 880, 882, 901, 909, 910, 922, 935, 937

orysones (n) prayers 1061

parauenture (adv) perhaps, not improbably 104, 1158

parsone (*in parsone of*) on behalf of 743

perdones (n) forgiveness of sins through the purchase of indulgences 301

perpende (v) consider 45

perquysytis (n) additional benefits 1031

Pessable (adj) moderate, sufficient 275

phariseyes (n) one of the ancient Jewish sects distinguished by their strict observance of the traditional and written laws and by their claims to superior sanctity 57, 752; *pharisaycall* (adj) 94

pleate (v) beg, implore; perhaps argue 176

pleineth (v) deplore 724

plente (n) fullness, perfection, completeness 786

plentuous (adj) both productive and generous 317, 338

pleyne (v) complain 880

poraile (n) poor 1594

posityfe (adj) arbitrarily or artificially instituted 1007

predicacion (n) discourse, assertion 56

precysely (adv) definitely, absolutely 220

prefe (n) ie, proof 747

presonnynge (vbl n) imprisonment 767

price (n) honour 276

priis (n) ie, price 1037

processe (n) narration, argument 942, 1054; procedure 916, 1018; *in processe of* in the course of 912

proctoures (n) defenders, guardians 855

procurators (n) managers, agents 1101

proferyd (v) offered 84

*prolle (v) ie, prowl, to obtain by stealth, cheating 251

proper (adj) accurate and thorough 1

proper (*in*) as one's own private property 735, 762

properte (n) ownership 785

proue (v) test, try 1352

prouocacyon (n) challenge, defiance, threat 85

prouynge (vbl n) probating 1033

purueaunce (n) provision, arrangements, beforehand 857, 863, 891; *purueyd* (v) provided 830; *purueynge* (ppl a) providing 1064

puysaunce (n) power 591

quarrell (n) cause 1278

quarterages (n) a friar's wages or pension received every quarter 301

quod a indeed, forsooth 224

rate (n) value or worth (ie, what is appropriate to their calling) 434

rechelesnes (n) lack of prudence or caution 1009

recyte (v) tell, declare 49

rehearce (v) relate, declare, state 267

renne (v) reign 1677

reprefe (n) censure, rebuke, reprimand 241; *Reprouynge* (ppl a) 668 *rerage (in to)* (n) in debt, in arrears 333

resident (adj) ie, residing 520

right as just as 1346

rightwise (adv) rightfully, correctly 919

roode (by th) an asseveration, by the cross 363

rude (adj) unlearned 515, 678

sacryng (vbl n) the ordination and consecration of persons to certain offices as of bishops, priests, etc 1035

sayde (adj) aforesaid 1189

* *scandalisacion* (n) the action of scandalizing 1266

science (n) knowledge 1366, 1375, 1376

seactes (n) religious orders or a religious following 121, 134, 647; see Commentary

season (afore) (adv) in earlier times 65, 320

sekirnes (n) security 883

sentence (n) an opinion pronounced on some question 29, 96, 1368

set vp (v) put up for sale or auction 292

skant (adv) scarcely, hardly 1455 (first recorded usage in OED is this tract)

slewthe (n) laziness 1594

some what (adv) a certain amount 122

smote (v) struck 1526

sore (adj) grievous 15; (adv) earnestly 20, 931

spritte (n) ie, spirit 1651

states (n) various orders of people 869, 871

stentyd (v) cut short, stopped 595

stondinge (ppl a) as regards 947

Stoutely (adv) stubbornly, vigorously 116; *stowte* (adj) 509

straytely (adv) strictly 572

sued (v) appealed 113; followed (see *ensued*) 695, 707, 787, 796, 898, 933

surete (for a) (n) certainty, fact 476

sustentacion (n) the action of maintaining well-being 280

symony (n) the practice of buying or selling ecclesiastical preferments 701, 932, 941, 1032

take kepe (v) pay attention, take heed 718

tardye (taken) (adj) caught in an error 501

temporalteis (n) temporal possessions 993 (2), 1005, 1176, 1226

temporalte (n) those not belonging to the priestly order 457, 1273

teneamentes (n) land, property 214

tokeninge (in) (ppl a) as a token or evidence 740, 794-5

tourmeyle (v) distress, torment 306

tradiciones (n) beliefs, customs 15

transitory (adj) not lasting, ie, of the world 120

trowe (v) believe, think 441, 717

tryde (v) ascertained 389

tuycion (n) tutelage, care 652

vade (v) ie, fade 132

vayne (adj) devoid of real value or worth 137

vicaries (n) priests in a parish acting on behalf of the real parson or rector (OED states that Wycliffe used the expression parsons and vicars [as here] in Works 1880, 76) 1131

vnavisely (adv) impudently, injudiciously 701

*vnequite (n) wicked, unfair 1092, 1095

vnkyndly (adv) improperly 734

vnlickly (adv) ie, unlikely 1262

vnryght (adj) improper, wrong 1665

vysage (n) face 425

wanne (v) earned 280, 285

want (v) lack 670

warantyse (n) the action of guaranteeing 660

warrante (v) to give assurance of a fact 358

wasse (v) ie, was 1188

wayte (n) watchman, sentinel 1118, 1122, 1124, 1130

wene (v) believe, suppose 72

whaye (n) watery part of milk 307

whit sonday the seventh Sunday after Easter observed as a festival of the Christian church in commemoration of the descent of the Holy Spirit on the day of Pentecost 1408

whygge (n) sour milk or whey 307

will (n) wish, desire 790, 1281, 1422

witholde (v) retain 1071

wolden (v) wished 1374; *wold* 1376; would 1492

woodnes (n) folly, recklessness 801

wote (v) know 247, 693, 733, 1553; *Wotest* 407; *woteth* 1424

wounder (adv) exceedingly 941

wousse (v) vouch, warrant, give assurance of a fact 501

wull (v) ie, will 361

younger (adj) youthfully innocent 727

Emendations

Abbreviations

A = Arber; B = British Library (*STC* 1462.5); O = Bodleian (*STC* 1462.3); H = Huntington (*STC* 3021); C = British Library (*STC* 3022)

30 Though ed: though A, B, O
55 manifestly. O: manifestly A, B
69 manyfestly. O: manifestly / A, B
98 Math .x. O: Mtah .x. A, B
105 oppressyd O: oporessyd A, B
125 theym O: thyem A, B
143 praye. O: praye A, B
150 praye. O: pray A, B
226 falshod. O: falshod A, B
239 *line not indented in A, B, O*
242 thefe ed: thefe. A, B: thefe / O
252 allwaye. ed: allwaye A, B: all waye O
275 Pessable O: Peaceable A, B
284 *lines properly indented in O but not indented in A, B*
290 Gatt O: Gate A, B
331 husbandemen O: husbandeman A, B
338 Plentuous A, O: Plentnous B
363 throode. O: the rode A, B
448 honour. ed: honour A, B, O
549 Husbondman. O: The husbandman. A, B
590 fast ed: fast. A, B, O
612 stoode. ed: stoode A, B, O
617 offence. ed: offence A, B, O

628 contrary. ed: contrary A, B, O

713 ryght. O: ryght A, B

839 laboure. O: laboure A, B

853 and O: And A, B

870 approuyd. ed: approuyd A, B, O

879 vndone. O: vndone A, B

884 clergye. ed: clergye A, B, O

887 assoyled. ed: assoyled / A, B, O

891 purueaunce O: purneaunce A, B

933 allmes. O: almes A, B

935 christes O: chhristes A, B

946 vpon ed: vppe A, B: vp O

946 no man O: no no man A, B

958 persone O: perone A, B

992–5 for as moche as they take theyr temperalteis fro theym. And thys takynge of ther temperalteis in to the handes of the clergye hath neuer the lesse malyce in hit selfe O: for as moch as they take their temperalteis in to the handes of the clergy hath neuer the lesse malice in it selfe. A, B

997–8 of kinde and of grace / as the clergye hath robbed and yet dothe the chirche of thes thre maner goodes. O: of kinde and yet dothe the chirche of thes thre maner goodes. A, B

1018 by chryste and his apostles. O: and his apostles. A, B

1027–8 of lordes / and apostasye O: of lordes / apostasye A, B

1040 Iesu. O: Iesu A, B

1052 lawes. O: lawes A, B

1055 vnhappynesse O: vnhappenesse A, B

1087 entremedleth O: entromedleth A, B

1097 worde O: wor= B: wor[d] A

1114 vs. A, O: vs B

1129 slombringe O: slomobringe A, B

1136 did. ed: did A, B, O

1158 perauenture. O: perauenture A, B

1164 stately. O: stately A, B

1171 slayne. O: slayne A, B

1262 detecte. ed: detecte A, B, O

1264 vnlickly O: vnlickly. A, B

1276 *In* B Gentillman *is in the left hand margin*

1303 langage. C, H: langage A, B

1306 ambitious A: ambitions B, C, H

1367 pullisshed. H: pullished A, B (C *handwritten addition*)

1380 Deute. A: Dente. B; Deutero. H (C *handwritten addition*)

1386 .xxxij. H: .xxij. A, B (C *handwritten addition*)

1392 men. ed: men A, B, H (C *handwritten addition*)

1449 gode. H: god A, B; god. C

1458 Alfred ed: Al[f]red A: Alred B, C, H

1513 othe. C, H: othe A, B

1517 englishe A: enhlishe B; englysshe H; Englyshe C

1518 them. C, H: them A, B

1590 Ebrewe. C, H: Ebrewe A, B

1608 eiusdem. ed: eiusdem A, B, H; eiusdem / C

1611 eiusdem. ed: eiusdem A, B, H; eiusdem / C

1620 CC.xxxiiij. ed: CCxxxiiij. A, B, C, H

1622 C.xxiiij. Also ed: C.xxiiij. also A, B; C.xxiiij. / also H; Cxxiiij. Also C

1625 .viij. C, H: .viij A, B

1626 emperowre. ed: emperowre / A, B, H; Emperour. C

1638 newe. C: newe / A, B, H

1642 Apostles. H: apostles A, B; Apostles. C

Variants

Abbreviations

A = Arber; B = British Library (*STC* 1462.5); O = Bodleian (*STC* 1462.3); H = Huntington (*STC* 3021); C = British Library (*STC* 3022)

33 Which] Who O
33 to be] is O
132 vade] fade / O
164 dayly] duely O
177 ought] aught O
191 oures] oure O
202 Your] your O
257 soules departed] deade soules O
295 of custome] a custome O
306 tourmoyle] tourmeyle O
452 denye] renye O
539 Cobham.] Cobbam. O
567 We shuld no thinge couet superfluously.] We shulde not couett superfluously. O
628 popes auctorite] popes hygh auctoryte O
712–13 seke by a nother waye to attayne it] seke it by a nother way to attayne] O
721 apostleshyp] apostleed O
725 *side-note in O* Ozee.
752 For as Christe sayeth Math. xxiij.] For as Christe sayeth in the thre and twenty Chaptre of Mathewe. O
773 fraunchyse are to gether] fraunchyse to gether / O
831–2 that he may] that may O

837 hadde] hath O

897 any state] any a state O

917 to the states] to tho states O

917 hathe] hadde O

938 leaue] lawe O

958-9 geuen to. How] geuen to / howe O

963 secular lordes / and] seculer lordes. And O

978 and dampnable synne /] and a dampnable synne / O

983 vnto christes] in to chrystes O

985–6 (saue Antichriste and his disciples)] saue Antichriste and hys
dysciples O

1005 nor geue] ne geue O

1055 That the people] That people O

1057–8 *side-note 14* hist. xxi. iij. ca. Cipriane] hist. xxi. [ij.] iij. ca. Cipriane A

1063–65 *indecipherable side-note in* O

1073 *side-note in* O Lu.x

1076 Christ Iesu /] Iesu Christe / O

1087 deades] nedes O

1094–5 ministre to the boordes of poore folke:] ministre to boordes of poore
folke. O

1101 deades] nedes O

1122 god will] will god O

1128 deades] nedes O

1132–3 with pouder of couetyse of worldly deades that they nether] with
pouder of couetyse of worldly riches and so occupied in worldly nedes that
they nether O

1184 ther his ryght] ther is ryght O

1203 Of mattyns / masse /] Of mattyns and masse / O

1258 (as they saye)] as they saye O

1271 Or withdrawe] Or to withdrawe O

after 1291 O *has* AMEN

1295 Englysshe.] Englysshe / H; Englysshe with the Auctours. C

between 1295–6 Cum priuilegio C

1314 thurste] truste C

1318 sore corrupte.] corrupte / C

1319–20 That ye may knowe that yt is only the inward malyce whiche they
haue euer had ageynst the worde of God.] That ye may knowe that yt is not
Tyndales translacyon that moueth them but only the inwarde malyce
whiche they haue euer had ageynst the worde of God. H; That ye maye
knowe / that it is not Tyndales translation that mouethe them / But only
the inward malyce whiche they haue euer had agaynste the word of god C

1325 the] these C

1330–1 not bycause] bycause C

1345 For] Or C

1350–1 the new lawe theuangely] the newe lawe and thevangely H; the newe Lawe and the euangely C

1358 tounge. But it] tounge. etc. It H; tonge. etc. It C

1359 (and we saued shuld be)] and we savyd shuld be H; and we saued shulde be / C

1369 is a cleane myrror] is as a clene mirror H

1372 blinde] blinded h

1384 intently] intentyfly H

1393 Chapter .xi.] the eleventh chapter. H

1407 your sonnes] our sonnes C

1407–8 your yong men] our yonge men C

1413 syns] sythe H; Sythe C

1419 I that may] I may C

1421 ther] our C

1423 forsothe] for soche C

side-note 26 here] beleue C

1433 almanye / and italy /] and almayne / italy h; and Almayne / Italy C

1436 Merland] morlande C

1437 Pope] Bysshop of Rome C

1439 vnto] into C, H

1445 ought it] ought not it C

1449 venerabilis] venerable C

1466 nor] ne C, H

1468 and therfore] Therfore C

1468 into englishe] into the Englyshe C

1471 one] a C

1482 to them] vnto them. C

1485 Gatryke /] Garryk / C

1505 adnulle] admyt C

side-note 31 nature] master C

side-note 32 trust bishop] trust a bishop C

side-note 33 lacking C

1536 oculis.] Oculis errere. C oculis. etcete. H

1541 not ne wyll] ne wyll C

1544–5 Rex est vicarius diuinitatis / et] Rex est diuinitatis: et C

1547 kyng desyer] kyng wolde desyre C, H

1552 men to] men for to C

1554 saythe. xxiiij] saythe the xxiiii C

1569 neuer] nen H; not C

1570 of the people] of people C
1575 and are traytors] and traytours C
1577 cruell] euyl C
1578 dayte] daye H; day C
1580 qui] que C
1581 wold] sholde C
1584 Ardemakan in the] Ardem if an the C
1588 the lawe of ower beleue in englishe.] the lawe in Englyshe. C
1588 Also they] And they C
1589 the Iewes] Iewes C
1591 the lewde] lewde C
1592 her] ther H; theyr C
1594 poraile /] people / C
1595 maye] manye C
1597 wrothe] were C
1597 langages] language C
1598 same contreys /] same / C
1599 or] and C
1599 among the hethen] amonge hethen C
1600 the merueylles] meruels C
1601 knowe] shewe C
1601 none] no C
1604 vt patet per] vt patet C
1606 vt patet per] vt patet C
1608 Ezechiell] Ezechium C
1617 to preache his] to preche the C
1618 vnto] to C
1618 nor langage.] nor yet language. C
1628 that Ierom] that that Ierom C
1629 to women moche] moche to women C, H
1638 and the newe.] and newe. C
1645 the litterall lettre that sleyth sowlys] literall lettre that it sleyth sowlys
    H; lyterall lettre that it sleyeth sowles C
1657 them selfes] themselfe C
side-note 40 my lordes say] my lordes of the spirytualte saye C
1667 in iniustitia detinent.] in iusticia detinetur C
1668 ower kyng / and to ower lordes] our noble kynge and to the lordes C
1672 lettre] lyttel boke C
1673 multyplyed for for] multyply it for C
1673 knoweth what] knoweth not what C
1674 with] by C
1675 vnto] to C

Appendix A

F.D. Matthew, *The English Works of Wyclif Hitherto Unprinted*, prints two parts of this tract in a work which he cannot specifically attribute to Wycliffe. Part one, which Matthew entitles 'The Clergy May Not Hold Property' (382–93), corresponds to 690–1042 in *A proper dyaloge*. Part two, designated 'Appendix' and entitled by Matthew 'On the Wrongfulness of the Clergy Holding Secular Office' (393–6), corresponds to 1057–1142 in *A proper dyaloge*. Throughout both parts of the tract are the editor's running side-notes plus what I assume are the tract's original side-notes, most of which point to biblical sources for the citations in the text.

In the collation which follows, I have compared that section of the copy-text of *A proper dyaloge* that corresponds to Matthew's two Lollard tracts named above. I have recorded all substantive variants, orginal side-notes, and the majority of accidental variants below. All Old and Middle English letters have been normalized.

692 doctrine] lore
692 be laufully] lefulli be
693 But] And
695 doctrine] lore
696 soch argumentes] siche nakid argumentis
700 churche] clergi
704 notwithstondynge seynt] not-withstondynge that seynt
704–5 *side-note in Matthew* Acts iii.
706 Actes] dedis
708 soch worldly goodes /] to that goode,
709 after any worldly] after worldly
710 kingdom] lordeschip
712 sayenge.] saiynge thus:

712–13 seke by a nother waye to attayne it /] sike it by an other title

715 lordshippe or no /] lordeschip,

716–17 *side-note in Matthew* 1 Peter v.

717 not sayde of trothe] sayde not of trowthe

724–5 *side-note in Matthew* Hosea viii.

725 se] loke

728–9 as a seruaunt.] a seruant.

729 of apostles] of the apostles

733 that clarkes] that and clerkis

735–6 *side-note in Matthew* Acts iv.

737–8 as wryteth Saynct Luke in the fourthe chaptre of the Actes] *lacking in Matthew*

741 and namely relygyous people] and religious, namely,

744 ouer thys] ouer alle this

749–50 *side-note in Matthew* John x. and xiv.

752 Math. xxiij.] *lacking in Matthew*

752–3 *side-note in Matthew* Matt. xxiii.

758 sayeth other wyse than it is in dede.] saith here other-wyse than it is.

762 same maner wyse] same wise

764 knyghtes fe] knyghtte

768 belongyd] bylongyd oonly

773 fraunchyse ar to gether /] franchisen to-gydir,

781 And so what so ever] And what-so-euer

791 some wretche] a wreche

793–4 he must loke to whom he shulde do almesse to] he most loke that he to whom he schuld do almes

795 *side-note in Matthew* Luke xiv.

797 will releue] releue

799 thos persones that] tho that

805 another people] eny peple

809 be ruled so] be so rewlid

809 *side-note in Matthew* Cor. viii.

810 receiue it. And] ressavyn it, and no tribulacion to tho that geuen it. And

811–12 *side-note* Quod superest date elemosinam. Luke xi.

813 regarde] rewarde

818–19 notwithstonding at that tyme the emperoure was hethen.] not-with-stondynge that the emperoure that tyme was hethen.

823–6 And though it had be so that the clergy myght haie occupyed thus worldly lordshyppe / and also though it hadde be no destruccion nor appey-rynge of any other state / yet it hadde be no allmes for to geue theym soche goodes] *lacking in Matthew*

838 tedious] tenefulle

840–1 *side-note in Matthew* Matt. vii.

843–4 howe and wher by they shulde lyue. For he dealyd the londe amonge the laye people] *lacking in Matthew*

849 in] on

850–1 *side-note in Matthew* Deut. xv.

860–1 *side-note in Matthew* Luke xiv.

862 vpon theym] *lacking in Matthew*

882 chryst / were it fully kepte.] criste, and desyren in grete party that this fayne and sufficient ordenaunce of criste were fully kepte.

888–9 *side-note in Matthew* Matt. vi.

895 by God] of god

906 oure realme nedy /] owre rewme

913–14 And many noble men because they lacke] And tho that ben lefte, bycause that hem lakkith

917 restoringe again of them] restorynge of hem

922–3 *side-note in Matthew* Judges xi.

923–4 *side-note in Matthew* Mark vi.

928–9 *side-note in Matthew* De questionibus veteris et nove legis.

933–4 And not sue theire folishe dedes] And not thus sue her predecessouris or progenitouris in her foly dedis

939 to swere for to] to swere to

945 vpon payne] vp payne

950–1 entayled to / ye although it be so that the parsone] entaylid to; ye allethough it be not so gouen for euer but for a litille tyme. And though it be so that the persone

966 yf prestes] if oure prestes

966–7 tythes because god graunted them to the kynred of leuy / yet ther argument is voide. For christe] tithis as goodis in a maner entaylid to hem, for als myche as god in the olde lawe had gone and entailed siche tithis to the kynred of levy and to noone other lyne; For criste

971 For Gregory the tenthe ordeyned] For as it is writen in policronicon, the seventhe boke, gregor the sexte ordenyd

972 tythes] thes tithis

983 vnto] in-to

985–6 (saue Antichriste and his disciples)] safe anticriste and his disciples,

992–3 robbe them for as moche as they take theyr temperalteis fro theym.] robben holy chirche, if thai withdrew the tithis from hem, for als miche as thai han take her temporaltes from hem.

994–5 malyce in hit selfe.] malice of robrye and cause of malice in it sijlfe,

996 *side-note in Matthew* Gen. iii.

1012 laye] layman

1015 kynde to] kynde for to

1023–4 for though they be lesse in one chirche they passe in a nother] (for though thai be lesse in oo chirche, thai passen in an-other)

1025 yf] and

1033 of testamentes and money for halowenge] of testamentis, for halowynge

1039 begynninge. No man] bigynnynge; 'Fundamentum aliud,' and *cetera* – 'No man

1057 by] thorow

1057 *side-note in Matthew* xxi q. iij cap. Ciprianus

1060–1 to preache gods worde / *lacking in Matthew*

1061–2 *side-note in Matthew* 2 Tim. ii.

1071 prieste of christ in] preste in

1072–3 *side-note in Matthew* Luke xvi.

1075 must be vntrewe] must nede be vntrue

1076 Christ Iesu] ihesu criste,

1085 *side-note in Matthew* 2 Tim. ii.

1086 deades] nedis

1090–1 *side-note in Matthew* Acts vi.

1094 folke:] men;

1097 *side-note in Matthew* iii. decre in fine.

1100 deades] nedis

1114 bounde] holden

1121–2 blowen his horne god will] blowe in his horne wille god

1127 deades] nedis

1129 perell to make] perelle to lordis to make

1130 slepers in lustes] slepers and slombreris in lustis

1130–1 and in slomebernes] *lacking in Matthew*

1132 deades that they nether] riches, and so occupied in worldly nediss that thai neither

1137 as sayeth Malach.] as saith the prophete malachie:

1137–8 *side-note in Matthew* Malachi ii.

1140–1 offices and busynes the messangeres] office the messangeris

1142 offices] office

1142 and etc.] *lacking in Matthew*

Appendix B

The following tract printed by Deanesly (439–45) is the original English text upon which is based 1357–1673 of *A proper dyaloge.* The Deanesly reprint is based on the Trin. Camb. 333, ff. 26–30 b manuscript, which Deanesly claims is the only complete version of the tract. There are some significant differences between the original and *A proper dyaloge*'s somewhat updated version. The original is printed here so that the reader can see the additions, alterations, and excisions made to it in the 1530 text. (Published by the Syndics of Cambridge University Press. Reprinted here with the permission of Cambridge University Press.) Deanesly has modernized all Old and Middle English letters for ease of reading:

Agens hem that seyn that hooli wrigt schulde not or may not be drawun in to Engliche: we maken thes resouns.

Ffirst seith Bois in his boke *De disciplina scolarium*: that children schulde be taugt in the bokis [of] Senek; and Bede expowneth this, seying children schulden be taugt in vertues, ffor the bokis of Senek ben morals: and for thei ben not taugt thus in her yougthe thei conseyuen yuel maners and ben vnabel to conseyue the sotil sciense of trewthe, seyinge the wise man: *wisdom schal not entre in to a wicked soule.* And moche ther of the sentence of Bede; and Algasel in his logik seith the soule of a man is as clene myrour newe polichid in wiche is seen sigt liche the ymage of man. But, for the puple hath not konynge in youthe, the[y] han derke soulis and blyndid so that thei profiten not but in falsenes, malice and other vices; and moche ther of this mater. O, sithen hethen philosofris wolden the puple to profeten in natural science, how myche more schulden cristen men willen the puple to profiten in science of vertues; for so wolde God.

Ffor, wane the lawe was gouen to Moises in the mounte of Synay, God gaf it in Ebrew for that al the pupel schuld vnderstonde it, and bad Moises to rede in unto hem, to the tyme thei vndurstondyn it. And he rede it, as is pleyn in Detronomie 31 . c . and Esdrias also redde it from morou to mydday, as it is pleyn in his ffirst boke 8 . c ., apertily in the stret; and the eeres of the puple weren entently gouen ther to and thei vnderstoden it. And this thei migt not haue done but if it hadde ben redde in ther modur tonge so that the pupel, hering, felle in to grete wepinge. In Deut. 32 . c . it is writen: *Aske thi fadris and thei schullen schewe to thee and thin eldris, and thei schulen sei to thee.* Also the profete seith *How many things he hath seid unto oure fadris: thei schul make hem knowen vn to her sonnes, and the sones that scholen be borne of hem schulen rise and schullen teche thes things,* to her sonnes. And thus Petre in his first pistile: *Be ye redi to fulfille to eche man that asketh youg in resoun, in feith and hope.* And al so Peter seith: *Euery man, as he hath taken grace, mynyster he forthe to other men.* And in the Apocalips it is writen: *The housebonde, and the wiffe seyn come; and he that hereth seith he cometh;* that Crist (that is heed of holi chirche) is the housbonde, and parfite prechouris and doctouris (that is the wiffe) clepen the puple to the weies of heuene, and iche man that herith clepe other. This this is confermede in Actus of apostilis, there as the apostilis weren but rude men and fischeris thei [al]legeden the prophecies; as Peter in the first chapiter seid: *The Hooli Goost be the mouthe of Dauid [spake] be [fore concerning] Judas that was the duke of hem that token Crist,* and more processe there. In the 2 . c . Peter seith *It is writen be the prophete Joel: It shcal be in the last daies seith the Lorde, I schal schede ougt of my spirit vpon iche flesche; youre sones and youre dougtteris schulen prophecie and youre yonge men schullen se viciouns* and more ther in process. Also in the iij. c . James seith, allegginge the profecie: *Aftur thes things I schal turne agene [and] I schal make vp the tabernacle.* And thus the apostilis, that ben clepid ydiotes be scripture, allegeden here and in many other placis the profecies. And of this it is notabile that the lewde puple in the olde lawe knewe of the lawe notwithstandig that God for synne hadde departed the tunges of hem, as it is opon in the ij. chapitur of Genesis. If god wole, he loueth not less vs cristen men in thes daies than he dide the pupel in the olde testament, but better, as he hath scheued be the mene of Cristis passioun and be the newe parfite lawe gouen to vs; and herfore on the witsondaie he gaf to many diuerse nac[i]ouns knowing of his lawe be [their] one tunge, in tokene that he wolde alle men knewe his lawe, to his worschipe and her profite. Ffor, as it is writen in the boke of Numbers, the II. c . wane Moises had choson seuenty elder men and the spirite of God rested on hem and thei profecieden, twey men, as Eldad and Medad, profeciden in castelis, and on seid to Moises: *Sir forbede hem* and he seide *Wat, enviest thu for me? w[h]o schal lette that alle the puple profecie, if god gif hem his spirite?* and in actus of apostilis, the II . c ., seith Peter, wane he had cristened Cornelie, and his felowes repreued hym therof, for he was an hethen man, he seid to hem, *If God hath gouen to hem the same grace that he hath geuen to vs, wiche beleuen in our Lorde Ihesu Crist, w[h]o am I that may forbede God.* And sent Poule seith in I Cor. 14 . c . *I wole euery man to speike with tunges more forsothe to profecie.* Also he seith: *I schal preye with spirit and I schal preie with mynde,* that is with affeccoun and with vndurstandinge; and this is myche better than al onli to haue deuocioun in wordes and not in vndurstanding. And this preueth the texte aftur, that seith: *how schal he sei amen vpon this blessing that wot not wat thu seiste?* and on this seith the doctor Lire. If the puple vnderstood the preyour of the prest, it schal the better be lade in to God and the more deu-outelie answere *amen.* Also in the same chapeter he seith: *I wole rather fyue wordes be spoken to the vndurstanding of men, than ten thousand that the[y] vnderstonden not.*

Also seuenti doctouris, with outen mo, by fore the incarnacioun translati-den the Bibile into Greek ougt of Ebrew; and aftur the ascencoun many trans-latiden al the Byble, summe into Greek and summe into Latyne. But seint Ierom translatide it out of Ebrew in to Latyne: w[h]os translacioun we vsen most. And so it was translated in to Spaynesche tunge, Frensche tunge and Alemayne; and other londes also han the Bibel in ther modur tunge, as Italie hath it in Latyn; for that is ther modur tonge, and be many yeeris han had. Worschipful Bede in his first boke *De Gestis Angulorum* 2 . c. tellith that seint Oswold kyng of Northeumberlond axide of the Scottys an holi pischop Aydan to preche his puple, and the kynge of hym self interpreted it on Englische to the puple. If this blessid dede be aloued to the kynge of al hooli chirche, how not now as wel augte it to be alowed a man to rede the gospel on Englische and do ther aftur? It was herde of a worthi man of Almaine, that summe tyme a Flemynge (his name was James Merland) translatid al the Bibel into Flemyche, for wiche dede he was somoned before the pope of grete enmyte, and the boke was taken to examynacoun and trwly apreued; it was deliuered to hym agene in conficioun to his enmyes. Also venerabile Bede, lede by the spirit of God, translatid the Bibel or a grete parte of the Bibile, w[h]os originals ben in many abbeis in Englond. And Sistrence in his fifte booke the 24. c . seith the euangelie of Jon was drawen into Englice be the for seide Bede; wiche euengelie of Ion and other gospellis ben y[e]t in many pla-cis, of so oolde Englische that vnnethe can any man rede hem; ffor this Bede regnede an hooly doctor aftur the incarnacoun seuene hundered yeer and xxxij. Also a man of Loundon, his name was Wyring, hadde a Bible in Englische of northen speche, wiche was seen of many men, and it semed too honndred yeer olde. Also sent Poule seith: *If our gospel is hid it is hid to hem that schal be dampned;* and eft he seith *he that knoweth not schal not be knowen of God.* Also Cistrence in his sext bok the i. c . seith that Al[f]rede

the kynge ordined opone scolis of diuerse artes in Oxenforde; and he turnede
the best lawes in to his modir tunge, and the sawter also; and he regned aftur
the incarnacioun eigt hundered yeer and seuenti and thre. Also seint Thomas
[Aquinas] seith that barbarus is he that vnderstandith not that he redeth in
his modor tunge and therfore, seith the apostile, *If I knewe not the vertu of
the voice to wome I speike, I schal be to hym barbarus and he that speiketh
to me barbarus,* that is to sey, he vnderstandith not that I sey, ne I vnderstande not wat he seith. Sum men thenkyne hem to be barbaros wiche han
not propur vnderstan[din]ge of that thei reden, to answere therto in her
modor tunge. Also he seith that Bede drew in to Englische the liberal artis,
leste Engliche men schuldon be holden barbarus. This seint Thomas, *super
primum posecicorum,* exponens hoc vocabulum Barbarus. Also the grett
sutil clerk Lyncolne seith in a sermon that bigynneth *Scriptum est de leuitis;*
If (he seith) any prest seie he can not preche, oo remedie is, resyne he vp his
benefice; another remedie is, if he wol not thus, record he in the woke the
nakid tixt of the sonndaie gospel, that he kunne the groos story and telle it to
his puple; that is, if he vndurstonde Latyne; and so [do] he this euery woke of
the yeer, and for sothe he schal profite wel. For thus preched the lord seyng,
Joh. 6 , *The wordes that I speike to youg ben spirit and lyf.* If for sothe he
vnderstode no Latyn, go he to oon of his neigtboris that vnderstandith, wiche
wole charitabily expone it to hym; and thus edifie he his flock, that is his
puple. Thus seith Lyncolne, and on this argueth a clerk and seith: If it is leue-
ful to preche the naked text to the pupel, it is also lefful to write it to hem;
and consequentliche, be proces of tyme, so al the Bibil. Also a nobil hooly
man, Richerde E[r]myte, drewe oon Englice the sauter, with a glose of longe
proces and lessouns of *dirige* and many other tretis, by wiche many Engliche
men hau ben gretli edified. And if he were cursed of God that wolde the
puple schulde be lewder either wors than thei ben. Also sire Wiliam Thorisby, erchebischop of York, did do to drawe a tretys in Englisce be a worschipful clerk w[h]os name was Gaytrik; in the wiche weren conteyned the
articulis of the feith, seuene dedli synnes, the werkes of mercy and the
comandements; and sente hem in smale pagynes to the comyn puple to lerne
this and to know this, of wiche ben yit manye a componye in Englond.

But ther ben summe that seien: If the gospel were on Engliche, men
mygten ligtly erre therinne. But wel touchith this holi man Richad Hampol
suche men expownyng this tixte: *Ne auferas de ore meo verbum veritatis
vsquequaque,* ther he seith thus: Ther ben not fewe but many wolen sustene
a worde of falsenes for God, not willing to beleue to konynge and better than
thei ben. Thei ben like to the frendes of Job: that, wiles thei enforsiden hem
to defende God, they offendeden greuosly in hym; and, thoug suche ben
slayne and don myracles, thei neuertheles ben stynkyng martirs. And to hem

that seien that the gospel on Enliche wolde make men to erre, wyte wele that
we fynden in Latyne mo heretikes than of ale other langagis; ffor the *Decres*
rehersith sixti Latyn eretikes. Also the hooli euengelistis writen the gospell
in diuerse langages, as Matheu in Indee, Marke in Ytalie, Luck in the partyes
of Achaie, and John in Asie aftur he hadde writun the Apocalips in the yle of
Pathomos; and al thes writun in the langage of the same cuntre, as seith Ardmakan. Also Ardmakan in the *Book of questiouns* seith that the sacrament
mai wel be made in iche comoun langage; for so (as he seith) diden the apostilis. But we coueteyten not that, but prey Anticrist that we moten haue oure
bileue in Englische. Also we that han moche comyned with the Jewis knowen wel that al mygty men of hem, in wat londe they ben born, yit they han
in Ebrew the Bible, and thei ben more actif of the olde lawe thane any Latyn
man comonli; yhe, as wel the lewde men of the Jewes: as prestis. But it is red
in comyne of the prestes, to fulfille ther prestes office and to edificacoun of
porayle that for slouthe stoudieth nogt. And the Grekis, wiche ben nobel
men, han al this in ther owne langage. But yit aduersaries of trewith seien,
wane men rehersen that Grekis and Latyns han al in ther owne langage, the
clerkis of hem speiken grammaticalliche and the puple vnderstondith it not.
Witte thei that, thoug a clerke or another man thus lerned can sette his wordis or Engliche better than a rewde man, it foloweth not her of that oure langage schuld be destried. It were al on[e] to sei this, and to kitte oute the
tunges of hem that can not speke thus curiosly. But thei schulde vnderstonde
that 'grammaticaliche' is not ellis but abite of rigt spekyng and rigt pronoun-
syng and rigt wrytinge.

But Frere Tille, that seide before thi buschop of Londoun, heerynge an hun-
drid men, that Jerom seide he errid in translatyng of the Bibel, is lyk to Ely-
mas, the wiche wolde haue lettid a bischope or a Juge to heere the byleue; to
w[h]om Poule seid: *O thou ful of al trecherie, and of al false teching* to turne
the buschop from the beleue, *thou schalt be blynde to a tyme.* This [is]
writun in the Dedus of the apostilis 13 . c . Ffor Jerom seith in the prolog of
Kynges: I am not knowyng to my self in any maner me to haue [erred, in]
changyng any thinge from the Ebrew trewith. Wel I wot, he seide sum tyme
that holy writ was false aftur the letter. But aftur, wane Austyn hadde writen
to him, and he to him agen, he grauntid wele that it was trewe, as he rehersith in a pistle, and in the Prolog of the Bibel; and was glad and ioyeful of his
translacoun; and therfor, wane he hath rehersithd al the bookis of the Bibel,
thane he seith in the Prolog of Penteteuke: I praie the, dere brother, lyue
amonge these, haue thi meditacoun in these, knowe noon other thing but
these. But Jerom hadde many enemyes for translating of the Bibel, as he
rehersith in the ffirst Prolog, to his enemyes thus: Whi art thou turmented be
[*sic*] enmeye? what stirist thou the willes of vnkunnynge men agens me? if it

semeth to the that I haue erred in myn translacion: aske the Ebrew councel, with the maisteris of diuerse citees. In the secunde Prolog he seith this: We seeyn (rehersing the sentence bifore), leest we ben seen to holde oure pes agens the ba[ckbi]tourus. And in the same he seith: We, hasting to oure contre, schullen passe with a deffe eere to the dedly soungyis of the mermaidens. And thus in many prologis he scorneth his enemyes and lettith not his hooly werk. But [he] seith: *I seide I schal kepe my weies that I trespas not in my tounge: I haue put keping to my mouthe wane the synfulman hath stande agens me.* These ben the wordis of Ierom rehersing the profigte.

Also it is knowen to many men that in the tyme of Kyng Richerd, whose soule God a soile, in to a parliment was put a bille be assent of two erchebischopis and of the clergie to anulle the Bibel that tyme translatid in to Engliche, and also other bokis of the gospel translatid in to Engliche; wiche, wanne it was seyn of lordis and comouns, the good duke of Lancastre Ion (w[h]os soule God asoile, for his mercy) answered ther to sharpely, seying this sentence: we wel not be the refuse of alle men; for, sithen other naciouns had Goddis lawe, wiche is lawe of oure byleue, in ther owne modur langage, we wolone haue oure in Engliche, w[h]o that euere it begrucche; and this he affermede with a grete othe.

Also the bischope of Caunturbiri, Thomas Arrundel, that nowe is, seide a sermon in Westimister there as weren many hundred puple, at the biriyng of quene Anne, (of w[h]os soule God haue mercy); and, in his comendynges of hir, he seide it was more Ioie of hir than of any whoman that euere he knewe; ffor, not withstanding that sche was an alien borne, sche hadde on Engliche al the foure gospeleris with the docturis vpon hem, and he seide sche hadde sent hem vnto him, and he seide thei weren goode and trewe, and comended hir in that sche was so grete a lady and also an alien, and wolde so lowliche studiee in so vertuous bokis. And he blamed in that sermoun scharpeli the necligence of prelatis and of other men, in so miche that summe seiden he wolde on the morowe leue vp his office of chaunceler and forsake the worlde; and than it hadde be the last sermoun that euere thei herde.

Bibliography

Those interested in Tyndale scholarship eagerly await the critical edition of his works now in preparation for the Catholic University of America Press under the general editorship of Anne M. O'Donnell, SND. Until volumes of that edition appear, critics will have to be satisfied with the Parker Society three-volume edition listed in my bibliography.

Editions of *A proper dyaloge* or parts thereof

A proper dyaloge betwene a Gentillman and an Husband man eche com-playnenge to other theyr mysreable calamyte through the ambicion of the clergye. 1529–30 Bodleian STC 1462.3

A proper dyaloge betwene a gentillman and a husbandman eche com-playnynge to other their misreable calamite through the ambicion of the clergye. 1530 British Library STC 1462.5

A compendious olde treatyse shewynge howe that we ought to haue the scripture in Englysshe. 1530 Huntington STC 3021

A compendyous Olde treatyse shewynge, howe that we ought to haue the Scripture in Englyshe with the Auctours. c.1538 British Library STC 3022

Reprints: *A proper dyaloge ...* ed F. Fry (London: Willis and Sotheran 1863); *A proper dyaloge ...* ed Edward Arber *English Reprints* 6 (London 1871; rpt New York: AMS Press 1966) 129–84; *Agens hem that seyn that hooli wrigt schulde not or may not be drawun in to Engliche: we maken thes resouns* (rpt in Deanesly of an original version of *A compendious olde treatyse*) 439–45; a sixteenth century version of *A compendious olde treatyse* is reprinted in Foxe IV 671–6; Bühler's version of the text is in *Medium Aevum* 7:3 (October 1938) 170–83.

Other References

Algazel's Metaphysics: A Mediaeval Translation ed Rev J.T. Muckle (Toronto: St Michael's College 1933)

Al-Ghazali's Book of Fear and Hope ed William McKane (Leiden: E.J. Brill 1962)

Ames, Joseph *Typographical Antiquities or The History of Printing in England, Scotland, and Ireland* 4 vols ed Thomas F. Dibdin; facsimile of 3rd ed 1810–19 (Hildesheim: Georg Olms Verlagsbuchhandlung 1969)

Arber, Edward *English Reprints* vol 8 (London 1871; rpt New York: ams Press 1966)

Aston, Margaret *Lollards and Reformers: Images and Literacy in Late Medieval Religion* (London: Hambledon Press 1984)

– *Thomas Arundel: A Study of Church Life in the Reign of Richard II* (Oxford: Clarendon Press 1967)

Ballads from Manuscript ed Frederick Furnivall 2 vols (London: Taylor 1868–73; rpt New York: AMS Press 1968)

Barlowe, Jerome, and William Roye *Rede Me and Be Nott Wrothe* ed Douglas H. Parker (Toronto, Buffalo, London: University of Toronto Press 1992)

Barnes, Robert *A supplicatyon made by Robert Barnes vnto henrye the eyght* 1531 (STC 1470)

Bately, Janet 'Lexical Evidence for the Authorship of the Prose Psalms in the Paris Psalter' *Anglo-Saxon England* 10 (1982) 69–95

Bedae Venerabilis Opera 6 vols in 10 *Corpus Christianorum, Series Latina* 111 vols (Turnholti: Brepols Editores Pontificii 1953–83)

Bede *A History of the English Church and People* trans Leo Sherley-Price (Harmondsworth: Penguin 1955; rpt 1962)

The Bible in Its Ancient and English Versions ed H. Wheeler Robinson (1940; rpt Westport, Connecticut: Greenwood Press 1970)

Brant, Sebastian *The Ship of Fools* trans Edwin H. Zeydel (New York: Columbia University Press 1944; rpt Dover Press 1962)

Brown, John *The History of the English Bible* (London: Cambridge University Press 1912)

Bruce, F.F. *The English Bible: A History of Translations from the Earliest English Versions to the New English Bible* (New York: Oxford University Press 1970)

Bühler, Curt F. 'A Lollard Tract: On Translating the Bible into English' *Medium Aevum* 7 (October 1938) 167–83

Burke, Peter 'The Renaissance Dialogue' *Renaissance Studies* 3 (1989) 1–12

The Cambridge History of the Bible ed P.R. Ackroyd and C.F. Evans vol 1 (Cambridge: University Press 1970)

The Cambridge History of the Bible ed G.W.H. Lampe vol 2 (Cambridge: University Press 1969)

Cavendish, George *Thomas Wolsey, Late Cardinal. His Life and Death Written by George Cavendish his Gentleman-Usher* ed Roger Lockyer (London: Folio Society 1962)

Chuilleanáin, Eiléan Ní 'The Debate between Thomas More and William Tyndale 1528–33: Ideas in Literature and Religion' *Journal of Ecclesiastical History* 39 (1988) 382–411

Clark, James Andrew 'The Bible, History, and Authority in Tyndale's *The Practice of Prelates*' *Moreana* 28 (July 1991) 105–17

Clebsch, William A. *England's Earliest Protestants 1520–1535* (New Haven and London: Yale University Press 1964)

Cole, Howard C. *A Quest of Inquirie: Some Contexts of Tudor Literature* (Indianapolis and New York: Bobbs-Merrill 1973)

Corpus Juris Canonici ed Aemelius Friedberg and Aemelius Richter 2 vols (Leipzig: Editio Anastatice Repeteta 1879)

Corpus Scriptorum Ecclesiasticorum Latinorum (Vienna 1868; rpt New York: Johnson Reprint 1965)

Coulton, G.G. *Five Centuries of Religion* 4 vols (Cambridge: University Press 1923–50)

The Crisis of Church and State 1050–1300 ed Brian Tierney (New York: Prentice-Hall 1964; rpt Toronto, Buffalo, London: University of Toronto Press 1988)

CWE = *Collected Works of Erasmus* vol 27: *Praise of Folly* ed Betty Radice (Toronto, Buffalo, London: University of Toronto Press 1986)

Daniell, David *William Tyndale: A Biography* (New Haven: Yale University Press 1994)

Day, John T. 'Proper Guidance in Reading the Bible: Tyndale's *A Pathway into the Holy Scripture*' *Moreana* 28 (July 1991) 131–43

Deakins, Roger 'The Tudor Prose Dialogue: Genre and Anti-Genre' *Studies in English Literature* 20:1 (1980) 5–24

Deanesly, Margaret *The Lollard Bible and Other Medieval Biblical Versions* (London: Cambridge University Press 1920; rpt 1966)

Deanesly/Bühler: see pp 111–12 note 21

Demaus, Robert *William Tyndale: A Biography* (London: The Religious Tract Society 1871)

Dick, John A.R. '"To Dig the Wells of Abraham": Philology, Theology, and Scripture in Tyndale's *The Parable of the Wicked Mammon*' *Moreana* 28 (July 1991) 39–52

– '"To Trye his True Frendes": Imagery as Argument in Tyndale's *The Parable of the Wicked Mammon*' *Moreana* 28 (July 1991) 69–82

Dickens, A.G. *The English Reformation* (1964; 2nd ed London: Batsford 1989)

Dicta Lincolniensis: A Selection of the 'Dicta Theologica' of Robert Grosseteste ed Gordon Jackson (Lincoln: Grosseteste Press 1972)

Dictionary of National Biography ed Sir Leslie Stephen and Sir Sidney Lee 63 vols (1885–1901; rpt London: Oxford University Press 1921–2)

Documents Illustrative of English Church History ed Henry Gee and William John Hardy (London: Macmillan 1910; rpt New York: Kraus Reprint 1972)

Donaldson, E. Talbot 'Chaucer the Pilgrim' *Chaucer Criticism* ed Richard Schoeck and Jerome Taylor (Notre Dame, Indiana: University of Notre Dame Press 1960) 1–13

Elton, G.R. *Reform and Reformation* (London: Arnold 1977)

English Lyrics of the Thirteenth Century ed Carleton Brown (Oxford: Clarendon Press 1932; rpt 1953)

The English Reformation Revised ed Christopher Haigh (Cambridge: University Press 1987)

The English Works of Wyclif Hitherto Unpublished ed F.D. Matthew (London: Kegan Paul, Trench, Trubner; EETS 1880; rpt Millwood, New York: Kraus Reprint 1973)

Eusebius *The Ecclesiastical History* vol 1 trans Kirsopp Lake; vol 2 trans J.E.L. Oulton (London: William Heinemann 1926; rpt Cambridge, Massachusetts: Harvard University Press 1953, 1957)

An exhortacyon to the dylygent study of scripture made by Erasmus Roterodamus. And translated in to inglissh. William Roye(?) 1529 (STC 10493)

Ferguson, Charles *Naked to Mine Enemies: The Life of Cardinal Wolsey* (London: Longmans, Green 1958)

Fish, Simon *The summe of the holye scripture and ordinarye of the Christen teachyng* (STC 3036)

Five Books on Consideration: Advice to a Pope trans John D. Anderson and Elizabeth T. Kennan *The Works of Bernard of Clairvaux* vol 13 (Kalamazoo, Michigan: Cistercian Publications 1976)

Foxe, John *The Acts and Monuments of John Foxe* ed George Townsend 8 vols (London 1843–9; rpt New York: AMS Press 1965)

Frith, John *A disputacion of purgatorye made by Iohan Frith which is deuided in to thre bokes* 1531 (STC 11386.5)

– *The Revelation of Antichrist* (STC 11394)

Froissart's 'Chronicles' ed and trans John Jolliffe (London: Harvill Press 1967)

From Ockham to Wyclif ed Anne Hudson and Michael Wilks (Oxford: Basil Blackwell 1987)

Gairdner, James *Lollardy and the Reformation in England: An Historical Survey* 4 vols (London 1908; rpt New York: Burt Franklin 1968)

The Gospels Gothic, Anglo-Saxon, Wycliffe and Tyndale Versions ed Joseph Bosworth 4th ed (London: Gibbings and Co 1907)

Gower, John *Confessio Amantis* ed Russell A. Peck (New York, Chicago: Holt, Rinehart and Winston 1968)

Graham, Richard H. 'Tyndale's Source and Tyndale's Originality: A Reading of *The Parable of the Wicked Mammon*' *Moreana* 28 (July 1991) 53–65

Gwyn, Peter *The Rise and Fall of Cardinal Wolsey* (London: Barrie and Jenkins 1990)

Haas, S.W. 'Simon Fish, William Tyndale, and Sir Thomas More's Lutheran Conspiracy' *Journal of Ecclesiastical History* 23 (1972) 125–36

Hall, Edward *Hall's Chronicle; Containing the History of England During the Reign of Henry IV and the Succeeding Monarchs, to the End of the Reign of Henry the Eighth* (London: J. Johnson 1809; rpt New York: AMS Press 1965)

Hammond, Gerald *The Making of the English Bible* (Manchester: Carcanet New Press 1982)

Heath, Peter *The English Parish Clergy on the Eve of the Reformation* (London: Routledge and Kegan Paul; Toronto: University of Toronto Press 1969)

Herford, Charles H. *Studies in the Literary Relations of England and Germany in the Sixteenth Century* (Cambridge: University Press 1886)

Higden, Ranulphi *Polychronicon Ranulphi Higden Monachi Cestrensis* 9 vols Rolls 41. *Rerum Britanniarum Medii Aevi Scriptores, or Chronicles and Memorials of Great Britain and Ireland During the Middle Ages* (Rolls Series) 91 vols (London 1882; rpt Wiesbaden, Germany: Kraus Reprint 1964)

Holinshed, Raphael *Holinshed's Chronicles of England, Scotland, and Ireland in Six Volumes* vol 3 (London: J. Johnson 1808; rpt New York: AMS Press 1965)

The Holy Bible: A Translation from the Latin Vulgate in the Light of the Hebrew and Greek Originals (London: Burns and Oates; Macmillan 1960)

The Holy Bible Revised Standard Version (New York: Thomas Nelson 1952)

Hudson, Anne 'The Debate on Bible Translation, Oxford 1401' *English Historical Review* 90 (1975) 1–18

– 'John Purvey: A Reconsideration of the Evidence for His Life and Writings' *Viator* 12 (1981) 364

– *Lollards and Their Books* (London and Ronceverte: Hambledon Press 1985)

Hume, Anthea 'English Protestant Books Printed Abroad 1525–1535: An Annotated Bibliography' in *The Complete Works of St Thomas More* vol 8 appendix B 1065–91

– 'A Study of the Writings of the English Protestant Exiles 1525–1535' (PH D diss University of London 1961)

- 'William Roye's *Brefe Dialoge* (1527): An English Version of a Strassburg Catechism' *Harvard Theological Review* 60 (1967) 307–21

Jack Upland, Friar Daw's Reply and Upland's Rejoinder ed P.L. Heyworth (London: Oxford University Press 1968)

John Wycliffe: The Holy Bible, Containing the Old and New Testaments ed Rev Josiah Forshall and Sir Frederic Madden 4 vols (Oxford: University Press 1850; rpt New York: AMS Press 1982)

Kahn, Victoria *Machiavellian Rhetoric: From the Counter-Reformation to Milton* (Princeton, New Jersey: Princeton University Press 1994)

King, John N. *English Reformation Literature: The Tudor Origins of the Protestant Tradition* (Princeton, New Jersey: Princeton University Press 1982)

Kingsford, Charles L. *English Historical Literature in the Fifteenth-Century* (1913; rpt New York: B. Franklin 1962)

Knowles, David *The Monastic Orders in England* 2nd ed (Cambridge: University Press 1963)

- *The Religious Orders in England* 3 vols (Cambridge: University Press 1948–59)

Knowles, David, and R. Neville Hadcock *Medieval Religious Houses in England and Wales* (1953; rpt London: Longman 1971)

Koszul, A. 'Was Bishop William Barlowe Friar Jerome Barlowe?' *Review of English Studies* 4 (1928) 25–34

Lane, Robert *Shepheards Devises: Edmund Spenser's 'Shepheardes Calendar' and the Institutions of Elizabethan Society* (Athens and London: University of Georgia Press 1993)

Langland, William *Piers the Ploughman* trans J.F. Goodridge (Harmondsworth: Penguin 1959) *The Vision of William Concerning Piers the Plowman* ed Walter Skeat 2 vols (London: Oxford University Press 1886; rpt 1954)

The Lay Folks' Catechism ed Thomas F. Simmons and Henry E. Nolloth (London: Kegan Paul, Trench, Trubner EETS 1901; rpt Millwood, New York: Kraus Reprint 1975)

Le Goff, Jacques *The Birth of Purgatory* trans Arthur Goldhammer (Chicago: University of Chicago Press 1984)

Lehmberg, S.E. *The Reformation Parliament 1529–1536* (Cambridge: University Press 1970) .

The Life of King Edward Who Rests at Westminster Attributed to a Monk of St Bertin ed Frank Barlow (London and Edinburgh: Thomas Nelson 1962)

The Major Latin Works of John Gower: 'The Voice of One Crying' and 'The Tripartite Chronicle' trans Eric W. Stockton (Seattle: University of Washington Press 1962)

Mandeville's Travels ed P. Hamelius 2 vols (London, New York, Toronto: Oxford University Press 1923; rpt 1961 EETS)

Marsilius of Padua 'Defensor Pacis' trans and intro Alan Gewirth (New York: Columbia University Press 1956; rpt Toronto, Buffalo, London: University of Toronto Press 1980)

Martin Luther: Selections from His Writings ed John Dillenberger (New York: Doubleday 1961)

McFarlane, K.B. *John Wycliffe and the Beginnings of English Nonconformity* (London: English Universities Press 1952)

– *Lancastrian Kings and Lollard Knights* (London: Oxford University Press 1972)

McLean, Andrew '"A noughtye and a false lyeng boke": William Barlow and the Lutheran Factions' *Renaissance Quarterly* 31 (1978) 173–85

Medieval English Lyrics: A Critical Anthology ed R.T. Davies (Evanston, Illinois: Northwestern University Press 1964)

Millus, Donald J. '"Howe Diligently Wrote He to Them": Tyndale's Own Letter, *The Exposition of the First Epistle of Saint John' Moreana* 28 (July 1991) 145–53

More, Thomas *The Complete Works of St. Thomas More* ed Louis L. Martz, Richard S. Sylvester, et al (New Haven and London: Yale University Press 1963–)

Mozley, J.F. *William Tyndale* (London 1937; rpt Westport, Connecticut: Greenwood Press 1971)

New Catholic Encyclopedia 17 vols (New York, London: McGraw Hill 1967)

The New Encyclopaedia Britannica 15th ed (Chicago, Auckland, London, Paris, Rome 1974; rpt 1985)

The New Testament. Translated by William Tyndale 1534 ed N. Hardy Wallis intro Isaac Foot (Cambridge: University Press 1938)

Norton, David *A History of the Bible as Literature* 2 vols (Cambridge: University Press 1993)

Ochino, Bernardino *Seven Dialogues* trans Rita Belladonna (Ottawa: Dovehouse 1988)

O'Donnell, Anne M. 'Philology, Typology and Rhetoric in Tyndale's *Exposition upon the V.VI.VII. Chapters of Matthew' Moreana* 28 (July 1991) 155–64

– 'Scripture Versus Church in Tyndale's *Answer Unto Sir Thomas More's Dialogue' Moreana* 28 (July 1991) 119–30

O'Donovan, Joan Lockwood *Theology of Law and Authority in the English Reformation* (Atlanta, Georgia: Scholars Press 1991)

The Owl and the Nightingale ed Eric G. Stanley (London: Thomas Nelson 1960; rpt 1966)

The Owl and the Nightingale ed J.W.H. Atkins (Cambridge: University Press 1922)

Pantin, W.A. *The English Church in the Fourteenth Century* (Cambridge:

University Press 1955; rpt Toronto, Buffalo, London: University of Toronto Press 1980)

Patrologiae Cursus Completus Series Latina ed J.P. Migne 221 vols (Paris: Apud Garnier Fratres 1844–1903)

Patrologiae Cursus Completus Series Graeca ed J.P. Migne 161 vols (Paris: Apud Garnier Fratres 1857–66)

The Penguin Dictionary of Saints ed Donald Attwater (Harmondsworth: Penguin 1965)

Peter, John *Complaint and Satire in Early English Literature* (Oxford: Clarendon Press 1956)

'Pierce the Ploughmans Crede' to Which is Appended 'God spede the Plough' ed Rev Walter Skeat (London: N. Trubner 1867; rpt New York: Greenwood Press EETS 1969)

Political Poems and Songs Relating to English History 2 vols ed Thomas Wright (London: Longmans Green 1859–61)

The prayer and complaynt of the Ploweman vnto Christ (STC 20036)

Political, Religious and Love Poems ed Frederick Furnivall (London: Oxford University Press EETS 1866; rpt 1965)

The Psalter or Psalms of David and Certain Canticles With a Translation and Exposition in English by Richard Rolle of Hampole ed H.R. Branley (Oxford: Clarendon Press 1884)

Religious Lyrics of the Fifteenth Century ed Carleton Brown (Oxford: Clarendon Press 1939; rpt 1952)

Religious Lyrics of the Fourteenth Century ed Carleton Brown (Oxford: Clarendon Press 1924; rpt and rev 1952)

Religious Pieces in Prose and Verse ed George G. Perry (London: Kegan Paul, Trench, Trubner EETS 1867; rpt 1914)

The Revelation of Antichrist Richard Brightwell (ie, John Frith) 1529 (STC 11394)

Richardson, Anne 'Scripture as Evidence in Tyndale's *The Obedience of a Christian Man' Moreana* 28 (July 1991) 83–104

The Riverside Chaucer ed Larry D. Benson (Boston: Houghton Mifflin 1987)

Roye, William *An exhortacyon to the dylygent study of scripture* (STC 10493)

Rupp, E.G. *Studies in the Making of the English Protestant Tradition* (Cambridge: University Press 1947; rpt 1966)

Sacramentum Verbi: An Encyclopedia of Biblical Theology ed Johannes B. Bauer vol 1 'Antichrist' 28–32; 3 vols (New York: Herder and Herder 1970)

Scarisbrick, J.J. *Henry VIII* (London: Eyre and Spottiswoode 1968)

Select English Works of John Wyclif ed T. Arnold 3 vols (Oxford: Clarendon Press 1869–71)

A Select Library of Nicene and Post-Nicene Fathers of the Christian Church ed Henry Wace and Philip Schaff, 2nd series (Oxford: James Parker; New York: Christian Literature Company 1893); vol 6 *The Principal Works of St. Jerome* trans W.H. Fremantle

Selections from English Wycliffite Writings ed Anne Hudson (Cambridge: University Press 1978)

Skelton, John *The Complete English Poems* ed John Scattergood (Harmondsworth: Penguin 1983)

Smeeton, Donald Dean *Lollard Themes in the Reformation Theology of William Tyndale* (Ann Arbor: Edward Brothers 1986) vol 6 of Sixteenth Century Essays and Studies

Smith, Preserved *Erasmus: A Study of His Life, Ideals and Place in History* (Harper 1923; reprinted New York: Dover 1962)

STC = *A Short-Title Catalogue of Books Printed in England, Scotland, and Ireland ... 1475–1640* ed A.W. Pollard and G.R. Redgrave (London 1926); 2nd ed W.A. Jackson and F.S. Ferguson completed by Katharine F. Pantzer 3 vols (London: Bibliographical Society 1976–91)

St. Augustine on the Psalms trans Dame Scholastica Hebgin and Dame Felicitas Corrigan vol 1 (London: Longmans Green; Westminster, Maryland: New Press 1960)

Stenton, Doris M. *English Society in the Early Middle Ages (1066–1307)* 3rd ed (Harmondsworth: Penguin 1962)

Stevenson, Francis S. *Robert Grosseteste, Bishop of Lincoln* (London: Macmillan 1899)

The Stoic Philosophy of Seneca: Essays and Letters trans and ed Moses Hadas (New York: W.W. Norton 1968)

Stow, John *A Survey of London* intro H.B. Wheatley (London: Dent; New York: Dutton 1965)

Strong's Exhaustive Concordance of the Bible compiled by James Strong (1890; rpt Nashville, Tennessee: Abingdon Press 1986)

Sturge, Charles *Cuthbert Tunstal: Churchman, Scholar, Statesman, Administrator* (London: Longmans, Green 1938)

Supplement to the Works of Geoffrey Chaucer ed Walter W. Skeat (vol 7 of *The Complete Works of Geoffrey Chaucer* (London: Oxford University Press 1897; rpt 1935)

Thomas, Keith *Religion and the Decline of Magic* (Harmondsworth: Penguin 1973)

Thomson, John A.F. *The Later Lollards 1414–1520* (London: Oxford University Press 1965)

The Thought and Culture of the English Renaissance ed Elizabeth M. Nugent (Cambridge: University Press 1956)

Three Books of Polydore Vergil's English History Comprising the Reigns of Henry VI., Edward IV., and Richard III. ed Sir Henry Ellis (Camden Society 1844; rpt New York and London: ams Press 1968)

Tilley, M.P. *A Dictionary of the Proverbs in England in the Sixteenth and Seventeenth Centuries* (Ann Arbor: University of Michigan Press 1950; 2nd printing 1966)

A treatyse of the donation gyuen vnto Syluester pope of Rhome, by Constantyne emperour of Rome 1534 (STC 5641)

Tucker, Samuel Marion *Verse Satire in England before the Renaissance* (New York: Columbia University Press 1908; rpt New York: AMS Press 1966)

Tudor Translations of the Colloquies of Erasmus (1536–1584) ed Dickie Spurgeon (Delmar, New York: Scholars' Facsimiles and Reprints 1972)

Tyndale, William *An Answer to Sir Thomas More's Dialogue 'The Supper of the Lord'* ed Henry Walter (Cambridge: University Press 1850) Parker Society

– *Doctrinal Treatises and Introductions to Different Portions of the Holy Scriptures* ed Henry Walter (Cambridge: University Press 1850) Parker Society

– *Expositions and Notes on Sundry Portions of the Holy Scriptures, together with 'The Practice of Prelates'* ed Henry Walter (Cambridge: University Press 1849) Parker Society

Tyndale's New Testament Translated from the Greek by William Tyndale in 1534 ed David Daniell (New Haven and London: Yale University Press 1989)

Tyndale's Old Testament, Being the Pentateuch of 1530, Joshua to Chronicles of 1537, and Jonah ed David Daniell (New Haven and London: Yale University Press 1992)

Valla, Lorenzo *'The Profession of the Religious' and Selections from 'The Falsely-Believed and Forged Donation of Constantine'* trans Olga Zorzi Pugliese 2nd ed (Toronto: Centre for Reformation and Renaissance Studies 1994)

Vickers, K.H. *Humphrey, Duke of Gloucester* (London: Archibald Constable 1907)

Wawn, Andrew 'Chaucer, *The Plowman's Tale* and Reformation Propaganda: The Testimonies of Thomas Godfray and "I Playne Piers"' *John Rylands University Library of Manchester* 56 (Autumn 1973) 174–92

– 'The Genesis of *The Plowman's Tale*' *Yearbook of English Studies* 2 (1972) 21–40

Wells, J.E. *First Supplement to a Manual of the Writings in Middle English* (New Haven: Yale University Press 1919; rpt 1952)

Westcott, B.F. *A General View of the History of the English Bible* 1905; 3rd ed revised Rev William A. Wright (New York: Lemma 1972)

Whether Secular Government Has the Right to Wield the Sword in Matters of Faith: A Controversy in Nürnberg in 1530 over Freedom of Worship and the Authority of Secular Government in Spiritual Matters trans James M. Estes (Toronto: Centre for Reformation and Renaissance Studies 1994)

White, Helen C. *Social Criticism in Popular Religious Literature of the Sixteenth Century* (New York: Macmillan 1944)

William Tyndale and the Law ed John A.R. Dick and Anne Richardson (Kirksville, Missouri: Sixteenth Century Journal Publishers 1994); vol 25 of Sixteenth Century Essays and Studies.

William Tyndale's Five Books of Moses Called the Pentateuch ed Rev J.I. Mombert (1884) rpt intro F.F. Bruce (Fontwell, Sussex: Centaur Press 1967)

Williams, Neville *The Cardinal and the Secretary* (London: Weidenfeld and Nicolson 1975)

Wilson, K.J. *Incomplete Fictions: The Formation of English Renaissance Dialogue* (Washington: Catholic University Of America Press 1985)

Woodward, G.W.O. *The Dissolution of the Monasteries* (London: Blandford 1966)

The Works of William Barlowe Including Bishop Barlowe's Dialogue on the Lutheran Factions intro and ed Andrew M. McLean (Appleford, Berkshire: Sutton Courtenay Press 1981)

Worth, Roland H. *Bible Translations: A History through Some Documents* (Jefferson, North Carolina and London: McFarland and Co 1992)

Index

Aaron 177
Abelard, Peter: *Sic et Non* 16
Abraham 211
Acton, Robert 198
Acts 191, 204, 214, 226, 227, 229, 230
Adam 154, 206, 207, 212
Aelfric 98
Africa 100, 213
Agnes 173, 240
Aidan, Bishop 229
Akiba, Rabbi 239
Alcibiades 109
Alcuin: *Conflictus veris et hiemis* 16
Alexander, bishop of Lincoln 216
Alisaundre 239
Alfred, King 15, 98, 167, 230
Al-Ghazali, Algasell 14, 164, 223, 224
Ambrose 73
Ames, Joseph: *Typographical Antiquities* 102
Anderby 232
Anne, Queen 169, 233
Antiochus, King 14, 164, 221
Antoninus 239
Antwerp 24, 31, 60, 79, 102, 181

Aquila 16, 172, 238, 239
Aquinas, Thomas, St 15, 16, 45, 167, 230, 231; *Summa Theologiae* 16
Arber, Edward 22, 36–7, 102–3, 110, 112, 231; *English Reprints* 102
Aristeas 227
Aristophanes 17
Aristotle 43, 231
Armachanus, Ardemakan 171, 236–7
Arthur, King 184
Arundel, Thomas, Archbishop 15, 37, 97, 98, 99, 117, 120, 169, 196, 221, 233, 234
Asaph, St 24
Aston, Margaret: *Lollards and Reformers* 26, 30, 33, 34, 86, 91, 119–20, 179, 195, 197, 198, 201, 219, 232, 234
Atkins, J.W.H., ed: *The Owl and the Nightingale* 16–17
Atleta 172, 240
Audelay, John 70
Augustine of Hippo, St 78, 147, 152, 170, 187, 199, 204–5, 209, 235; *City of God* 205; *Confes-*

sions 205; *St. Augustine on the Psalms* 205

Augustinians 78, 187

Babylon 171

Bacon, Roger 227

Ball, John 118

Ballads from Manuscript 72–3, 117, 185; *Now a Dayes* 72–3, 185; *The Ruyn' of a Ream'* 72–3

Banckes, Rycharde 102, 106

Barlowe, Jerome 18, 23–4, 24–6, 27–8, 30, 31, 32, 38–9, 51, 55, 61, 62–70, 76, 85, 95, 99, 109, 110, 111, 112, 174, 180; *Rede Me and Be Nott Wrothe* 18–21, 22, 23, 24–6, 27–8, 29–30, 31, 32, 38–9, 51–9, 62, 70, 75, 76, 85, 86, 99, 109, 110, 111, 112, 114, 174–5, 176, 180, 185, 188, 189, 190, 196, 220, 222, 224

Barlow(e), William 24–5, 110

Barnes, Robert: *A supplicatyon made by Robert Barnes vnto henrye the eyght* 112

Basil, Basyle, St 157, 214

Bately, Janet 98, 230

Bath 89, 98, 230

Bayfield, Richard 23, 27, 110

Beaufort, Henry, bishop of Winchester 195

Becket, Thomas à 217

Bede 15, 42, 98, 164, 167, 223, 229, 230; *De Gestis Anglorum* 167; *Ecclesiastical History* 15

Benedictines 231, 235

Berengar 82

Bernard(e), Bernerde, Bernard of Clairvaux, St 10, 146, 202–3; *De consideratione* 10

Beverly, Beuerly 85, 198

Bevis of Hampton 43, 113, 224

Bodleian Library 24, 102–3, 105

Boethius, Boetius 14, 42, 164, 223

Bohemia 221

Bonaventure 45

Boniface III, Pope 179

Bonner, Bishop 23

Bownd, Nicholas 112

Boxted 23

Bradley, Henry 74

Bradwardine 82

Braybrocke, Robert 233

Bristol 110

Broune, Ihon 198

Brown, John 232

Bruis, canon of Bedford 217

Brunton, Thomas 118

Bugenhagen, Peter 200

Bühler, Curt 16, 33, 34, 36, 37, 38, 42, 44, 45–50, 96–7, 111–12, 113, 223, 224, 225, 227, 231, 232, 240

Burke, Peter 108, 109, 111

Burton 230

Bury St Edmunds, seynt Edmundes bury 110, 195

The burying of the Mass. See *Rede Me and Be Nott Wrothe*

Butler, William 97

Caesar 80, 206

Calixtis, St 218

Cambridge 34, 53, 219, 228, 237, 238, 239

The Cambridge History of the Bible 227, 228, 237, 238, 239

Canterbury 89, 190, 193, 197, 230, 234

Canvil, Joselin 218

Capito, Wolfgang 20, 21

Carmelites 77, 187

Carolingian era 16
Carthage 213
Carthusians 201
Cavendish, George: *Thomas Wolsey, Late Cardinal. His Life and Death Written by George Cavendish his Gentleman-Usher* 117
Caxton, William 218
Cecyle, Cecilia 173, 240
Cesarea Philippi 181, 227
Charles the Great 186
Chaucer, Geoffrey 19–20, 67–8, 74, 176; *The Canterbury Tales* 67, 74; *General Prologue to the Canterbury Tales* 67
Chester 89
Chichester 24
Chuilleanáin, Eilean Ní 17
Cistercians 167, 172, 202, 216, 218, 230
Clebsch, William 22, 23, 26, 52, 60, 109, 110, 115, 181, 219
Clement 211, 216
Cole, Howard: *A Quest of Inquirie* 114
Comestor, Peter 228
Comodus 239
Compton, Sir William 190
Constance 202
Constantine, Constantyn(e) 90, 117
Corinthians 45, 191, 206, 227, 229, 230–1, 236, 240
Cornelius, Cornelij 166, 227
Cornhill, William 218
Coulton, G.G. 186
Cranmer, Thomas, Archbishop 229
Crowley, Robert 77
Cyprian, Cipriane, St 12, 155, 156, 199, 200, 213

Dalton, John, of Pickering 232

Dante 82
Daniel(l) 171, 172, 229, 238
Daniell, David 42, 48, 49, 113, 174; *Tyndale's Old Testament* (ed) 113
David, St 89
Davies, R.T. 70–2
Daw, Friar 187
Deakins, Roger 19–21, 109
Deanesly, Margaret 16, 33, 34, 36, 37, 38, 42, 44, 45–50, 96, 97–9, 103, 111–12, 113, 120, 188, 221, 223, 224, 225, 227, 228, 229–30, 231, 232, 233, 234, 236, 240
Demaus, Robert 188
Demetrias, Demetriadis 100, 172, 240
Deuteronomy 165, 207, 224, 225, 226
Deventer: Jakob von Breda 223
Dick, John: 'To Dig the Wells of Abraham' 114
Dickens, A.G.: *The English Reformation* 22, 76, 82–3, 85, 101, 108, 110, 116, 119, 197
Dionyse, St 199
Dominican 77–8, 181, 187
Donaldson, E. 67
Dublin 234
Duns 41, 45,
Durham 73, 89, 94, 230

Easton, Adam 118
Ecclesiastes
Eck, John: *De purgatorio contra Ludderum* 115
Edward the Confessor 93, 169, 235
Egbert, King 201
Egypt 177, 199
Eldad 165, 226
Elias 181
Ely 89, 234

England 26, 27, 31, 56, 58, 64, 66, 72, 73, 92, 93, 94, 95, 109, 110, 151, 160, 168, 179, 187, 188, 189, 194, 195, 197, 198, 199, 201, 208, 219, 220, 221, 222, 229, 234, 235

Erasmus, Erasmian 17–18, 19, 67, 99, 109, 113; *Colloquies* 19, 109; *Paraclesis* 99; *Peregrinatio Religionis Ergo* 67; *Praise of Folly* 113

Erastian 82, 91

Esdras, Esdre 165, 171, 225

Estes, James M. 116

Ethelwulf 201

Ethiopia, Ethiope 172

Eugenius, Eugenie 10, 146, 202

Eusebius 238

Eustochia(ium) 100, 172, 240

Eve, Eue 154, 206, 207, 212

Exeter 89, 230

Exodus 177, 199, 214, 224, 230, 237

Ezekiel, Ezechiell 157, 171, 214

Ezra 225, 229, 238

Fabyan 189

Ferguson, Charles: *Naked to Mine Enemies: The Life of Cardinal Wolsey* 117

Ferrer, Bonifatius 228

Fiore, Joachim de 212

Fish, Simon: *The summe of the holye scripture and ordinarye of the Christen teachyng* 100; *A supplicacyon for the Beggers* 8, 31–2, 52, 59–66, 69, 81, 85, 86, 88, 92, 94, 95, 99, 114, 116, 175, 179, 180, 183, 184, 186, 187, 191–2, 193

Fisher, John 219; *Assertionis Lutheranae confutatio* 115, 181

FitzRalph, Archbishop 82, 236

Fleming, Richard, bishop of Lincoln 36–7, 112, 169, 234

Forshall, Josiah 48, 197

Foxe, John 22–3, 34–6, 37, 100, 108, 111, 112, 114, 182, 195, 197, 201, 211, 215, 216, 217, 218, 219, 221, 222, 229, 231, 233–4, 235, 236, 239; *Acts and Monuments* 22, 34, 37, 219; *The Story of M. Symon Fish* 114

France 109, 118, 198, 201, 215, 221,

Francis, St 187

Franciscans 73, 181, 187

Frederic, Emperor 216

Frith, John 191; *Antithesis* 113; *A disputacion of purgatorye* 115, 180–1; *A Pistle to the Christian Reader* 121; *The Revelation of Antichrist* 52, 100, 115

Froissart's Chronicles 118

Fulda 228

Furnivall, Frederick 73

Gabriel 145, 202

Gardiner, Stephen 53

Gascoin, Thomas: *Dictionario Theologico* 234

Gatryke, Gaytrik, Gaytrynge, John 168, 231

Gaudentius 240

Genesis 43, 188, 207, 212, 229, 237

Gerald of Wales 91

German(y), almanye 15, 18, 20, 108, 109, 160, 216, 228

Gethsamine 106

Giles, Gyles, St 194, 197

Godfray, Thomas 19, 75, 110

Gower, John: *Confessio Amantis* 68, 212; *Vox Clamantis* 69

Grapheus, Johannes 31, 60
Gratian: *Decretum aut concordia discordantum canonum* 16; *Decretum Gratiani* 235
Gregory of Nazianzus, St 157, 214
Gregory x, pope 12, 81, 153, 211, 230
Grosseteste, Robert, bishop of Lincoln 10, 15, 206, 231
Guildford, Sir Henry 190
Guy of Warwick 113
Guyart des Moulins 228
Gwyn, Peter: *The Rise and Fall of Cardinal Wolsey* 117

Habakkuk 229
Hadas, Moses: *The Stoic Philosophy of Seneca* 223
Hadrian, Emperor 172, 239
Hales, Alexander de 45
Hall, Edward 190–1, 193, 195–6, 197, 198
Hamelius 191
Hartel, Guilelmus 213
Heath, Peter 93, 117
Hector 43, 224
Heggeley (Lincolnshire) 234
Henrician Reformation 74, 75, 82
Henry ii 160, 201, 217
Henry iii 216
Henry iv 198
Henry v 9, 13, 142, 194, 196, 197, 198, 215
Henry vi 195
Henry vii 73
Henry viii 12, 22, 26, 34, 52, 64, 76, 81, 85, 112, 114, 115, 116, 117, 175, 185, 189, 191, 192; *Assertio Septem Sacramentorum* 115
Herbert, J.: *Postilla super Biblia* 227

Hercules 43, 224
Herford, Charles 17–18, 19, 21, 108, 109
Herod(e) 152, 196, 209
Herodias 209
Hessen 24, 33, 106, 173
Hester 172
Hexapla 239
Higden, Ranulphi: *Polychronicon* 16, 178, 211, 218, 228, 229, 230, 235, 239
Holbein, Hans 17
Holinshed, Raphael 191, 194, 195
Homer: *Iliad* 202
Hood, Robin, robyn hode 42, 43, 44, 112, 113, 202, 224
Hosea, Osee 146, 203
Hoveden, Roger 218
Hudson, Anne 96; *The Debate on Bible Translation* 33, 112, 113, 120; *Lollards and Their Books* 82, 111; *Selections from English Wycliffite Writings* 81, 87, 89–90, 111
Hugh, Huge, St 32, 145, 201, 202; Hugh of Cluny 201; Hugh of Lincoln 201
Humber (river) 95
Hume, Anthea: 'English Protestant Books Printed Abroad' 22, 24, 26, 31, 34, 52, 60, 79, 102, 108; *English Protestant Exiles* 25; 'William Roye's *Brefe Dialoge*' 20–1, 174
Humphrey, Humfrie, Humfray, duke of Gloucester 8, 141, 195
Huntingdon Library 102–3, 106
Hutten, Ulrich von 17–18, 109

Iambres, Jambres 4, 126, 177
Iannes, Jannes 4, 126, 177

Ieffraye 18, 29, 30, 53–5, 56–9, 178, 188, 222
Iosue of Iudicum 172
Ipswich 85
Ireland 194, 233, 234, 236
Isaiah, Isaie, Esaye 126, 171, 172, 177, 229
Italy(ian) 15, 100, 109, 216, 227, 228
Iulianos 178

James 189, 202, 204, 240
James I of Aragon 228
Jephthah, Jephta 208, 209, 210
Jeremiah, Jeremias, Jeremy 172, 181, 229, 238
Jericho 239
Jerome, Hieron, Ierom, St 16, 73, 120, 171, 172, 199, 237, 238, 239, 240
Jerusalem 226, 230, 239
Job, Hiob 168, 229, 232, 238
Joel, Iohell 166, 171, 226
John the Baptist 181, 209
John of Gaunt 117
John of Jandun 82
John, Ihon, duke of Lancaster 15, 169, 195,
John, Ihon, Iohan, King 8, 13, 65–6, 140, 160, 179, 193, 194, 218
John, Ihone xxii, pope 160, 215, 216
John, Ihone, Ihonn, St 49, 139, 167, 170, 171, 177, 182, 191, 196, 199, 202, 204, 209, 219, 220, 226, 229, 230, 233, 236, 237, 240
Jonas 43, 178, 181
Joses 189
Joshua, son of Nun 226, 229
Joye, George 79
Juda, Iuda, Jude 153, 189, 211, 240
Judges 208, 229

Judith, Iudithe 171, 237

Kahn, Victoria 20
Katheryn, Katherine 173, 240
Keyser, Martinus de: The prayer and complaynt of the ploweman vnto Christ: written not longe after the yere of our Lorde M and thre hundred 79
King, John N.: English Reformation Literature 112
Kings 191, 229
Kirkby, Margaret 232
Knowles, David: The Monastic Orders in England 91, 95; Religious Houses 93; Religious Orders 62, 83, 87, 93, 119, 186
Koszul, A. 25

Lambeth 111, 201, 206
Lane, Robert 76
Langland, William 67, 68, 76, 117, 185; Piers the Plowman 68
LeGoff, Jacques: The Birth of Purgatory 180
Lehmberg, S.E. 113, 189, 190, 193; The Reformation Parliament 113
Leicestershire 197
Leo x 219
Liechtensteyn, P. 224
Lincoln 85, 89, 148, 167, 169, 216, 218, 231, 234
Lockyer, Roger 117
Lollard(s), Lollardy 3, 4, 9–10, 11–13, 19–20, 26, 27, 28, 30, 31, 32, 33, 34, 36, 37, 46, 50, 53, 68, 74–6, 79–84, 86–91, 95, 96, 97, 101, 108, 113, 115, 117, 118, 119, 179, 186, 189, 191, 195, 197, 198, 201, 210, 219, 221, 227, 231, 232, 234, 236

Lombard, Peter: *Sentences* 16
London, Londoun 8, 47, 55, 59,
    73, 89, 110, 139, 142, 168, 195,
    197
Louis of Bavaria 83, 160, 215, 216
Lucian 17
Lucifer 154, 212
Lucye, Lucy 173, 240
Luft, Hans (Johannes Hoochstraten)
    3, 24, 33, 35, 36, 37, 39, 50, 100,
    106, 108, 112, 113, 121, 173
Luke 49, 77, 141, 146, 166, 171,
    176, 196, 206, 207, 208, 213, 226,
    229, 237
Luther, Martin 83, 99, 109, 115,
    120, 200, 203, 219; *Das Siebend
    Capitel S. Pauil zu den Chorinth-
    ern (An exhortacyon to the
    dylygent study of scripture)* 99;
    Freedom of a Christian 203;
    Repeal of Purgatory 115
Lutheran(e)s 9, 28, 31, 75, 80, 115,
    119, 144, 200
Lutterworth 197
Lyne, Roger 231
Lynn 110
Lyons 93, 187
Lyra, Lyre, Nicholas 15, 45–6, 113,
    227

Machabeijs, Machabees 164, 191,
    221
Madden 48, 197
Malach(i) 158, 215
Malerni, Niccolo 228
Malmesbury, William 99
Mandeville, Sir John: *Travels* 191
Map, Walter 91
Marborow, Marlborow, Marburg 24,
    33, 36, 102, 106, 108, 173
Margaret 173, 240

Mark, Marcke 137, 171, 175, 189,
    209, 229, 237
Marsilius of Padua 118; *Defensor
    Pacis* 11, 82–91, 216
Mary, St 189
St Mary's Abbey 231
Matthew, Mathew(e) 77, 127, 128,
    147, 171, 179, 181, 182, 196, 199,
    203, 204, 205, 206, 207, 208, 209,
    228, 236
St Matthew's Ipswich 85
Matthew, F.D. 9, 12, 32–3, 103, 111,
    177, 179, 181, 200, 201, 202, 211,
    215; *The Clergy May Not Hold
    Property* 32; *The English Works
    of Wyclif* 9, 214; *The English
    Works of Wyclif Hitherto Un-
    published* 103
Maximien 75
McFarlane, K.B.: *John Wycliffe and
    the Beginnings of English
    Nonconformity* 94, 117, 119;
    *Lancastrian Kings and Lollard
    Knights* 118
McLean, Andrew 25; *The Works of
    William Barlowe Including
    Bishop Barlowe's Dialogue on the
    Lutheran Factions* 110
Medad 165, 226
Medieval English Lyrics 69–70
Mel, John 23
Melchisedec 211
Merland, Iames (Jacob van Maer-
    lant) 15, 166, 228; *Rijmbijbel*
    228
Mersey (river) 95
Migne, J.P. 214, 223; *Patrologia
    Latina* 223
Milman, Dean 68
Mombert, J.J. 49, 113
More, Sir Thomas 8, 19, 20, 23, 25,

26, 31, 37, 45, 46, 53, 60, 61, 62–3, 92, 97, 99, 108, 111, 114, 115, 116, 174, 175, 176, 179, 180, 181, 183, 184, 185, 186, 187, 191–2, 193–4, 195, 215, 219, 220, 221, 227
- *The Complete Works of St. Thomas More* 20, 23, 25, 26, 111
- *Confutation of Tyndale's Answer* 219
- *A Dialogue concerning Heresies* 37, 99, 220
- *Responsio ad Lutherum* 115
- *The supplycacyon of soulys* 8, 60, 61–3, 180–1, 184, 191, 194, 215
- *Utopia* 19
Moses, Moyses 40–2, 47, 48, 49, 126, 137, 149, 165, 177, 204, 206, 211, 224–5, 226, 229
Mozley, J.F. 188

Nehemiah 225, 229
Neotus, Abbot 230
Nero 75
New Catholic Encyclopedia 187
Nineve 235
Netherlands, the 109, 224
Newerk 218
Niger, Randulphus 218
Nolloth, Henry 231
Norbury, John 117
Norfolk 114
Normandy 118, 235
Norton, David 111, 120–1
Norwich 89
Numbers 226
Nun 226
Nuremberg, Nurnberg 83, 116

Ochino, Bernardino 109
Ockham, Ocham, William 116, 118–19, 216

O'Donnell, Anne 113
O'Donovan, Joan 116
Oecolampadius 115
Oldcastle, Sir John (syr Ihon oldecastle) 8, 91, 141, 194, 195, 197, 198
Olivet 177
Origen 16, 172, 238, 239; *Hexapla* 238
Oswald, Oswolde, St, king of Northumberland 167, 228
Outremeuse, Jean d' 191
Oxford 33, 78, 97, 99, 111, 216, 221, 230, 231, 233, 236

Palmer, Thomas 33, 97, 111
Paris, University of 228
Pantin, W.A. 93, 94, 95, 116, 117, 118, 237; *The English Church in the Fourteenth Century* 117
Paul, Paule, Polle, St 15, 39, 45, 46, 71, 126, 138, 141, 148, 156, 166, 167, 170, 173, 177, 218, 237
St Paul's Cathedral 197, 219, 233, 234
Paul's Cross 22, 110, 188, 219
Paula 100, 172, 240
Payne, Peter 33
Peckham 231
Perry, George 231
Peter, John 67, 76
Peter, Simon Peter, St 15, 74–5, 88, 118, 145, 146, 165, 166, 181, 199, 202, 203, 222, 226, 240
Pharisees 4
Philip, brother of Herod 209
Philip IV of France 82
Piers the Plowman 117, 118, 224
Pilate 196, 219
Plato 43

The Plowman's Tale 19–20, 74–6, 110, 176
Pollard, A.W. 185
Polydore Vergil 195, 198, 218, 219; *Three Books* 195
Polyphemus 109
Portugal 109
Prince of Wales 117
Proverbs of Solomon 229
Psalms 205, 221, 229, 232, 235, 240
Ptolemy II Philadelphus, King 227
Purvey 14, 33, 34, 96, 111, 197, 234; *De Versione Bibliorum* 33

Rastell, John: *A New Boke of Purgatory* 115, 181
Rayomond 45
Reading 110
Revelation 191, 202, 211, 222
Rhine (river) 110
Richard I, King 201
Richard II, King 9, 10, 15, 32, 80, 91, 102, 103, 145, 168, 198, 199, 201, 233
Rolle, Richard (the heremyte of Hampole) 15, 98, 168, 231–2; *Psalter* 98
Richmond 85
Roland, Song of 224
Roye, William 18–21, 22, 23–4, 24–6, 27–8, 30, 31, 32, 38–9, 51, 52, 55, 61–70, 76, 85, 95, 99, 109, 110, 111, 112, 120, 121, 174, 180; *A Brefe Dialogue Bitwene a Christen Father and his stobborne Sonne* 20–1, 24, 31, 52, 174; *A Disputation between the Father and the Son* 22; *An exhortation to the diligent studye of scripture* 121, 190, 220, 222; *Rede Me and Be Not Wrothe*: see Barlowe, Jerome

Rudby (Yorkshire) 85
Rupp, E.G. 22, 25, 26, 27, 110
Ruth 172

Salisbury 85, 89, 216, 217
Samuel 229
Sasima 214
Sawtre, William 197
Scarisbuck, J.J. 117
Schott, Johann 22
Scotland 222
Scotus, Sedulius: *De rosae liliique certamine* 16
Seneca, Seneke 14, 42, 164, 223
Senlac Hill 110
Serene 172
Severus 239
Shakespeare 109, 198
Sigonio, Carlo: *De Dialogo* 19
Simmons, Thomas 231
Simon of Swineshead 189, 218
Sinai 165
Skeat, Walter 68, 74, 77–8
Skelton, John 70, 76, 85, 117; *Phyllyp Sparowe* 70
Sleaford 234
Smeeton, Donald 113
Smith, Preserved 109
Smithfield 220
Socrates 109
Solomon 208
Southwell 85
Spain, Spanish 15, 109, 228
Spenser Edmund: *Shepheardes Calendar* 76
Spurgeon, Dickie: *Tudor Translations* 109
Stanbridge: *Vulgaria* 188
Standish, Henry 73

Stanley, Eric, ed: *The Owl and the Nightingale* 16–17
Starkey, Thomas: *Dialogue between Pole and Lupset* 19
Stephen, Steuen of Blois, King 160, 216
Stevenson, Francis 206
Stokesley, Bishop 53, 60, 110, 115
Strassburg 22, 228
Straw, Jack 118
Sturge, Charles 120, 188
Suffolk 114
Swithune, St 145, 201, 202, 231
Sylvester, Syluester, Pope 90, 117
Symmachus, Simacus 16, 172, 238, 239

Taystek, John de 231
Theocritus 16
Theodosion, Theodotion 16, 172, 238, 239
Thessalonians 189
Thomas, Keith: *Religion and the Decline of Magic* 112
Thomson, John: *The Later Lollards* 76, 118, 119
Thorisby, William, Archbishop of York 15, 168, 231, 232
Thorpe, William 22, 37, 211; *Defence* 37
Thynne, William 74
Tilley, M.P. 188, 202
Timothy 126, 177, 196, 204, 213, 214
Tobias, Tobye 171, 229, 237
Trent 217
Trinity College, Cambridge 34
Troilus 43, 224
Trojan War 224
Tudors 19, 21, 30, 119
Tunstal, Cuthbert, Bishop of

Durham and London 8, 13, 30, 47, 53, 60, 73, 96, 97, 120, 188, 196, 219
Tyler, Wat 118
Tyndale, Tindal(e) 9, 13, 14, 20, 22, 27, 30, 31, 34, 37, 38, 39–50, 52, 55, 73, 79, 81, 85, 86, 96, 97, 99, 100, 111, 112, 113, 114, 115–16, 117, 120, 121, 163, 174, 175–6, 177, 178, 179–80, 181, 182–3, 184, 187, 188, 195, 196, 198, 199, 200, 202, 212, 214, 218–19, 220, 222, 224, 227, 236
– *Answer to Sir Thomas More's Dialogue* 37, 40, 45, 113, 198, 199, 200, 227
– *Compendious Treatise* 37
– *Doctrinal Treatises* 4, 39, 40–2, 43–4, 47, 48, 49, 52, 178, 179, 182–3, 184, 188, 196, 199, 202, 212, 218–9, 220, 224, 227, 236
– *Epistle to the Romans* 20, 175
– *New Testament* 9, 13, 14, 20, 30, 31, 42, 47–9, 50, 55, 96, 97, 111, 174, 188, 219, 220
– *Obedience of a Christian Man* 31, 43, 44–5, 50, 52, 81, 113, 114, 121, 176, 180, 181, 182–3, 184, 187, 188, 199, 202, 212, 224, 227, 236
– *Old Testament* 43
– *Parable of the Wicked Mammon* 31, 39, 40, 43, 50, 52, 111, 112, 181, 214, 218–19
– *The Practice of Prelates* 117, 175, 178, 179, 182, 195, 198, 222

Ullerston, Richard 14, 33, 34, 96, 111, 120
Upland, Jack 187
Uthred of Bolton 118

Valla, Lorenzo 90–1; *Declamatio* 90
Vies, castle 216
Virgil 16
Vulgate 174, 225, 228, 236, 237, 240

Wales 198
Waltham 230
Warham, William, Archbishop 52, 53, 114–15
Watkyn 18, 30, 53–4, 58–9, 178, 188
Wawn, Andrew: 'Chaucer, *The Plowman's Tale* and Reformation Propaganda' 19, 20, 74, 75; 'The Genesis of *The Plowman's Tale*' 74
Weert, Jan de 228
Wells, J.E. 85, 231
Wessex 201
Westminster, Westmester 169, 218, 233, 234, 235
Westminster Hall 81
Whitaker 68
Williams, Neville: *The Cardinal and the Secretary* 117
Winchester 89, 201, 202
Wisdom 223, 236
Witham (Somerset) 201
Wittenberg 200
Wollore, David of 95
Wolsey, Thomas, Cardinal 12, 18, 27, 52, 55, 76, 85, 94, 108, 114, 117, 174–5, 179, 185, 189, 219

Woodward, G.W.O. 186, 192
Worcester 35, 89
Worth, Roland 228
Wycliffe, Wickliff, Wicliffe 9, 13, 32, 48, 68, 78, 81–3, 84–6, 93, 94, 97–8, 99, 116, 118, 119, 120, 179, 181, 182, 183, 186, 187, 189, 197, 198–9, 200, 201, 202, 205, 206, 207, 210, 211, 212, 215, 221, 231, 233, 234, 236
– *De nova praevaricantia mandatorum* 86
– *Determinacio ad argumenta Johannis Outredi* 87
– *The English Works of Wyclif* 183, 186, 187, 200, 201, 202, 205, 206, 210, 211, 212
– *Tractatus de Pseudo-Freris of Dominion* 183
– *Wycliffe Bible* 13, 48, 97–8, 197
Wykeham, William of 94
Wynter, Thomas 85
Wyrynge 168, 233

Yale 25
York 85, 89, 231, 232, 233, 234

Zebedee 202
Zechariah 191
Zwingli 115